Women and the Women's Movement in Britain, 1914–1999

Second Edition

MARTIN PUGH

First edition 1992
Reprinted 1993, 1996
Second edition 2000

 Published by
MACMILLAN PRESS LTD
Houndmills, Basingstoke, Hampshire RG21 6XS
and London
Companies and representatives
throughout the world

ISBN 0–333–73265–0 hardcover
ISBN 0–333–73266–9 paperback

A catalogue record for this book is available from the British Library.

This book is printed on paper suitable for recycling and made from fully managed and sustained forest sources.

10   9   8   7   6   5   4   3   2   1
09   08   07   06   05   04   03   02   01   00

Printed in Hong Kong

 Published in the United States of America by
ST. MARTIN'S PRESS, LLC.,
Scholarly and Reference Division,
175 Fifth Avenue, New York, N.Y. 10010

ISBN 0–312–23491–0 (cloth)

To the memory of
my mother
and my grandmother

Acknowledgements

None of those who have helped me in connection with this book should be assumed to subscribe to the interpretation or to the emphasis of the author. However, I must express my thanks particularly to Johanna Alberti and Elizabeth McCarty who took time off from their own work to read and comment on many of the chapters. I also appreciate the advice and suggestions on particular points made by Hugh Berrington, David Doughan, Sheila Hetherington, Patricia Hollis and Marion Jones. As always, colleagues at several institutions contributed to the end product by their observations on papers read at the universities of Edinburgh, Glasgow, East Anglia, Leeds and Newcastle. I would also like to record how much I have benefited from the published work of other scholars, particularly Olive Banks, Brian Harrison, Elizabeth Roberts, Harold L. Smith, Elizabeth Vallance, Jill Liddington, Jane Lewis and Jeffrey Weeks.

I am glad to express my thanks to the staff of that indispensable source for women's history, the Fawcett Library, for their help over several years, notably David Doughan, Catherine Ireland, Susan Cross, Penny Baker and Veronica Perkins. I am also grateful for the assistance given by archivists at the British Library Newspaper Library (Colindale), the Brynmor Jones Library at Hull University, the Cambridge County Record Office, Churchill College, Cambridge, Conservative Central Office, the Blair Atholl Estates Office, Glamorgan County Record Office, the Mitchell Library, Glasgow, the National Library of Wales and the Newcastle University Special Collections.

Finally, I should like to thank the British Academy (small Grants in the Humanities) and the Newcastle University Research Committee and Staff Travel Fund for their financial support for the research visits undertaken in connection with the book.

M.P.

Contents

List of Tables

x   *List of Tables*

Preface to the Second Edition

*'Women's history need not be confined to separate shelves. Its themes
should inform not just the history of women but that of men too.'*

Jane Rendall, *History* 75, 243, p. 72

The first edition of this book (1992) was written very much with this
intention in mind. I aimed to examine the interaction between three
overlapping spheres in twentieth-century British society: first, the
organised women's movement, second the wider and less-politically
involved female population, and third, the male-dominated political
establishment. On the one hand, many conventional questions posed by
historians cannot be tackled adequately without a recognition of the
centrality of women's role; on the other hand, an evaluation of the evolution of the women's movement cannot progress satisfactorily in isolation from the forces and ideas surrounding it. In retrospect the chief
themes pursued still seem to me to be valid and important: the successive generations among feminist activists, the apparent paradox presented by women's achievements after 1918 with the evidence of
decline at the formal organisational level; the difficulties of working
within the political system while maintaining a radical cutting edge; the
significance of domesticity as a positive, not simply a negative, force in
women's lives. I posed the question how far the year 1918 was a major
turning-point both for the women's movement and in terms of its wider
implications for British politics and society, and I suggested that historians had been reluctant to see the period as the 'age of women'.
According to Cheryl Law this meant that I had 'dismissed the period'.[1]
She, presumably, misunderstood, or else decided not to go on to read
the book, since in many ways (and not only in this book but in other
publications) I tend to take a rather positive view about the impact of
women and feminism on wider changes and issues. But I also recognise
that the relationship between any cause and the wider society is
complex and sometimes elusive. It is comparatively easy, for example,
to approach the institution of marriage by examining criticisms of it by
feminists, but things become much more problematical when this is put
in the context of the extraordinary (and unexplained?) popularity of
marriage and motherhood among twentieth-century British women. It is
also notorious that assessments of pressure groups and causes over
short periods are highly misleading. To examine the women's movement from, say, 1919 to 1928 is to unearth a record of achievement and

growth; but this is to avoid the problems presented by the pattern of development during the subsequent decade.

Like most radical movements feminism presents long-term cycles of development; and this seems much more obvious from our perspective at the end of the century. I am therefore grateful to Jonathan Reeve for suggesting that I should extend the book by writing two new chapters. In looking at the emergence of Women's Liberation one is immediately struck by the importance of new generations within the movement; but on the other hand some familiar questions of tactics and of ideology seem to reappear in this period. Thus, the 1990s has seen a debate about the 'New Feminism' whose critics regard it as rather complacent and maternalist much as Eleanor Rathbone's opponents did in the 1920s; there is also currently a real dilemma over how far women should concentrate on exploiting their much higher profile within the parliamentary system and how far this implies succumbing to the fatal embrace of the British political Establishment with its legendary skill at smothering radicalism by adopting it. But to see the problems is not to be pessimistic. I have noticed that male authors of the women's movement are apt to attract criticism for not taking it seriously enough if they suggest the movement suffered from decline, weaknesses or divisions. This is scarcely reasonable; are historians to suspend the critical faculties they freely apply to the study of male organisations when they come to women's movements? With this in mind my chapters on Women's Liberation and Feminism in the Era of Thatcherism ought to be read with care. The argument is broadly that the apparently hostile climate of the last twenty years has been far less inimical to feminism than is generally assumed; even at its height Thatcherism proved unable to stem women's advances, and may even be said to have accelerated progress albeit unintentionally. Consequently the dilemmas facing the movement today are, in many ways. the dilemmas posed by success not by failure.

Chapter 1   Women and the Women's Movement before 1914

Perhaps the most conspicuous effect of the research and writing about nineteenth-century women in recent years has been the undermining of traditional assumptions about the separate spheres inhabited by the two sexes in British society. The received wisdom of middle-class Victorians had woman as dependent, passive, the 'Angel in the House', separated from public life and confined to home, marriage and morality. It has become increasingly clear that this is based upon prescriptive literature which is often highly misleading as a guide to women's lives. Even the official census showed that 55 per cent of single women and 14 per cent of married women were in paid employment in the Edwardian period. For the majority of women work, both inside and outside the home, was a necessary part of their lives, though not a continuous one. It is also clear that marriage was a significantly *less* common feature of Victorian women's lives than it was to be during the twentieth century. At any point in time three in every ten adult women were single and one was a widow. The average age of marriage was rather late, and by the turn of the century avoidance of marriage appeared to be growing, albeit slightly. As a result of early male mortality married life often turned out to be a brief affair, and consequently the one-parent family led by a woman seems to have been common. Much to the consternation of the Victorian male establishment, some married couples deliberately chose to have smaller families in this period. From 1870 when the birth rate stood at 35 per thousand, it fell to 29 by 1899 and to 24 by 1913.

What was the relationship between these developments amongst women and the emergence and growth of an organised women's movement in the Victorian era? Some links seem obvious. The acute problems of unmarried middle-class women in supporting themselves stimulated the 'Ladies of Langham Place' to initiate a series of campaigns for women from the 1850s onwards. It was the successors of this respectable movement who provoked the damning verdict of the Pankhursts many years later: 'so staid, so willing to sit, so incorrigibly leisurely'. Yet we have come to see not only how long a history the women's movement has in Britain, but also how successful the early feminists were even in the period when women remained outside the pale of the constitution. The catalogue of reforms and advances includes divorce law reform in 1857, the Married Women's Property Acts in 1870 and 1882, the winning of the local government vote in 1869, the extension of elementary, secondary and university education to women from the 1870s, rights in the custody of children in 1873, the right to judicial separation and maintenance in 1878, the raising of the age of consent to 16 in 1885, the repeal of the Contagious Diseases Acts in 1886, and the widening of access to employment in shops, schools, offices, the civil service, and even the medical profession. This is not to minimise the disabilities still suffered by British women, but by any standards this was a formidable record of improvement. Not all the changes can be attributed primarily to the pressure exerted by feminists. In education, for example, women were to a large extent the beneficiaries of a wider movement for reform, especially in elementary schooling. Pat Thane has also suggested that many of the legal changes which helped women were essentially the result of the movement to rationalise the judicial system rather than the result of concern for women.[1] Moreover, it was the maturing of the economy which generated many of the jobs in the service sector which women occupied.

If we no longer underrate the late Victorian feminists there is conversely a tendency to exaggerate their radicalism and to measure their ideas by the yardstick of current beliefs. For example, Susan Kingsley Kent's study of the constitutional suffragists claims that behind a demure front they aspired to the overthrow of marriage and sexual conventions.[2] However, most empirical work puts them in a quite different perspective: determined but cautious reformers struggling to win support in a society which was far from favourably disposed to feminism. This is underlined by several important studies of marriage and employment. Joan Perkin has argued in her study of Victorian marriage that upper-class ladies actually enjoyed a rather liberated life style. She also suggests that since most working-class wives played a central role in the family inferior legal status as married women was largely irrelevant.[3] Similarly, Elizabeth Roberts has examined women's attitudes towards work and found little basis for the familiar view of women as victims of the industrial revolution which separated them from work and confined them to the home.[4] On the contrary, it has been demonstrated that working-class women adopted a multitude of strategies to maintain family income, that they were often skilled managers of money and that they made the key decisions in the family's life. Their attitudes towards work outside the home remained largely negative; it was sometimes a necessity, but improvement for them consisted in being able to remain at home. Thus, the women's pressure groups spoke only for small middle-class minorities on several major issues, not for women in general.

Lydia Becker summed up the dilemma when she observed: 'a great lady or a factory woman are independent persons – personages – the women of the middle class are nobodies.' However, much of the work done by historians concentrates on the middle class, and on small radical minorities within the middle class. There is obviously a danger in this of producing an unbalanced history. It is, of course, difficult to avoid this initially because it is always the articulate minorities who leave a literary trail of evidence for the historian to follow. But we have begun to reach the stage in women's history where the big battalions amongst the female community remain relatively hidden from history. This is being corrected. Studies have begun to appear of such organisations as the Mothers' Union (400,000 members), the Girls' Friendly Society (240,000 members and associates), and the Primrose League (upwards of half a million female members) – often by male historians.[5] Beside them the feminist pressure groups were tiny. Of course, the large groups tended to be domestic, maternal and conservative in character. Yet we can hardly, on this account, neglect them, otherwise it becomes impossible to explain satisfactorily the history of women in Victorian and twentieth-century Britain. It has, in fact, become increasingly apparent that the home was not as isolated from the public world as conventional wisdom liked to believe. The work of Anna Davin, to take one excellent example, shows how women's position as mothers forced them higher up the political agenda from the late Victorian period onwards.[6] Domesticity, in fact, emerges not simply as a negative factor in women's lives, but as an important formative force which contributed to the changes in the public and political status of women. Perhaps the best example of an organisation that set out consciously to take up the concerns of ordinary married women and attempt to turn them into 'political' questions was the Women's Co-operative Guild. Though not yet very large, it proved to be an important link between the majority of women and the world of women activists.

It was Millicent Fawcett who increasingly urged her fellow women's suffragists not to be apologetic about domesticity, motherhood and the distinctive experience these imposed upon women:

> we do not want women to be bad imitations of men; we neither deny nor minimise the differences between men and women. The claim of women to representation depends to a large extent on those differences. Women bring something to the service of the state different from that which can be brought by men.[7]

This proved to be a more efficacious tactic than attempting to argue that the two sexes enjoyed the same attributes and qualities. It capitalised upon the male belief in woman as the morally superior half of society; her influence in the sphere of politics could hardly be other than beneficial. It also chimed in neatly with the actual route being followed by large numbers of conventional Victorian and Edwardian women who were in fact using their base in domesticity to advance into the public realm. This was conspicuous in the area of philanthropic activity which led women by degrees into the habit of poor law visiting and, after 1869, into a new role as voters and elected councillors in local government. Patricia Hollis's invaluable study of this subject has shown how women's role as pioneers of such policies as introducing school meals, subsidising milk or providing outdoor relief for the elderly thrust them into the centre of *national* politics during the Edwardian era.[8] Similarly women managed to carve out for themselves a key role within each of the three political parties as speakers, canvassers and fund-raisers, without renouncing their conventional occupations as wives and mothers. As a result one can say that by the turn of the century the whole notion of separate spheres for the two sexes had to a considerable extent ceased to correspond with reality.

One tangible sign of the shift in opinion engendered by these developments was that after the turn of the century a majority of members of parliament supported women's suffrage in one form or another. The argument over the basic principle had essentially been won. There remained, of course, the intractable task of determining the details as to how many women should vote and on what qualifications. But in essence the Edwardians were haggling over the details. All of which puts a different perspective on the dramatic climax to the struggle for the vote in the shape of the militant campaigns of the Women's Social and Political Union (WSPU). The important role traditionally claimed by the Pankhursts has not, so far, recovered from the careful analysis of their organisation by Andrew Rosen.[9] Their suffering and sacrifice made an indelible impression that can never be forgotten; but history is an unsentimental business, and it has clearly exploded many of the more extravagant claims made by the suffragettes. Pankhurst claims that they had won public opinion to their side scarcely seem consistent with the antagonism towards them amongst working-class women which Jill Liddington has discussed in her valuable study of Lancashire.[10] Nor does it square with the growing hostility of the crowds and the defeat of the Pankhurst-backed candidate at the Bow and Bromley election in 1912. Always a small organisation, the WSPU split repeatedly until it became a mere rump of personal followers of the Pankhurst family. Nor, ultimately, did militant tactics succeed in shaking the resolve of the government on women's suffrage; rather they alienated, if only temporarily, much of the support built up amongst politicians for enfranchising women.

On the other hand recent work has had the effect of placing the constitutional movement for women's suffrage in a much more positive light. It was the National Union of Women's Suffrage Societies (NUWSS) that at last began to grow into a mass movement with over 50,000 members from about 1909. Ironically, this was probably the most significant achievement of the Pankhursts; many women who did not wish to be associated with militancy nonetheless felt impelled to signify their support for the suffrage by joining the more moderate organisations. Further, a number of writers have drawn attention to the importance of the change of tactics by the NUWSS around 1912.[11] They made a conscious effort to bring round some of the trade unions and other working-class leaders to active support for women's suffrage; biographies both of working-class women such as Selina Cooper and of middle-class socialists such as Isabella Ford have shown how, after being somewhat alienated by the unhelpful attitude of the labour movement, suffragists concentrated their efforts on Labour in the last years of peacetime.[12] In particular an electoral pact between the members of the NUWSS in 1912 marked the end of the non-party stance of the suffragists; this was a shrewd innovation because it threatened to undermine the electoral co-operation between the Liberal and Labour parties on which the life of the Asquith government entirely rested. Consequently, as Sandra Holton has shown in her recent analysis of the subject, even the prime minister was being prised away from his stubborn resistance to enfranchisement by 1914.[13] Thus when war broke out in August of that year, the solution to the problem – creating a franchise for the wives of workingmen – was already well within the politicians' sights.

Chapter 2 The Impact of the Great War

Each society sees the Great War in a different light. For the participants it understandably represented upheaval and confusion in every aspect of life. From the perspective of the 1920s and 1930s the destructive aspects of war appeared uppermost; it was only too easy to blame the perceived changes – political instability, economic weakness and moral decline – upon the conflict. But as we have drawn away in time so the constructive significance of the Great War has loomed larger. Another mass war and the social changes to which it gave rise confirmed this impression. The shift of perceptions culminated by the 1960s in a new Whiggish view of modern British history as a series of progressive steps, in each of which a major war provided the chief engine, leading to the achievement of full employment and the welfare state. Women, as a newly participating group, stood to benefit from the levelling effect of twentieth-century wars.[1] However, since the 1960s the work of the 'lumpers' who built up this interpretation has been largely dismantled by the 'splitters' of the historical profession. Sceptics and feminists have noticed a circular quality to the argument, and wondered why women who supposedly underwent a dramatic liberation during 1914–18 had to be 'liberated' all over again in 1939. While women clearly experienced certain changes during the twentieth century it now seems clear that change was not consistently in one direction. The welfare state itself proved to be a mixed blessing for women: Sir William Beveridge may have been a great reformer but he was no feminist.

Thus in analysing the relationship between women and the First World War a number of questions must be asked. How far are 'wartime' changes attributable to developments that preceded the war? Were the changes lasting or merely ephemeral? Were they qualitative or simply quantitative – an important question in connection with women's employment? Can one generalise about shifts in the attitudes of women, employers and politicians? Finally, how far did the victorious outcome of the war help to frustrate the pressures for change by reinforcing traditional ideas and values about the position of women in society?

Patriotism and the Women's Movement 1914–1915

In one sense the events of August 1914 proved to be decisive: in a matter of days the 'sex war' had been swamped by the Great War. For a government embroiled in the problems of industrial militancy, the imminent civil war in Ireland and the persecution of suffragettes under the 'Cat and Mouse' Act, war came as a relief. The strikes faded; the Home Rule legislation was suspended; and on 7 August the home secretary announced a royal amnesty for all those imprisoned for assaults in connection with recent strikes and for offences committed by militant suffragettes. This novel sign of statesmanship reflected a shrewd expectation that 'prisoners of both classes will respond to the feelings of their countrymen and countrywomen in this time of emergency and that they may be trusted not to stain the causes they have at heart by any further crime or disorder.'[2]

The Women's Social and Political Union required no further encouragement to effect its escape from the dilemma in which its leaders had been embroiled. Christabel Pankhurst returned from her exile in Paris, and within days her mother announced a suspension of activities: 'It is obvious that even the most vigorous militancy of the WSPU is for the time being rendered less effective by contrast with the infinitely greater violence done in the present war.'[3] Such swift reversals came easily in the autocratic WSPU. In the democratically run NUWSS readjustment took longer. Caught, like many organisations, in a pre-war posture, the NUWSS participated in the great Peace Meeting in London on 4 August. However, it soon extricated itself from this stance, and before long the moderate suffragists, too, were offering their support for the war effort and the suspension of their campaign: 'We know that a War Government cannot busy itself with legislation for franchise reform', declared Mrs Fawcett; as time passed this conviction hardened and she felt that with a coalition government in 1915 there was 'practically no chance of a new franchise being introduced'.[4] In this way the two sides withdrew from their confrontation over women's suffrage, and feminists embarked upon the transition from peace to war.

For many of the better-off women in Britain the immediate effect of war was to increase the already considerable scope for philanthropic work; but the sudden sense of national crisis lent a new urgency and a higher prestige to this traditional activity. There followed an immense flowering of organisations in which women played a prominent role: the Red Cross Society, the Belgian Refugees' Fund, the Prince of

Wales Fund, Queen Mary's Needlework Guild, the Soldiers' Parcel Fund, and innumerable local Patriotic Funds, Sewing Guilds, Soldiers' and Sailors' Dependents' Funds and Wounded Soldiers' Entertainment Funds to mention but a few. In addition some new bodies were both staffed by women and expressly for the benefit of women, such as the Duchess of Marlborough's Women's Corps founded in August 1914 with a view to relieving distress among middle-class women. It soon began to supply the authorities with items urgently needed, from khaki shirts to sandbags, and helped to produce goods formerly imported such as toys. As middle-class committee women became drawn irresistibly into these organisations the suffrage societies inevitably wound down their activities. NUWSS membership fell by some 20,000 to 33,000 by 1916. Mrs Fawcett, though vulnerable to criticism for failing to maintain pressure on the politicians, calculated that restraint at this stage would earn dividends: 'Let us show ourselves worthy of citizenship whether our claim to it be recognised or not.'[5]

In fact signs of a shift in official attitudes towards women began to manifest themselves in 1915 during the discussion over the National Registration Bill. Some MPs argued against the inclusion of women in the scheme on the grounds that as women were not voters they had no obligations to the state, but this was rejected, much to the jubilation of the suffragists: 'The inclusion of women in the National Registration Bill is the first Government recognition of the fact that women can render effective aid to their country in wartime.'[6] In the event some 50,000 women registered their availability for work by April, while the canvassing that was necessary in order to compile a register was largely performed by female volunteers, for many of whom it was a natural extension of parish visiting or political canvassing. Thus 1915 marked a second stage in the move away from Edwardian confrontation: the absorption of women into the official war effort. Many aristocratic ladies and middle-class women, already prominent for their expertise or political work, became involved in the machinery of government. The National Service Department provided employment for May Tennant, already a factory inspector, for the militant Lady Rhondda (Margaret Haig), and for the anti-suffragist Violet Markham. Lady Londonderry presided over the Women's Legion and the Women's Land Army, Katharine Furse over the WRNS and the VADs, and Helen Gwynne-Vaughan over the WRAF. In addition women active in the Labour movement played a conspicuous role, especially in government departments and official committees reporting on food, health, employment and reconstruction, notably Mary Macarthur, Susan Lawrence, Mrs Pember Reeves, Margaret Bondfield and Beatrice Webb.

The only question seemed to be how far women should go in backing the war effort and neglecting their pre-war objectives. In the main the ex-suffragette leaders went from one extreme to the other with an unequivocal abandonment of suffragism for the patriotic cause. 'We want to make no bargain to serve our country', declared Mrs Pankhurst, dropping her recent past through the trapdoor of history:

> never throughout the whole of that fight did we for one single moment forget the love we had for our country or did we relax one jot of our patriotism ... one of the mistakes the Kaiser made, one among many, was that he thought under all circumstances the British people would continue their internal dissensions.[7]

By October 1915 their journal the *Suffragette* had been replaced by *Britannia*, a platform for the advocacy of military conscription, the war of attrition and the internment of enemy aliens. The Pankhursts' new strategy involved speaking from recruiting platforms, hounding alleged traitors in the public service, and attaching themselves to Lloyd George who, as the new minister for munitions, was anxious to absorb women workers into the engineering industry. In the summer of 1915 he encouraged Mrs Pankhurst to organise a mass march by women demanding to be allowed to perform such work; he provided the necessary finance and agreed to meet a deputation. As a result a body of some 20,000 women marched from Westminster to Blackfriars on 7 July complete with martial music and a pageant of the allied nations.[8] This admirably served Lloyd George's purpose in impressing his colleagues – and no mention was made of women's suffrage. The march also led to further public work by the Pankhursts as stump orators in the industrial districts where they preached the government's message: work hard for the war effort and ignore the traitors who were fomenting strikes. In this way the Pankhursts shrewdly attached themselves to the one politician whose star was rising, and effected a satisfying transition from public enemies to arch-patriots.

For the constitutional suffragists, however, the path proved much less smooth. Although Mrs Fawcett had quickly asserted the pro-war stance of the National Union, her organisation contained too many opponents of war for unity to prevail for long. Some suffragists took inspiration from the initiatives which began in the United States with a meeting in Washington in January 1915 under Jane Adams and Carrie Chapman Catt, the president of the International Suffrage Alliance.

This gave rise to a meeting at The Hague at which women from twelve countries set up a Women's International League for Peace and Freedom (WIL), and planned a congress designed to push the belligerent powers towards a negotiated peace.[9] In April 1915 the National Union suffered the resignations of eleven leading members who supported these initiatives, including Helena Swanwick, Catherine Marshall, Maude Royden, Isabella Ford, Margaret Ashton and Kathleen Courtney.

What significance should be attached to this development? The National Union seceders joined women such as Charlotte Despard, Ethel Snowden and Mrs Bruce Glasier in forming a Women's International League in Britain to work for peace as the Union of Democratic Control was already doing among men. Largely women of Labour or radical Liberal credentials, these women were the ones who had given most support to the Election Fighting Fund (EFF) and co-operation with Labour since 1912. Inevitably their loss left the National Union leaning somewhat more to the right by the end of the war; meanwhile it weakened the EFF strategy, compounding the difficulties of sustaining it during the wartime political truce. It was not until March 1918 that the EFF was formally wound up. Meanwhile the work of Arthur Henderson, a cabinet member after May 1915, in pushing for women's enfranchisement maintained the spirit of the pre-war alliance. But by 1917 the strategy effectively lapsed partly because franchise reform was now being achieved, but also because of the new initiatives undertaken by the Labour Party involving the creation of a nation-wide political machine and individual membership; Labour simply outgrew the pact with the NUWSS. During the 1920s many feminists maintained their role both in the party and in women's organisations, but in time most felt drawn towards the former. Meanwhile the NUWSS reverted to its traditional non-party stance.

On the other hand the significance of divisions over the war for the achievement of women's suffrage is less clear. Since a number of studies have been made of anti-war women and none of patriotic women the historian must be careful of misrepresenting the situation. In Britain the anti-war movement as a whole remained a very small and unpopular one; the WIL itself claimed only 2458 members in 1916 and 3687 by 1918.[10] Study of the work of a strong critic of government policy such as Sylvia Pankhurst in the East End of London puts pacifism into perspective. Sylvia found herself in complete opposition to the raucous patriotism of her sister. By 1917, amid the excitement caused by the revolution in Russia, she had become associated with the move to establish soviets in Britain. But it seems clear that while East

Enders accepted her charitable work they refused to be drawn to her anti-war views; cut off from all substantial working-class organisations Sylvia managed to maintain her tiny group only by donations from a handful of middle-class ladies.[11]

It is all too easy to make misleading assumptions about pro- or anti-war feeling during the Great War. For example, from her work in the 1930s and the Second World War one might suppose Vera Brittain to have been amongst critics of war in 1914. But her diary, as opposed to the impression given in her more widely read *Testament of Youth*, makes it clear that this was not so. She was in fact a strident supporter of the war effort, keen for her brother to enlist for the sake of his honour – in opposition to her father whom she subsequently painted as the conventional figure.[12] This serves as a warning against the assumption that Mrs Fawcett and the leading NUWSS figures such as Ray Strachey, Eleanor Rathbone and Lady Frances Balfour represented a mere rump of right-wing pro-war opinion. That would not be consistent with the fact that it was the opponents of war who withdrew, feeling that they could not overturn a decision against participation in the Hague meeting made by the large Council of the National Union.[13] Clearly many women felt rather torn over the issue, regretting the war but accepting the necessity for it. Many judged that it would be bad tactics to involve the National Union and thus the suffrage cause in the controversy over war and peace. Thus a woman of left-wing views, Selina Cooper, could decide to stay with the NUWSS despite her strong sympathy with the proposal for a negotiated peace.[14] Mrs Fawcett believed that an international gathering of women to promote peace would probably divide along national lines and tend to make women seem ridiculous. She had always worked on the basis that suffrage would be damaged if the politicians were allowed to damn it by association with other causes; and she was left in no doubt on this score by Lord Robert Cecil, a leading suffrage supporter, who warned her of the loss of political backing if she allowed the National Union to participate in peace rallies in August 1914.[15] The radical suffragists of the Women's Freedom League made much the same judgement about the need to give women's suffrage a clear run unimpeded by pacifist connections.[16] They appreciated that the anti-suffragists were hoping to be able to claim both that women could not contribute to the defence of their country and that they were natural opponents of war. The defeat of a proposal for conscription in Australia, which was widely attributed to female voting in the referendum, provided potentially dangerous ammunition for them. In Britain, however, it was immensely advan-

tageous for the suffragist cause that when the franchise issue returned
to the top of the agenda in 1917 such arguments could not credibly be
made. By then the well-publicised patriotism of the Pankhursts, and the
assiduous work of thousands of women for the war effort cut the ground
from under the feet of the antis. The mounting irritation of the League
For Opposing Women's Suffrage is well captured in an outburst in
1915:

> They sew and knit comforts for the soldiers, but with such a perpetual
> running accompaniment of suffragist self-laudation that they might as well
> embroider the sacred name of Mrs Pankhurst or Mrs Fawcett on every sock
> and every muffler, so as to give notice to the soldiers as well as to the country
> at large that Suffragism alone has the trademark of thoughtful and benevolent
> patriotism.[17]

Thus, in spite of the organisational drift of suffragism and the diversion
of its members into war work, there were grounds for believing that if
suffragists kept their machine ticking over they would eventually enjoy
an opportunity to capitalise upon the public sympathy that had been
stirred by women's patriotic conduct.

Continuity: Housekeeping and Motherhood

Even in 1918 when some 6 million women were officially in paid
employment, the substantial majority of women still remained at home.
Far from detracting from their traditional role, war crystallised conventional assumptions about the proper relations between the sexes.
For most women the early days of the crisis were dominated by the
frantic rush to volunteer by their male relations and by the alarming rise
in food prices with which they had to contend. Both underlined the
indelible facts of life as seen by conventional people of both sexes: man
as fighter and woman as housekeeper. Yet it would be a mistake to
assume that a renewed emphasis on domesticity was wholly unhelpful
to the women's cause. At the least it served to focus the attention of
government and the press on the female population of the country.
    During the 40 years before 1914 the British people had enjoyed a
rising standard of living based on imports of cheap food. Much of this
soon ceased to be available, or became expensive, and consequently the
suppliers and manufacturers exhorted housewives to maintain their
usual level of expenditure for fear of creating unemployment amongst
the workers employed in the consumer goods industries. The commercial world soon began to tap a rich vein of patriotism amongst all those

who were denied a direct role in the military conflict. Thus Lifebuoy Soap would 'carry you to victory over Germs and Microbes of Disease ... Enclose a Tablet in your next parcel to the Front: he will appreciate it.' Tommy Atkins appeared 'still A1 and on the Active List – Thanks to Beecham's Pills'. And the suppliers of Perrier Water urged customers to 'Fight to the Finish in war and trade' by ditching German mineral waters in favour of French. In such ways were women invited to take a vicarious pride in the battles from which, for the most part, they were irretrievably separated.

The role of women as spenders and consumers grew more significant from February 1915 when Germany imposed a submarine blockade on the British Isles, thereby reducing the country to a supply of food sufficient to last only four months by early 1917. Hence the manu-facturers' efforts were rapidly overtaken by the propaganda both of private individuals and of the government. Expedients for increasing home supplies, limiting prices and rationing of food formed part of the eventual strategy. But the instinctive response of authority to the crisis was that of generations of Victorian do-gooders: to place the respon-sibility firmly upon the British housewife to control her expenditure and use scarce resources more rationally. As early as October 1914 a National Food Economy League began a campaign to avoid wastage of food and fuel; it generated recipes, handbooks, demonstrations and advice on nutrition. Its propaganda elevated woman into the centre of events:

> A great responsibility has fallen today on everyone who has to do with the buying, cooking and using of food. Waste ... is at all times folly, but at such a time as this ... it is unpatriotic ... baking at home is urged as a national duty at this time.[18]

As the author of the *Win the War Cookery Book* declared with unconscious irony:

> The British fighting line shifts and extends and now *you* are in it. The struggle is not only on land and sea; it is in *your* larder, *your* kitchen and *your* dining room. Every meal *you* serve is now literally a battle.

These efforts were duplicated by many other bodies including the NUWSS Patriotic Housekeeping Exhibition which dispatched lecturers across the country, and the Food Reform Association which established Food Reform Shops in the provinces. But by the end of 1916 the voluntary propagandists' work was subsumed under a new department for food under Lord Devonport which sponsored a Food Economy Campaign headed by the Hon. Maude Lawrence. Its characteristic innovations were the Local Food Committees and 'National Kitchens' for communal cooking. Housewives were invited to display a Pledge Card in their window: 'In honour bound we adopt the national scale of voluntary rations.' Slogans such as 'Eat Less and Save Shipping' were clear enough, but 'Eat Less, Masticate More and Save a Pound of Bread per Person per Week' must have puzzled some. The working-class woman received a deluge of novel but actually rather complicated recipes for scalloped parsnips, barley rissoles, bean fritters, bread made from potatoes, oats, maize and beans, and concoctions of soup and nettles. Meanwhile the wealthy were advised to leave the cheaper items for manual workers: 'Today the true patriot who can afford it will eat asparagus not potatoes.' There is no reason to suppose that most housewives took the slightest notice of all this propaganda; its chief function was to give status and employment to those who purveyed it. The generation of 1914 had grown accustomed to eating meat fairly regularly, and retained a healthy suspicion of food that smacked of workhouse cuisine. When black pudding was rationed there turned out to be so little demand for it – a sign that by 1917 housewives had more cash in their pockets – that it was soon deleted from the list of rationed items. Higher family incomes arising from plentiful wartime employment seem to have raised expectations about the quality of food. J. M. Winter has analysed the evidence for improved conditions in the shape of falling infant mortality rates, better health among schoolchildren and greater life expectancy for non-combatants.[19] Yet although housewives seem to have made their own decisions about feeding the family without literal regard for official advice, few could have been in doubt about the *importance* of their work as an integral part of the national struggle.

The dominance of domesticity is underlined when one looks at the behaviour of women in the rural sphere. In spite of the attention given to women who joined the Land Army (see pages 23–4) it is significant how few were involved; by December 1917 only 7000 were at work after the intense propaganda about boosting home food supplies. In contrast women responded much more readily to a parallel innovation in the form of the Women's Institutes (WIs). First established in Anglesey in 1915 the idea for the WIs originated in Canada and had long been seen as a means of injecting fresh life into apathetic agricultural districts. This long-term aim fitted perfectly into the immediate wartime need for promoting the economical use of food and the preservation of surpluses, and for extending the rural labour force by encouraging women to develop gardens and smallholdings for vegetables, hens, bees, pigs and rabbits. In the event the WIs succeeded in tapping the interest of married rural women who refused to be dragged away from their homes for the Land Army and similar schemes.[20] By 1918 some 760 WIs had been established with 50,000 members. Moreover, the WI proved to be an *enduring* institution and not one of the ephemera of wartime; as such it tells us a good deal about the typical attitudes and aspirations of British women.

War also impinged on the traditional concerns of women in that it posed a severe threat to expectations of married life, as the casualty figures soon began to record the terrible toll of husbands and boy friends. This came on top of a period of considerable concern over the supply of British husbands. Males, after all, comprised six out of every ten of those who emigrated each year, and the war, with its official death toll of three-quarters of a million men, appeared to have exacerbated the problem. In fact assumptions that large numbers of women would be denied the chance of a married life receive little corroboration from the statistics (see pages 222–3). However, at the time the fears were real enough, and they manifested themselves in the boom in hasty wartime marriages and the subsequent tendency for women to marry older men than before. The key point is that British women of the war generation were by no means in retreat from the institution of marriage, as the inter-war trend in its favour suggests. Yet contemporaries focused upon marriage not just because they feared it was somehow in decline, but because of the behaviour of married couples in steadily reducing family size. This was, of course, a well-grounded fear, for birth rates had been falling since the late 1870s (see page 89). During 1915–19 they dropped sharply as a result of the disruption of family life. Consequently population and the attitudes of women towards their traditional function of motherhood became an abiding issue in this period.

In this respect, though, war experience simply compounded existing fears and policies. At least since the 1890s, when infant mortality rates reached a peak, local Medical Officers of Health had been promoting improvements in child welfare. The Boer War turned the spotlight upon the poor physical condition of the urban population, thereby encouraging government to concern itself more with the nation's children; hence the introduction of training for midwives (1902), school meals (1906), medical inspection of schoolchildren (1907), compulsory notification of births (1907), the Children Act of 1908, and municipal schemes for the provision of cheap and hygienic milk for babies. No doubt the emphasis here was more on children than on mothers, but if the state required a larger and fitter population for economic and imperial purposes it could not entirely neglect the role of motherhood. Already by 1914 the rearing of children had become a matter of duty and patriotism.

One recognition of this was the inclusion of the maternity grant towards the expenses of childbirth in Lloyd George's 1911 National Insurance Act. In the same spirit he had hoped to include pensions for widows in his scheme. The 'endowment of motherhood' as a way of relieving the burden of young children on family budgets had been advocated by Fabians and other Edwardian reformers. 'Let us glorify, dignify and purify motherhood by every means in our power', declared John Burns, president of the Board of Trade. Pressure groups such as the Women's Co-operative Guild decided to take politicians at their word and capitalise upon the fashionable belief in raising the status of the mother in society. When they interviewed Herbert Samuel, the new president of the Local Government Board (LGB), in 1914 they found that they were pushing at an open door. The result was that by July Samuel had circularised the local Public Health Committees offering a 50 per cent subsidy for expenditure on maternity and infant welfare. During the war Samuel's policy was extended at greater cost, so that by 1917 the LGB was setting standards of provision such as the employment of at least one Health Visitor for every 500 births. While it would be misleading to see these initiatives as a product of war, it does seem that the wartime situation helped to accelerate the implementation of a social policy at a time when competition for scarce resources might have been expected to curtail it.

Yet this policy for women heralded no shift in male conceptions of the female sex; rather it entrenched more deeply the traditional emphasis on woman as wife and mother. Feminists cheerfully

Table 2.1   Infant Welfare Provision 1911–1918

	Infant welfare centres	Health Visitors
1911	100–150	
1912	150–160	
1913	200	
1914	350	600
1915	570	690
1916	850	810
1917	1100	980
1918	1290	1350

Source: LGB figures, Imperial War Museum, WEL 1/2.

acquiesced in this if only for tactical reasons. Mrs Fawcett saw infant welfare as a form of national service equal to that of the fighting men.[21] The Women's Co-operative Guild maintained its maternity campaign throughout the war, and with excellent timing published in 1915 a volume of evidence (*Maternity: letters from working women*) which gave a moving account of the cost to the health of working-class mothers of producing the nation's children. Even more striking was the appearance of a National Baby Week Council under Lord Rhondda (chairman), Lloyd George (president) and Waldorf Astor (vice-president). 'It is more dangerous to be a baby in England than to be a soldier in France' warned one of its posters. In 1917 the Council launched National Baby Week and propagated the case for a new ministry for health. Lord Plunkett's Babies of the Empire Society aimed to promote maternal and infant health by breast-feeding and the provision of nurses trained for infant welfare work. The National Society for Day Nurseries advocated state finance both for nursery schools and for mothers' pensions. Much practical work was also done in setting up day nurseries, for example Sylvia Pankhurst's scheme to take over a public house in the Old Kent Road and rename it 'The Mother's Arms'. This is a reminder that baby-care propaganda was not simply a male imposition upon working-class women. A working-class feminist like Selina Cooper threw herself into Baby Week in spite of the fact that it diverted her from her other work for the Women's Peace Crusade.[22]

A more radical shift of attitudes is reflected in the National Council for the Unmarried Mother under Mrs H.A.L. Fisher. Pointing to the very heavy mortality rates among illegitimate children it urged reforms to allow unmarried mothers to obtain maintenance from fathers, and the provision of accommodation to enable such women to work and keep their children. The terrible drain of manpower seemed to make this a necessary investment for the future. Nine months after the first wave of volunteer soldiers had departed the nation woke up to the existence of thousands of young, unmarried but pregnant women. Their plight was taken up by the War Babies and Mothers league which sought state intervention both to give material help and to remove the stigma of bastardy from them. As the Unionist MP Ronald MacNeil put it:

Sacred as are human life and character at all times, the present wastage of the most vigorous of our manhood sets a stamp of exceptional value on the approaching increment of population. No effort should be spared to secure that these children come into the world under healthy conditions, and are reared so as to be a credit, both morally and physically, to the country; and it is not less imperative that the mothers, both for the children's sake and for their own, should be saved from the degradation which too often follows a single lapse from virtue ... . Very many of the men whose children are about to be born have already amply redeemed their fault by giving their lives for their country and for us ... but let it be frankly acknowledged that the women are no more blameworthy than the men.[23]

Against the background of such feelings the passage of the 1918 Maternity and Child Welfare Act comes as no surprise. Now the local authorities were required to appoint committees for maternity and child welfare on which working women were directly represented. The act also widened the powers of local authorities by allowing grants for home helps, lying-in homes, food for expectant and nursing mothers and children, crèches and day nurseries, convalescent homes and hospital treatment for children up to five years.

Discontinuity: Women and Wartime Employment

Women's employment provides much the most dramatic and tangible indication of change in the lives of British women during the First World War. Yet in order to assess the significance of this phenomenon one has to analyse attitudes towards women's work by all four interested parties: government, employers, trade unions and women themselves, both middle- and working-class. Their various responses help to explain both the extent of the changes and their failure to survive the special circumstances of war.

Initially the effect of war was to disrupt the usual pattern of employment. This reflected the concentration of women in sectors such as clothing and the luxury trades in which demand fell away quite sharply. As a result some 50,000 women, normally employed, found themselves out of work by March 1915, according to Violet Markham. In response to this, feminists adopted certain defensive measures designed to maintain the limited footing women enjoyed in the labour market. Writing in *Women's Industrial News* Clementina Black drew attention to the wealthy women who had stepped in as unpaid volunteers to sew garments for the troops, thereby depriving poor women of their livelihood.[24] This led to the establishment of Queen Mary's Work For Women Fund, led by Lady Crewe and Mary Macarthur, whose object was to finance work schemes for women unemployed as a result of the war, to assist with emigration to Australia, and to pay for periods of retraining and the supply of home helps.[25] The Fund laid down 'ideal' terms of employment including a maximum 40-hour week and a rate of 3d. per hour or up to 10 shillings a week, which was actually *below* the rates set by several of the Trade Boards introduced to improve conditions in the 'sweated' industries. In this sense the Fund stood in the tradition of late-Victorian public works schemes – it was not supposed to compete with normal employment opportunities. For non-manual workers the Society for Promoting the Employment of Women sponsored the Educated Woman's War Emergency Training Fund which sought to retrain governesses and journalists for clerical positions, and to organise hostels for women suddenly obliged to move in order to find work. Thus during the first nine months of war the emphasis lay in trying to develop employment within the existing range of women's occupations.

However, before long pressures for change became irresistible. By January 1915 some 2 million men, from a total male labour force of 10.6 million, had joined the armed forces. Yet while the military authorities pressed for more men, the government suddenly wished to increase greatly the supply of munitions. The new minister responsible, Lloyd George, cast around for expedients, for he appreciated that many skilled workers in engineering had already volunteered. In the long run conscription would help to bring some key men home, but in the short run it threatened to drain industry of manpower even further. Hence Lloyd George's co-operation with the Pankhursts in publicising the need for more women in industry. But others had been making the same point for months. In January Lady Londonderry's letter to *The Times* on the need to use women to remedy the shortage of agricultural labour generated much support; and Mrs Fawcett wrote to Asquith to urge that women be allowed into the higher reaches of the civil service.[26] By May, when Lloyd George took office, 50,000 women were already registered officially as available for war work. Meanwhile he had negotiated a voluntary deal with the trade unions, known as the Treasury Agreement, whereby they acquiesced in, among other things, the entry of unskilled workers, including women, into jobs traditionally held by skilled men. This subsequently gained the force of law as the Munitions of War Act.

As a result of the various efforts by employers, government and women's organisations a sharp increase in female employment began to occur by 1916. It should be noted that the figures issued by the Board of Trade in 1918 (see Table 2.2) give an incomplete picture in that they show a much lower total for working women in 1914 than the usual 4.8 to 4.9 million. The report evidently neglected the most important women's occupation – domestic service. In fact female servants

Table 2.2   Increases in Women's Employment 1914–1918

Industry/ occupation	July 1914 Men	Women	July 1918 Gain + or loss -	Gain or loss %
Building	920,000	7,000	+ 22,000	320.2
Mines & quarries	1,266,000	7,000	+ 6,000	89.0
Metal industries	1,631,000	170,000	+ 424,000	249.2
Chemicals	159,000	40,000	+ 64,000	158.9
Textiles	625,000	863,000	− 36,000	− 4.2
Clothing trades	287,000	612,000	− 44,000	− 7.3
Food,drink & tobacco	360,000	196,000	+ 39,000	19.8
Paper & printing	261,000	147,000	− 6,000	− 4.3
Wood industries	258,000	44,000	+ 35,000	80.6
Other industries	393,000	89,500	+ 61,000	68.4
Total industrial occupations	6,163,000	2,176,000	+ 565,000	25.9
Government establishments	76,000	2,000	+ 223,000	10150.0
Gas, water & electricity under local authorities	63,000	600	+ 4,000	704.3
Agriculture	800,000	80,000	+ 33,000	41.3
Transport (including municipal)	1,161,000	18,200	+ 99,000	545.4
Banking, finance & commerce	1,401,000	505,500	+ 429,000	84.9
Professional occupations	127,000	50,500	+ 69,000	136.5
Hotels, pubs, cinemas & theatres	199,000	181,000	+ 39,000	21.2
Civil service incl.Post Office	244,000	66,000	+ 168,000	254.4
Local govt. incl. teachers	376,000	196,200	+ 30,000	15.5
Total for all occupations	10,610,000	3,276,000	+ 1,659,000	50.6

Source: Board of Trade *Report on the State of Employment in all Occupations in the United Kingdom in July 1918.*

diminished by 400,000, from 1,658,000 to 1,258,000 during the course of the war. Consequently the true net increase in employment is nearer 1,259,000 rather than the 1,659,000 given in the Board of Trade Report. In total the number of women officially employed rose from 4.93 million before the war to 6.19 million by July 1918, an increase of 23.7 per cent. While this was obviously a considerable increase in such a short period, it should not be exaggerated. Most of the working-class women were *already* involved in employment outside the home, or had previously been employed prior to marriage, or were teenage girls just about to take up their first job; to this extent the experience was not necessarily novel or significant. The point is underlined by the returns made by employers showing the sources of their wartime labour supply, which showed that only a small minority comprised women not previously in employment.[27]

Much, however, can be said on the positive side. Wartime offered women a wider range of jobs, thereby enabling some to abandon low-paid or unattractive work, notably in domestic service or the sweated trades, for work offering higher pay and sometimes status; but general-isation is difficult, for as we shall see, wartime wages were often very low. Women who resented the long hours and lack of freedom in domestic service often felt factory work represented an improvement in that their obligations to their employers were tightly circumscribed; this may help to explain why munitions girls put up with the refusal to grant them equal pay with men. Appreciation of better conditions of work was even more apparent for those who went into offices during the war. Even munitions workers enjoyed being able to sit down through-out the day – a pleasant contrast to the day of a servant spent running up and down with heavy and dirty items. This is a reminder that for many wartime workers the move was not obviously towards heavy 'male' jobs but towards something that seemed quite appropriate for a woman. Employers were not slow to conclude that some jobs usually classed as 'skilled' could in fact be picked up by dextrous females in a very short space of time, and this led to changes in the status or classification of the work concerned. In industries such as engineering, where the government interfered, women gained certain tangible benefits in the form of provision of meals, toilets and even crèches. It is also significant that official surveys of the health of women workers by 1918 pronounced that, contrary to popular fears, they had not suffered physically from their wartime efforts except in certain special cases where dangerous substances had been handled.[28]

How deep and lasting an impression did wartime work make upon the women involved? Some clearly saw their jobs as a change, even an adventure, others were simply doing what their mothers told them to do; many expressed satisfaction with their work either because of the improved conditions, or because of the sense of involvement with the patriotic cause which it gave them, while others behaved as housewives had always done – taking the opportunity to supplement the family income at a time when their husband's income had suddenly diminished. Their attitudes can only be assessed adequately by taking account of women's inter-war behaviour in the labour market. Studies such as those by Elizabeth Roberts tend to underline that while employment outside the home was a normal part of life experience for working-class girls, nothing changed their long-term goals or expectations. Work was an *interlude* before and during marriage, but no more than that. This is borne out by the absence of any strong or concerted effort to *retain* their jobs as the end of the war approached; women had always expected to vacate them for the returning men, especially those officially stated to be replacing men.

However, these qualifications do not have the same force when applied to many of the middle-class girls for whom wartime work was often a far more novel and unsettling experience. Though many entered occupations which they would never have dreamt of pursuing in normal circumstances, some were encouraged to seek a long-term career. Their families increasingly accepted the desirability, or even necessity, of their finding some means of supporting themselves after the war, fearful, perhaps, of a dearth of marriage partners, or of their own inability to support daughters out of dwindling family resources. The girls themselves were influenced as much by the social consequences of taking up a career as by the economic. A wider and more independent personal life often appeared to be the chief gain of the war years, so much so that, as feminists subsequently discovered, middle-class women were apt to regard the emancipation of their sex as an accomplished fact by the inter-war period.

However, generalisation is hazardous, for women's attitudes varied a good deal from one occupation to another. The most positive response appears to have been aroused by typing and clerical work. This, of course, was far from novel, for it had been a buoyant sector for women's employment since the 1870s. During the war both private commercial firms and the civil service substituted women for men. Their work proved relatively pleasant – according to critics, because they had insufficient to do – and the pay was modest. A government typist earned around £1 a week, and good shorthand typists, women clerks and telegraphists between £1 and £2. Perhaps the most striking change was the apparent rise in status. This may have been connected in part with the publicity accorded to the nation's foremost secretary – Frances Stevenson. Certainly Lloyd George's readiness to break with convention by appointing a woman aroused much interest, especially after he became prime minister in 1916. Stevenson began to become a role model. In girls' colleges it was noticed that educated girls no longer required persuasion to take up secretarial posts. It now became fashionable for a girl shorthand typist to aspire to higher things by styling herself a 'lady secretary'.[29] However, it became clear during the 1920s and 1930s that while there were plenty of jobs for women in this area they were essentially low paid, and were to take women no further than acting as assistants to men in authority.

A very different significance can be attached to work on the land during the First World War. Following Lady Londonderry's initiative the big county families threw themselves enthusiastically into the recruitment of women into the agricultural labour force. Under Lord Selborne, who served as minister for agriculture from May 1915, women were canvassed and registered by a network of county committees, and a voluntary body, the Women's Land Service Corps, was set up in 1916 to train them. In January 1917 this was overtaken by the Women's Land Army, the official agent of the ministry, which awarded badges, armlets, stripes and certificates at a series of military-style rallies in each region.

Yet while the leaders of county society welcomed the chance to serve on committees connected with this effort, the significance for those directly involved in the Land Army was minimal. Selection boards turned down girls whom they believed to lack the high moral character needed for life on lonely farms, and issued recruits with stern instructions: to behave 'like an English girl who expects chivalry and respect from everyone she meets'. Girls were not permitted to enter public houses, to smoke in public or to go about with their hands in their pockets. They were often required to be in bed by 9.30 p.m. in summer and 9.00 p.m. in winter, though the rules were flouted. Accommodation was often very poor, and Sunday was the only day off. In return for these privations the girls received the official minimum wage of 18 shillings in 1916, which was raised to 20 shillings by 1918 or to 22 shillings for those who acquired a certificate of training. In practice, however, farmers preferred to pay by the hour, often as little as 3d. or 4d.; in Lincolnshire deductions of 11 shillings were made for board and lodging from 16–20 shillings weekly pay.[30] Working-class girls were simply not prepared to put up with these conditions: the work was too akin to domestic service, and only revived prejudice about the 'degradation' of agricultural labour.[31] Consequently, in counties close to major towns they opted for less restrictive work in offices or factories. In particular they seem to have feared placing their names on a register and being dragged away to serve on farms miles from their homes.[32]

Oddly enough the most enthusiastic recruits for the land were those from non-manual backgrounds in teaching or shops, influenced perhaps by a vision of the romantic shepherdess or milkmaid, or simply by a desire to see a different part of the country for a short time. Some professional, university educated women gave up jobs paying £220 to £400 per annum for the Land Army, but encountered a wall of prejudice amongst many farmers, some of whom actually sent them back home. Even for those who stayed agricultural work was clearly seen as a purely temporary affair, an interruption in one's career and not a long-term option. As for the employers, their attitudes were very mixed. An official survey in 1916 found more counties where farmers remained hostile to women workers than favourable ones. In several areas farmers preferred to solve their labour problems by having boys released from school at 12 years old (and many were), or by bringing old age pensioners back to plough the land![33] Impervious both to patriotic propaganda and to experience, they continued to insist that women lacked the strength for ploughing, that they would 'run off home when a shower of rain came on', and that they were an expensive form of labour. Here there was to be no breakthrough against well-entrenched prejudice.

In industrial employment the issues were similar though more complicated. The immediate question is how far the war years altered employers' views on women's capabilities. It has to be remembered that even in traditionally 'male' industries many of the women performed what were regarded as 'female' jobs. For example, in iron and steel women took on clerical work initially; on the railways they were already clerks but now issued tickets and acted as porters; even in munitions they were used on packing at first. However, they soon moved beyond these jobs. In industries where women were already numerous they acquired a portion of the heavier work; and in engineering skilled men's work was soon rearranged so as to reduce the element of skill or make greater use of machinery. Thus, the number of women officially stated as replacing men reached 897,000 by October 1916 and 1,064,000 by 1918. These figures suggest that after the rapid influx in

1916 things settled down: there were strict limits not to what the women were capable of, but to what trade unions and employers would tolerate. Thus by the end of the war five-sixths of women were probably doing 'women's' work. An official survey on substitution concluded that there were seven trades where women had been introduced into at least some branches of work which appeared suitable for them on a long-term basis; in addition there were sixteen where women had already worked before the war, and twenty-one, including chemicals, glass, paper and milling, in which women workers were still considered to be unsuitable.[34] The rate and extent to which women were absorbed varied not only between industries but within industries according to the extent of government intervention. In munitions, for example, by October 1916 women had increased by almost 300 per cent in government-controlled establishments, but by only 36 per cent in uncontrolled ones; in chemicals the rise was 244 per cent in controlled and 49 per cent in uncontrolled ones.[35] Almost inevitably, then, the withdrawal of government intervention after the war was, in itself, likely to curtail the permanent impact of women's wartime work.

These views were to some extent influenced by opinions about the quality of women's work, which were mixed. Among the munitions firms complaints were raised about poor time-keeping by women, though men were by no means free from criticism; this was usually attributed to difficulties in travelling to work, and sometimes to pressure of domestic duties or excessive illness amongst women. It is noticeable that some of these ideas were not substantiated by investigations of women's health. Winston Churchill, later minister of munitions, evidently assumed that both men and the women introduced into the industry were less efficient than those they replaced, though, again, this seems to have been more prejudice or politics than fact. Managers of gas works considered women workers superior to those men currently available as clerks or for reading meters and collecting accounts, but as inferior to the normal male labour force. In commercial establishments the verdict on women employed by banks and insurance offices was favourable but patronising in the sense that they were seen as perfectly competent for routine typing and shorthand, or as cashiers and book-keepers. Some of them were to be retained after the war, but they would be in posts without responsibility and certainly not in managerial positions. One bank summed up the situation:

> they have proved a very floating population ... too many only regard their earnings as so much pocket money and throw up their work on the slightest pretext.[36]

It need hardly be said that these remarks echo ominously through the inter-war years.

In a sense these views represent the undercurrent running through the war. Historians have often taken notice of the more conspicuous but misleading praise bestowed by the press. Newspapers undoubtedly liked women for providing fresh copy and giving a new twist to their attempts to boost morale; they therefore praised them but in a patronising way:

> We like to see some slip of a girl, very official in her Post Office uniform, with white-topped cap jammed down over her eyes, sitting perched up on the high seat of a red mail van.[37]

Moreover, girls who handled horse-drawn vehicles or drove motor vans for the Royal Mail were largely upper- and middle-class; they could be the more easily tolerated because their role was regarded as purely temporary.

Another distinct indication of women's own attitudes towards work and its long-term implications lies in their participation in trade unions. Some of the key figures of wartime, including Mary Macarthur and Margaret Bondfield, had considerable experience of building up union membership amongst women which by 1914 stood at 358,000 (largely in textiles) compared to 3.8 million for men. Thereafter women's membership grew at a faster rate than that for men. This was partly a reflection of the fact that they started from a much lower base, and also of the fact that many were moving from sectors notoriously difficult to organise, such as domestic service, into large-scale manufacturing industry where organisation was relatively strong. As a result 1.2 million women had joined trade unions by 1918 compared to 5.3 million men. Out of a total of 1264 separate unions, 6 were exclusively female and 347 mixed in membership as against 204 in 1912. This was the nub of the question: should women organise separately or throw in their lot with the men? On the whole leaders like Macarthur and Bondfield, who were by now being drawn into the national hierarchy of the labour movement, felt inclined towards amalgamation with the men. But progress was limited by the traditional hostility of trade unionists towards women whom they regarded as unskilled, low-paid workers used by the employers to hold down wage levels and to frustrate their own aspirations to a 'family wage'. Some unions calculated that women should be encouraged to join for fear that employers might be tempted to outflank the unions by taking on even more women; membership of the National Union of Clerks was 26 per cent female by 1918. But many, such as the Amalgamated Society of Engineers (ASE), continued to exclude women. They judged that if women were to become permanently entrenched in the union the effect would be to depress the general level of pay in the industry; it was better to treat their presence as special and temporary. Hence the importance of the specific undertaking given by the government in the Treasury Agreement that dilution of labour would be terminated at the end of the war. Nonetheless women clearly derived some benefits from the bargaining by Macarthur and the National Federation of Women Workers who obtained a minimum wage of £1 a week for munitions workers. Later the spread of Whitley Councils helped to improve conditions in some of the industries where organisation was weak. Yet in spite of their experience five-sixths of female workers remained outside the unions, partly because they felt alienated by male hostility, but also because they never regarded their jobs as more than a temporary expedient.

The question of rates of pay was clearly fundamental to trade union attitudes to women. Before 1914 the typical female employee received around one-half of the wages of a man in both manual and non-manual occupations. Although the Trades Union Congress had passed a resolution in favour of equal pay as far back as 1888, they paid no more than lip service to the idea. Even the National Union of Teachers had refused to campaign for equal pay, thereby provoking a breakaway by many of its women members. At the very least the First World War turned equal pay for women into a major issue for the first time. The government found itself obliged to face the problem as a result of its desperate need to recruit unskilled labour without antagonising the existing workforce. Employers instinctively took advantage of the situation; for example women working on the trams in Newcastle-upon-Tyne were offered only 15 shillings in contrast to 28 shillings for men, until they threatened industrial action. Initially women entering munitions work received only 2½d. an hour – a sweated wage. Naturally the ASE and other unions insisted that women should receive equal pay where they were genuinely replacing men, otherwise they would refuse to co-operate with the government's strategy of diluting the labour force. Yet as Harold Smith has pointed out, neither Lloyd George nor the unions advocated abandoning sexual discrimination in pay when they made the Treasury Agreement in 1915.[38] What they did agree upon was that existing rates for each job should not be undermined, which appeared to open the way to equal pay for women. As so often happened there was a good deal of ambiguity as to the real meaning of the deal Lloyd

George had reached. It emerged subsequently that he was prepared to insist that women be paid equally when employed on piece work, but they would not receive equal time rates. In practice employers kept them out of piece work, and paid them half to two-thirds the male rate for time work in spite of the fact that on operations calling for fast, dextrous and repetitive actions women often proved superior to men. Of course, women's representatives were not included in the Treasury Agreement, and although subsequently Macarthur and Sylvia Pankhurst tried to pin Lloyd George down they were unable to extract anything except a commitment to a minimum wage for women, which they felt was treated more as a maximum. Lloyd George insisted that 'for some time women will be unskilled and untrained, and they cannot turn out as much work as men can who have been at it a long time'. Thus employers were free to take women at low rates which Lloyd George believed necessary in order to encourage them to exploit this extra source of labour. In practice it also proved a simple matter to modify or divide most of the skilled jobs, or to introduce new machinery so that the women employed could not be said to be performing the same role as men and therefore not entitled to the same pay. In this way Lloyd George managed to satisfy both employers and trade unions. His ministry held to its basic belief that equal pay 'is a social revolution which ... it is undesirable to attempt during war time'.[39]

As for women themselves, they largely accepted discrimination in pay and the practice of awarding higher increases to men during the course of the war. It was not until 1918 that blatant discrimination in the form of higher bonuses for men in munitions and the refusal of any bonus at all to women on buses and trams provoked protests and even brief strike action. The government reluctantly backed down over the bus and tram workers, and appointed a new committee to look into female wages. But by this time munitions work was about to be wound up. By the end of the war no real change had taken place except in the sense that feminists had been thoroughly aroused to the nature of the problem they faced on equal pay. Bondfield, Eleanor Rathbone, Beatrice Webb and the others involved had concluded that the very notion of 'equal pay for equal work' was too vague and easily evaded to be worth fighting for.

The final aspect of women's wartime work which must be considered is the manner of their departure from it, though this is more thoroughly examined in a later chapter. Popular reaction against the women evidently gained strength towards the end of 1917 in the form of a good deal of press comment on the inadequacies of girl typists; much of their work was now said to be of very poor quality, and government offices in particular were supposedly overstaffed. Here one may discern the origins of the anti-waste campaigns and the post-war attack upon 'flappers'. Some ministries were already weeding out their female employees – a policy which coincided with the passage through parliament of the bill which gave votes to older women. By the spring of 1918 a good deal of thought was already being devoted to demobilisation at the end of the war, particularly to the conflict between the need on the one hand to find work for discharged men during a period of economic disruption, and on the other hand the expectation that some women would wish to continue their employment if only because of the loss of male breadwinners during the war. In fact the reports on substitute labour prepared for the Ministry of Reconstruction suggested that especially in clerical occupations women would voluntarily surrender their jobs for ex-soldiers; no serious opposition was anticipated – it was rather the threat of demobilised men that commanded official attention.[40] Official assumptions were, if anything, reinforced by the views expressed by the Labour movement at this stage. The Joint Standing Committee of Industrial Women's Organisations, which included Ramsay MacDonald, J.R. Clynes and J.H. Thomas as well as Macarthur, Bondfield and Susan Lawrence, agreed on the need for compulsory reductions in the working week for women, balanced by improvements in wages by means of trade boards and an agreed minimum in order to prevent any detrimental effect on men's pay.[41] Most sweeping were the recommendations of a trade union conference held in March 1918 which bluntly concluded that women's industrial work must be consistent with the interests of their family life. They might be encouraged into textiles, confectionery, boot and shoe making, laundry work, domestic service, shops and clerical work, but should be legally banned from many trades which were quite unsuitable for them.[42] Married women were to be excluded from employment, but given pensions in respect of disabled husbands and dependent children. Finally the union leaders favoured tighter protective legislation. Existing factory legislation permitted a 12 hour working day for women; this should be reduced to 8 hours for five days with 4 on Saturdays. Thus before the guns had ceased to roar in France male-vested interests already had their heavy artillery in place on the domestic front. Most of the issues which were to trouble the women's movement between the wars had been raised by 1918; and ominously for women, entrenched male interests already planned not just to recover ground temporarily conceded during the war, but to deny women some of their pre-war footing in the employment sphere.

Women in Uniform

Perhaps the development which crystallised both female aspirations and male apprehensions about sex roles most effectively was the female adoption of uniforms during the course of the war. The bridgehead into the world of official uniforms had in fact already been established in the Edwardian period by nurses under the auspices of the Voluntary Aid Detachments (VADs). These evolved in connection with the army reforms of Richard Haldane, assisted by his sister Elizabeth, both of whom regarded women as full citizens and as part of the nation's defences. Hence the VADs, of whom two-thirds were female, were organised under the Red Cross and attached to the Territorial Army. By 1914 there were nearly 50,000 of them. But as Anne Summers has argued, wartime legend about the VADs can distort their significance.[43] With young girls the VAD's role was undoubtedly popular; indeed some of their accounts echo those of youthful soldiers like Julian Grenfell in glorying that they were young enough to enjoy the opportunity presented by the war. But the VADs, in common with the many other forms of uniformed service, were very much the preserve of upper- and middle-class girls, who welcomed the sense of freedom and status their work bestowed, but for whom it was not the path to a career. Moreover, men believed that the VADs should be confined to hospital work at home if at all possible. As Dr Elsie Inglis found when she proposed to take nurses into military hospitals, Florence Nightingale might never have existed: 'My good lady', purred the War Office official, 'go home and sit still.'[44] Of course she successfully offered her services to the French and Serbians, and in due course women did play a courageous role in the war zone; but even they failed to shake these imperturbable male notions of superiority.

As always the route towards a prized official uniform for women lay through voluntary activities. And by tradition it was easier for aristocratic ladies to advance down this road. The ubiquitous Lady Londonderry succeeded as, for example, head of the Women's Legion and as Colonel-in-Chief of the Women's Volunteer Reserve. Formed in February 1915 the WVR was simply intended to provide assistance with first aid, transport, air raids, telegraphy and signalling. But it consciously aped the military. Its officers had to be saluted and addressed as 'Sir'; and members enjoyed khaki uniforms, puttees and felt hats:

> They are quite serious these women volunteers, and although uniform is compulsory, we are told that they are by no means to be a merely ornamental corps, though, of course, they will be that.[45]

The effort to maintain a light, patronising tone towards these initiatives showed signs of increasing strain as volunteer bodies mushroomed during 1915; for the fact was that to most men who, after all, lacked the status of a uniform, these women represented an embarrassment and perhaps a threat. Thus the War Office succeeded for some time in keeping them strictly apart from the military as merely enrolled civilians. This, however, meant that by 1917 the voluntary agencies had become so deeply entrenched that the task of the National Service Department in recruiting women proved frustrating. The Women's Army Auxiliary Corps, formed in January 1917 in order to supply clerks, cooks and domestic workers to the army, attracted the names of 35,000 women by 1918; but only 18,000 of these actually agreed to abide by the terms laid down for service. The press, volatile as ever, was quick to pounce on this, denouncing the 'idle girls of villadom' for failing to become WAACs.[46] Too many middle-class girls, it was claimed, preferred to spend a morning or two helping in a hospital while maintaining a full complement of servants to do their own housework. After the WAAC came two much smaller organisations, the Women's Royal Naval Service in November 1917 whose recruits might tackle clerical, household, postal, garage, storekeeping, electrical and engineering work, and the Women's Royal Air Force in April 1918. Three-quarters of the WRAFs were engaged in clerical and domestic jobs, though some became drivers, fitters, welders and carpenters working on the aeroplanes.

All of these women enjoyed a prestigious uniform, military discipline and an official hierarchy corresponding to that in the male service; thus Katherine Furse as Director of the WRNS was officially equivalent to a rear admiral, and Helen Gwynne-Vaughan, Commandant in the WRAF, was on a par with an air commodore, her deputy with a group captain. But the line was still drawn short of combat. The WRAFs were known as 'Penguins' – because they did not fly. 'As a matter of fact', explained the *Daily Express*, 'flying is not a woman's job ... they always lost their heads in a sudden emergency.'[47] For men the uniformed woman posed a threat to masculinity; she could be tolerated if she acted essentially as a helpmate to the men in the fighting forces, though even that proved too much for traditionalists. When Helen Gwynne Vaughan attempted to recruit an officer's wife for the WRAF, she met with a magisterial rebuff: 'Madam, my wife is a truly feminine woman'.[48] Lady Londonderry complained of the behaviour of male porters who invariably squeezed her out of lifts when she wore uniform; and she even found herself turned away from the front door of a big house to the tradesman's entrance by an indignant maid who later explained: 'I thought you was one of them 'orrible Army women.'[49]

In the long run, however, uniformed women connected with the forces probably made less impact than those who penetrated the ranks of the police force. The opportunity was created by the effects of wartime work in gathering together large numbers of young soldiers and young working girls, and allowing them to develop a free social life. Fears about rising immorality aroused the traditional moral strand within the feminist movement:

> the girlhood of the country was thrown off its balance – the crowds of khaki-clad men who were gathering together to fight for King and country ... all excited its imagination ... . This unfortunately in many instances was expressed by foolish, giddy, irresponsible conduct. The National Union of Women Workers realised that this behaviour of the young girls might result in leading them into grave moral danger; and it determined to save them from their own folly.[50]

After a meeting of the National Council of Women in 1914 under Maria Ogilvie Gordon the first Women's Patrols were established in London; by February 1915, 900 patrols were in action. They frequented military camps, ports, parks, public houses and cinemas where opportunities for drunkenness and sexual immorality presented themselves. At the same time a similar initiative was being taken by Miss Margaret Damer Dawson, a middle-class philanthropist, and Miss Nina Boyle, a Women's Freedom League organiser. But they wished to give women a professional, not merely an amateur policing role. Women's vulnerability to ill-treatment at the hands of the police had long led feminists to demand entry into the force. But Miss Dawson quickly appreciated that the concern over growing immorality during wartime strengthened their case, and she seized upon an official request for special constables to press her idea on the Chief Commissioner for the Metropolitan Police. Though reluctant to admit women on account of the bad relations between his men and the suffragettes, he agreed that the ladies might recruit Women Police Volunteers (WPVs) to help in dealing with Belgian refugees, women at railway stations and street disorders. A Mrs Edith Watson became the first woman to wear a police uniform.

These developments had a two-fold significance. First, the patrols and WPVs proved attractive to suffragettes and suffragists. This is scarcely surprising, for the war focused attention on the old double standard in sexual attitudes. Male authority simply assumed that the cause of immorality lay with the female sex. In Plymouth the Watch Committee proposed the revival of the notorious Contagious Diseases Acts which had been abolished in the 1880s. Regulation 40D under the Defence of the Realm Act (DORA) made it an offence for a woman with venereal disease to have sexual relations with a member of the armed forces. Military commanders began to restrict the movements of women in their areas. In Cardiff they were banned from public houses between 7.00 p.m. and 6.00 a.m., and even cleared from the streets after 7.00 p.m. In Grantham women were restricted to their homes from 8.00 p.m. to 7 a.m. – and the authorities enjoyed the power under DORA to enter houses in order to check on the presence of non-residents. Those arrested for breaking the curfew found themselves prosecuted and subject to 62 days imprisonment.[51]

It is somewhat paradoxical that much of the work of inspecting houses, following couples from public houses to their lodgings, and quartering parks in order to intervene between supposed 'prostitutes' and their clients was done by women. One patroller explained: 'there was a spice of adventure in it, and women might claim their right as members of the Church militant to take their part in the fight against sin and misery.'[52] Yet the satisfaction of the participants and the favourable reports on women's patrols issued by chief constables are somewhat at odds with the marked reluctance to employ women in the police after the war. Even in 1917 women police had been appointed in only twelve boroughs, largely in areas dominated by munitions works like Carlisle, or swamped by new military camps like Grantham. With the special sanction of wartime patriotism they were seen to have gained a dangerous new freedom to interfere with male behaviour, even if women were invariably the ostensible targets; few wished to place their employment as police on a permanent footing. An indignant comment on unnecessary interference with soldiers and their girl friends enjoying summer evenings in Hyde park captures the mood:

> Just strapping young fellows cuddling their sweethearts ... yet, stalking these lovers, are the women patrols ... . In the police court any Saturday morning you may hear the story of their work, and if it does not revolt you, then indeed we have lost all that remains to us of our respect for womanhood ... this prying behind the trees in Hyde Park, this patrol with the lantern and the muckrake, this stolid recital of filthiness, let us keep them out of it![53]

No doubt much of this was wounded male pride, yet there are grounds for thinking that the patrols homed in on innocent behaviour which was easier to tackle than the real crime of the urban areas. Resignations by women from the WPV during 1917 suggest that the experiment was not always the success it was officially claimed to be. Certainly one can see in the outraged reactions of men one important strand in the upsurge of hostility towards feminists in the post-war years. Many girls shared their feelings. After long hours at work the attentions of young soldiers were by no means unwelcome to them; and they too began to see the patrols as the work of frustrated spinsters or men-haters. Much of the explanation for the hostility of the younger generation towards feminism between the wars has its origins in this experience.

Women's Enfranchisement and the Separate Spheres

Under the terms of the Representation of the People Act of 1918 parliament bestowed the vote upon women aged 30 and above who were themselves local government electors or who were married to local government electors. This measure enfranchised some 8,479,156 women in the British Isles as against 12,913,166 men, giving the women a 39.6 per cent share of the total. Great as this advance clearly was one should notice the two qualifications: the age limitation and the decision to tie most women's rights to their husbands. The historian therefore has to explain both why this concession was made and why it took the peculiar form that it did; the apparent illogicality of the compromise seems almost to echo that of 1867 when householders in boroughs, but not in counties, received the vote, thus inviting a further reform in a few years.

As in most historical questions a number of explanations present themselves, and though historians disagree about them they are not all mutually incompatible by any means. Nonetheless there are grounds for attributing much more importance to some than to others. The first part of one's explanation for women's enfranchisement in 1918 is that the ground for it had been so thoroughly prepared before 1914. As is evident from the experience of a country like France, in the absence of a well entrenched campaign even the mass participation of women in a life-and-death war failed to make women's votes a matter of concern. But to draw attention to the pre-war build up is not simply to note the urgent political need for Asquith and his colleagues to resolve a question which posed a growing threat to their position. It is also to see that before the outbreak of war the lines of the *precise* solution to the problem had already emerged. The question was one of detail: on what terms were women to be enfranchised? The answer emerged in W.H. Dickinson's 1913 bill which included the vital proposal to enfranchise *wives*. This was the element incorporated into the 1918 Act which removed the fears of Liberal and Labour politicians about the potential danger of creating more Conservative votes by confining the qualification to single or propertied women. With the solution to the dilemma in sight what was needed by 1914 was a bill in a form which could pass – that is in a government measure.

The second part of the explanation is that during the war the opportunity for enfranchisement of women was created by the concern of the politicians to give votes to *men*. This arose because the war took many men away from their normal residences to the armed forces or to new jobs. As a result of this they disrupted the 12-month residence requirement which was necessary for the majority of electors who qualified as householders and lodgers. These movements interrupted the work in 1914 on which the new register of voters for 1915 was to be based. Thus from an early stage governments faced the prospect of massive disfranchisement of existing male voters. This they could not tolerate because of the very real prospect of having to conduct an election during the war, as had been done in 1900. For political reasons, therefore, they felt more or less obliged to find ways of changing the registration system to bring male voters back onto the lists. This was not, perhaps, technically a franchise reform but it was so close to it that advocates of the women's case in cabinet, notably Arthur Henderson, Lord Robert Cecil and Sir John Simon, inevitably raised wider questions. Now it was generally assumed, especially in view of the frustrating experiences over franchise reform before 1914 and the rivalry between the parties, that it would be impossible to resolve the issues during wartime. This of course was the judgement made by Mrs Fawcett among others. And for some time it seemed that this would prove to be correct. However, by the summer of 1916 the Conservatives, now partners in Asquith's Coalition, had grown increasingly restive about the whole conduct of the war. They anticipated a change of government which might well require an election. Therefore some solution to the shrinking register of voters had to be found. In the end the solution was what in retrospect looks simple. An all-party conference under the Speaker of the Commons, J.W. Lowther, was appointed to devise a comprehensive set of proposals.[54] Working expeditiously during the autumn of 1916 it reached a broad agreement by January

1917 on wide-ranging reforms including a simplified residence qualification for men giving them virtually full adult suffrage, a big
reduction in plural voting, special measures to enable servicemen to
vote, a sweeping reform of the boundaries of the constituencies and
many other innovations. Towards the end of their work they dealt with
women's suffrage, anxious not to throw away their achievements by
disagreement over this one item. By 15 to 6 the members voted in
favour of the principle of giving some votes to women; they rejected
equal suffrage with men by 12 to 10; and finally voted narrowly in
favour of W. H. Dickinson's proposal to enfranchise women local
government voters and wives of such voters. Yet, fearful about the
dangers of women becoming a majority, they also thought it prudent to
add a further control in the form of a maximum age limit, suggesting
either 30 or 35.[55] This was the scheme which was subsequently
accepted by the House of Commons by a vote of 387 to 57 and by the
Lords by 134 to 71.

These developments should be taken into account when assessing a
third explanation for women's enfranchisement put forward by Sandra
Holton, that it was due to the campaign and pressure exerted by the
women's movement during the war.[56] The argument here is not unlike
that over the role of the popular agitation during the 1866–7 crisis; and
the obvious flaw in Holton's view is that parliament evidently took up
the issue primarily to enfranchise men, not women. Moreover, as we
have also seen, there was virtually no campaign by the women during
1914 and 1915; indeed this period undoubtedly made it easier for
politicians to climb down without too much loss of face by 1916. In
1916 the women's campaign did revive somewhat – stimulated by
parliamentary initiatives as had been the case in 1866–7 – but whether
the campaign was significant in the sense that it actually influenced
politicians is debatable. Clearly the WSPU had all but ceased to
function. In the critical year – 1917 – Christabel Pankhurst spent six
months in the United States while Mrs Pankhurst prepared for a
propaganda trip to Russia. The National Union kept an eye on the
cabinet, and by May 1916 Mrs Fawcett judged it time to send Asquith a
letter on the suffrage; she was much encouraged by his response in
which he insisted that there was no intention of introducing franchise
legislation but that if it were done it would be 'without any prejudge-
ments from the controversies of the past.'[57] Thereafter the NUWSS and
the WFL encouraged their members to write to ministers pressing for
the vote, and there were meetings between the women and sympathetic
MPs including W.C. Anderson, Sir John Simon, W.H. Dickinson and

Lord Robert Cecil. But even now the NUWSS offered to accept any purely registration reform the cabinet proposed, provided that no franchise measures were included; this would have allowed them merely to bring back men onto the register if a practical way could be found. Nor did Asquith feel obliged to meet any of the deputations Mrs Fawcett tried to press upon him. This scarcely amounted to very strong pressure on the government. This is not surprising since, as a number of observers commented, there was no head of steam in the country over the issue. As the War Emergency Workers National Committee had told Sylvia Pankhurst in 1915, 'the public mood is far too much centred on war matters to concern itself very much about suffrage'.[58] Even in 1917, when the issue had gained much more public attention, apathy still reigned. Selina Cooper and another NUWSS organiser, Annot Robinson, who believed in the complete enfranchisement of working women, decided to try to arouse the women munitions workers in Lancashire and Yorkshire to sign a petition for women's suffrage. But Cooper soon admitted it was a 'thankless task' as most girls were quite happy to accept whatever parliament offered.[59]

Once the Speaker's Conference had been appointed the initiative passed out of the women's hands. Although Mrs Fawcett had two allies on the Conference in Dickinson and Simon, she was apparently kept in the dark about its progress. At length Dickinson revealed the decision taken on women's suffrage merely by saying it was 'something substantial upon which to build'. He strongly urged her to:

> do all you can to induce women to see that it will be bad tactics to fall foul of the Conference because it may not have done all that they expected. The whole matter will need the most careful handling so as to avoid the risk of the Government having an excuse for saying that as it [is] impossible to satisfy the advocates of W.S. they refrain from dealing with W.S. at all.[60]

In short she was advised against bargaining over the terms of reform. Now although Mrs Fawcett resented both the age limit and the effective exclusion of daughters living at home, she did in fact acquiesce, as did virtually all suffragists with the exception of Sylvia Pankhurst, who continued to argue for full adult suffrage. Thus, when she led a deputation of some 22 suffrage societies to meet Walter Long, the minister responsible, she concentrated not on the *terms* of enfranchisement but on the *form* that the legislation would take. She offered to cease all agitation for a wider franchise if the cabinet would include the Speaker's proposals in its bill.[61] At this point the suffragists were exercising some effective pressure in the sense that Long undoubtedly desired to settle the whole question and thereby avoid the reappearance of a women's agitation after the war. Even so, the government adamantly refused to do any more than include a women's suffrage clause in the bill. No whips were to be brought out in its support, and if the Commons were to reject the clause the cabinet would go ahead with the rest of the measure. Since Lloyd George refused to move from this position, and even the Labour MPs declined to insist on the inclusion of women[62] Mrs Fawcett gracefully backed down: 'we should greatly prefer an imperfect scheme that can pass'. Thus when all the evidence is added up the pressure from extra-parliamentary forces looks meagre, especially by comparison with some of the earlier reform crises in British history.

A fourth line of explanation for enfranchisement is the most obvious one of all: people had simply changed their minds in the sense that male prejudice against women had melted in the face of revelations about their capabilities during wartime and their contribution to the war effort. Though superficially attractive this is much harder to demonstrate than one might suppose and was, moreover, disparaged by several women activists including Helena Swanwick, Cicely Hamilton and Elizabeth Robins.[63] It is scarcely sufficient to point to the flattering comments made by politicians about women's work – which were often contradicted privately. It has to be shown that the re-evaluation of women's role was fundamental and lasting. Yet, as has already been noted, as early as 1917 a reaction against women workers was under way; any delay in granting women the vote would have left their cause exposed to the unsympathetic climate of 1919. Thus even at its height the shift in attitudes towards women was a fragile phenomenon. Traditional prejudices continued to flourish in spite of, or even because of, the unusual wartime roles performed by women. Indeed for many people the war seems to have had the effect of reawakening conventional notions about the separate spheres: 'we women were brought back to the primitive conception of the relative position of the two sexes', wrote Catherine Hartley, 'again man was the fighter, the protector of woman and home. And at once his power became a reality.'[64] Clearly the glorification of the fighting man was not simply an expedient of anti-suffragist males, anxious to hold the line against reform. Even amongst women it was commonly considered that men deserved priority treatment because they had fought. In 1916 when Sir Edward Carson proposed to make military service the qualification for voting Mrs Pankhurst authorised a Tory MP to announce in parliament that she would accept a measure to enfranchise servicemen even if women were still excluded: 'Could any woman face the possibility of the affairs of the country being settled by conscientious objectors, passive resisters and shirkers?'[65] This is why 1916 was such a dangerous year for the suffrage cause; for politicians did, indeed, give priority to the men, as is abundantly clear from three specific innovations they subsequently made. They disfranchised conscientious objectors for five years, enfranchised 19-year-old boys who had seen active service, and introduced schemes for absent and proxy voting for servicemen still abroad at election time.

Women's own attitudes towards their ability to contribute to national defence are particularly interesting, in that they show a remarkable continuity before, during and after the war. For example, as Anne Summers has pointed out, if women's part in the war effort led to the granting of the vote one would expect to see some signs of conversion to suffragism on the part of those involved in VAD and similar work before 1914. In fact there appears to be an inverse relationship between the two since the female leaders of the VADs such as Lady Tullibardine, Lady Wantage, Lady Jersey and the Duchess of Montrose remained markedly anti-suffragist. Similarly, the male politicians who were aware of the importance of women nurses in wartime seem not to have been influenced; they assumed the women would volunteer whether enfranchised or not.[66] During the conflict itself women often found it impossible to see their own role as equal to that of men. Katherine Furse, in spite of her major contribution, admitted, 'there was always a queer haunting feeling in my heart that as women we were profiting by the sacrifice of men.'[67] Such sentiments were echoed well into the 1920s by Lady Tullibardine, then Duchess of Atholl, when she opposed equal franchise for women:

> no one will dispute that the proposal means that women will be in the majority on the Parliamentary register. When I reach that point I cannot forget that the preponderance ... will have been largely due to, or at least greatly increased by, the fact that we lost 740,000 precious lives of men in the Great War and that that war is still taking its toll of ex-servicemen ... to propose a great extension of this kind looks like taking advantage of the heroic sacrifices of those men.[68]

Ultimately the decision lay with male politicians. Yet ascertaining their real opinions about women is no easy matter. It must be remembered that it was quite possible for men to accept votes for women, if the implications appeared to be limited, without necessarily abandoning their basic beliefs about the role of the two sexes. Several prominent anti-suffragists such as Walter Long have been identified as wartime converts; yet Long's private correspondence shows that his underlying hostility towards women's enfranchisement remained unchanged – he was simply making a tactical retreat in the face of a limited reform in order to avoid the possibility of something worse as generations of reluctant Tories had done before him.[69] On the strength of two parliamentary speeches in 1916 and 1917 Asquith appears to be the outstanding example of a politician who had fundamentally revised his views on women. In fact his opinions, as opposed to his political judgement, were unwavering. His comments on the women electors at Paisley in 1920 might have been written in 1885:

> There are about fifteen thousand women on the Register – a dim, impenetrable, for the most part ungetattable element – of whom all that one knows is that they are for the most part hopelessly ignorant of politics, credulous to the last degree, and flickering with gusts of sentiment like a candle in the wind.[70]

Yet Paisley's male voters he considered to be 'among the most intelligent audiences I have ever had'! What makes these remarks so striking is that they were made at a point when Asquith's political comeback was being accomplished by means of the acclaimed political talents of his *daughter*, Violet. If this failed to inspire a revision of his ideas on women in politics or to induce a more generous view, nothing would. In this light the historian cannot but look rather critically upon the bland compliments freely bestowed by politicians such as Asquith upon women's wartime work. The inescapable fact is that when faced with the necessity of effecting an embarrassing retreat from his long-held position of opposition to women's suffrage Asquith invoked fashionable patriotic eulogy as a reasonably dignified expedient; but it was little more than that.

Most MPs of this period have left no clear record of their views on the issue except, perhaps, in the form of their votes in the House of Commons. It is therefore possible to gain an approximate indication of the shift of opinion by comparing the parliamentary division on the women's clause on 19 June 1917 with members' behaviour on the Conciliation Bill in 1911. Both divisions took place in circumstances that were comparatively favourable for the women, for in 1911 the suffragettes had also suspended militancy, albeit briefly, in order to give the bill a fair chance. It transpires that of the 387 members who voted in favour of women's suffrage in 1917 only 169 had voted in 1911, 151 in favour and only 18 against the bill. Of the 57 members who voted against women's suffrage in 1917, 25 had participated in the

1911 division of whom 21 had opposed and 4 supported the bill. Thus in a total of 194 members involved in both divisions 18 had moved in favour and 4 against women's suffrage, a net gain of 14. While this corroborates the view that political opinion moved in favour of the women's cause during the war, it suggests that the shift was of very modest proportions. However, this is not surprising, for the parliament of 1917 was basically the one that had been elected in December 1910, modified somewhat through by-elections; like its predecessors the 1910 parliament already enjoyed a *suffragist* majority. The change that did occur after 1914 is to be explained, especially on the Liberal side, by the fact that the *terms* of the 1917 measure reflected their wishes much more closely than those of the Conciliation Bill. For the Conservatives, who had recorded pro-suffrage votes on a number of occasions since the 1880s, the objection to franchise extensions had been a matter of *class* rather than sex. Once they had been led to accept a vote for nearly all working-class men there was no strong reason of party interest to deny it to women. At worst they were expected to vote as their husbands did, and at best to be rather more inclined towards Conservatism.

Ultimately the politicians' behaviour in 1917 seems to reflect, if anything, the strength of traditional ideas about women as housewives and mothers rather than any radical re-evaluation of their role. If domesticity did not exactly help it at least moulded the final form which the women's franchise actually took. The heightened awareness was to have political implications for women in the sense that motherhood was held to constitute war service too. Indeed Earl Grey actually urged the Speaker's Conference, of which he was a member, to bestow an additional vote upon all married men and women who had produced four children on the grounds that such people had had 'an additional experience of life and their vote is therefore of more value. Further they have rendered a service to the state without which the state could not continue to exist.'[71] Such remarks were, of course, only consistent with the long-standing preference expressed by Liberal and Labour reformers for including the wives of workingmen in whatever changes might be made, and the traditional hostility towards bestowing the vote upon spinsters. Moreover, these preferences are reflected in the decisions actually made by politicians in 1916–17. Historians who wish to place the emphasis on women as wartime workers have to explain why parliament deliberately chose to *exclude* the young women who had performed such conspicuous service in the munitions factories. They of course were largely single; politicians tended to equate the flapper with feminism – incorrectly as it turned out – and feared that she might well use her political influence to defend her footing in industry and to retreat further from marriage and motherhood. On the other hand politicians felt much more comfortable about the woman over 30 to whom they gave the vote; she was more likely to be married, to have children and to have no lasting interest in employment or a career. In short she appeared to be a stable element in a changing world, one who was unlikely to seek to promote radical, feminist issues in parliament if enfranchised. As the history of the inter-war period shows, this judgement was not without some shrewdness. What makes this explanation of political motivation ultimately credible is that it follows very much the pattern of thought and behaviour exhibited in connection with the enfranchisement of men. In 1866, for example, Gladstone had reached the conclusion that certain carefully chosen workingmen were responsible individuals whose inclusion within the political system would tend to strengthen rather than destabilise it. In much the same spirit the politicians of 1918 took a finely calculated risk.

Chapter 3   Strategy and Tactics of the Women's Movement in the 1920s

Looking back from the perspective of 1928 the equal rights feminist, Ray Strachey, admitted that in 1917–18 suffragists had been too exhausted and distracted to realise that the tide was turning decisively in their favour.[1] Until a very late stage the life-and-death struggle with Germany absorbed their thoughts. After the comparative ease with which parliament granted the vote came a greater surprise: in October 1918 MPs conceded, almost without debate, the right of women to sit in the House of Commons, preferring to settle the issue rather than leaving it to Returning Officers to decide whether to accept women's nominations as valid. Hard on the heels of this coup came the December general election. There followed a scramble to find a few women candidates, and constituencies willing to take them, but there was no time for a serious effort to place women in winnable seats.

This period of confused and hectic activity allowed little real opportunity for the feminist leaders to think through the new situation. What should be their next step? Up to 1914 the movement had been, in effect, held together by concentration on the franchise; now it seemed logical to try to realise the broader goals of feminism. But feminists found themselves in a dilemma often faced by successful radical movements in British history. In the aftermath of a victory the forces of reform were easily dissipated unless some alternative means could be found to rally support and thus maintain the momentum. The reform of 1918 certainly invites comparison with the 1867 Reform Act. Both were illogical measures, sustained at the time by a certain ephemeral political rationale, which positively invited further legislation. Thus by 1884 the householder and lodger franchises had been extended from boroughs to counties. Similarly after 1918 the anomaly of the 30-year age limit provided one clear target to aim at. Yet it was insufficient as the basis for a great campaign. Those feminists for whom the vote was essentially symbolic grew complacent, thinking the struggle for women's emancipation effectively over but for the details. But many recognised that the immediate question was whether to concentrate on achieving equal suffrage or to widen the range of demands. The latter was naturally attractive both because it was more likely to inject fresh enthusiasm and because, in view of the 8 million new women voters, it might be expected to produce results. Many women's questions would now, surely, become practical politics at last.

Yet behind this lay the problem of deciding by what *means* to capitalise upon women's presumed influence. A wider agenda implied a proliferation of pressure groups devoted to specific causes. Would they require a new umbrella group to co-ordinate their activity or would the existing ones suffice? Or was it appropriate in the new circumstances to be more ambitious and pioneer a new political party as the vehicle for women's aspirations? Then there was the associated question as to the kind of methods to be employed. In the light of women's enfranchisement had the balance of advantage shifted away from militancy towards constitutional methods? If women now enjoyed a footing within the pale of the constitution was the logical next step to work through the existing political parties to achieve goals and abandon separate women's organisations?

The Demise of the Militant Tradition

Almost alone amongst women's leaders the Pankhursts scarcely paused to think through these problems. For them perpetual motion was the only tactic, and opportunism the chief philosophy. Thus as their role in the war reached a plateau in 1917 they began to chart a route into the post-war world. As early as November 1917 they decided that the vote was in the bag, and the time had come to plan for their future careers. In a speech at the Queen's Hall Christabel announced:

> when certain influences are seeking to herd the coming women voters into the wrong political camps, we ... are the people upon whom falls the duty and responsibility of starting the Women's Party ... by starting fair and square the Women's Party can avoid many of the mistakes that men's parties have made in the past.[2]

There was undoubtedly some shrewdness in this initiative. In the circumstances of 1917–19 with trade union expansion, widespread industrial militancy and mass enfranchisement, even a Labour leader like Arthur Henderson was disquieted at the potential for a revolutionary situation. Christabel simply exploited the greater fears of the right. She gained funding for her Women's Party from the British Commonwealth Union (BCU), favourable propaganda from the Northcliffe press, and the sympathy of the leaders of the Coalition government. Lloyd George reminded Bonar Law that the Pankhursts had been 'extremely useful' to the government in the industrial areas where they had 'fought the Bolshevik and Pacifist element with great skill, tenacity and courage'.[3] The Pankhurst name might be a valuable asset in seeing the Coalition through a general election.

In practice coalitionism was the real rationale for the new party. Its literature in the election billed Christabel as the 'Patriotic Candidate' not the Women's Party candidate; and the only women's question referred to was improved housing. For the most part her propaganda concentrated on the standard causes of the far right – making Germany pay for the war, removing aliens from government departments and essential industries, curtailing the work of shop stewards and trade unions, and opposing Irish Home Rule. Clearly the Women's Party was a mere masquerade, a deviation from feminism and not a development from it, the origins of which were apparent in the rightward drift of Pankhurst politics well before 1914. Christabel's object in forming a party was essentially to strengthen her bargaining power vis-à-vis Lloyd George and to attempt to obscure the fact that there were no candidates except herself. Like the WSPU it was a personal vehicle: 'we have no constitution beyond the fact that our leaders are Mrs Pankhurst, Miss Christabel Pankhurst, Mrs Flora Drummond and Miss Annie Kenney'.[4] Yet the party served its immediate purpose. Lloyd George successfully urged Bonar Law to offer Christabel a free run in the Conservative seat of Westbury in Wiltshire. She, however, switched her attention to the newly created constituency of Smethwick where, after much grumbling, the local Conservative candidate withdrew. Standing as the officially approved Coalitionist Christabel fought a characteristically belligerent campaign, attacking her Labour opponent as pro-German and appealing to women to wage a crusade against Bolshevism. In the event she lost by 700 votes.

The new party strategy, culminating in the defeat at Smethwick, is significant in three main ways. The first is personal. At first sight Christabel's performance looks impressive in that she came the closest to victory of any of the women's candidates in 1918, apart from the Sinn Feiner elected in Dublin. Closer inspection modifies this impression, however. In 1922 Smethwick saw another straight contest between Labour and a right-wing Coalitionist. While throughout the country Labour improved its position markedly in 1922, in Smethwick the party's share of the poll fell back. In 1918 the Labour candidate had evidently done well, probably because he was up against Christabel. It is not difficult to see why. The Pankhursts had tackled working-class seats before, notably at Bow and Bromley in 1912 where their high-handed approach had helped to alienate George Lansbury's support. But the Pankhurst capacity for self-delusion blotted out such lessons.

During the war Christabel had convinced herself that her tours of the industrial districts had turned the workers away from militancy and Bolshevism – notwithstanding the evidence of rapidly growing strike action from 1916 onwards. Thus she insisted on standing in the West Midlands where Labour was to score several victories and near-misses in 1918. Ironically she had turned down the offer of Westbury where, with the 'Coupon' and no Tory opponent, she could hardly have lost. She had almost certainly thrown away the chance to become Britain's first woman MP by sheer political misjudgement.

Secondly, the election result immediately put the Women's Party on the slippery slope. By 1919 the BCU had concluded that Christabel was not a vote winner and withdrew its funds. Moreover, for Christabel the humiliation of defeat proved too much. In 1919 the party folded and she began her retreat from public life, rationalising her behaviour by saying that it was not possible to change the world by means of women's enfranchisement because democracy itself was now so decayed.[5] The rapid demise of the initiative inevitably had a dampening effect on those other feminists interested in a new party for women.

Thirdly, one must consider the wider implications for the women's movement and militancy. We have already noticed how the Pankhursts rapidly lost their grip on women's suffrage after 1914. Soon a virtual Pankhurst diaspora was under way. Christabel went abroad, recanted her faith in women's suffrage and discovered religion.[6] In the United States she found a ready reception in her new role as God's appointed representative dedicated to the second coming of Christ. Meanwhile Mrs Pankhurst found herself without means of material support. She too embarked on American tours and by 1921 had become a lecturer for the National Council for Combating Venereal Disease in Canada. When she returned to Britain in 1926 she had become a staunch Conservative, and in order to spite Sylvia in the East End of London, became adopted as candidate for the hopeless seat of Whitechapel. She died in 1928 before the election came. Sylvia, buried in her work in London, had moved as far to the left as Christabel had to the right. She was involved in the Leeds soviet in 1917, briefly joined the Labour Party and contributed to the formation of the British Communist Party. Repudiating the soviet tactics of co-operation with parliamentary socialism she visited Russia in 1920 where Lenin was to castigate her ideas as an 'infantile disorder'. Her complete inability to co-operate with any section of the Labour movement rapidly reduced her to the leadership of a tiny personal organisation. It was not until the 1930s that Sylvia discovered her last great cause: the restoration of the emperor Haile

Selassie to his throne after the Italian invasion of Abyssinia, which occupied her for the rest of her life. Finally there was the youngest sister, Adela, who had been dispatched to Australia where she, too, pursued a bewildering variety of issues. In 1916 she campaigned against conscription, was active after the war in industrial strikes, but fell out with the unions and by 1929 had decided to make a stand against Communism with a new 'Guild of Empire'. In the Second World War she campaigned to persuade Australians to adopt a pro-Japanese policy, a bizarre twist even by Pankhurst standards.

While these twists and turns underline the shallowness of Pankhurst politics and their ceaseless search for self-promotion, their careers do have considerable negative significance: all were decisively lost to the women's movement. But was this simply a reflection of Pankhurst idiosyncrasy or more typical of the militants after 1918? Certainly the pre-war impetus was never recaptured. Annie Kenney married and left public life. Flora Drummond founded the Women's Guild of Empire in 1928, an organisation dedicated to opposing strikes and Communism. A distinct contingent of former suffragettes, of whom Mary Richardson was the most prominent, joined the British Union of Fascists. This left a dwindling band of women who gathered for the celebratory reunions organised by the Suffragette Fellowship, but who ceased to be active campaigners. Only the more left-wing ex-militants such as Emmeline Pethick-Lawrence, Dorothy Evans and Monica Whately advanced beyond the cause of suffrage. Thus the Women's Freedom League, which had originated as a more democratic breakaway from the WSPU in 1907, continued to function much as before. However, the WFL's militancy had always been of a carefully defined kind which took the form of non-payment of taxes rather than violence. The most striking feature of the WFL was its loyalty to the equal rights tradition of feminism as is shown by the continuing emphasis on equal franchise and resistance to protective legislation. After 1918 its campaigning methods were of a conventional form indistinguishable from other women's groups.[7] Indeed the WFL found itself handicapped by its inability to carve out a distinctive role; this was reflected in the 1920s by its small and dwindling membership, a severe shortage of funds, and a heavy reliance upon a handful of leaders including Dr Elizabeth Knight, Florence Underwood and Helena Normanton.

A more significant attempt to effect the transition to post-war politics originated with a group of women centred around Lady Rhondda (Margaret Haig). Daughter of D.A. Thomas, the Liberal MP, she had been brought into her father's business affairs and took a particular interest in his newspapers. Though a WSPU member her participation in militancy had been of a rather nominal kind as her memoirs make clear.[8] After working at the Ministry of National Service during the war she found herself by 1918 with a good deal of money, business experience, an interest in the press but no immediate challenge. She therefore decided to establish a new feminist journal, *Time and Tide*, which was launched in 1920 under the editorship of Helen Archdale. The new paper made its pitch on the basis that the national press was merely the instrument of political parties, that it failed to treat men and women equally and was written by men with merely self-conscious inserts for women. *Time and Tide* proposed to combine discussions of the standard political questions of the day with articles of feminist interest, as well as book reviews, theatre, music, gardening and sport. Its pages were filled by a distinguished range of contributors including Rebecca West, Vera Brittain, Winifred Holtby, Elizabeth Robins, E.M. Delafield, Virginia Woolf, Rose Macaulay, Cicely Hamilton and Helena Swanwick.

Yet how far *Time and Tide* may be seen as an extension of the militant tradition is questionable. Its distinctiveness lay in the emphasis on an *independent* role for women in public life. It regretted that Lady Astor wore a party label, and argued throughout the 1920s that it was still a mistake for women to join parties while they remained so low down the political agenda. Instead women should somehow band together as voters and force the parties to change their priorities.[9] However, *Time and Tide* never tried to promote a women's party. As the 1920s wore on it was increasingly reduced to criticising the parties for failing to place women in winnable seats and women politicians for giving excessive loyalty to their male leaders.[10] Although *Time and Tide* proved to be a success as a journal, it never developed into a major weapon for feminism. Lady Rhondda's approach was sternly up-market: 'a first-class review', she boasted, 'is read by comparatively few people, but they are the people who count, the people of influence.'[11] At a time when 8 million women had recently obtained the vote this was a surprisingly elitist strategy to adopt. Others with less feminist, or anti-feminist, ideas were ready to exploit the women's market. Led by the *Daily Mail* the national press spawned its women's pages, dedicated to domestication, while still opposing equal franchise. Meanwhile the women's magazines expanded rapidly in number and in circulation. According to the editor of *Woman* Lady Rhondda was 'completely mystified' by the success of such magazines.[12] As a result no attempt was ever made to launch a popular feminist paper. Even at its lofty level

Time and Tide soon faltered, perhaps responding to the pressures of the market. After 1928 when equal franchise had been won, Rhondda commented that she 'felt free to drop the business. It was a blessed relief that one had not got to trouble with things of that sort any more.'[13] Indeed the journal's feminist agenda does not seem to have outlived the 1920s, though it did retain a number of female contributors. During the 1930s it developed into an independent journal for current affairs and reviews.

However, Rhondda's work did not end here. One of the magazine's roles was to provide a platform for a new organisation, the Six Point Group, founded in 1921. With Rebecca West and some other ex-militants in its ranks this can be seen as, in some sense, the successor to the WSPU. Yet the Six Point Group's militancy was carefully circumscribed; and it is better understood in terms of the *equal rights* tradition of feminism. The organisation took its name from the six immediate areas of reform for women: (i) the position of the unmarried woman and her child; (ii) the widow with children; (iii) the law on child assault; (iv) unequal rights of guardianship enjoyed by married parents; (v) unequal pay for men and women teachers; (vi) inequality of opportunity for men and women in the civil service. This reflected both a judgement of what was attainable in the early 1920s, and the fact that no single issue was big enough to dominate women's activities. Branches of existing feminist organisations who were invited to join the Six Point Group objected that it was merely duplicating their own work unnecessarily.[14] But, echoing the WSPU, the new body contended that the successors to the NUWSS were ineffective campaigners and that reform must come through government legislation, not private members' bills; to this end women's efforts must be co-ordinated through a single body and concentrated on a limited list of realistic measures.[15]

In terms of tactics the nearest approach to militancy involved the publication by the Six Point Group of 'Blacklists' of MPs who had been the worst opponents of women's interests, and a 'White List' of the best supporters, for the general elections of 1922, 1923, 1924.[16] Women were urged to set aside party loyalty and work to defeat the Blacklisted members. In 1922 for example they had the satisfaction of reporting that of 23 MPs on the Blacklist 9 had been defeated, 2 stood down and only 12 had been re-elected. In practice, however, this was only a shade more coercive than the pressure being applied by the constitutionalists at this time, though their emphasis was perhaps rather more on supporting friends of women's causes. Friction between the organisations was not, therefore, of any great consequence, especially as the Six Point Group remained a small organisation concentrated in and around London.

Thus, even taking the WFL and the Six Point Group into account, it can hardly be said that there was a return to Edwardian forms of militancy after 1918. Militancy might well have been provoked by, for example, the widespread sacking of married women in the early 1920s. The local authorities responsible for such discrimination would have been vulnerable targets for such tactics. Yet no one tried to resuscitate the old campaign. Age, infirmity and loss of interest by many ex-suffragettes is only part of the explanation. In spite of public protestations to the contrary, militants were not always convinced that their methods had worked; more to the point, they seemed less likely to be effective in the new conditions in which women enjoyed the vote. Ultimately, as Rhondda herself said, the vote had been essentially a symbol of women's alienation from the parliamentary system; once it had been removed they never felt the same outrage and antagonism, notwithstanding the indignities and discrimination women still suffered.

From Suffrage to Equal Citizenship

After the war – as in the Edwardian period – the National Union of Women's Suffrage Societies stood at the centre of the women's movement. But it had become virtually a one-issue organisation, and now that that issue had been partly removed some fresh initiatives seemed called for. However, the NUWSS was a more democratic institution than the WSPU and took more time to reassess its position. Two new steps were adopted. Firstly, the NUWSS symbolised its intention of promoting a wider programme than simply the franchise by taking a new name, the National Union of Societies for Equal Citizenship (NUSEC) and defining its objective as to 'obtain all other reforms, economic, legislative and social as are necessary to secure a real equality of liberties, status and opportunities between men and women'. Secondly, it accepted the need to extend the reach of the feminist movement. Before the war Eleanor Rathbone had perceived that when women eventually won the vote most would require encouragement and education in order to make use of their new influence. It was not clear that the existing organisations were best equipped to handle this role, and so Rathbone pioneered the Women's Citizens Association (WCA) in Liverpool in 1913 with a view to increasing the level of awareness amongst women who had not been connected with feminist organisations. In the summer of 1917 at a meeting under Mrs Maria Ogilvie Gordon it was decided to establish the WCA as a national body and by 1918 branches were being formed in the country. One of the Women's Citizens Association's most important practical tasks lay in encouraging women to participate in local government, and it was logical for it to absorb the branches of the Women's Local Government Society when that body disbanded. With its largely middle-class and non-party character the WCA clearly enjoyed a lot of common ground and common personnel with the existing feminist groups. Indeed in 1924 the WCA decided to merge with NUSEC, an indication that in spite of its ostensibly distinct role it was really catering to the same audience of educated middle-class feminists, rather than extending the range of the movement. For example, a working-class NUSEC organiser, Selina Cooper, found that in a Lancashire town like Nelson it was virtually impossible to sustain a WCA amongst the working women of the community.[17]

However, during the early 1920s there seemed to be ample grounds for optimism. The doors of parliament suddenly yawned wide as politicians sought to know what the women were thinking. Mrs Fawcett retired in 1920, giving way as president to the vigorous Eleanor Rathbone. Although Rathbone eventually led the movement towards what was called the 'New Feminism', it should be stressed that in the 1920s there was a good deal of continuity with the Edwardian pattern. As yet NUSEC appeared to be firmly within the equal rights tradition of feminism; it remained strongly wedded to parliamentary methods, indeed it considered that its skill and experience in this respect would bring great dividends after enfranchisement; it clung to the non-party strategy; and it continued to co-operate closely with male political allies.

Although NUSEC's programme for the 1920s rapidly grew rather ambitious, the plan was to concentrate on a limited number of issues each year according to what seemed feasible. Equal franchise continued to be a focus throughout the decade. Amongst the inequalities targeted were the opening of the professions and the civil service to women (a goal only partly achieved by the 1919 Sex Disqualification (Removal) Act), equal pay especially for teachers, equal guardianship over children, the equal moral standard (by which was meant the laws on divorce, solicitation and prostitution), and equal treatment in the honours list. NUSEC also campaigned to defend the right of married women to employment, and to resist protective legislation; this latter eventually produced a major split in 1927 and initiated the shift to the 'New Feminism'. Finally NUSEC espoused the separate taxation of married women, Lady Astor's bills to control sales of alcohol, proportional representation (a way of facilitating the election of women), and the provision of birth control advice, though this received little attention in this period, and, perhaps most importantly, widows' pensions. This last issue was a harbinger of the shift that was to come in the end of the decade, but as yet the emphasis still lay with the equal rights reforms.

How were these objectives to be attained? Partly by influencing the policy of the political parties – NUSEC's traditional role – but also by promoting the election of women committed to a feminist programme. Yet in both cases the strategy assumed a non-party stance. In the immediate aftermath of war NUSEC clearly retained a footing in each camp. Staunch Liberals included Margery Corbett Ashby, Margaret Wintringham and Mrs H.A.L.Fisher; Ethel Snowden, Edith Picton-Turberville and Mary Stocks represented Socialism; and Lady Selborne, Dame Helen Gwynne Vaughan and Lady Frances Balfour the Conservatives. There also remained many women such as Fawcett, Rathbone or Kathleen Courtney who were rather detached from or hostile to party politics.

Strictly speaking the NUWSS had abandoned its non-party stance in 1912 in favour of co-operation with Labour. Yet for many of the leaders this had been a marriage of convenience; indeed Rathbone and others had briefly resigned over the policy. The sudden achievement of women's suffrage in 1917 meant that the Election Fighting Fund policy never had to be tested at a general election, so that in 1918 NUSEC offered support to suitable women candidates regardless of party. Though there was apparently no recrimination over this tacit abandonment of Labour it does appear that the enfranchisement of women accelerated the migration of some left-wing activists, such as Ellen Wilkinson, into party politics; moreover the split over the war in 1915 had already led some radical women like Isabella Ford and Margaret Ashton away from NUWSS. As a result the centre of gravity after the war had moved somewhat to the centre-right. This was underlined in the early 1920s by an apparently close association between NUSEC and David Lloyd George who clearly cultivated the movement and was sympathetically treated in the new journal, the *Women's Leader*. This was, however, more an indication that Lloyd George was expected to deliver some of the reforms NUSEC wanted than a long-term commitment.

At the Coupon Election some fifteen women candidates stood in

England, Scotland and Wales including one Conservative, one Women's Party, four Labour, four Liberals, and five Independents. There had been too little time to secure seats for women, and most of the women stood in hopeless constituencies. One of the strongest was Mary Macarthur in Stourbridge, where but for her untimely death she would probably have been victorious in 1922. Several of the women failed to stick to good prospects. For example, had Violet Markham (Liberal) fought Mansfield again or Mrs Despard (Labour) fought Battersea North both might have enjoyed the victory that fell to their respective parties in 1922. The five Independent candidates in 1918 stood in affluent London seats (Chelsea, Richmond, Hendon and Brentford) and in the equally hopeless Glasgow Bridgeton, polling from 5 per cent to 20 per cent of the votes cast. After 1918 Independent women candidates were rarely promoted, the chief exception being Rathbone who stood in East Toxteth in 1922 under WCA auspices, and was eventually elected in 1929 for the Combined English Universities. Only the combination of a special electorate and the single Transferable Vote system made her success possible. Clearly a women's party never appeared feasible, perhaps for financial as much as political reasons, and it seemed less complicated to lend extra support to women fighting under the party flag. In practice, however, this tactic proved by no means easy. Not all feminists were willing to accept a party label. None of the parties was keen to nominate women; and some of the few who were adopted proved insufficiently feminist to merit support from NUSEC.

To a large extent candidates were simply beyond NUSEC's influence. However, several early strokes of luck obscured the difficulties. Two by-elections in which women successfully filled their husbands' seats – Lady Astor at Plymouth Sutton in 1919 and Mrs Wintringham at Louth in 1920 – buoyed up the NUSEC leaders. Both were feminist, their evident co-operation in parliament augured well for an informal women's party, and Wintringham's victory as an orthodox Liberal was widely interpreted as proof that women would in fact be vote-winners for their parties after all. Once the foothold had been established there was some pressure on each party to get its best women into the Commons.

Yet the momentum generated by Astor and Wintringham was not really sustained. The problem was partly a Conservative one. They enjoyed the most winnable constituencies, but the women they produced often had no noticeable feminist credentials, even Astor having no history of work for women's suffrage. At Berwick in 1923 Mrs Hilton Phillipson declined to endorse NUSEC policies; and both she and the Duchess of Atholl, also elected in 1923, voted against bills to grant women equal franchise. At Southend in 1927 Lady Iveagh refused to reply to NUSEC's questions, and they were reduced to supporting her on the grounds that she was, at least, a woman.[18] In the same year Mrs Pankhurst undermined NUSEC's work in by-elections by holding meetings for the Conservative candidates at the same time as its own meetings for women. Nor were the resources sufficient to make a wide impact. A rally in 1920, attended by Astor and Lloyd George, designed to appeal for funds to promote women MPs, raised a mere £200.[19] In any case it emerged in due course that Conservative candidates did not want the money.

Opportunities to back Labour candidates were rather greater, if less likely to succeed; but here, too, problems emerged. At the Northampton by-election in 1920 the *Woman's Leader* could not conceal its dismay that Margaret Bondfield conducted her campaign around the conflict of labour and capital like an orthodox party candidate, with virtually no mention of women's questions.[20] Bondfield was, nonetheless, regularly supported, as indeed was Arthur Henderson at his by-election in Newcastle East in 1923. But socialists like Jennie Lee simply refused to respond to NUSEC approaches even from local branches.[21] One difficulty was that when NUSEC gave public support to a woman they were assumed to be backing her party too; thus the feminist Labour candidate at Stroud, Edith Picton-Turbervill, found that the local SEC had cancelled its meeting for her because of opposition by women supporters of the other parties. Consequently, as early as 1924 Rathbone proposed abandoning the attempt to concentrate on seats where women were standing.[22]

The alternative was to propagandise the parties at large. For example, NUSEC extracted pledges of support from the party leaders on equal franchise – and then kept reminding them of the need to live up to their promises. On the approach of a general election each party chairman or chief whip would be tackled and urged to incorporate the NUSEC programme into the manifesto – which the Liberal and Labour parties did to some extent. It was also easy at first to subject by-election candidates to questionnaires and sometimes to hold joint meetings on women's questions. The response of candidates at the Paisley by-election of 1920 shows how, under the spotlight, male politicians were all too prone to producing identical answers – which rather cut the ground from under the women's feet (see Table 3.1). In time, however, candidates took the measure of the new women electors and they grew more resistant. At the Bosworth by-election in 1927, for example, the

Table 3.1 The Paisley By-election, 1920

UNANIMITY

The following answers were given by the candidates at the Paisley Election to the questions put to them by representatives of the National Union of Societies for Equal Citizenship.

1. Do you support the equal moral standard for men and women and will you watch legislation dealing with the social evil with a view to the establishment of a real and not merely verbal equality between the sexes in the laws and their administration?

Mr MacKean (Unionist)	Mr Asquith (Liberal)	Mr Biggar (Labour)
Yes, certainly.	Certainly.	Certainly.

2. Are you in favour of the further extension of the franchise to women by lowering the age limit, and making the qualification the same as for men?

Yes.	Certainly.	Certainly.

3. Are you in favour of giving the same nationality rights to women as to men?

I am.	Qualified assent.	Certainly.

4. Are you in favour of the separate taxation of the incomes of married women?

I am.	Yes, certainly.	No.

5. Are you in favour of the equal guardianship of children by both parents?

Certainly.	Yes.	Certainly.

6. Are you in favour of the full professional and industrial freedom of opportunity for women?

I am.	Yes, certainly.	Yes, with reservations.

7. Are you in favour of giving men and women equal pay for work of equal value?

Certainly.	Certainly.	Certainly.

8. Are you in favour of giving the wife in Scotland full control over her property as well as her income, as is the law in England?

Yes.	Yes.	Yes.

three candidates simply issued a joint refusal to respond to NUSEC's questions. Local societies were more likely to be able to engage their candidates' attention. At the 1923 general election some 65 societies were reported to be active in 120 constituencies, and a similar number in 1924. But this was obviously not a very extensive effort and fewer than half the NUSEC branches were involved. The Glasgow society explained that they had abstained simply because their members were working for their respective parties.[23] Thus, the pressure both on the parties and on behalf of individual women candidates amounted to a small-scale operation. In 1924 NUSEC promoted just 14 women, and the same number in 1929. The distribution on this occasion is an indication of the difficulties of pursuing a non-party strategy, for there were six Labour women (Susan Lawrence, Picton-Turbervill, Monica Whately, Ellen Wilkinson, Margaret Bondfield and Eleanor Stewart), six Liberals (Mrs Wintringham, Mrs Corbett Ashby, Lady Stewart, Mrs Hornabrook, Miss M.E. Marshall and Mrs C.B. Alderton), one Conservative (Lady Astor) and Rathbone as an Independent. The figure of 14 should be set against the total number of women candidates which was 41 in 1924 and 69 in 1929. A combination of inadequate resources and hostility from the parties was gradually strangling the election policy. While NUSEC chose to regard the election of eight women in 1923 as a triumph, it is not clear that these victories, any more than the four in 1924 or the fourteen in 1929, owed anything of significance to the work of the women's pressure groups.

The Women's Party in Local Government

In contrast to parliamentary politics local government appeared to present a much more satisfactory theatre for women's public participation after the war. Since the 1870s women had been winning elections at this level especially in School Boards and Boards of Guardians. The 1918 Representation of the People Act increased the number of women local government electors from 1 million to 8.5 million. When she attained the age of 30 a woman could now register on the basis of her husband's local government qualification. Alternatively, at the age of 21 she could be registered on the strength of a personal qualification during the six months up to 15 December or 15 June as (i) an occupier, as owner or tenant, of land or premises; (ii) a joint occupier of land or premises; (iii) an occupier of unfurnished lodgings; or (iv) an inhabitant of a dwelling house by virtue of office or employment.

Table 3.2 Women Elected to Local Authorities in England and
Wales 1914–1937

	1914	1923	1930	1937	% of total
County Councils	7[a]	68	138	242	5
City and Borough Councils	19	213	439	599	5
London Boroughs	22	116	289	253	15.8
UDCs	11	104		225[b]	4.5
			308		
RDCs	200	353		334[b]	4.6
Total	259	754	1174	1653	5.4
Boards of Guardians	1536	2323	–	–	

[a]   Women were not eligible for election until 1907.
[b]   Returns for UDCs and RDCs incomplete. If women were represented in the
same proportion as on bodies for which returns were made there would be an
additional 684 giving a total of 2346.
Sources: The Women's Year Book 1923–24; Memorandum, Central Women's
Electoral Committee (1924); Billington Greig Papers 281; Ray Strachey (ed.),
Our Freedom and Its Results (1936).

There seems to have been a long-term increase in women's representation on local elective bodies which, with some interruptions, was
sustained throughout the inter-war period. This began in 1919 when
elections were resumed after the wartime truce; for many women their
public wartime work had just come to an end or was about to, and
municipal politics offered at least one alternative form of activity. From
their foothold in the pre-war period women extended their presence so
that they were represented on almost two in every three local authorities by the late 1930s (see Table 3.3).

However, two qualifications must be made to this picture. The first is
that the local government reforms of 1929, which replaced the elected
Boards of Guardians with the Public Assistance Committees of local
authorities, dealt a severe blow to female participation, since the
Guardians had always comprised the lion's share of elected women –
over three-quarters in 1923 for example. The gains made on other
bodies clearly came nowhere near to compensating for this loss.
Secondly, in spite of the increase in the number of women councillors,
they remained at only 5 to 6 per cent of the total by 1937, a surprisingly
low proportion in some ways. No doubt their position in the House of
Commons was even weaker – 1.5 per cent in 1935 as against a high

Table 3.3   Distribution of Women on Elective Local Authorities

	1914 Local authorities with women members		1937 Local authorities with women members	
	with	without	with	without
County Councils	32	30	57	4
City and				
Borough Councils	124	200	231	140
London Boroughs			28	–
UDCs	73	730	147	126
RDCs	228	364	152	70
Boards of				
Guardians	550	90	–	–
All	1007	1414	615	340

point for the inter-war period of 2.4 per cent in 1931. But in view of the fact that women had roughly 50 years experience in local politics one might have expected them to have capitalised on their position more extensively. In some ways local government appeared more attractive, or at least attainable, than the House of Commons. It was easier and less expensive to get elected. The office was more manageable from the point of view of a woman tied to a home. Some, such as Ruth Dalton who had experience of the London County Council and the House of Commons, also felt that one could play a more constructive and satisfying role than as an MP. This helps to explain why local government experience failed to provide many women with a route of advance to parliamentary candidatures. Certainly some MPs, including Susan Lawrence, Ellen Wilkinson, Thelma Cazalet Keir and Eleanor Rathbone, had previously served on local authorities, but this does not appear to have assisted them in obtaining parliamentary nominations.

Most importantly, many women appreciated the relative absence of party control in local authorities. Lists published by the *Woman's Leader* in 1921 suggest that a majority of the women elected were still Independents,[24] and contemporary comment indicates that some women resented party discipline and rigid allegiance to party. This sometimes reflected a lasting cynicism, especially amongst middle-class women, as a result of the frustrating struggle for the vote, and was especially pronounced among Liberal women in the 1920s.

On the other hand, in clinging to their independence women were swimming against the tide, since after the war the party machines steadily increased their grip on local politics. This was partly the result of Labour's dramatic expansion from 1919 which meant that in many places municipal elections took the form of a Labour-versus-the-rest battle. Although this created new opportunities for Labour candidates the party could still be choosy. It is significant that otherwise well-qualified Labour women such as Selina Cooper and Hannah Mitchell were turned down as municipal candidates because they were regarded by the party as too feminist and as insufficiently amenable to discipline.[25] Nor were the circumstances of the 1920s entirely auspicious in local government. Controversies over the dismissal of married women employed by the councils, or the provision of information on birth control at local maternity clinics quickly isolated feminists from most male politicians. Further, ratepayers sometimes regarded women as liable to promote excessive expenditure because of their enthusiasm for education or health and child welfare provision. Consequently feminist candidates encountered difficulty in periods such as 1920–1 when 'Anti-Waste' became a fashionable cry, especially as women voters were thought to be the mainstay of retrenchment campaigns.[26]

Nonetheless, local government clearly provided an attractive field of endeavour for many feminists, and interestingly it demonstrated the limited viability of the idea of a women's party. This form of women's politics was most nearly realised in those urban areas which contained a substantial base of educated, middle-class women. For example, the conspicuous strength of women in London was a feature both before and after the war. There a body called the Women's Municipal Party had been established which took advantage of the post-war situation very effectively. By the 1930s one in six councillors in the London Boroughs was a woman, as was a similar proportion (24 in 144) on the London County Council. Other towns went some way down this road. In Glasgow, for example, several groups including the Women's Citizens Association, Women's Suffrage Society, the National Council for Women and the British Women's Temperance Association, decided to set up a Women's Local Representation Joint Committee in 1919. Its function was to secure the election of women to local bodies by finding suitable candidates, appealing for funds and supplying canvassers.[27] Though only a loose federal organisation this committee usually managed to secure the election of three or four women each year. But it suffered from a certain reluctance to stand amongst many of those invited. Moreover, its credentials as the women's party were undermined by the fact that a larger number of women stood for Labour. As a result the committee's Independent women looked a little like an anti-

Labour front, drawn as they were from middle-class women from Liberal or Conservative backgrounds. Further, the issues they took up, notably the employment of married women, made them rather antagon-istic to the local Labour forces. This was something of a contrast to the national position in that most of the parliamentary candidates backed by NUSEC were anti-Conservative by the late 1920s. In the long run this inconsistency could not be sustained, hence the Glasgow members increasingly withdrew from the promotion of candidates at both municipal and parliamentary level. A more extreme case was that of Newcastle and Gateshead. Here all but one of the women councillors were Labour representatives. Most were, indeed, the wives of Labour councillors. They concentrated on health, sanitation and maternity on the council, leaving topics like finance strictly to the men. In short, loyalty to the Labour movement largely precluded feminism or any challenge to the status quo.[28]

A different social and political configuration made a town like Cambridge a much more congenial theatre for independent feminists. Here the Women's Suffrage Society was supplemented in 1918 by a Women's Citizens Association acting as an umbrella organisation to which some eighteen local women's societies affiliated, including the Women's Liberal Association. This latter point underlines the extent to which women Liberals could be detached from their party after the war. Under WCA auspices the first woman, Mrs Keynes, was elected to the town council in 1918. By 1929 seven women had been returned, all as Independents, as well as four to the County Council. Attempts were also made to persuade local Women's Institutes to encourage their members to stand for rural district councils. At every election, whether parliamentary or municipal, candidates were subjected to ques-tionnaires on women's issues. As a result something approaching a real women's party may be said to have existed in Cambridge in this period. Clearly the university formed a vital source of personnel; Labour was not very strong and the Liberals evidently weak in the post-war years. Consequently the candidates were invariably radical Liberal women with marked pro-Labour sympathies who enjoyed straight contests with Conservatives. They appealed for votes on the basis that they were women, non-party and non-businessmen. Almost all the NUSEC issues as well as the promotion of women police were advocated in the 1920s. This made for a fairly coherent social-political platform which was electorally realistic and successful by comparison with Glasgow because of the relative weakness of the conventional parties.

Even in Cambridge, however, the strategy proved difficult to sustain in the long run. As the 1920s wore on there seemed to be less room for women candidates in that potential nominees often refused to stand against sitting councillors. All parties, including the Liberals, began to object to Independent women, and the result was a withdrawal of some women from the Independent platform in favour of a party label.[29] 'The mind of the average elector does not seem to understand that Independence in municipal affairs is compatible with partisanship in Parliamentary politics', complained one activist. Thus, although by the 1930s the WCA, with 700 members, still flourished, it was on the retreat even in Cambridge.

The Alternative: Party Politics

Throughout the inter-war period feminists found themselves rather torn between their traditional, indirect approach to politics – using a non-party organisation to bring pressure to bear on the politicians – and the more direct method – exploiting the position of women within the political establishment. Up to a point both tactics could flourish side by side, especially under the auspices of NUSEC. Even loyal party women found the existence of non-party women's groups supportive and comforting; as we have seen, party candidatures for women proved elusive, and in any case, experience undermined confidence in them. Scepticism was particularly marked among Liberal feminists, influenced partly by sheer disillusionment with their party leader, and also, no doubt, by the poor prospects of Liberal candidates of either sex between the wars. They played a major part in keeping the women's organisations going in this period.

Yet, by the end of the 1920s, when the feminist groups were dwindling in size, the main party organisations for women were reaching a peak. The Conservative and Labour parties clearly exercised a powerful attraction. Women such as Ellen Wilkinson and Selina Cooper had always hoped to be able to pursue feminism *and* socialism simultaneously, and at last the opportunity to do this appeared to have arrived. Thus during the early 1920s it was reported that in the constituencies women were deserting non-party organisations for the political parties. Some argued that there was no longer a need for separate feminist groups, either because the parties were in the process of absorbing much of the feminist programme, or because the agenda of feminism, while perfectly acceptable, was rather peripheral by comparison with the great issues of national politics. Up to a point feminists appear to have accepted the force of these arguments. As the *Woman's Leader* admitted:

> the items on NUSEC's agenda are, for the most part, not considered, even by the most ardent feminist, as being of such outstanding importance as the great problems in foreign politics of international peace and reparations, and in home politics of unemployment, housing and public health.[30]

However, the confidence of the party women sits uncomfortably with the meagre share of representation meted out to aspiring female candidates. Is it not rather puzzling that so many politically ambitious women should have been able to justify their continuing loyalty to parties still dominated by men? Seen in its context, however, their attitude is explicable. Although the momentum of the women's movement was about to slow down, in the early 1920s it must have seemed as though the pace of reform was, by comparison with previous decades, *increasing*. Nor were expectations immediately after the war very high. Gratifying as it was to have the legal right to sit in the House of Commons, many politically aware women were more interested in innovations designed to allow them to play a full and formal part in their respective party organisations.

Self-interest plainly dictated that the parties would respond to this aspiration. There was naturally a good deal of speculation about the loyalties of the new women voters, but the peculiar nature of the 1918 election made it difficult to draw any firm conclusions. Indeed the situation was not unlike that prevailing after 1867 in that all the parties felt the need to establish contact with the new electors, most of them remote from the parliamentary world. It was not clear that this involved no real concession of power by men until the dust had settled over the reforms that followed the extension of the franchise.

The Conservative and Unionist Party took up the question of reorganisation at a special conference at the end of November 1917. With the Representation of the People bill now certain to become law, and the prime minister constantly looking for an opportunity to hold a general election, this had become an urgent necessity. Plural voting had been greatly reduced, and the electorate multiplied by three times by a large influx of young and working-class voters. However, the party had not won an election since 1900. The explosion of trade union membership and the anticipated rise in Labour candidates threatened a result similar to the 1906 landslide.

On the other hand, in view of their extensive experience since the 1880s in recruiting hundreds of thousands of women for the Conservative cause under the Primrose League and, more recently, the

Women's Unionist and Tariff Reform Association (WUTRA), the party had some reason to regard the new women voters as the compensating feature of the electoral innovations of 1918. It certainly enjoyed a far larger organisational base amongst women than either its Liberal or Labour rivals. Yet so far women had participated as auxiliaries to the army of Conservatism. Both the Primrose League and the WUTRA enjoyed close connections with the National Union of Conservative Associations through their leading personnel, but remained constitutionally at arm's length. The question, then, was whether this should give way to amalgamation with the organisation in London and, more controversially, in the constituencies.

At national level the adjustment went fairly smoothly. The basic principle adopted was that women should receive one-third of the representation at each stage of the organisation. The WUTRA transferred its headquarters to the Central Office as the Women's Unionist Organisation, and by 1928 the women's department employed 29 staff and was training many women as organisers. Within the National Union the women were represented by a Women's Advisory Committee under Lady Edmund Talbot whose chief task was to form new women's branches and to organise the annual women's conference. It had the right to submit resolutions of its branches to the National Union and to the cabinet.

Both the Women's Unionist Organisation and the Primrose League received direct representation on the National Union's Central Council and the Executive. Constituencies were entitled to send three representatives to the Council for every 80,000 voters, of whom one was to be a woman. At the annual conference of the party female representation exceeded one-third during the inter-war years; and from 1920 the conference elected 21 members of the Council of whom 7 were women. The Executive included 6 members chosen by the party leader of whom 2 were women, and Council selected a further 32, including enough women to bring the total number to 16 of the 48 members.

Most of the agonising occurred over the relationship between the party and its women at constituency level. At the 1917 conference Sir George Younger argued that women must take part in selecting candidates and not just in working for them. But were they to be admitted as members of the Association on the same footing as men, as had been the practice in the Primrose League, or should they join separate Women's Unionist Associations linked to the constituency committees? In the debates on this issue a clear division of opinion emerged. On the whole, opponents and former opponents of women's suffrage advocated the creation of a single Unionist organisation incorporating both sexes. This surprisingly equalitarian formula reflected their acute fear that separate organisations would generate friction and competition between the sexes over choice of candidates and policy. 'I dread more than anything else the possibility of there arising in this country a Women's Party and a Men's Party', declared one delegate, while another warned against doing 'anything that suggests for a moment that women represent different interests from men or require a different policy'.[31] Against this supporters of women's suffrage and some of the party agents who had experience of working with WUTRAs pointed out that the sexes had invariably co-operated. This, indeed, was the real lesson of the Primrose League's activities since the 1880s: large numbers of Conservative women, including many suffragists, had devotedly worked for the party's causes and candidates without attempting to press women's demands upon the party.[32] Eventually it was decided to allow the constituencies flexibility over this sensitive issue; thus they could either have a separate women's branch or appoint a Women's Divisional Advisory Committee to deal with the interests and activities of the female members.

These elaborate arrangements could not entirely conceal the fact that women were effectively confined to the sphere of the National Union and its committee structure. Its functions – organisation and propaganda – had been performed by women for several decades; all that had changed was that women were now formally incorporated into the party apparatus. They would not impinge upon the parliamentary sphere except indirectly through a consultative body known as the Women's Parliamentary Committee, comprising the wives of MPs. The idea of this was to keep the women in touch with what was being done for them in parliament, and thereby to counter any demand for a woman's party.[33]

In the Labour movement organisations for working women such as the Women's Co-operative Guild and the Women's Trade Union League had been rather peripheral politically though individuals like Mary Macarthur and Margaret Bondfield were winning acceptance by their work on the industrial front. A few women members of the Independent Labour Party (ILP) and the Fabians became affiliated members of the Labour Representation Committee, but the general absence of individual membership in the constituencies made it difficult for women to join the Labour Party as such. However, during the Edwardian period the party leaders recognised that their failure to mobilise women supporters was a major cause of their organisational weakness, and to remedy the problem they established a Women's Labour League in 1906. By 1914 the WLL had around 4000 members in 100–120 branches and received an annual subsidy of £100–150 from the National Executive of the party.

In April 1917 a WLL subcommittee under Dr Marion Phillips made proposals to the NEC as to how Labour might organise women in response to the parliamentary reform measures then before the Commons. In the summer this initiative was overtaken by Arthur Henderson's resignation from the cabinet which led to a comprehensive overhaul of the party's constitution.[34] This reorganisation of the Labour Party affected the women in three main ways. In the first place the decision to create a common pattern of constituency parties based on individual membership immediately opened an avenue of participation for women largely unavailable hitherto. There followed a rapid growth of female membership during the early 1920s, admittedly from a very low level, bringing the total to nearly 100,000 by 1922 and an estimated 150,000 by 1924. This suggests that in the 1920s a majority of the individual members of the party must have been women. This advance was slightly marred by what some considered a patronising distinction made in the membership subscription – 1 shilling for men but only 6d. for women – which clearly implied a lower status for the latter. Objections were, however, overcome by the practical argument that the higher fee would only deter poorer women from joining.[35]

Secondly, the women's branches were now reconstituted as women's sections of the constituency Labour parties and were represented on their local executive committees. Thus, like the Conservatives, they were tied firmly into the party structure while maintaining a separate hierarchy of their own involving Women's Advisory Councils in each region and an annual conference from October 1918. At the centre the Women's Department, one of seven, was headed by the Chief Woman Officer, Dr Marion Phillips, from 1918, and backed by eight organisers. The women's organisation could send resolutions for consideration by the party conference but as these had to go through the NEC there was a fairly effective check as in the Conservative Party's system. Like their Conservative counterparts some Labour women had reservations about the establishment of sections for women. However, the party view, expressed by Phillips, was that if Labour was to recruit ordinary women hitherto inexperienced in political work a good deal of encouragement and education would be required; this could be more quickly and effectively accomplished in separate sections where it would be a central object. Otherwise there was a danger of women being attracted into other organisations for women and diverted from politics altogether.[36]

In the event many of the existing Labour women activists accepted Phillips' proposals even if they did not subscribe to her thinking. The middle-class socialist-feminists wished to maintain a degree of independence and, as one put it, 'be at liberty to go with the progressives not find [themselves] tied to what might be a retrograde party'. Clearly the separate sections helped remove some of the impetus towards what might have become a women's party at this crucial stage. But the arrangements portended a struggle between the orthodox party women and the more individualistic feminists on the left.

Thirdly, under the new party constitution adopted in 1918 women were given four representatives on the twenty-strong National Executive Committee. But the procedure now was that these should be chosen, not by their own organisation, but by the party conference as a whole. The first members in 1918 were Ethel Snowden, Ethel Bentham, Susan Lawrence and Mrs Harrison Bell, the last being replaced in 1919 by Mary Macarthur. This system, of course, was designed to give effective power to the trade unions, and in the long run it generated dissatisfaction in the women's organisation amongst those who felt that only the most orthodox were chosen to represent women.

However, in the circumstances of 1918 the balance between integration with the party and the maintenance of a separate identity for women seemed to have been well struck. In both Labour and Conservative parties the actual role of women may have been less novel than the rhetoric suggested; but the point is that they acted swiftly enough to check what might have been a move towards a new party for women. Each party set aside resources to build up women's membership, offered a career structure, and created a hierarchy of participation even if it did not lead very near to the centres of power; and both managed to build upon the existing pattern of women's party political work by involving them in the organisational expansion in the 1920s. The old ruling class, and the new, still knew the art of the timely concession.

Why Was There No Women's Party in Britain?

The notion of a separate political party for women is apt to be dismissed without serious consideration. Both male and female scholars, reflecting, no doubt, the pronounced British belief in party, tend to regard the idea as unrealistic. Yet 40 years after their enfranchisement women were represented in parliament by a mere 25 women MPs. From this perspective it is not obvious which would have been the more realistic course. It is difficult to think that women's political position would have been any *weaker* if they had taken the risk of launching a new party back in 1918. There was nothing inevitable about the strategy actually pursued by the women's movement after the Great War. The historical record shows that political parties have been based upon philosophies, social class, religion, language, regional and national loyalty; and some of the most significant parties – the Indian National Congress, the Irish Nationalists, and even the British Labour Party – seemed an unrealisable dream for considerable periods of time. In post-1918 Britain women enjoyed a 40 per cent share of the electorate, a well-defined programme and philosophy, and a wealth of practical experience. There was nothing inherently improbable about turning this potential into a new party. Moreover, the widespread belief that the war had somehow rendered the old parties obsolete and discredited, which was a feature of the years 1917–19, created an air of expectation that at least one new party would appear. At the time, as we have seen, politicians, especially the Conservatives, took the prospect of a women's party very seriously. Many Liberals, already accustomed to opting out of their party in local elections even before 1914, were ripe recruits. And although Labour, buoyed up by its recent declaration of independence, was less vulnerable than the older parties, it is clear that many of the socialist-feminists provided potential leaders for a women's party. During the early 1920s – the optimum time for an initiative – politicians could not be certain whether women would vote as a bloc or align themselves behind their male relations along existing party lines. At the very least a women's party at this stage would have helped to squeeze additional concessions out of the conventional parties. Each displayed some anxiety not to be outflanked when its rival managed to return a new woman MP to the Commons. And politicians were quick, if not necessarily correct, to attribute election results such as those of 1923 and 1929 to the preferences of women electors.

It is also often forgotten that feminists and politicians had, or thought they had, an example in front of them at the end of the war. The women's movement in the United States of America had developed along similar lines to that in Britain; and British radicals had in the past shown themselves very willing to learn from the American example. Thus it did not go unnoticed by feminists that from 1916 a 'National Women's Party' (NWP) existed in the United States. Of greater significance was the new League of Women Voters (LWV) established in 1920 as the successor body to the National American Women's Suffrage Association. While the NWP remained a small organisation and went into decline after 1919, the LWV was very large and led some British feminists to conclude that by 1921 American women had done a better job of converting their organisation into a political machine.[37] On closer inspection the LWV looks less impressive, and its difficulties seem to anticipate those of the British movement. It was weakened by divisions over issues like protective legislation, and increasingly slipped into welfare politics. What was not easy to appreciate at the time was that the energy which the LWV put into great moral causes, such as peace and prohibition, tended to divert it from feminism although it appeared to be working with the grain of party politics.

In the event the opportunity to establish a new party in Britain was let slip, and this is what must be explained. Basically the women's movement could not start with a clean slate. It already comprised a multitude of organisations amongst which the feminist ones were dwarfed in size by those whose ideology was more ambiguous but which pulled in the numbers – for example the Women's Institute with over 300,000 members by 1937, the Conservative women with 1 million by the late 1920s, or women's trade unions which numbered between 700,000–900,000 between the wars. To tap this sort of strength for political purposes seemed an intractable problem, hence the belief that a period of educational work amongst women was essential. In addition the existing women's organisations fell into several distinct, and sometimes conflicting, families. At the centre lay the equal rights feminist groups. Though several of them amalgamated, new single-issue bodies continued to emerge such as the Open Door Council (1926) and the National Birth Control Council (1930). Then there was a cluster of women's organisations chiefly involved with the Labour movement. Thirdly came a range including the Mother's Union, the WIs, and Townswomen's Guilds which stretched all the way from the anti-feminism of many of their rank and file members to the feminism of some of their leaders. A similar mixture of sentiment could be found amongst the last family – those groups based on professions and occupations of various sorts. This huge range of women's organisations derived some coherence and co-ordination from three sources: common personnel, some universally supported causes, and several umbrella groups. Individuals such as Nancy Astor and Eleanor Rathbone clearly managed to maintain their connections across much of the spectrum, while a less well-known woman like Lady Gertrude Denman created an important if fragile bridge between the WIs and the campaign for birth control. Particularly vital were women such as Dorothy Jewson – active in the Labour Party and in the feminist causes; Monica Whately even managed to be both a Labour candidate and a prominent figure in the Open Door Council and the Six Point Group which were particularly critical of Labour views. Moreover, although feminist issues such as protective legislation and birth control proved divisive, it is noticeable that one or two moral crusades were capable of drawing in women from virtually the entire range of organisations, notably disarmament and the League of Nations, women police, and the cinema and censorship.

Finally, the increasingly fragmented efforts of the women's groups gained a certain degree of co-ordination from three umbrella organisations during the 1920s. The first of these was the National Council of Women (NCW) whose origins lay back in the 1880s when it had been known as the National Union of Women Workers. In spite of its name it was not a trade union organisation. It linked together a wide range of charitable and religious organisations for women. By 1914 it had expanded to take in 1450 affiliated societies including suffragists and anti-suffragists, local government groups, women's settlements and colleges, temperance reformers and women's trade unions. In this way the NCW came to represent a uniquely wide range of women in social and political terms. It gradually became less philanthropic and more political in character. For example by the Edwardian period it was encouraging women to stand in local elections and pressurising the parties to select them. However, in the 1920s it suffered two defects. First, it failed to retain all the groups connected with the Labour movement though it invited them to participate. Second, it remained a loose federation lacking an effective executive capable of concentrating pressure on specific issues. This was perhaps an inevitable result of its size – it was too widely drawn to be really coherent.

The second umbrella group – which clearly detracted from the strength of the NCW – was the Joint Standing Committee of Industrial Women's Organisations (JSCIWO) which by 1923 incorporated twenty-three bodies. It basically served the institutions of the Labour movement. This was its strength, in that it made for coherence, and its weakness, in that it became somewhat antagonistic to other women's organisations. The other flaw in the JSCIWO lay in the weakness of the Labour Party itself; had Labour enjoyed office more often and made better use of its limited opportunities the JSCIWO might have loomed much larger in this period.

The third attempt at an umbrella organisation was known as the Consultative Committee of Women's Organisations (CCWO). Its origins lay in a NUWSS initiative in March 1916 when they were trying to co-ordinate the various suffrage societies' efforts over electoral reform. However, after a meeting in January 1918 to consider joint action over other women's issues there seems to have been a hiatus until the spring of 1921 when Lady Astor called a conference to reform the organisation. Forty-nine societies affiliated, including NUSEC, NCW, the Six Point Group and the Conservative and Liberal women, but not the Labour women or the Women's Co-operative Guild. It also enjoyed the backing of several male politicians such as Major J. Hills, MP and W.H. Dickinson who urged the Consultative Committee to resist any temptation to launch a political party. What the Committee did do was to set up a parliamentary committee two-thirds of whose members were MPs, to establish a fighting fund to promote flying columns to campaign in the constituencies of MPs hostile to women's demands, and to try to secure the election of candidates supporting equal rights legislation.[38] In essence the Consultative Committee represented an extension of the work of NUSEC and the Six Point Group both in aim and methods. It did, however, suffer withdrawals by its affiliated bodies, notably the Women's Institutes which declared that the Committee's subjects were outside their own scope. In 1926 the Midwives' Institute, the Total Abstinence Union, the Association of Headmistresses and the Conservative Women's Reform Association also withdrew. The most disruptive issue was birth control. Proposals to make information on this subject available to mothers at local maternity clinics were instrumental in alienating the Mothers' Union and the St Joan's Social and Political Alliance from the Committee.

The other side to the Consultative Committee's work lay in cultivating the politicians. Here Nancy Astor played a leading role in trying to bridge the gap between feminists and male politicians by organising regular monthly 'At Homes' as an alternative to formal confrontations and deputations. Yet it proved difficult to keep a balance between the political and the social. Some feminists complained that Astor's events became too lightweight because they were swamped by society ladies. She countered criticism by claiming the MPs would hardly attend if they were faced with a phalanx of 'serious women'![39] Nonetheless the combination of NUSEC's traditional pressure group work with Astor's easy entry into high political circles made for a reasonably effective organisation in the 1920s. The CCWO could claim credit for a substantial number of reforms although momentum was inevitably lost once the more widely acceptable measures were settled. As questions such as birth control began to loom larger the more lukewarm feminists fell away. Even Astor, who clearly had aspirations to lead a women's party at Westminster, as her initiatives after the 1929 election show, was fairly tepid on such topics.

In this context the failure to attempt a new party for women is comprehensible: the women never felt driven to so extreme or ambitious a remedy. This is a reflection partly of the strength of party loyalties in Britain, the habit of working for party causes, and the timely concessions made around 1918 to accommodate women supporters. It may also be that the social divide was always too great to bridge; feminism always had difficulty mobilising working-class women even without the opposition of an organised labour movement. It is also the case that the psychological moment for launching a new party was fairly short – by 1924, when four general elections fought under women's suffrage had elapsed, it had definitely passed. Thus the Pankhursts' brief experiment in 1917–19 was of some importance, for nothing discredits a good idea as effectively as premature or inept revelation. Finally, one must recognise that many feminist leaders with their long experience of dealing with the established parties had some grounds for believing that they were likely to achieve their aims by working along broadly the same lines as before. It is easy, in retrospect, to argue that the non-party approach had become anachronistic; it underestimated both the dominance of party politics after 1918, and the speed with which the enemies of the women's movement would regroup their forces within the establishment.

Chapter 4   The Anti-Feminist Reaction

War had had the effect of focusing attention upon women in general
and young women in particular, and after 1918 the popular press kept
them in the public eye. If, as some contemporaries believed, the whole
experience had unsettled the relations between the sexes, then it was
almost inevitable that there would follow a debate over the proper roles
of men and women in peacetime. In this debate we can distinguish three
broad views. Many men and some prominent anti-feminist women,
reacting sharply against the entire wartime experience, simply wanted
everything put back in its proper place; thus men must recover lost
ground in employment and women devote themselves to their homes.
The magazine *Home Chat* breathed a sigh of relief: 'Now we are
feminine again'. A second and intermediate position was held by those
women, including many feminists, who had long accepted the fundamental differences between the sexes. For them war had not changed
anything so much as sharpened their perception of the relations
between men and women. While it was a matter for satisfaction that
women had laboured in the war, war itself was the especial work,
indeed crime, of man; as women their responsibility lay in using their
political power for peace and conciliation in the post-war world. This
approach culminated in the kind of argument used by Mary Stocks, an
articulate critic of 'equal rights' feminism between the wars, when she
contended that no sensible woman would wish to take equality to the
length of joining her country's armed forces on the same footing as
men. At the far end of the spectrum stood those feminists for whom sex
equality remained the paramount goal. For them war had proved their
case as to the capability of women, but had by no means settled the
question; male-vested interests remained too deeply entrenched. As
Rebecca West put it:

> I am an old-fashioned feminist. I believe in the sex war. ... When those of our
> army whose voices are inclined to coo tell us that the day of sex-antagonism
> is over and that henceforth we have only to advance hand in hand with the
> male I do not believe it.[1]

This awareness of the dangers of a reaction amongst the mass of women,
carelessly glorying in their new-found freedom, is reflected in the post-
war writing of Cicely Hamilton, actress, author and former suffragette:

> It would be a mistake to imagine that we, of the enfranchised twentieth
> century, are proof against the danger of a return to femininity, and the
> dependence femininity implies ... the flow of every tide is followed by its

ebb. ... The crop-haired young women of the present day who array themselves in gym suits, run, jump, and swim – they may live to see their daughters falling over draperies, languishing in flounces or filling up doorways with hoops ... ere they know what they are doing they will have lost the precious right to show their legs! And woman, once more, will be a legless animal – and reduced to the state of dependence implied by her unfortunate deformity![2]

Femininity and Feminism

However, in spite of, or perhaps because of, the experience of 1914–18, the uncompromising views of West and Hamilton were rejected by large numbers of women. They saw feminism as a threat to their femininity. Charlotte Haldane poured out her contempt for the 'war-working type of women – aping the cropped hair, the great booted feet, and grim jaw, the uniform, and if possible the medals of the military man'.[3]

This charge was developed in the writing of Arabella Kenealy who claimed that the underlying object of the women's movement was masculinism, that is the training of women in order to enable them to compete with men in every sphere. In her view female subjection was a blessing ordained by Nature.[4] Between the wars such women persistently emphasised the distance between 'proper women' on the one hand and on the other, the feminist who was by implication a spinster. Witness Janet Courtney's account of the Women's Institutes movement which she pronounced to be feminine not feminist because 'it contains too large a proportion of married women'.[5] This stereotyping was to prove a considerable handicap to the women's movement during this period, and one has the impression that some feminists played to their weakness. Lady Rhondda's scathing comments on married women are a case in point: 'lacking in vitality ... rather vapid conversation ... what a world in which a whole class of human beings is condemned to a life which turns the majority of them into devitalised bores ... the kept-wife has no raison d'être as a person.'[6]

Of course, critical feminists were often themselves reacting to another stereotype which attracted a great deal of attention during the 1920s: the ultra-feminine, shallow-minded flapper. The visible signs of this phenomenon included the craze for dancing and cinema-going without chaperons, the fashion for dieting and slimming and changes in dress design which seemed to favour the flat-chested, narrow-hipped figure. 'The modern girl is a slim as a lamp post', declared the *Daily Mail*, which emerged as the foremost authority in this field. Typically, it drew the connection between her physical attributes and her responsibility for the 'lower standard of morality' of the post-war period: 'the social butterfly type has probably never been so prevalent as at present. It comprises the frivolous, scantily clad "jazzing flapper", irresponsible and undisciplined.'[7]

For the average girl, cheap dances, cinema tickets and copies of fashionable clothes were but a pale echo of the social life enjoyed by the wealthy. The atmosphere of the 'roaring twenties' is well captured by magazines like *Vogue* and *Eve* which clearly catered to the upper-class female. Founded in 1920, *Eve* encouraged its readers to pursue a relentless round of shopping, hunt balls, tennis, golf, ski-ing, sailing, shooting and flying, and regularly regaled them with 'Tennis tattle from the Riviera', 'People who count at Cannes', and '*Eve* and her car'. *Eve* was prepared to be serious about fashion and gardening, but its awareness of new horizons for women was only rarely perceptible. Presenting one of its full page portraits of Asquith's daughter, Violet, with her two children, *Eve* explained, as though introducing readers to an unfamiliar breed: 'Lady Bonham-Carter is an intellectual, and, according to rumour, is likely to enter the political arena in the near future.'[8] Clearly *Eve's* challenge to conventional notions about the sexes was confined to the social sphere: the emancipated woman drove her own motor car, she did not stand for parliament. This reflects a not uncommon assumption that the political side of women's struggle was now essentially over; those who continued to fight such battles were indelibly associated with the gloom of strong-mindedness and spinsterhood.

That many feminists found themselves at odds with ordinary women in their attitude towards women's social life was to a large extent a direct result of the experience of wartime, in that the opportunities available to young working women to enjoy themselves and seek boy friends and husbands led to friction with the various patrols and women police volunteers, many of whom were erstwhile suffragettes and suffragists. Yet, as we know, feminists' eagerness to participate in such wartime work was but a reflection of the long-standing concern about morality within the women's movement. For them freer relations between the sexes, especially if it involved earlier and easier sexual activity, was overwhelmingly in the interests of men. Although most had to discard their uniforms after 1918, their concerns about the double standard in sexual morality remained undimmed. As a result they earned an unfortunate reputation as interfering, strait-laced and

priggish older women, keen to deny to younger generations the heterosexual pleasures they themselves had never had.

Even before 1914 a debate had been simmering within the ranks of
feminism about the whole value of sex and marriage. Perhaps the most
effective spokesperson for those who thought women should deliberately opt for spinsterhood was Cicely Hamilton, who had written
Marriage as a Trade in 1909. In this she characterised marriage as a
sordid deal in which a woman sold her body in return for her keep but no
wage; for many women sexual intercourse was simply not a necessity,
and in any case, it entailed the unacceptable risk of venereal disease.
The signs of a retreat from marriage during the Edwardian period
suggested that the message was getting across. However, even before
the war women were being offered a wholly different view of their
sexuality by men like Havelock Ellis, author of *The Psychology of Sex*,
and socialist-feminists such as Stella Browne and Dora Marsden, the
editor of the *Freewoman*. They challenged Victorian assumptions about
women as sexually passive, arguing instead that sex was as essential to
their health and pleasure as for men's. *Freewoman* bitterly attacked the
spinster as 'the barren sister, the withered tree, the acidulous vestal' and
deplored her influence in schools.[9] Stella Browne declaimed:

> It will be an unspeakable catastrophe if our richly complex Feminist
> movement with its possibilities of power and joy, falls under the domination
> of sexually deficient and disappointed women, impervious to facts and logic
> and deeply ignorant of life.[10]

While both sides in this dispute expressed extreme minority views,
Browne's positive attitude towards sex was much closer to post-1918
ideas, as the runaway success of Marie Stopes' *Married Love* suggests.

However, many leading feminists felt alienated from the younger
generation of women. As Mary Agnes Hamilton observed, it was
dismaying for feminists to see young girls eagerly applying cosmetics
in public and generally showing their desire to gratify the male sex.[11]
'They have ruined their beauty by a clown's splash of lipstick, bloody
claws and the everlasting dental grin', complained Helena Swanwick.
'The emancipation of today displays itself mainly in cigarettes and
shorts', noted Sylvia Pankhurst. Even Mrs Fawcett inveighed against
the women's pages of the national press for their 'inane observations on
the length of skirts or the shape of sleeves'.[12] Clearly a wide gulf had
opened up between the serious-minded feminist and the flapper who
took for granted the gains that older women had fought so hard to win.

Masculinity and Feminism

From the male perspective the craze for clothes and dancing on the part
of young women was clearly reassuring in so far as it pointed to a return
to femininity. But the vigorous pursuit of an independent social life
seemed a little threatening in the context of a number of attempts to
invade the male sphere or compete with male authority. From the pages
of *Good Housekeeping* Lord Birkenhead pompously denounced 'This
Intrusion of Women' into the fields of politics, the law, employment
and even sport.[13] Certainly women were being encouraged to take up
golf, athletics, cricket or rowing; magazines like *Good Housekeeping*
and *Eve* gave much prominence to the lady motorist, which must have
antagonised the majority of men for whom a motor car was still out of
reach. The 1920s also saw female mountaineers scaling Kilimanjaro
and the Eiger; while in 1927 a Miss Mercedes Gleitz became the first
woman to swim the English Channel, a feat soon emulated by others of
her sex. Perhaps even more publicity attached to the female pilots such
as Lady Heath and Lady Bailey who flew the London to Cape Town
route. Most celebrated, of course, was Amy Johnson for her solo flight
to Australia in 1930 after only 50 hours flying experience. Rather
tactlessly she proceeded to beat her own husband's record for the flight
to Cape Town in 1932. The strain which this competition put upon their
marriage led them to undertake joint flights, but they divorced in 1938.
From this the women's magazines drew a moral: no good could come of
attempts to play roles for which nature had not fitted women.

In retrospect the excitable and often crude language in which the
defensive reaction against women was expressed during the 1920s
seems out of proportion to the real changes which were taking place.
How can one account for the concern especially over young women
after 1918? To some extent the issue was deliberately orchestrated by
influential elements in the national press particularly in papers owned
by Alfred Harmsworth (Lord Northcliffe), his brother Harold (Lord
Rothermere) and Lord Beaverbrook. They were largely responsible for
popularising the term 'flapper', in a derogatory sense, especially to
denote the young, unenfranchised woman, though women's magazines
like *My Weekly* used it in a neutral way when referring to clothes to 'fit
the Flapper' and 'more Flapperstyles'. The key fact is simply that
young women, conspicuous during the war, had been providing the
press with good copy. What changed after the war was the light in
which they were presented. For several years it had suited proprietorial
purpose to depict women in terms of patriotism and national unity. But

by the time of the armistice they had already begun to change tack with alarming speed. Where recently they had heaped praise on women they now began to identify them in a threatening light as a section of the population lacking true public spirit. To some extent women became merely scapegoats or weapons made to serve the political purpose of press barons. For example, Northcliffe's sudden switch in favour of women's suffrage in 1916 was not unconnected with his desire to destroy the Asquith government over the electoral register; similarly attacks upon the costs of unemployment benefit for women from 1919 may be seen in the context of the anti-waste campaign against Lloyd George; and the furore over equal franchise after 1927 provided the *Daily Mail* with another stick with which to beat Stanley Baldwin.

A second strand in the debate about young women was simply the sheer numbers – 'Our Surplus Girls' as the *Mail* began to call them from 1919. As a result of wartime male losses the traditional excess of women over men in the population rose to 1.9 million, a shift which was widely believed to constitute a serious political and social problem. By 1921 there were 1176 women to every 1000 men in the 20–24 years age group and 1209 to every 1000 in the 25–29 years age group. Many of these women would inevitably seek permanent paid employment, and hence try to retain their wartime jobs at a time when work would be desperately needed for men returning from the forces and those made redundant by the collapse of industries linked to war production. Hence the sudden resurrection of mid-Victorian expedients such as mass emigration for 'superfluous' women by the *Mail* and other newspapers.

It was also feared for a time that women might exploit their new political muscle to defend their position in the labour market. Already in 1919 the enfranchisement of those under 30 years old was widely taken for granted, and politicians of all parties showed themselves anxious to establish their credentials as supporters of equal suffrage. This particular question did not come to the fore until the spring of 1927 when the home secretary, William Joynson-Hicks, announced a government bill on the subject. This provided the opportunity for an unusually bitter and relentless attack upon women in general and 'Votes for Flappers' in particular. The *Daily Mail* had already familiarised readers with the idea of the 'sex war'; its scaremongering tactics built upon this by highlighting the number of extra women voters in various constituencies: 'Men Outnumbered Everywhere'. It went on to argue not just that women would dominate elections, but also since the young women comprised an incorrigibly irresponsible and ignorant section of the population, they would easily be manipulated by socialist propaganda.[14]

The third kind of rationale behind the reaction against women lay in concerns over morality and the future of the British family. As more women sought careers, it was claimed, fewer would settle down to marriage. Corroboration for this was found in the patent determination of so many females to enjoy a fuller social life and to adopt a more self-confident and assertive approach to sexual behaviour. During the war much alarm had been engendered by the growing opportunities for girls to engage in sexual relations outside marriage, and the increasing familiarity with methods of preventing pregnancy; this removed the traditional pressure to get married at a time when economic conditions favoured the single, self-supporting girl. Symptoms of this supposed tendency towards immorality were popular films and novels written by women such as Elinor Glyn and Ethel M. Dell: 'They have made the world safe for pornography; declaimed the *Daily Express* in a typical outburst.[15] The real fault with the so-called 'sex novel' was that its author cast women as heroines who pursued an adventurous sex life – by implication women in general were encouraged to make the same escape from passivity.

Contemporary critics detected an ominous connection between looser moral standards and changes in the physical appearance of young women. Arabella Kenealy attributed this to wartime experience:

> Many of our young women have become so de-sexed and masculinised, indeed, and the neuter states so patent in them, that the individual is described (unkindly) no longer as 'she' but as 'it'. ... Cruelty lies in the fact, however, that the womanhood of many will have been wrecked quite needlessly by the strain of superfluously strenuous drill and marchings, scoutings, signallings and other such vain and fruitless imitations of the male.[16]

Soon the press began to warn of the consequences of this unnatural experience:

> With short hair, skirts little longer than kilts, narrow hips, insignificant breasts, there has arrived a confident, active, game-loving, capable human being, who shuns the servitude of household occupations ... this change to a more neutral type ... can be accomplished only at the expense of the integrity of her sexual organs.[17]

Barbara Cartland summed it up more succinctly when she said that the new slimline girl would have weak babies, if she had them at all.[18] And, as always, the medical profession stood ready to lend a spurious scientific respectability to anti-feminist propaganda; one Guy's Hospital consultant pronounced that 'in trying to look like boys women of the present day destroy the character of their sex ... they are poor creatures sheathed from throat to hips in rubber'.[19] Some politicians were even prepared to speak in public about their fears over the presumed connection between the single woman, feminism and lesbianism. In 1921 the House of Commons approved an amendment to the Criminal Law Amendment Bill which would have made homosexual acts between women illegal as they were between men. Professing great reluctance to bring the topic to members' attention, the MPs spoke of the lesbian as a lunatic who ought to be incarcerated or possibly incur the death penalty so that she might be eliminated from society. They hesitated only for fear that severe punishment would publicise lesbianism and thereby give dangerous enlightenment to women presently ignorant of the very idea.[20] In the event the amendment failed to become law only because the government refused to accept any major alteration to what had been an 'agreed' bill. However, feelings ran so high that members preferred to lose the entire measure rather than pass it without the anti-lesbian clause.

Part of the explanation for these excitable and intolerant views lay in the belief that changes amongst women were undermining masculinity; while girls grew more boyish, the young men seemed increasingly languid, effeminate, intellectual and passive. Thus Kenealy argued:

> The male becomes emasculate when the women invade his domain. And with the increasing hugger-mugger of the sexes, it grows, every day, more and more difficult for men to escape into the bracing, invigorating environment and moral of their own sex ... if they are to cope with the new Feminism men must needs look to their laurels and produce a new Masculinism. For truly these weak-chinned, neurotic, young men of the rising generation are no match for the heavy-jawed, sinewy, resolute young women Feminism's aims and methods are giving us.[21]

This kind of comment persisted throughout the inter-war period. Barbara Cartland recalled that young men back from France had often sought the reassurance of marriage; if thwarted they became emotional and dramatic even to the extent of threatening suicide.[22] In an article on 'This Generation of Men' Vera Brittain commented on 'the charming ineffectiveness of so many present-day husbands'. She argued that men who had survived the war or been too young for it suffered from poor physique and a lack of vitality and public spirit; they often had to be supported by their wives, and as a result we were heading for a matriarchal society.[23] These far fetched remarks did, of course, have some basis in the emotional and physical damage done to so many young men by war experience. The maimed, gassed, shell-shocked or demoralised male, unable to pick up the thread of civilian life was too common a sight to escape attention in the 1920s. Many men, perhaps genuinely afraid that wartime experience had caused lapses in their manliness, covered their fears with an outward show of hostility towards women. It is well established that soldiers frequently felt resentful towards other men who had stayed at home and taken advantage of the extra pay to be obtained during the war. All the more strongly did they react against women who had done the same, notwithstanding that at the time women's work had been lauded as a vital patriotic contribution. Further, for the many men who had not, in fact, fought and who consequently lived with a sense of guilt, it was only too tempting to associate themselves vociferously with their own sex and join in a general male attack upon female usurpers.

Demobilisation

Few contemporaries would have disagreed with the view that the re-establishment of male self-respect after 1918 hinged upon men's role as workers and breadwinners for their families. Consequently demobilisation came as an inevitable check on women's prospects. Faced with some 4 million men, anxious to return to their homes, the authorities agreed to demobilise more rapidly than was thought prudent. The 1919 Restoration of Pre-War Practices Act represented the fulfilment of pledges the government had given on dilution of labour; but the expulsion of women workers was also applied to establishments which had not even existed before the war. The government set an example by forcing female civil servants back into routine work in order to reserve the more attractive positions for returning servicemen. The Association of Women Clerks protested that women were being expelled for the benefit of men who had not always seen active service.[24] In a deputation to Lloyd George Lady Rhondda contended that women were invariably better trained and more efficient than the men who were replacing them; she also pointed out that many were widows of servicemen, now obliged to support a dependent family, and that some, at least, of their work was quite new, and as such ought not to be affected by pledges given to pre-war employees.[25] Ministers were by no means entirely unsympathetic to this case, but did little to help. When challenged in his capacity as financial secretary to the Treasury to explain why the government continued to employ married women whose husbands were in work, Baldwin responded, slightly apologetic, that the complete loss of female employees might not be 'compatible with efficiency and economy'. But this was contemptuously swept aside. 'It is news that our public offices are flooded with indispensables', sneered the *Edinburgh Evening News*, and it went on to demand the sacking of 'this class of social scroungers'.[26] Baldwin subsequently promised a deputation of women trade unionists that he would dismiss women of independent means and those supported by husbands.

The ineffectiveness of women's response to these pressures was partly a reflection of the equivocal feelings amongst leading women themselves. In her capacity as a member of the Ministry of Reconstruction committee on female employment Susan Lawrence endorsed the official view of the necessity for dismissing married women, and accepted that while men should be paid on the basis that they had families to support, women should be regarded as though single.[27] Lilian Barker, the superintendent at Woolwich Arsenal, pronounced that the 'first duty was to the soldier – the man who had done his bit for the past four years – and who would now be wanting to return to his normal occupation'. In spite of the implication that the munitionettes had not been doing their duty too, the girls seem to have accepted their dismissal from Woolwich, at a rate of 1500 a week from January 1919, without protest. Though many expressed regret at the termination of their wartime work, they also felt that a break would be welcome; in the interval many became married, while others considered alternative forms of employment. What emerges forcefully from all the reports in the immediate post-war years is the pronounced reluctance of young women to accept jobs in domestic service, laundry, dressmaking, tailoring and millinery. Many refused to work in these occupations even if it meant losing their out-of-work donation, and only sheer necessity forced some of them back by 1920. They found themselves victims of the notion, which had gained strength from the middle-class typists and nurses of wartime, that the working girl required only pin money since she was really supported by her father. Some employers took advantage of this to offer wages so low that many women declined the offer; even the London County Council made a point of denying to its women teachers the post-war salary increase it introduced for men.

The friction inevitably generated by the ruthless removal of women from their wartime role was only partly mitigated by the out-of-work donation, set at 20 shillings for women and 24 for men. Even this was denied to girls in the Land Army if they left voluntarily. Munitionettes received two weeks pay in lieu of proper notice and a train ticket to their homes. Soon, however, employers began to complain that they could not obtain female labour, and blamed the donation for this problem. In any case the donation was shortly replaced by the extended system of national insurance benefits. However, the path for women who wished to claim benefit proved stony. They were not eligible unless they had paid national insurance contributions before the war. If they declined the offer of a post in domestic service they immediately lost benefit. Many tried to avoid this by refusing to admit that they had been in service before 1914, but only one in five of those who appealed against a decision to withdraw payment was successful.[28]

This was the situation that attracted the first vitriolic attack upon women in the national press during the summer of 1919. Within a matter of months the patriotic munitions girl had been transmogrified into an anti-social parasite. 'Scandal of the Proposed Retention of Flappers while Ex-Soldiers Cannot Find Jobs', screamed a typical headline in the *Daily Sketch* on 28 June. Yet with its characteristic inconsistency the popular press also criticised women when they *did* abandon their jobs because of the benefits some of them received. Thus the *Daily Mail* reported: 'Paying Women Not To Work. Honest Toil Shirked. Idling on the Dole'.[29] Even *The Times* joined in with reports about the 21,000 women clerks said to be receiving the out-of-work donation in April 1919 while firms in the City were crying out for staff.[30] By encouraging its readers to write in with examples and opinions about unoccupied women the *Mail* kept the issue alive, and found enough ammunition to help sustain what became a dangerous campaign against excessive government expenditure. By 1922 women had been excluded altogether from benefits unless their family income fell below 10 shillings a week; and as the conditions grew more stringent many women simply ceased to register with their local Labour Exchange. In this way they began to lose out in the struggle for scarce resources within a very short time of acquiring the vote.

Beneath the rhetoric the pattern of employment for women in the immediate post-war period is clear enough. During the first few months of 1919 the rapid loss of jobs through demobilisation was mitigated somewhat by the brief boom in consumer goods industries especially where no agreements with the unions existed, or where the work was unattractive to men. Even so, half a million women were unemployed by the spring. The picture unfolds in the weekly reports compiled for the Ministry of Labour in each region. In Glasgow the Govan Exchange noted at the start of January that 900 women had just lost their jobs, but 'no local demand exists for women's labour except in domestic service which is very unpopular'; and in the south-east and London a number of employers were reported to be refusing to take women recently employed on war work on the grounds that they had 'tended to lower the pre-war standards'.[31] Although women comprised a substantial majority of the unemployed during 1919, in the perception of politicians unemployment was a male and not a female problem; the 353,000 ex-servicemen still without jobs by November loomed much larger in their calculations. Thus the process of steadily weeding out women continued until it was overtaken by the onset of a slump in 1920. This proved particularly serious for women in view of the collapse of some textile businesses. Yet as 1920 wore on and the depression deepened the Ministry of Labour ceased to report separately on women's employment. During 1919 alone 195,000 women had, in fact, been placed in domestic service by the Labour Exchanges, and by 1921 this was, once again, the largest occupation for women. In January of that year half a million women were officially out of work, and by January the following year the total was down to 370,000. Many had stopped registering, a tacit recognition of their marginalisation in the aftermath of war.

Housekeeping as a Profession

If the negative aspect of the post-war approach to women involved attempts to push them out of the labour market, the positive aspect was a renewed emphasis upon the traditional function of woman as the manager of her household. Though clearly not novel this strategy developed in several ways after 1918; it involved an attempt to elevate the status and prestige of housekeeping, and it was now extended across the social scale to middle-class women just as much as to working-class ones. All were increasingly seen as professional housekeepers whether they were paid or not.

As an occupation domestic service had long dominated female employment; but it also enjoyed widespread approval because it was regarded as providing a fine training for future wives. By 1891 there were 1,759,000 women domestic servants in England and Wales alone. But from this peak the total slowly subsided to 1,662,000 by 1911, and well before 1914 the 'servant problem' had become a matter for discussion and concern. The traditional supply of willing girls drawn from rural districts into the town houses of the wealthy was dwindling; and many young women displayed an increasing reluctance to submit to the conditions and pay generally offered to a female domestic. The war, however, greatly increased the level of debate about domestic service, initially because of the disruption experienced by many households as girls were attracted away to factories and offices. After 1918, as we have seen, the discussion in the press grew very critical when proprietors gave full vent to the feeling that married women who were not satisfied with their husbands' wages should take up the 'proper and natural employment' that was so freely available to them. In December 1918 the Ministry of Reconstruction appointed a Women's Advisory Committee on problems of recruitment and retention of servants; and throughout the 1920s the question was taken up by public figures ranging from Lady Londonderry and the Duchess of Atholl on the right to Susan Lawrence, Mrs Pember Reeves and Marion Phillips on the left. A measure of agreement emerged over the reasons for the unpopularity of domestic service. The long hours and loneliness contrasted with the comparative freedom of most factory or office work where a girl's obligations to her employer were strictly limited. Also, the low status was now deterring potential servants; the dress was widely resented, and the tendency to refer to a girl by her Christian name rather than her surname now seemed patronising to many. However, no consensus existed over the critical issues. Susan Lawrence, for example, believed that nothing would change unless the government insisted on a minimum wage and a maximum working week – interventionism which Lady Londonderry refused to countenance.[32] The interest in domestic service shown by the Fabian Women, the Women's Co-operative Guild and the Labour Party Women's Sections is significant. Clearly the WCG saw the issue in terms of providing 'home helps' in order to relieve the pressure and strain upon pregnant mothers. Labour was influenced partly by the recognition that domestic service would remain an essential occupation for women, and if they continued to be put off the competition with men for scarce jobs would be exacerbated. In addition female domestics were one of the least organised groups of workers, and hence most susceptible to influence by employers. While both the Transport and General Workers and the National Union of General and Municipal Workers accepted women domestics, they had never succeeded in recruiting more than a tiny fraction. Labour's own analysis of the problem placed great emphasis on the low wages, long hours and contempt shown by other workers for domestic service. But it also advocated formal training as a means of raising status, and placement by Labour Exchanges rather than private agencies.[33] In the event the government went no further than supporting training schemes organised by the Central Committee on Women's Training and Employment. Until 1924, however, girls who joined this scheme had to agree to take a job in service, and as a result few were recruited. The government also paid the cost of a uniform for 4000 servants, but this did not get over the resentment against the typical dress worn. Consequently the chief recruiting agent was necessity. After the loss of one in four domestic servants during the war, the numbers returned to just 1,600,000 by 1931. This reflected a temporary return to work by *older* women, obliged to replace the wages of unemployed husbands. Nothing really altered the declining popularity of the occupation amongst young women; and one has the impression from books such as E.M. Delafield's *Diary of a Provincial Lady* (1947) that the difficulties of both finding and retaining properly qualified servants remained a preoccupation throughout the inter-war period.

The other side of this particular coin was, of course, that many middle-class women were obliged to manage without or with far less domestic help than their mothers had been accustomed to enjoy. Thus, while fruitless efforts were being made to raise the status of the paid domestic, some rather more successful propaganda was directed towards both the middle-class and the working-class housewife designed to persuade her of the necessity for managing her household in a *professional* fashion.

The chief agency for such propaganda was the women's magazine. A flourishing press had existed since the mid-Victorian period in which women were encouraged to take pride in their skills as household managers. Those designed for working-class girls like *Home Chat* (1895) or *My Weekly* (1910) relied upon a set formula of romantic fiction leavened by articles on fashion, cookery and household tips; and the appearance of *Peg's Paper* in 1919 is an indication that there was still much life in this type of publication. Many such magazines had flourished quite oblivious to the controversies over women's emancipation, by sticking to their belief that woman found her true vocation only in marriage and the home. If there is any change at all after 1918 it is in the form of a shift of emphasis away from the somewhat fuzzy, idealised view of married life towards a more practical approach. This is reflected in the titles of the many new papers that sprang up in the 1920s –*Woman and Home, My Home, Modern Woman, Modern Home, Wife and Home*. Above all it was the new journal *Good Housekeeping* (1922) which launched an influential campaign to elevate the whole status of household management in Britain.

'We are on the threshold of a great feminine awakening', declared

the enthusiastic editors in their first edition in 1922. 'Apathy and levity
are alike giving place to a wholesome and intelligent interest in the
affairs of life, and above all in the home.'[34] This rather bold and
confident tone reminds us that magazines like *Good Housekeeping*
often saw themselves as promoting the emancipation of women
between the wars. Alice Head, who took over as editor in 1924, was a
suffragist and, clearly, a successful career woman. But she was no
crusader for women's rights, and her whole approach reflected the
security and status of her own position rather than an appreciation of
the general lot of British women; thus she cheerfully published Lord
Birkenhead's attacks upon women's new role on the grounds that the
controversy would build up interest in her journal; she did not show a
feminist's concern that his writing in *Good Housekeeping* reinforced a
far wider onslaught upon feminism throughout the press at this time.[35]

In the event the 'awakening' to which *Good Housekeeping* summoned
its readers in 1922 was not so much a new departure for women as an
improved competence in the performance of the traditional functions of
the majority of women. In effect readers could take a correspondence
course in home-making by subscribing to the magazine, learning how
to manage their resources, raise the quality of their cookery and
needlework, and take full advantage of new products, especially
mechanical household aids, which were tested in the Good Housekeeping Institute. There can be little doubt of the high quality of advice
and information offered; many journals subsequently copied, but did
not match, its style and material. Amongst middle-class women, who
formed its natural market, its reach was eventually formidable. By
1950 fully half of all women in households whose income fell within the
£440–£1000 range read *Good Housekeeping* regularly or occasionally.[36]

For women the wider significance of such a magazine lies in its
aspiration to lift traditional household management skills to almost
professional status. In a sense this was bound to be flattering to many
women who found themselves driven back to the home after their
wartime experiences. It also seemed rather practical at a time when
middle-class women began to experience problems in finding well-
trained domestic staff. On the other hand the claim that 'there should be
no drudgery in the house. There must be time to think, to read, to enjoy
life' begins to look a little hollow as the pages of *Good Housekeeping*
unfold. Take a typical early piece by Viscountess Gladstone on 'The
Model Housewife'. In this she recommended the housewife to draw up
a proper budget with estimates of expenditure under various heads; she

advised women to do more laundry at home and to make their own furniture polish; she pointed out that if wives always bought food themselves, as French women did, they would get exactly the right amount and so avoid waste. There was, in fact, almost no end to advice of this sort. Yet the chief effect was inevitably to add to the burdens of many women both by promoting higher standards and by steadily filling up with housekeeping the time that might have been devoted to wider interests. It is indeed true that a preoccupation with house and home did not altogether preclude wider horizons. During the 1920s *Good House-keeping* carried articles by many feminists including Mrs Fawcett, Rebecca West, Lady Rhondda, Helena Normanton, Ellen Wilkinson and Margaret Wintringham, as well as other women prominent in public life such as Violet Bonham-Carter, Frances Stevenson and Lady Londonderry. In this way attention was drawn to women who had proved to be successful in spheres other than the purely domestic. But this element in *Good Housekeeping* certainly diminished as the decade wore on, while household management steadily expanded. In the long run the magazine reflected ever more common ground with the general run of women's journals between the wars.

Population and Motherhood

Fears about a decline in both the mental and physical capacity of British women to fulfil their role as mothers was a characteristic of the inter-war period. The rather apocalyptic tone often adopted even in weighty analyses such as Enid Charles' *The Twilight of Parenthood* is particularly striking; blaming the prosperous classes for trying to encourage the poor to emulate their own preference for the small family she declared they had 'moulded the destiny of a civilisation which has lost the power to reproduce itself'.[37] As in the era of 'national decadence' it was fashionable for a time to dredge up historical analogies for present and future dilemmas. Thus Kenealy contended that the ancient civilisations of Greece and Rome owed their decline and downfall to feminist dominance which led to a 'decline of mother-power'; progress, on the other hand, coincided with periods marked by a 'rising level of womanly character and virtue' and a 'high observance of woman's functions of home and motherhood.'[38] This attitude was echoed at the political level. As late as 1935 Neville Chamberlain went out of his way to justify his proposals for increasing the married man's tax allowance and raising allowances in respect of the second and all subsequent children in terms of easing the position of the family:

> I must say that I look upon the continued diminution of the birth rate in this country with considerable apprehension. At the present time it may seem that we have here a larger population than we are able to support in England. ... But I have a feeling that the time may not be far distant ... when the countries of the British Empire will be crying out for more citizens of the right breed, and when we in this country shall not be able to supply the demand.[39]

How to remedy the situation? Clearly the first part of the solution lay in ensuring that as many women as possible got married, preferably young. If Barbara Cartland's account is to be believed young girls after the war came under a good deal of direct pressure to do so. She herself claimed to have been unceremoniously tackled by a 45-year-old colonel on the Isle of Wight in 1919; this proved to be only the first of 49 proposals of marriage in the period up to 1927 when she finally accepted an offer – not before time, one feels.

Not surprisingly, those women who attained prominence in careers outside the home and marriage were regarded as something of a threat. Even so respectable a figure as Nancy Astor received very muted acclaim in the women's magazines for fear that she might be taken as a role model. *Home Chat*, for example, conceded that with her special advantages Lady Astor experienced no great difficulty in combining her work as an MP with that of the mother of six, but warned: 'most wives and mothers will be quite content to follow these pioneers at a very considerable distance'.[40] Starting from the conviction that marriage was the 'Best Job of All' such papers as *My Weekly* gave solemn consideration to the question 'Should A Girl Propose?' Significantly in 1919 the answer to this was very much in the affirmative, taking into account the special circumstances of large numbers of ex-soldiers returning home broken in health and spirits and presumably lacking the determination to do their duty.[41] At the same time these years were characterised by a good deal of inconsistent advice to girls. While encouraged to take the initiative they were also criticised for embarking too lightly on marriage without appreciating how different it would be from courtship; injunctions to the young woman to raise the standard of her housekeeping went blandly along with criticism for failure to maintain her physical attractiveness:

> There always seems to be something underhand about things if a girl will perk and preen before marriage, and afterwards not trouble whether he sees her in a soiled dress or not.[42]

Table 4.1 Crude Birth Rate[a] (England and Wales) 1901–1931

1901–5	28.2	1920–1	24.0	1927	16.6
1906–10	26.3	1922–3	20.1	1928	16.7
1911–14	24.1	1924–5	18.6	1930	16.3
1915–19	19.4	1926	17.8	1931	15.8

[a]i.e. births per thousand of the population.

However, doing her duty by her husband was, in contemporary opinion, but part of her wider responsibility to the state itself. Ever since the late 1870s the birth rate had been gradually declining in Britain, but during 1915–19 it suffered an unusually sharp drop. After an equally steep rise in 1920–1 there was a return to the existing pattern. As a result of this long-term trend by 1933 one authority calculated that the 'net repro-duction rate' had reached 0.75, and the population had practically ceased to increase. If fertility remained constant, succeeding generations would experience a decline in the population of England and Wales from 45 million to a mere 6 million in 200 years.[43] In order to maintain even a stable population, it was suggested, each woman should bear an average of three children.

The question was how to reach this desirable goal? Population propagandists strongly favoured an early start in childbirth – at the age of 17. Once a woman was diverted into a career she might be reluctant to return to motherhood, and as Barbara Cartland claimed, 'scien-tifically a woman only attains her full development after giving birth to a child'.[44] By 1921 the National Baby Week Council had over a million members and a thousand local committees organising baby shows and competitions, pram parades, slide lectures and child welfare exhibi-tions.[45] But the idea of young and repeated motherhood ran into the grim statistics on maternal mortality which remained stubbornly high between the wars. This put governments under pressure to encourage mothers in rearing families. They shied away from family allowances, home helps and birth control for obvious reasons. They also made what capital they could with the doctors' view that women themselves were often to blame for high infant mortality rates because they did not breast-feed their babies as much as in the past. Working women were especially criticised in this respect. On the other hand the politicians did concede more resources in the shape of grants to support local maternity and child welfare clinics. By 1937, 54 per cent of mothers attended a clinic, though many received only a perfunctory examina-tion.[46] Professional pressure to hospitalise pregnant women, which was

supported by women's organisation at this time, resulted in a gradual
increase in the proportion of births that took place in hospitals from 15
per cent in 1927 to 25 per cent in 1937 and 54 per cent by 1946.[47] In
addition a number of local authorities distributed milk both to children
and to pregnant women between the wars.

Women's Employment and the Depression

Although feminists of all shades regarded employment as central to the
next stage in women's emancipation, they found themselves on the
defensive in this area throughout the 1920s and 1930s. They were the
victims of a number of forces beyond their control which determined
the level of employment among women. The first of these was simply
the state of the economy and the labour market. Inter-war fluctuations
pulled women in opposite directions. On the one hand prolonged and
widespread unemployment clearly hindered women indirectly in that it
stiffened male antagonism to the female worker. The depression also
directly undermined the textile industry which had been a major source
of jobs for women. On the other hand, the growth of long-term male
unemployment inevitably drove women out to work, as it had always
done, in order to feed and clothe their families. In this way the period
kept alive the habit of temporary, sporadic work for women.

The second influence was the range of attitudes and expedients
adopted by male authority in the shape of husbands, employers, trade
unions and governments. This too was mixed. Early encouraging signs
such as the Sex Discrimination (Removal) Act of 1919 rapidly proved
to be a broken reed in the face of the resurrection of obstacles such as
the bar on married women and further protective legislation. By and
large the period saw a retreat from the positive view of women in the
labour force that had flourished during the war. At its crudest the attack
was articulated by Lord Birkenhead who expressed the common view
that any working woman deprived a man of a job and thereby prevented
him from establishing a family. As late as 1933 Sir Herbert Austin, the
motor car manufacturer and former MP, was still advocating the
sacking of *all* women workers as a solution to the problem of
unemployment.

The third factor was the capacity and qualifications of women for the
work available, and the aspirations and attitudes they themselves
adopted towards paid employment. In educational terms the major
battles had already been won by this time, although a few islands of

reaction still remained such as Cambridge University which continued to refuse to admit women as full members throughout this period. A small number of women did take advantage of the 1919 Act to penetrate the ranks of the professions. Probably more important was a growing acceptance of the desirability amongst middle-class families of some occupation for their daughters, partly because of financial difficulties in supporting them after the war, and also because of fears that husbands would be in short supply. By the 1930s the middle-class girl was likely to take for granted that she must be able to support herself, even if she did not intend to do so for long, and this, indeed, represented emancipation for many. It is also significant that women began to complete their families in a shorter space of time because they had fewer pregnancies, which offered greater opportunities to seek employment outside the home. However, some women were inhibited from taking advantage of this by the ideology of domesticity. If a mother had fewer children she was often to find that they remained dependent on the parental home for longer and that she was required to concentrate her attention upon them more than ever.

The net result of all the conflicting influences upon women's employment may be seen in the national statistics both for the number of workers who were women and for the number of women who were 'workers'. Considered from the perspective of the British labour force the striking feature of women's role is its stability (Table 4.2). There is a little more fluctuation in the proportion of women who worked outside the home in this period (see Table 4.3). These figures explode the notion that the First World War represented a revolution in

Table 4.2 Women as a Percentage of the British Labour Force 1911–1961

1911	1921	1931	1951	1961
29.6	29.5	29.8	30.8	32.4

Source: A.H. Halsey (ed.), *British Social Trends Since 1900* (1988), p.106.

Table 4.3 Participation Rates of Women in the Labour Force 1911–1961 (%)

1911	1921	1931	1951	1961
35.32	33.12	34.20	32.72	37.49

Source: A.H. Halsey (ed.), *British Social Trends Since 1900* (1988), pp. 166–72.

women's employment in Britain. Once the transition to peace had been accomplished there were actually *fewer* women going out to work than there had been in the Edwardian period. The modest recovery thereafter seems only to have restored the pre-war participation rates.

However, the national statistics do conceal some shifts in the pattern both in terms of the type of employment obtained by women and in terms of the age and marital status of women workers. For example women made major gains in clerical and related work where they comprised 21 per cent of the work force in 1911 but 44–46 per cent between the wars. In the same period they also improved their position slightly amongst higher professionals (from 6.0%, to 7.5%), and amongst the inspectors and foremen category (from 4.2% to 8.7%). However, women declined as a proportion in two major sectors, the lower professionals, which largely comprised teachers and nurses (from 63% to 59%), and amongst manual workers (from 30.5% to 28.8%). In general the deteriorating sectors reflect the impact of the depression, while the improving sectors suggest the effect of legal changes.

In terms of age there was a trend towards a higher level of employment amongst women in their late teens, twenties and early thirties; but the older age groups show a decline. The sharp reduction of widows and divorcees who took paid employment probably reflects the impact of the 1925 Widows' Pensions Act which brought relief to many hard-pressed women who had traditionally been obliged to find jobs in order to keep their children out of the poor law system.

Amongst married women only 9.6 per cent had been employed according to the 1911 census; this fell to 8.7 per cent in 1921 but rose to 10.0 per cent in 1931, an interesting if slight change because it occurred in the face of a widespread ban on employing married women. The dismissal of women on becoming married was by no means unknown before 1914, but the practice seems to have been more than restored after the war. This was especially the case with local authorities who frequently sacked women teachers, doctors and manual employees such as cleaners. In the civil service tradition held it to be desirable for a woman to leave on marriage, but outside the Post Office this was not always operated as a policy, partly because it would have wasted the services of skilled workers. In 1921, however, the government succumbed to pressure and drafted regulations to restrict all future civil service recruits to single and widowed women. Subsequent enquiries in 1929 and 1933 produced no major change in this policy. Between 1934 and 1938, for example, only eight women were retained in employment after their marriage on grounds of special qualifications or experience.[48]

On the other hand the effects were not very great; for example, in the four years up to 1934 less than 4 per cent of female civil servants actually retired each year because of marriage. In 1930 Winifred Holtby noted with understandable irritation the results of a survey of 7000 women employed in the civil service by the Civil Service Clerical Association which showed that a very large majority supported the marriage bar.[49] Clearly such findings undermined the feminist case and strengthened the hand of politicians for it corroborated the view that most young women regarded low paid employment as a temporary interlude prior to marriage.

In the case of women teachers, whose total numbers fell from 187,000 in 1921 to 181,000 in 1931, the argument about not losing the advantage of experienced employees was particularly strong. Yet the pressure exerted on their behalf was often rather muted. In Cardiff for example, the Women's Citizens Association sent a deputation to the City Council in 1922 to ask them to keep the door open for exceptional cases and for women obliged to return to work to support dependants. The Council agreed not to apply an iron rule, but insisted 'it will be expected that women teachers will tender their resignations on marriage'; the Council then decided whether the special needs of the school and the role of the individual teacher justified retention.[50]

Feminist organisations felt outraged at the sacking of highly qualified professionals such as Dr Miall Smith, an assistant medical officer dismissed by St Pancras Borough Council in 1921. The Sex Disqualification Removal Act had stated that: 'A person shall not be disqualified by sex or marriage from being appointed to or holding any civil or judicial office or post.' In spite of this, however, Sir John Simon gave his opinion to NUSEC that a case of wrongful dismissal on behalf of Dr Miall Smith would fail; the Act did nothing to infringe a local authority's right to *dismiss* for whatever reason.[51] Nor was further legislative redress now possible. Sir John Newman's 1927 Married Women's Employment Bill, which simply proposed to prevent dismissal of married women in the public services, was opposed by the government and rejected by 84 votes to 63. Critics argued that local authorities believed women to be less efficient workers after marriage, and that the bill was, in any case, not supported by the women civil servants themselves.[52] In time governments found further ways in which to discriminate against married women. The 1931 Anomalies Act modified National Insurance so that a married woman who lost her job had to satisfy more stringent terms in order to draw benefit than single women or men. As a result 180,000 married women failed to qualify for benefits in the first year of the scheme in spite of the fact that they had made contributions towards it.

However, the slight rise in the number of married woman at work in 1931 suggests that the negative pressures should not be exaggerated. Unfortunately the absence of a census for 1941 obscures the extent to which the positive trend continued during the 1930s. Ray Strachey, who monitored developments for the Women's Employment Federation, certainly discerned a steady trend towards more women workers during this decade.[53] She attributed this partly to the more positive attitudes amongst the middle classes where it was increasingly acceptable for the young wife to work whilst her husband was struggling to establish himself in his business or profession. Obviously this was perfectly compatible with the centrality of marriage. The trend towards an earlier age for marriage and the reduction in family size facilitated the growth of this combination of work and domesticity for middle-class women. Strachey also found comfort in the fact that amongst single women the trend towards employment continued after 1918 though at a slow pace. Amongst the 25–34 years age group 92.2 per cent of single women were employed by 1921 and 93.4 per cent in 1931. It seemed as though the era of the dutiful daughter confined to the family home to care for aged parents was finally drawing to a close, though some women simply added the burden of a job to their family responsibilities.

On the other hand, Strachey found less cause for satisfaction in the *quality* of women's contribution to the labour force, especially their foothold in the professions. In the legal profession, for example, debate about the admission of women had been joined during 1917. Lawyers' reluctance to allow women into clerkships in solicitors' offices looked like self-pleading, especially as women had demonstrated their capacity to study law at universities. Helena Normanton forced the pace by presenting herself at the Middle Temple, only to be rebuffed. The 1919 Act was clearly intended to open the way for such women and the result was that by 1935 there were some 116 female solicitors and 79 barristers. The slowness of progress was similar in the medical profession, already in theory open to women. From a total of 477 in 1914 the number of women doctors had grown to 1253 by 1921 and to 2810 by 1931. Yet women practised largely as GPs because hospitals continued to resist appointing them. But the most controversial and flagrant attempt to circumvent the spirit of the 1919 legislation was in the civil service. There had never been much difficulty in employing women in lowly posts; the real battle was in opening the higher grades of the civil service to university educated women. The Haldane Committee on the

Machinery of Government urged that women be allowed to sit the examinations for Class 1. But the Gladstone Committee on Recruitment into the Civil Service argued, on the contrary, that women could not stand the strain and required more sick leave than men, that the wastage rate was very high because of marriage (a fine example of male illogicality), and that it would never be possible for women in senior positions to keep control of men in subordinate roles. In the event the government of Lloyd George took advantage of the loophole in the 1919 Act which permitted it to present Orders in Council to introduce special rules governing admission to the civil service. In spite of a debate in the Commons in May 1920, in which MPs universally supported a motion of Major J. Hills to allow women equal opportunity of employment in the civil service and local government, the government instituted a separate scheme for admitting women in July of that year. Claiming that open competition would place women at a disadvantage they opted for a mixture of selection boards and examinations. Separate establishment lists were kept for women, and they were consequently excluded from the general seniority lists which would lead to the highest posts in the civil service. These policies and practices, combined with the marriage bar, help to explain why the progress of women in the professions was disappointing during the inter-war years.

Nor were feminists entirely happy about the evidence that more young girls were seeking jobs, because their work mainly remained low-level and temporary rather than part of a career pattern. This is underlined by the oral evidence uncovered by historians such as Elizabeth Roberts which shows considerable continuity of attitude; employment was still seen as unattractive and as something that a woman could gratefully turn her back on if her husband's income permitted.[54] Clearly the developments within the inter-war economy proved a somewhat mixed blessing. The contraction of the great capital goods industries – coal, iron and steel, ship-building and railways – removed jobs that were disproportionately held by men. The declining profitability of the textile industry was the one which hit women's employment significantly. On the other hand the growth sectors of the economy were in the services where women already enjoyed a strong position, and increased their hold, and in consumer goods industries involving a good deal of light, unskilled production line work for which women were as well suited as men. In both sectors, however, feminists' reservation was that the women were rushing into jobs at a very young age, without trying to take advantage of education and training, and consequently were perpetuating their status as low-level, low-paid, temporary workers.

The war experience had done much to stimulate feminist concern over inequalities of pay. They took some comfort from the report of the War Cabinet Committee on Women in Industry in December 1918 which recommended that the government should encourage industry to adopt equal pay by implementing the policy among its own employees first; if employers chose to plead that women were less productive workers than men the burden of proof should lie with them.[55] However, the Coalition government resorted to the claim that the state of the national finances ruled out the extra expenditure involved in equal pay, a line that was used repeatedly by all governments down to the 1950s. During the inter-war years women did enjoy equal pay in a limited number of professions including the law, medicine, the press, the stage and parliament. But in industry there was only a slight improvement on the Edwardian situation (see Table 4.4). Chronologically the pattern seems clear. In the 1920s when many women showed themselves reluctant to accept work on poor terms, there was a modest improvement in their pay relative to that of men; but by 1931 this gain had been checked and gave way to a slight falling back thereafter as sheer necessity forced them to take the jobs available.

From 1920 onwards supporters of equal pay concentrated their efforts on teaching and the civil service because their case was strong in these occupations and because the decision lay within the government's immediate power. In 1936 Ellen Wilkinson succeeded in winning the support of the Commons for equal pay when 31 National Government supporters defied their leaders. The issue became frustrating in the same way as the suffrage had been: many MPs found it easy to record a vote for the women's cause in the knowledge that any decision could be promptly crushed by a vote of confidence in the government. In the case of the teaching profession the stubbornness of the authorities was particularly striking. In 1919 the minister, H.A.L. Fisher, established a

Table 4.4 Average Earnings: Females as a Percentage of those for Males 1906–1935

Industries	1906	1924	1931	1935
All industries	43.7	47.7	48.3	48.0
Textiles	58.5	56.1	56.0	55.9
Clothing	46.3	49.1	50.2	51.2
Food, drink & tobacco	41.5	48.1	48.7	47.0
Paper, printing	36.4	38.6	39.4	37.3
Metal industries	38.1	44.7	47.6	45.7

Source: A.L. Bowley, *Wages and Incomes in the U.K. since 1860* (1937).

new system for settling pay in the shape of the Burnham Committee, only 5 of whose 44 members were women. This simply perpetuated the existing discrimination against women teachers; indeed, when new salary scales designed to take account of inflation were adopted in 1920, the gap between men's and women's pay was allowed to grow. In response to a deputation from the National Federation of Women Teachers in May 1920 Fisher contrived to give the impression that he favoured the principle of equal pay, but was hamstrung by the cost. They could hardly instruct local authorities to grant equal pay until the central government had done so for its employees.[56] In any case he needed the money for the children themselves, a form of moral blackmail much resorted to by his successors. Behind Fisher's emollient approach the official view as expressed by the permanent secretary was blunter; if obliged to give equal pay, he claimed, local authorities would tend to appoint men rather than women teachers, especially to the more senior posts, because they would rather have a man for their money. Further he used the argument that was common throughout industry, that men needed higher pay because they had greater responsibilities in the form of dependent family members. Drawing on the 1921 Census Eleanor Rathbone exploded this claim (Table 4.5).

In spite of such evidence, however, women's pay continued to be widely regarded as no more than a supplement to that of their husbands or as pocket money that a young girl might spend on luxuries. There is an assumption that their willingness to work for low wages made women particularly attractive to employers in the expanding light industries especially in the south and the midlands during the 1930s. However, the fairly stable position of women in the labour force is a caution against exaggerating the impact of the new consumer goods industries. This is a relatively under-researched area, but one valuable study has been made of the pattern of employment in Slough, a typical

Table 4.5 Family Background of Men over 20 Years in England and Wales 1921

%	
26.6	Bachelors
34.0	Married men or widowers with no children under 16 years
16.0	Men with one dependent child
10.5	Men with two dependent children
6.2	Men with three dependent children
6.7	Men with four dependent children

Source: E. Rathbone, *Wages Plus Family Allowances* (1925), p.2.

centre of growth industries such as food processing, chemicals, pharma-
ceuticals, electrical goods, furnishings and motor vehicles. It is something of a surprise to find that in 1931 women comprised only 32 per
cent of the total labour force in Slough, though they reached 41 per cent
in food and fell to 12 per cent in motor construction.[57] In view of the
need for manual dexterity and the irrelevance of strength and skill in
much of the work one might have expected women's share of employment to have been more than 2 per cent greater than it was nationally.
One plausible explanation for this would be the pressure exerted by
trade unions in order to safeguard the interests of their largely male
members; but the relative weakness of the unions in places like Slough
tends to undermine this view. The attitude of the employers may well be
the more important factor. Part of the reason for concentrating new
industry in the south was the preference for non-unionised labour
which could, of course, apply to female labour even more strongly.
There is some evidence that non-unionised firms used a higher proportion of female labour, but this is not very marked or a general
pattern. While employers often displayed a liking for women workers
as both amenable and cheap this was less significant in an area like
Slough where wage levels for men were already somewhat below the
national average. Moreover, even women could be undercut by youths
employed at rates substantially below adult wages. Especially where
the young male was a newcomer to the area and remained uninvolved
with the unions he often proved the ideal recruit.[58] This is also
consistent with the preference shown by employers in shops and offices
for young girls rather than mature women.

Notwithstanding the bias in favour of youth the expanding trading
estates clearly provided a relatively promising sector for women's
employment. But nationally women struggled to hold their ground
especially in manufacturing industry. As each phase of the depression
unfolded they appear to have suffered disproportionately. Even during
the 1920s their share of jobs in manufacturing industry fell from 26 to
22 per cent. According to a reply given to Nancy Astor by Margaret
Bondfield in February 1931 women experienced heavier unemployment
than men in most industries (Table 4.6).

In spite of their new status as parliamentary voters women were
evidently more vulnerable than men to the effects of the economic
depression. This is heavily underlined by the manner in which inter-war
governments tightened up the existing regulations governing the terms
of women's employment in industry. Many feminists had long resented
'protective legislation' which categorised them with children as persons

Table 4.6   Unemployment by Gender in Selected Industries,
February 1931

Industry	Male unemployment (%)	Female unemployment (%)
Pottery	35.5	47.2
Cotton	45.6	48.4
Wool	26.4	28.4
Linen	28.3	35.5
Drink	8.4	16.3
Tobacco	5.2	9.3
Food	11.1	21.3
Rope, hemp	20.1	25.1

Source: Astor Papers 1416/1/1/899.

requiring special help over their conditions of employment. It seemed as though politicians and trade unionists were using the slump as an excuse to impose further restrictions on women by reducing their maximum working week and excluding them from occupations which involved lifting heavy weights and handling dangerous substances. For example, they were kept out of paint manufacture on the grounds of potential lead poisoning to which men were allegedly less susceptible. The 1920 Employment of Women, Young Persons and Children Act prohibited night work, which had the effect of closing the newspaper trade to them. Such discrimination provoked the establishment of the Open Door Council in 1926. However, in its debates with the trade unions the ODC was damned as a middle-class feminist body, and never really mobilised the support of the working-class women for whom it attempted to speak. Consequently it does not appear to have enjoyed much success. As late as 1937 parliament passed another Factory Act to impose a maximum 48 hour working week on women.

It is clear that the trade unions had a rather poor record of defending the interests of their female members between the wars. During the war union membership among both sexes had risen sharply. But after 1918, while the upsurge amongst men continued for two years, female membership stagnated. Once the slump had set in by 1921 membership fell for both sexes until around 1934. Thereafter, men's membership increased much more rapidly than women's (see Table 4.7). The figures suggest that women had not been favourably impressed by their experience inside the movement. The war had generated one important development in the form of amalgamations such as that between the National Federation of Women Workers and the National Union of

Table 4.7   Trade Union Membership: Men and Women 1918–1939
(in millions)

	Men	Women
1918	5.3	1.2
1920	7.0	1.3
1921	5.6	1.0
1925	4.6	0.8
1933	3.6	0.7
1936	4.5	0.8
1939	5.2	1.0

General Workers in 1920. As a result by 1921 four out of ten of the unions affiliated to the TUC included female members. Women became better entrenched within the organisation, and several such as Margaret Bondfield (National Union of General Workers), and Julia Varley (Transport and General Workers Union) achieved prominent positions in the national leadership. However, in the long run the advantages of mixed unions seemed dubious. Few unions were willing to treat women's interests as priorities. Even the National Union of Teachers, a majority of whose members were women, failed to protest against the poor post-war pay scales for women. On the whole women paid lower subscriptions and received lower benefits; and in spite of a few token leaders, they were excluded from influence over their unions' policies. When the General Strike came in 1926 women were often not called out – a clear sign of their marginal role in male eyes. Recruitment efforts were concentrated upon men, and even Bondfield found herself confined to handling propaganda and provident schemes for women.[59] For Bondfield herself an escape route presented itself in the form of her elevation first to the General Council of the TUC and then to parliament and the cabinet. But behind her the womens' rank and file dwindled.

By the end of the 1930s perhaps the most that could be said was that women's position in the labour force had not deteriorated as badly as it might have done. But the feminist organisations could claim little credit for this. In the employment sphere they seemed unable to exert much political influence. Their most constructive role lay in working through organisations like the London Society for Women's Service and the Central Committee on the Training of Women in order to improve access to existing job opportunities and careers. Beyond that Vera Brittain and Monica Whately propagated the idea that no guilt attached to the working wife and mother; but it was to be some years before this view became widely acceptable.

Chapter 5   The Domestication of British Politics

During the summer of 1917 when the enfranchisement of women was becoming an accepted fact, Millicent Fawcett urged Helena Swanwick to start tackling the next problem: the organisation of women voters with a view to subjecting the political system to effective pressure on women's issues. 'I remarked on the difficulty of organising what doesn't exist', recalled Mrs Swanwick, to which Fawcett replied, 'Oh. I shall retire and watch you all floundering.'[1] The question remains largely unexplored by historians: how much difference did the enfranchisement of women really make? Any answer must involve consideration of a number of distinct themes: changes in the style and agenda of politics, the extent of the success of the women's movement in achieving its legislative goals, the motivation and tactics of the political parties in managing the influx of women into the system, and the actual impact made by women in electoral terms.

Women and the Agenda of Politics

Social historians, especially those interested in leisure, have discerned a certain shift in the direction of respectability and sobriety during the nineteenth and twentieth centuries. This is not without significance for political history. Politics, after all, has long been a hobby for many people, as opposed to a profession, and the traditional British parliamentary election was, from one perspective, no more than a festival, a show and a market for the community; it was characterised by noise, drinking and sporadic mob violence. Hence the Victorian assumption that the election was outside the sphere of ladies. But in the last twenty years of the nineteenth century Eatanswill gradually passed away, assisted no doubt by legislation designed to limit expenditure and undue pressure upon the voters. As elections became more sober and decorous, so the view that participation in them would detract from the womanly qualities steadily lost its force. But women were not only the beneficiaries of the change: they helped to accelerate the trend. By their very presence as canvassers and speakers, and as electors and candidates in local government, they helped to render traditional behaviour anachronistic and counter-productive. By the early twentieth century the number of petitions over parliamentary elections had begun to

dwindle, and the culmination came in 1918 when parliament felt ready
to risk introducing one-day polling throughout the country; in spite of
the greatly increased electorate, indeed perhaps because of it, fears of
disorderly conduct had clearly diminished greatly. The slightly eerie
quietness when the new voters went to the polls in December 1918,
which a number of politicians noted, heralded a new era. As the 1920s
unfolded the political parties began to rely rather less upon the
traditional mass rally and the physical mobilisation of supporters on the
streets; these techniques gave way to the subdued door-to-door canvass
and the meticulous identification of the new Absent Voters – work at
which women were believed to excel. Soon it became easier for the
leaders to communicate with voters by means of the wireless, and
politics shifted from the public platform to the home. In this way the
whole style and ambience of electoral politics became more congenial
for the typical British woman.

Moreover, the change in style was accompanied by an even more
significant development in the substance of politics. Since the 1880s
the conventional issues of male politics – the great constitutional, legal,
religious and moral questions – had been giving ground to concern over
poverty, standards of living, social welfare, unemployment and the
management of the economy. The critical boost to this shift had come
with the social and financial innovations of the Edwardian Liberal
governments. But the momentum had been maintained by the pressure
of wartime interventionism. Finally the rise of the Labour Party as the
second party in the state in 1918, coinciding as it did with the mass
enfranchisement, convinced most politicians that neglect of social and
economic questions could well prove fatal. Consequently in the inter-
war period such matters as pensions, housing, unemployment and
unemployment benefits occupied the central position in popular political
debate. Obviously there were counter-pressures including the sudden
anti-waste campaign shortly after the war, reductions in income tax and
efforts to balance the budget by retrenchment; but these only set limits
to the phenomenon. It is not insignificant that even on the Conservative
side a political reputation could now be made, as was Neville Chamberlain's, at the Ministry of Health, an office that did not exist until 1919.

In the era of the benign and interventionist state women inevitably
occupied a more central position than they had enjoyed in the Victorian
era. Back in the 1880s the Women's Co-operative Guild had set itself
the task of turning the concerns and interests of ordinary married
women into political issues. By the 1920s their successors began to
reap the benefits of the strategy:

There has never been a time when women were not interested in politics ... for are not politics bound up with all that woman is most concerned with – housing, food prices, the education of her children, the health of her family? What women have to realise is that the State is nothing but a larger home, and that its problems, duties and responsibilities should be considered in the same spirit of mutual helpfulness as in the home.[2]

When Eleanor Barton wrote these words she commanded widespread assent right across the political spectrum. This is clear from the emphasis given by candidates of all kinds to topics such as widows' pensions and house-building in this period; the latter is especially interesting as one of the few issues on which the views of housewives were actively sought. In this way domesticity continued to carry women towards the top of the political agenda. It may be thought that this was no more than a means of confining women to a new, but tightly drawn sphere within politics. There is something in this; but is it entirely clear who was victim and who was victor? Politicians could not take up domesticity without seriously limiting their own room for manoeuvre. Readjustment inevitably caused most strain on the Conservative side: 'we have a new electorate which is interested in Social and Moral Issues', insisted Nancy Astor. But though irritated by Astor there is no doubt that the leadership heard the message. Under Baldwin the Conservatives consciously played down their traditional role as defenders of the British Empire against internal and external threats; and as early as 1921 the party's Principal Agent identified the underlying change in the electoral struggle:

The women's vote is having a narrowing effect upon politics, making them more parochial and is, at the moment, reducing them to bread and butter politics and the cost of living ... their votes will probably be given on purely home questions ... while Imperial and foreign issues will leave them cold.[3]

Women and the Peace Movement

If women's impact on the agenda of politics was characteristically through domesticity, this was by no means the only form that their involvement took. By far the most important exception is their participation in campaigns for peace, disarmament and the League of Nations during the 1920s and 1930s. The effect of the Great War in stimulating the formation of such groups as the Union of Democratic Control and the No Conscription Fellowship, and the anti-war literature of the late 1920s and 1930s has long been studied. However, women activists are not to be seen simply as followers behind a predominantly male movement for peace. They had a history of their own as campaigners for peace which went back to the Quaker Peace Societies of the 1820s and the Olive Leaf Circles of the early Victorian period. Female opposition to war culminated in Emily Hobhouse's famous exposure of the British methods of subduing the Boers in the South African War at the turn of the century. Particularly amongst Liberal and Socialist women one finds the conviction that wars and the military machines and diplomacy that stood behind them were the peculiar work of men. By extension they often argued that women as mothers felt a special interest in the maintenance of peace, and that their wider involvement in national politics would help to eliminate war as a weapon in international affairs. This represented one strand in the broader view of women as the more civilised and morally superior sex.

Even before 1914 British feminists enjoyed close connections with women activists in Europe and America through the International Woman Suffrage Alliance (IWSA). Faced with the disaster of a major war in which Britain was a key participant a number of them immediately opted to join the Union of Democratic Control which campaigned for a negotiated peace and a settlement without vindictive terms. Others worked through the ILP and the No Conscription Fellowship. However, the distinctive contribution was made from 1915 onwards when efforts began to convene a meeting of the IWSA to bring together women from the combatant countries on neutral territory. In Britain supporters of this initiative included Helena Swanwick, Maude Royden, Margaret Bondfield, Marion Phillips, Margaret Llewelyn Davis, Kathleen Courtney, Emmeline Pethick-Lawrence, Charlotte Despard and Elizabeth Cadbury – clearly drawn from a wide range of women's organisations. Although only three British women managed to reach The Hague for the congress organised by the IWSA, a new Women's International League for Peace and Freedom (WIL) was established under the chairmanship in Britain of Mrs Swanwick. A further development came in 1917 in the form of the Women's Peace Crusade which sprang up spontaneously out of the mingled resentment caused by conscription, heavy casualties, food prices and the high cost of housing.[4] As with some of the male wartime protests and strikes of this period the momentum behind the Women's Peace Crusades was by no means exclusively pacifist in nature; much reflected frustration at the material consequences of the war upon women's daily lives. By contrast the WIL reflected a more consciously political ideology. But it was essentially that of middle-class women and a small minority at that.

Like the UDC and the ILP, the Women's International League made courageous attempts to argue the case for a saner approach to foreign affairs in a hostile climate, but its actual membership in 1916 stood at only 2458, and at 3576 by 1917. Far more women had involved themselves in such organisations as the Voluntary Aid Detachments and the Women's Patriotic League before 1914 and, when the crisis came, more seemed inclined to regard war as an opportunity for women than as something that perpetuated the subjection of their sex. Peace campaigners such as Emmeline Pethwick-Lawrence found it difficult to translate wartime protests into votes for anti-war candidates in 1918 even amongst women (see page 147).

When peace came the WPC dwindled rapidly – a sign of its essential connection with the immediate discomforts of war. The WIL maintained its activity throughout the period though on a relatively limited basis; even in the 1930s it claimed around 3500 members and had obviously been overshadowed by more popular peace movements of the period. Women's role in this activity between the wars was both through mixed organisations and through women's groups. Examples of the former include the League of Nations Union, the No More War Movement, which was formed in 1921, and the famous Peace Ballot of 1934 in which women played an essential part as canvassers. Also the Women's Sections of the Labour Party identified strongly with the socialist critique of war as a manifestation of the crisis of capitalism, and they adopted the view that any government which threatened to embroil the country in another conflict should be resisted by a refusal to bear arms.[5] Amongst the more distinctively female expressions of anti-war sentiment are the various Peacemakers' Pilgrimages which were organised during the summer of 1926 when some 10,000 women representing a wide range of organisations gathered in Hyde Park from all over the country. This activity was stimulated partly by the Locarno Pact and by the news that the League of Nations was to establish a Disarmament Commission. Feeling that the British government and its foreign secretary, Austen Chamberlain, were somewhat unenthusiastic about arbitration and disarmament, the women determined to maintain pressure by demonstrating women's concern through a succession of local pilgrimages during 1927. Some of the most active campaigners were women of the Women's Co-operative Guild which enjoyed a membership of some 67,000 by 1930. Its members were antagonised by the profiteering to which the previous war had given rise. The WCG developed a number of distinctive campaigning methods including the Peace Celebrations held during Armistice Week from 1927 onwards, the sales of Peace Handkerchiefs and Tablecloths, and the sale of White Poppies, wreaths of which were laid at war memorials on Armistice Day during the 1930s.[6]

But probably the most typical and respectable form which women's participation took was simply their membership of the League of Nations Union (LNU), whose membership rose from a quarter of a million in 1925 to a peak of 406,000 by 1931 and which thereafter fell back to under 200,000 by 1939. The LNU clearly provided a congenial form of participation for women such as Vera Brittain who became a regular speaker on its platforms in the 1920s. This of course is to some extent a reflection of its respectable reputation. It was vaguely internationalist in character rather than pacifist; as the Peace Ballot of 1934 was to demonstrate, many of its followers supported the use of sanctions against aggressor states and were antagonised by the failure of the British government to back collective security through the League. Consequently the range of women's organisations prepared to support the LNU extended as far as the Women's Institutes and the National Council of Women; with Lord Robert Cecil as its president the LNU could even appeal to Conservative women. Significantly NUSEC included the League of Nations among the reforms for women which it published in its statement of objectives in 1928. One can only interpret this as another sign of the faith many women had that the League would, by preventing future wars, serve the wider purpose of creating a society that would be more congenial for women.

Politicians could not but be impressed by the public manifestations of anti-war sentiment on the part of women. It was not uncommon for a women's peace campaign in each locality to draw together women from the Labour Party, the Liberal Association, the Women's Citizens and the WIL as well as those involved in temperance work or the WI. By crossing the bounds of social class and political opinion in this way women underlined the public concern over disarmament and the central position of women within the movement. Those who stood outside felt somewhat vulnerable. Some of the more right-wing Conservative women, for example, complained that their case for treating the League of Nations with scepticism was simply going by default because their leaders had failed to counter what one woman called the 'sloppy sentiment about the League of Nations', and ignored the possibility that it 'could be used to destroy the British Empire'.[7] In spite of such warnings it does appear that politicians allowed themselves to be carried along with the peace movement for some time. Increasing numbers of candidates, especially in 1929, felt it necessary to commit themselves to peace in their election addresses, and a number of them specifically linked the cause of peace to the interest of women voters. One of the advantages enjoyed by Ramsay MacDonald at this time was his superior record as foreign secretary in 1924 in working to reduce tension between France and Germany over reparations and the Ruhr. The expectation that he and Arthur Henderson might succeed at the Disarmament Convention at Geneva was an important part of Labour's appeal in 1929. Consequently the Conservatives could not afford to be outflanked on this issue; hence the elevation of the personable Anthony Eden as minister with special responsibility for disarmament in 1934. Several governments of the period recognised women's interest by appointing Mary Agnes Hamilton, Mrs Swanwick, the Duchess of Atholl and Margery Corbett Ashby as delegates to the League of Nations. However, women's groups encountered resistance within the League of Nations bureaucracy, and with the exception of Dame Rachel Crowdy who became head of the social section, women failed to rise far up the hierarchy.

   While it would be an exaggeration to see the inter-war peace movement as essentially the product of the women's movement, there clearly existed a mutually advantageous relationship between the two. To put it no higher, women remained a very visible element in the campaigns against war, and their participation went a long way towards keeping the League and disarmament near the top of the agenda, especially in the late 1920s and the first half of the 1930s. Simultaneously the cause of peace gave women a platform and a degree of authority within what would conventionally have been regarded as male territory, and although by 1939 only a handful of women such as Vera Brittain were to maintain their opposition to war, they never entirely lost the position they had won.

The Significance of the Women's Legislation of the 1920s

In the late 1920s Mrs Fawcett looked back on a career now stretching across half a century with an understandable sense of satisfaction. To her it seemed that politicians' attitudes towards women had changed radically:

> Those of us who had worked in the lobbies and Committee Rooms of the House of Commons ... were conscious of this improvement from the very moment when the Representation of the People Act, 1918, received the Royal Assent. We were no longer there on sufferance, but by right. ... Democracy is a great teacher of manners.[8]

By way of corroboration for her claims she pointed out that parliament had enacted just four measures to improve the position of women during the first 18 years of the century and then only after prolonged effort on the part of women's groups. By contrast the decade after 1918 had triggered an avalanche of reforms (see Table 5.1). Clearly there can be no hard and fast definition of women's legislation. It seems surprising that the lists published by feminist organisations at this

Table 5.1   Women's Legislation 1918–1929

1918   *The Parliamentary Qualification of Women Act*
(Allowed women to be elected as members of parliament)
The Registration of Midwives Amending Act
(Modified the Act of 1902)
Affiliation Orders (Increase of Maximum Payment) Act
(Increased the sum payable by a father for an illegitimate child from 5 shillings to 10 shillings weekly)

1919   *The Sex Disqualification (Removal) Act*
(Abolished all existing restrictions upon the admission of women into professions, occupations and civic positions including appointment as jurers and magistrates)
Nurses Registration Act
(Compulsory registration of all who practised as nurses)

1920   *Married Women's Property (Scotland) Act*
(Extended to Scotland rights already enjoyed in England and Wales)
Maintenance Orders (Facilities for Enforcement) Act
(Enabled women to recover sums payable under maintenance orders from men living in other parts of the empire)

1922   *Married Women (Maintenance) Act*
(Allowed a woman a maximum of 40 shillings for herself and 10 shillings per child under a separation order)
The Infanticide Act
(Removed the charge of murder for a woman guilty of killing her child where it was shown that she was suffering from the effects of her confinement)
Criminal Law (Amendment) Act
(Abolished the defence that a man had reasonable cause to believe that a girl was over the age of 16 except for men under the age of 23 and in connection with a first offence. Raised the age of consent for indecent assault from 13 to 16. Extended from six to nine months the period during which proceedings could be taken in cases of criminal assault)
The Law of Property Act
(Enabled husband and wife to inherit equally the other's property. Placed mothers on an equal footing with fathers as to inheritance of property from intestate children)

1923 *Matrimonial Causes Act*
(Allowed a wife equal grounds for divorce (i.e. adultery) with a husband)
The Bastardy Act
(Increased maximum payments by a father from 10 to 20 shillings under an affiliation order)

1925 *The Guardianship of Infants Act*
(Provided for equal rights between the sexes with respect to guardianship of infants)
The Widows, Orphans and Old Age Contributory Pensions Act
(Provided a 10 shillings weekly pension for widows of insured men who died after January 1926, for existing widows of insured men with children under 14½ years, and for insured men and women aged 65–70 or wives over 65 of such men. Also provided Children's Allowances of 5 shillings for a first child and 3 shillings for each subsequent child, paid to existing and future widows in respect of children up to the age of 14½ or 16 if in full time education)
The Summary Jurisdiction (Separation and Maintenance) Act
(Extended the grounds on which either partner in a marriage could obtain a separation order to include (1) cruelty, (2) habitual drunkenness, (3) enforced co-habitation by a partner suffering from venereal disease. Also abolished the requirement that a wife must leave her husband before applying for a separation order)

1926 *Adoption of Children Act*
(Introduced the principle that a court must satisfy itself with the circumstances of an adoption)
Registration of Midwives and Maternity Homes Act
(Provided for inspection and registration)

1927 Nursing Homes Registration Act

1928 *Equal Franchise Act*
(Abolished the age qualification for women parliamentary electors. Allowed a woman to register as an elector in respect of her residence)

1929 *Age of Marriage Act*
(Raised the age of marriage for both sexes to 16.

time omitted the 1921 Act which permitted a woman to marry her deceased husband's brother which obviously put them on an equal footing with men who already had the right of marriage with a deceased wife's sister. On the other hand the lists often do include the 1923 Intoxicating Liquor Act, which banned sales to those under 18 years, and the 1926 Legitimacy Act which legitimised children born out of wedlock if their parents subsequently married. Neither of these appear to qualify as feminist reforms, they were simply issues involving children in which some women had taken an interest. In its catalogue of women's legislation the Conservative Party listed the 1920 Women and Young Persons Act which excluded women from employment involving contact with lead – a measure naturally repudiated by many feminists.

Setting aside reservations about which measures to include, the record of legislation does seem a formidable one for a single decade; and it is difficult to escape the conclusion that it is attributable to the effect of women's enfranchisement in altering the priorities of the politicians. It had been suggested that a number of the reforms would probably have been achieved before 1914 had not the women concentrated their efforts upon the suffrage campaign.[9] One can certainly see some elements of continuity between the pre- and post-war phases. We know, for example, that Lloyd George wished to include widow's pensions in his 1911 National Insurance Act. The state registration of nurses represented the culmination of a very prolonged campaign whose success almost certainly owed more to the death of Florence Nightingale and to the war than to women's enfranchisement. It is also true that Victorian women had succeeded in tackling male vested interests in spite of their own expulsion from the electorate. In this respect there is a useful comparison between the 1922 Criminal Law Amendment Act and the great campaign of Josephine Butler to repeal the Contagious Diseases Acts. Both represent steps towards the equal moral standard to which feminists aspired. Yet although some politicians stubbornly defended the male freedom to exploit women sexually, even in the 1920s, their position was seriously undermined. Whereas in the 1870s it had been difficult to persuade most MPs to consider the issues involved in the Contagious Diseases Act seriously, by the 1920s the anti-feminists had been reduced to a beleaguered, if reasonably effective, minority. Feminists could realistically contemplate a two- or three-year campaign rather than decades of painstaking effort before attaining their object.

Whatever qualifications may be made about each individual measure this scarcely seems to detract from the sheer number of bills introduced during the 1920s. The range can only partly be explained in terms of a redeployment of efforts that had previously been focused almost exclusively upon the franchise question. For the activists the quality of legislation seemed to reflect a greater willingness to listen to women's demands on the part of politicians, and a readiness to put pressure on the government. A case in point was the debate on 5 August 1921 on a motion by Major J.W. Hills in favour of equal opportunities for women in the civil service. It was tempting to take refuge in the view that this matter had been dealt with by the 1919 Sex Disqualification (Removal)

Act. Yet in the face of opposition from the Treasury a succession of speakers supported Hills, and the government at length backed down for fear of being defeated in the lobbies. While the government still enjoyed scope for evasion and prevarication on the issue, such debates understandably encouraged the women to believe that they now enjoyed far more political muscle.[10]

Certainly there was no significant change in the tactics employed by women's organisations after 1918. NUSEC, for example carried on its steady pressure through a parliamentary secretary, Eva Hubback, who closely monitored parliamentary business and fostered contacts with sympathetic MPs whom she briefed on key bills and parliamentary questions. NUSEC maintained a series of specialist committees to concentrate on such issues as the civil service, equal franchise, the status of wives and mothers, married women's employment and women MPs. Their quiet work was complemented as and when appropriate by more public pressure in the form of rallies, delegations to ministers, circulars to MPs and candidates, and joint ventures with other women's organisations. The effort usually culminated in the introduction of a bill by a backbencher, as in the past, but in the 1920s this was often overtaken by a government measure. As always this work crossed the party divide; and although several of the new women members, notably Astor and Wintringham, were very co-operative, they were clearly not essential to NUSEC's parliamentary work. They invariably relied upon sympathetic men to take up their case, including Conservatives (Major Hills, who sat on NUSEC's executive, and Sir Robert Newman), Liberals (Frank Briant and Sir John Simon), and Labour (Ernest Thurtle and Fred Pethwick-Lawrence).

In some ways the most difficult of the women's issues during the 1920s was equal franchise. Whereas measures dealing with guardianship, maintenance or even divorce could be seen as answers to strictly limited and discrete grievances, the franchise was of potentially far wider significance. Before making women a majority of the electorate politicians wished to be reasonably certain of the use that women might make of their position. Nor was the 30 year age limit regarded as especially illogical at the time; after all the parliamentary vote had, in practice, been concentrated upon the older men as a result of the householder qualification and the late age of marriage. It was still widely believed that 21 was too young an age for both sexes. Consequently franchise reform was not a priority during the early 1920s. The politicians strove to obscure this by an elaborate exercise in shadow-boxing; each side brought forth backbench bills designed to prove their credentials as reformers and embarrass their opponents. In 1919 Labour included equal suffrage in its Women's Emancipation bill which was scuppered by the government's Sex Disqualification Removal bill. In 1920 a Labour backbencher introduced an equal suffrage bill which passed on second reading with all-party support; Lord Robert Cecil did the same in 1922. However, the Coalition government resorted to the traditional argument that a major increase in the electorate should be followed swiftly by a general election, and therefore pronounced reform premature. NUSEC concluded that nothing but a government bill would succeed, and from 1921 onwards it concentrated its efforts on persuading the prime minister to receive a deputation from MPs. By the autumn of 1922 Lloyd George had agreed, but the political crisis and sudden dissolution of parliament intervened. The new premier, Bonar Law, reiterated his personal support for equal suffrage, and the Liberals joined Labour in placing the proposal in their official programme. In 1923 it was the turn of a Liberal member, Isaac Foot, to introduce a bill, this time backed by a memorial signed by over 200 MPs and a large demonstration at Westminster Hall addressed by Astor, Bondfield and Wintringham for the three parties. However, neither Baldwin nor MacDonald saw fit to include equal suffrage in the King's Speeches that were prepared for the 1924 parliament. William Adamson (Labour) brought in a bill which was struggling in committee by the summer but appeared to have been rescued when the MacDonald government indicated its willingness to take responsibility for it. However, in the autumn MacDonald fell from office. The one real gain that NUSEC managed to squeeze out of the 1924 election was a pledge from Baldwin of Conservative support for equal suffrage and the offer of a new Speaker's Conference if they returned to power.[11] This pledge gave the new prime minister a respectable reason for excluding the issue from the 1925 King's Speech and for opposing further Labour bills on the subject. Although his prevarication increasingly antagonised the women's organisations, they could do little more than organise some large rallies and remind Baldwin regularly of his public pledge. Nothing happened during 1926 in parliament, and when the 1927 speech from the throne neglected to mention women it began to appear that there would be insufficient time to enact a reform and prepare the new register before the next general election. In March 1927 Baldwin promised a deputation that he would make an announcement before Easter. The problem was that Baldwin by no means dominated his cabinet in the period, and several ministers such as Austen Chamberlain and Winston Churchill still disliked women's enfranchisement. With a large majority and a five-year term ahead of him Baldwin, not un-naturally, had preferred to let the matter rest for as long as possible. Eventually he used his 1924 pledge to twist the arms of his recalcitrant colleagues: he could not ultimately renege on his promise. Thus it was in April 1927 that the home secretary announced a bill to enfranchise women on the same basis as men.

This was the signal for some sustained attacks on the 'woolgathering schemes' of the Baldwin government by the premier's enemies, notably in the *Daily Mail*. Over several months a battery of claims was made; that the government had a mandate only to impose economies and fight Bolshevism, that no demand for reform existed in the country, that young women paid little taxation and would strengthen the pressure for extravagant expenditure, that neither the cabinet nor Tory MPs supported reform, and that the change would herald a revolution because it would make women a majority in every constituency. Only the last of these claims was likely to make politicians pause. In an editorial on 'Why Socialists Want Votes for Flappers' the *Daily Mail* sought to frighten Tories about Labour's ability to manipulate thousands of impressionable young females. It followed up with reports that Conservative agents were in despair about their electoral prospects, and scare stories suggesting that specific Tory seats, currently held with comfortable majorities, were likely to be lost.[12] Significantly, however, the *Mail* failed to find more than a handful of Tory MPs ready to oppose equal suffrage. This left the paper rather isolated and increasingly hysterical in its opposition. The fact was that in 1924 Conservatives had managed to win 48 per cent of the poll when women comprised over 40 per cent of the voters. It scarcely seemed credible that the additions to the electorate being proposed could have the disastrous impact predicted, especially as the party would enjoy some credit for having introduced the reform as well as several other measures for women. Already 9 million women enjoyed the vote, while under 5.3 million remained unenfranchised. But of the latter nearly 2 million were actually *over* 30 years of age, leaving around 3.5 million in their twenties. Thus the 'flapper' voters around whom the controversy centred comprised no more than 11–12 per cent of the new electorate in 1929. Consequently not even the *Mail* could keep the momentum going, and as a result the bill passed into law relatively smoothly in 1928.

So far we have concentrated upon the sheer quantity of legislation for women which was concentrated into the decade up to 1929. It remains to evaluate the qualitative significance of this achievement. In this connection at least three major qualifications must be entered: first there is the ideology that lay behind the women's reforms, second the limitations in terms of the type of issues *not* taken up, and third the fluctuating impact of women's interests over the inter-war period as a whole.

When considering the thinking behind the legislation of the 1920s one has to take account of the bi-partisan character of the support. Why was it apparently so easy for Conservative, Labour and Liberal politicians to combine on these questions? While each party included some staunch feminists, they never enjoyed enough influence to convert the majority of their colleagues to their way of thinking; even the women MPs often neglected to press a distinctive women's line in parliament (see pages 196–9). Nor is it sufficient to argue that they were simply fearful of the consequences of refusing to offer reforms to women. There was obviously an element of that especially in the early 1920s, but politicians' firm refusal to tackle a range of issues of central concern to the women's organisations indicates that they retained the capacity to choose and to determine the priorities. There is, in fact, no mystery as to why certain topics were chosen. Some – such as legislation on midwives and nurses, married women's property, divorce and even the suffrage – may be understood essentially as extensions of existing legislation which were no longer seen as very controversial. Beyond that, however, the bulk of the legislation is linked by a common theme: it bears upon the role of women, in a legal and a material sense, as mothers and wives. This was undoubtedly the perspective through which most politicians preferred to view women. For Conservatives, for example, there seemed little reason, subject only to the need to restrict national taxation, to oppose such legislation. Indeed reforms calculated to assist and strengthen the mother's role in raising her children merited Conservative approval as likely to help maintain the home and the family. Such an objective fitted comfortably within the party's ideology and programme. 'I firmly believe that the progress of a nation depends upon a contented fireside', declared the Conservative candidate for Huddersfield in 1922. His colleague at Smethwick wrote:

> I appeal to you, Ladies, as a son, a husband and a father. We men value you for the sacredness of the home ties which you maintain. Keep our homes for us. ... We shall be happier in them than we can hope to be in any Communistic barrack.

For its part the Labour Party supported the full range of women's measures enacted under Coalition and Conservative governments; its candidates added only the rider that they had adopted the reforms first and that they would extend and improve them when they came to

power. Measures that assisted the ordinary mother-and-housewife
could be represented as one aspect in Labour's wider programme
designed to raise the living standards of the working-class community.
Thus the party's appeal to women was little more than a mirror image
of the Conservative approach, based upon the sanctity of home and
family: 'Women, for the sake of your children turn out the Conservative', exhorted the candidate at Hertford in 1922. At Wellington in
1923 Labour's standardbearer proclaimed:

> The home is a *sacred institution* and can only be kept sacred by the devotion,
> happiness and love of the Mother. *Motherhood is the pivot of our National
> Life.* The Labour Party comes and sits at their firesides and their tables and
> deals with things of real importance. We say *Take the taxes off the people's
> food* and thus lighten the Woman's burden.

This tendency to invest women and motherhood with moral
superiority – a very Victorian habit of course – extended to the Liberals
too. Their candidates were prone to assume that women took an
especial interest in temperance and in peace: 'Women possess by their
votes, and still more by their womanly influence, an immense power
for good', wrote the Thornaby Liberal in 1922. Like Labour the
Liberals also saw woman as Chancellor in the family: 'Men make
houses but Women make Homes' as the Sparkbrook candidate put it in
1922. Consequently for Liberals the reappearance of free trade as an
issue in 1923 intensified concern with housewifely politics: 'Women
will be quick to see that a vague promise of more employment for some
is as nothing against a certain rise in the weekly bill of every family.'
In this context the ideological basis for the women's legislation of
the 1920s becomes reasonably clear: there was none. Mainstream
politicians found it possible to support the reforms without in any way
subscribing to feminist views at all. Conservative, Labour, and Liberal
approached the measures from their own ideological perspectives,
bending but never breaking their party's traditional view. In this way a
bi-partisan programme of reform became entirely feasible.
The second qualification to be made is really a corollary of the first.
We learn a good deal about politicians' attitudes towards women and
their priorities by examining those issues that they *declined* to tackle
between the wars. These include equal pay, the bar on the employment
of married women, protective legislation, women police, the admission
of peeresses to the House of Lords, the nationality of married women,
separate taxation for married women, birth control and family allowances. Admittedly the record was not quite as bleak as this catalogue
suggests in that something was achieved on several of the items. For

example, in the late 1930s the National government finally agreed to
legislate so as to permit a woman who married a foreign citizen to
retain her British nationality, though the war intervened before the bill
had been passed. The subject of birth control hardly ever won a mention
during the 1920s either in parliament or at elections, for all parties
conspired to prevent it becoming an issue; even a politician as sympathetic as Lloyd George, who was willing to meet Marie Stopes and,
moreover, appears to have practised some form of birth control,
declined to be publicly associated with the question. From 1922 when
the question was raised as a result of the sacking of Nurse Daniels in
Edmonton for providing birth control information to a patient, ministers of health, including Neville Chamberlain and John Wheatley,
simply stonewalled. They argued that birth control was beyond the
proper functions of the local maternity clinics, and that the public funds
on which they depended could not be used for such a purpose without
express authorisation from parliament.[13] Although they modified this
position in 1930, it was not the result of parliamentary pressure. Few
MPs were willing to risk antagonising Catholic voters; and Ernest
Thurtle's 1926 bill on birth control was defeated by 167 to 82 votes. In
1927 however, the House of Lords approved a similar measure by 57 to
44, an indication both of their freedom from electoral disapproval and
of the fact that the upper classes were much more accustomed to
practising birth control.

How, in general, are we to account for the difficulties faced by the
women's organisations in pressing the politicians to take up their
causes? The economic climate explains a good deal. The extension of
legal restrictions on female employment, the endless prevarication over
equal pay for teachers and civil servants, and the maintenance of the
marriage bar were all symptoms of the defensive mood engendered by
the prolonged economic depression. Some causes were also handicapped by their limited appeal amongst women themselves. For
example, the case for allowing married women to be taxed separately
from their husbands was of little immediate concern to most working
wives.[14] Lady Rhondda's campaign to gain membership of the House
of Lords for peeresses like herself had even less impact. Rhondda based
her claim on the 1919 Sex Disqualification (Removal) Act which stated
that:

A person shall not be disqualified by sex or marriage from the exercise of any
public function, or from being appointed to or holding any civil or judicial
office or post, or from entering or assuming or carrying on any civil
profession or vocation.

In March 1922 she took her case before the Committee for Privileges which accepted her plea for admission.[15] The Solicitor-General, Sir Gordon Hewart, concurred. Normally such a ruling would have settled the matter, but the Lord Chancellor referred the matter back to the Committee whose membership was increased; Hewart was also replaced by Sir Ernest Pollock who opposed Lady Rhondda's case. The decision was soon reversed. Since only a handful of women were affected the question made no further progress.

The resistance encountered by the advocates of family allowances and women police is particularly significant for what it tells us about inter-war attitudes towards women; since both these issues elicited some sympathy from conventional politicians they are good indicators of the crucial boundary separating what was practical politics from what was not. Although family allowances could be advocated, like widows' pensions, simply as a social reform designed to assist hard-pressed members of the community, the original rational behind the proposal was a *feminist* one. Consequently, for most of the inter-war period the Labour Party followed the trade unions in resisting family allowances (see pages 137–8). Conservatives, naturally apprehensive about the cost of such a reform, never felt pressured to keep up with their opponents on this issue as they had on widows' pensions. In addition, the idea was not universally approved even by the women's organisations themselves.

Women's role in police work had originated during the First World War, but its survival in peacetime proved to be a surprisingly uncertain prospect. The arrangements had evolved in a typical English confusion of different authorities. In the first place there were a number of wartime women's patrols, some voluntary and part-time, others full-time and paid; they were largely financed by voluntary sources. Then there was the Women's Police Service which had been established to assist with munitions works. All of these were strictly temporary forms of police work and none of the participants enjoyed the status of police constables. In addition there were the Metropolitan Police Women Patrols attached to Scotland Yard, the Official Policewomen who though paid by the police authorities were not sworn in and the Official Women Police Constables who were appointed and sworn in by the authorities.

In spite of a report by the Home Office Committee of Enquiry of August 1919 in favour of making women a permanent part of the police force, the cabinet was clearly inclined to allow the experiment to wither after the war. This evidently began to occur anyway in that a number of the local authorities terminated the employment of the women police in the early 1920s. To some extent this reflected local financial pressures, but it was also a sign of male resentment towards women who enjoyed the authority and status conferred by a uniform. Chief Constables who disbanded their female force usually claimed that there was insufficient work to justify their continued employment. By 1924 the Police Federation of England and Wales had reversed its position and now pronounced women as useless and policing as 'a man's job alone'. In response to this the women's organisations pointed out that lack of work only occurred where women had been deliberately excluded from performing certain duties. The case for employing women police was partly the traditional moral-feminist one. It was seen as essential to use women in cases involving young girls vulnerable to prostitution, for taking evidence from females where sexual offences were involved, especially assault, for searching women prisoners and for watching those attempting suicide. In addition reports by chief constables indicated that women were used in a clerical capacity to collate crime records, take evidence in shorthand and type reports, as well as for interviewing and escorting women, and in plain clothes detective work where a male-and-female team enjoyed the advantage of being less conspicuous than the all-male one.[16]

However, in 1922 the Geddes Committee identified expenditure on women police as a target for economy, and for a time the complete scrapping of the system appeared a probability. At this point the women's organisations made good use of the two MPs Lady Astor and Mrs Wintringham, as well as Sir Arthur Steel-Maitland, who repeatedly raised the matter in the House of Commons. At first the home secretary, Edward Shortt, rejected their plea to retain a nucleus of women police which might be expanded when the financial situation permitted. However, Shortt was sufficiently embarrassed by the cross-questioning to take refuge in the suggestion that matters could be left to local discretion. Thus, although half the police authorities employing women terminated their contracts, women retained a toehold in the force. The issue was kept alive at the local level by Women's Citizens Associations and other women's groups.[17] At national level the case was advanced by the National Council of Women and the Women's Freedom League, who gave evidence to the 1928 Royal Commission on Police Powers and Procedures, by one or two controversial legal cases, and by a deputation of sympathetic MPs in 1932. As a result some 45 of the 183 police authorities still employed women by 1939. Nonetheless, the numbers involved were small; in the mid-1930s 49 women were employed by the Metropolitan Police, 103 in the English borough and county authorities, and 22 in Scotland against a national total of nearly 65,000 male police officers.[18]

This extensive range of setbacks and thwarted campaigns suffered by women's organisations between the wars enables us to set the women's legislation of the 1920s into its proper context. The concentration of reforms, especially in the first half of the decade, suggests strongly that they were being won from an ebbing tide. By about 1930 it had turned decisively, and this is borne out by the relative paucity of measures for women during the subsequent decade. In part this may have been simply a reflection of the success in eliminating many of the immediate objectives of the women's movement. But it is also an indication of an adjustment in the politicians' perception. The concentration of elections during the 1920s provided a test for dire predictions about the effect of women's enfranchisement; with a little experience all parties took confidence in their capacity to handle the new element in the system.

This brings us to the third major qualification to be made about post-1918 reforms for women. Politicians' susceptibility fluctuated over time. A crude measure of this may be found in the attention devoted to women's interests in the parties' general election manifestoes. However, a much better indicator of the salience of women lies in the election addresses published by the candidates themselves. Since candidates could rarely discuss all the issues mentioned nationally, the choices they made tell us a good deal about their own priorities and calculations. In particular this source enables us to assess just how far candidates felt obliged to address themselves specifically to the female electorate, which issues they concentrated on, whether the approach varied from one party to another, and whether the pattern changed over time.

Not surprisingly, in the Coupon Election of December 1918 two out of three candidates felt that the occasion called for some mention of women electors (see Table 5.2). Typically this took the form of extending a welcome and encouragement to make use of their votes, and paying tribute to women's efforts during the war. A number of male candidates evidently judged it worthwhile to remind women of their past record of support for their cause: 'I am not a wartime convert to women's suffrage,' wrote Gordon Hewart (Liberal) pointedly. Even in 1922 Sir John Simon (Liberal) reiterated his solid record of support for women's issues. Conversely, those who had resisted enfranchisement decided to disarm critics with flattery: 'My opinions on the suffrage question have been honourably held and always frankly stated', declared one Conservative, 'and I have yet to learn that honesty and frankness do not appeal to women.' In 1922 the Caithness and Sutherland Liberal confessed to his previous anti-suffragism but conceded rather patronisingly that he now felt that women used their vote responsibly. Similar sentiments were echoed by a number of Conservatives at this election; one said that women had 'fully justified the granting of the franchise to them', another complimented them on the 'intelligence and ability shown by women in public affairs'. Personal connections with women quickly became an established feature of election literature in that candidates frequently published photographs of themselves with wives and children, and printed messages from their wives. 'I am better able to understand your difficulties and problems', purred the Conservative at Wandsworth Central in 1922, 'by the helping guidance of my wife whom many of you know as your true and genuine friend.' None, however, equalled the endearing tribute of the wife of a Conservative

Table 5.2   Women Electors and Party Candidates at General Elections 1918–1931[a]

Election	Candidates who mentioned women (%)		Candidates who did not mention women (%)	
1918	64		36	
1922	46	which comprises (%): 23 Conservatives 49 Liberals 74 Labour	54	which comprises (%): 77 Conservatives 51 Liberals 26 Labour
1923	39	which comprises (%): 17 Conservatives 48 Liberals 58 Labour	61	which comprises (%): 83 Conservatives 52 Liberals 42 Labour
1924	63	which comprises (%): 59 Conservatives 52 Liberals 78 Labour	37	which comprises (%): 41 Conservatives 48 Liberals 22 Labour
1929	67	which comprises (%): 86 Conservatives 43 Liberals 73 Labour	33	which comprises (%): 14 Conservatives 57 Liberals 27 Labour
1931	16		84	

[a] The sample of election addresses used here is drawn from the National Liberal Club Collection. This collection slightly under-represents the Labour Party's share of candidatures nationally and, since Labour was more inclined to mention women in the 1918–24 period, the figures here may be said to understate the extent to which women were mentioned to a modest degree.

candidate in 1922 who assured the electors of Kidderminster: 'I chose him fifteen years ago for better or for worse, and have never regretted my choice.'

However, the novelty soon wore off. In the three elections to 1923 the proportion of candidates who directed an appeal to women fell steadily from 64 to 39 per cent which seems a curious comment on the steps actually being taken in parliament to legislate for women in these years. The Conservatives who, until 1924, were consistently the least likely to make an appeal to women voters may well have felt somewhat inhibited by being in office for most of the time; they could not risk arousing expectations they were unlikely to fulfil. Indeed, some already felt confident enough to make a virtue of their unresponsiveness, as witness one candidate in 1922 who wrote:

> I make no special appeal on questions of policy to the women voters. ... I have learned that they have come now to a full appreciation of the meaning of the franchise, and recognise that they should cast their votes on the basis of a common citizenship with men.

Conversely, not only did a majority of Labour candidates consistently address themselves to women voters, but a number actually claimed that Labour was the 'Women's Party', which exposed them to some criticism following their brief term in office in 1924. However, all three parties' candidates reflected the same trend towards fewer appeals to the women in the early 1920s. The Liberals, no doubt, showed relatively little change, but this is because in 1923 many of them were prompted by a conviction that the defence of free trade gave them an especial advantage with the housewife with her concern over food prices.

Rather suddenly the downward trend was arrested in the election of 1924. This was a feature of all three parties, but the Conservative switch of emphasis is most striking. This reflected what appeared to be the lesson of the 1923 election result – that housewives had reacted against the prospect of a rising cost of living and could not be neglected in future. This message naturally reinforced politicians' existing predilection for regarding women as essentially domestically oriented. In 1929, when the influx of new voters presented an obvious motive for appealing to women, there was in fact only a slight move in this direction. On that occasion the parties moved in different directions. While a slightly lower proportion of Liberal and Labour candidates mentioned women, the Conservatives showed another major shift towards an appeal to women. They had clearly judged it expedient to draw attention to the Baldwin government's record on equal franchise, widow's pensions, improved maternity benefits and other reforms for women. This was a little awkward for Labour. MacDonald's government had failed to introduce a suffrage bill and had only got as far as preparing a measure for widows' pensions. Nonetheless many Labour candidates raised these very issues. They invariably claimed the credit for equal franchise on the grounds that they alone had been consistent supporters of the proposal. They strongly criticised the widows' pensions scheme on the grounds that as there were so many exemptions it required drastic improvement. This appears to have been playing to their own weakness. However, since the reform had been introduced in 1925 it may be that by 1929 it was, to a degree, already being taken for granted, and so dissatisfaction with the details created an opportunity for the Opposition.

On the other hand the political salience of women's issues did not survive the impact of the crisis of 1931. In that year women were pushed not only down but off the agenda by the great majority of candidates. Taking their cue from the national leaders they simply treated 1931 as a one-issue election on the National government's appeal. Perhaps more significant is the impression given by Dr Stannage's study of the 1935 election that there was no real recovery of women's issues. Labour's manifesto came the closest to an appeal to women with a few brief references to maternal mortality, health services and lower rents. However, an analysis of the campaign suggests that candidates concentrated on socialism, disarmament, the League of Nations, tariffs, the cost of living, unemployment and housing though Labour candidates showed more inclination to mention maternal mortality in connection with health.[19] Although several of the leading issues were of obvious relevance to women it was not the women's interest that was stressed. The parties were, in short, well on the way to marginalising women's politics by 1935, and in so far as their interests featured it was in the form of proposals for assisting them in the performance of their duties as housewives and mothers.

In fact the character and quality of political propaganda directed at women in this period is as telling as the quantity. Even when a high proportion of candidates made an appeal to women it is fair to say that in most cases this amounted to a brief reference, sometimes only a sentence or a line, towards the end of the election address, though some supplemented this with separate leaflets for women electors. Regardless of party the politicians displayed a pronounced tendency to select the same issues for women (see Table 5.3). Not unexpectedly the question of equal franchise figured consistently in propaganda up to

1929; but it was rapidly overtaken by widows' pensions from 1923 and also by maternal and child welfare in 1929. These two issues, taken in conjunction with the rise of cost-living questions, indicate a pattern amongst the politicians of convergence upon an essentially domestic view of women's politics. This trend is strongly underlined by the literature produced by all three parties' national organisations for the new women voters in 1929. While the Conservatives defended their record of reforms, and the opposition parties attacked the problems faced by women, they reflected a common assumption that female voters were wives and mothers concerned with welfare, prices and their homes. Conversely the attention given to feminist causes, which had been at least a minor feature of the 1918 election, seems to have diminished. Equal pay, for example, occurred in the literature of over a

Table 5.3   'Women's Issues' at General Elections 1918–1929[a]

	Issues most frequently mentioned by those candidates who made a specific appeal to women electors in their addresses	(%)
1918	Equal pay	27
	Equal suffrage	18
	Widows' pensions	14
	Equal entry to professions	13
	Family allowances	7
1922	Equal suffrage	33
	Widows' pensions	23
1923	Widows' pensions	33
	Equal suffrage	25
	The cost of living	20
1924	Widows' pensions	82
	Equal suffrage	31
	The cost of living	18
	Equal guardianship	7
1929	Widows' pensions	61
	Maternity and child welfare	40
	Equal suffrage	27
	Peace	9
	The cost of living	8
	Equal pay	3

[a]   Based on election addresses of the three main parties in the National Liberal Club Collection.

quarter of those who mentioned women in that year; but by 1922 it had fallen almost completely out of sight – an ominous sign of candidates' reluctance to risk antagonising the male voters. Similarly, when they tackled the unemployment question, even under paragraphs headed 'Women Electors' (which was an unusual association), they almost never considered it as a problem of *women's* unemployment; rather they presented unemployment policies that were seen as relevant to women because it was in their interest that their *menfolk* should enjoy regular work. The few who referred to protective legislation to regulate women's employment clearly took it for granted that this was *attractive* to women and not a cause for grievance as many feminists believed. At the most one finds that small numbers of candidates advocated reforms on guardianship, illegitimacy, divorce and family allowances, though it is virtually impossible to find one prepared to mention either birth control information or the admission of women to the police force.

One is bound to conclude from all this that if politicians felt apprehensive about the new women voters in 1918 the mood soon changed. The experience of three successive general elections from 1922 to 1924 served both to restore their nerve and to suggest a relatively safe strategy for handling women's politics. No distinct party or bloc vote emerged which might have forced them either to confront women or to go beyond the existing range of domestic issues. Thus the parties successfully defined the terms of the debate so that it focused upon widows' pensions, the franchise, maternity benefits and the cost of living. Once the list of acceptable topics had been tackled by 1928 there was therefore no compelling reason to delve deeper into the field of women's politics. The reforms of the 1920s represent, therefore, a vigorous burst of activity in what had become a nearly exhausted seam by the end of the decade. It is an inescapable conclusion that by 1930 feminist politics had been decisively marginalised; and the centrality of women's issues in the form of material benefits for wives and mothers depended essentially on the maintenance of social welfare and the standard of living at the top of the agenda in British political debate.

Conservative Politics for Women

With the restructuring of its machinery in 1918 and the adoption of a low membership fee the Conservative Party effectively decided to compete with the Labour Party as a mass organisation. Inevitably the participation of women would go a long way to making this feasible. Hence the adoption of the principle of one-third representation to women at all levels of the party organisation. In view of their extensive traditional role as allied forces of the party in bodies such as the Primrose League and the Tariff Reform League it is not surprising that Conservative women adapted to this post-war system with little friction. Many of the women experienced in the Primrose League already felt the time was ripe to move from association to formal membership of the party; hence the swift transformation of many habitations into local branches of the Women's Unionist Organisation after 1918.[20] There followed a period of rapid growth which resulted in a women's membership of 1 million by 1928. Thereafter membership stabilised for several years; it fell below the million level by 1933 and subsided to 940,000 in 1934.[21] This reflects a similar pattern of growth and decline to that of the Labour Womens' Sections.

Table 5.4   Branches of the Women's Unionist Association

1921	1922	1923	1924
1340[a]	2102	3600	4067

[a] Incomplete record.
Source: Annual Reports, Women's Unionist Association

This impressive organisation was presided over by a Women's Advisory Committee at Conservative Central Office. By 1932 the party had 126 female Divisional Organising Secretaries in its employment, over 100 of whom held the approved certificate of training from the party. Since the 1880s women volunteers had represented a major advantage for Conservatives both in electoral work and in social activities between elections. There was therefore a large measure of continuity between the pre- and post-war situations. What was really different was that the women's role had become even more important. This is partly for the obvious reason that women had acquired votes and were soon to become a new 'majority' to set against the working-class majority to which Labour now laid claim. But it was also because the hugely increased electorate presented all parties with serious problems in maintaining contact and mobilising support. Although some of the traditional work of cultivating the electoral register had been rendered superfluous, there were new tasks such as rounding up the Absent Voters which called for quiet, meticulous work on the part of ladies with time to spare. Further, the pressure placed on Conservative constituency associations to raise more of their funds rather than relying upon one or two wealthy benefactors promoted an evolution from the traditional Primrose League 'entertainment' to the fund-raising social events which were to become so characteristic of twentieth-century Conservative associations. In such activities the female members were, as always, the essential ingredient. So successful was the Conservative Party in recruiting women that by the 1930s the party conference turned its attention on several occasions to the problem of attracting more men! 'The men have had a bad name ever since women became politically minded (laughter and cheers)', observed one delegate. Proposals for setting up a Men's Branch to give the downtrodden sex equal representation were earnestly debated; but women appear to have maintained their numerical dominance in Conservative associations down to the present day.[22]

From 1920 women also occupied a prominent role in the work of the party nationally. From that year the conference elected twenty-one representatives to sit on the Central Council of whom one-third were women: Mrs Neville Chamberlain headed the list followed by Lady Selborne. It is noticeable that among the candidates for the Central Council in 1920 there were eleven husband-and-wife teams of whom Lord and Lady Gisborough and Sir W.H. and Lady Goschen were both successful. Similarly the new system provided for one-third of the local association delegates at the annual conference to be women. The records show that this was indeed the case. In 1927 for example, 36 per cent of the listed delegates were women, and in 1930 some 38 per cent. This was in a total conference membership of 2700 and 3800 respectively. Women rapidly became prominent both in the body of the hall and on the platform; Lady Iveagh served as chairman in 1930 for example. From 1920 onwards women also appeared as speakers in conference debates. In 1924 they actually comprised one-third of all speakers, though thereafter their contribution diminished. From the point of view of their physical presence women undoubtedly loomed larger in the Conservative Party than in either the Labour or Liberal parties. This of course reflects the fact that they found it congenial in purely *social* terms. By comparison the more aggressively male ambience of the inter-war Labour movement, dominated as it was by trade unionists, proved rather less comfortable for women. Conservative ladies often enjoyed the advantage of their social class that put them on an equal footing with leaders of the party; some, like Mrs Chamberlain, owed their position at least in part to the status enjoyed by their husbands. However, inter-war conferences also show the advance of another type of Conservative woman, typified by Miss Irene Ward, now rising up the hierarchy by establishing professional careers in the party.

Clearly there are grounds for the view that the extensive role of women within Conservatism was essentially a matter of social activity rather than political as in the Labour Party. In November 1922 Mrs Bridgeman, the chairman of the WUA, welcomed Bonar Law, the party leader, to a women's election rally by expressing her gratitude that he was willing 'in the midst of his occupations and preoccupations to find time to address an audience of women'.[23] In view of women's role as voters in the election her tone seems not only deferential, but positively antiquated. However, the behaviour of the party members in this period was so varied that generalisation is rather difficult. At the annual party conferences genuine debates took place in which no great deference was shown towards the parliamentary leadership. Moreover the women were by no means confined to traditional women's subjects; they featured prominently in debates on the great issues that mattered to Conservatives – Ireland, the menace of Bolshevism, House of Lords reform, India, empire trade and the state of the party organisation. At the same time the conferences of the 1920s considered proposals dealing with such topics as equal franchise, equal guardianship, widows' pensions and the Criminal Law Amendment Bill, on each of which conference adopted the women's view. After 1930 issues of this sort clearly slipped down and even off the agenda, which, of course, is consistent with the general pattern for the decade rather than a feature special to Conservatism. As amongst Labour women politicians there seems to have been a division between those who were chiefly interested in politics, that is the issues that concerned their male colleagues, and those who wished to promote women's politics. Prominent among the latter were Lady Selborne and Viscountess Astor; the latter especially intervened repeatedly on social reform questions and the raising of the school-leaving age to 16. It was largely because of the frequency of her speeches and the gratuitously provocative remarks she made that Astor found herself severely heckled at party conferences. Her reception at Women's Unionist conferences was no less hostile: 'Be still and listen', she snapped at her tormentors on one occasion in 1932.

However, the impact of women's participation upon the Conservative Party's overall strategy was limited. During the early 1920s the party was obviously quick and effective in mobilising women, but relatively slow in adapting itself politically. Fewer women became Conservative candidates, fewer Conservative candidates made a specific appeal to women; and the party leaders were slower than their rivals to incorporate parts of the NUSEC programme into their national manifestoes.[24] But by 1924 the party was on a fast learning curve. Dismayed at what appeared to be a loss of women's votes they suddenly produced a new section on 'Women and Children' in their manifesto which covered guardianship, maintenance, adoption, women police, and widows' pensions; at the same time Baldwin also produced his pledge on equal franchise. By 1929 the party had taken care to arm itself with a catalogue of reforms for women, and also pointed to a 10 per cent cut in the cost of living and reductions in income tax. By 1935 the party seemed to have settled on its approach to women; it was hardly necessary to refer to them specifically, provided that the cost of living, housing, pensions and education showed improvements. In short Conservatives showed themselves responsive, within certain well-defined limits, to what they perceived to be women's interests.

What is less clear is whether the women's Conservative organisation exerted any distinctive pressure upon the party. By far the most satisfying means of integrating the party's perspective on woman as mother and housewife with the existing Conservative ideology and programme was found in the subject of empire trade. This idea received considerable stimulus from the British Empire Exhibition at Wembley in 1924 which led to a variety of practical political activities, notably participation in Empire Day every May, the promotion of Empire Shopping Weeks and Empire Pageants. The Central Office supplied thousands of Empire Boxes containing samples of food produced in the colonies which local branches then used in their own exhibitions and placed on display in the shopwindows of sympathetic grocers.[25] Such a theme had obvious advantages. The pageantry maintained one of the appealing aspects of earlier Primrose League work. The emphasis on food and shopping enabled the party to translate political principle into tangible form for ordinary members. Indeed empire trade was, in a real sense, the Conservative mirror image of the kind of work being done by the Women's Co-operative Guild and the Labour Party Women's Sections on the left. It married the humdrum activities of the housewife with the political priorities of the party. This materially helped in maintaining a substantial women's organisation while avoiding the danger of contamination by feminist thinking.

In common with the other parties the Conservative women's organisation included a minority of determined feminists. But the mainstream of the movement displayed a characteristic suspicion towards women's organisations and causes. Even the Women's Institute was regarded as a disturbing source of anti-Conservative propaganda because of the interest it took in questions such as housing and the League of Nations: 'the Women's Institutes are a splendid power for good but they want keeping straight'.[26] Debates on equal suffrage and

the need to adopt more women as candidates often took on a surprisingly Victorian tone as some women delegates argued that men
were 'fundamentally political animals, more mature than women as
well as broader and more balanced in their views'.[27] Less surprisingly
the Conservative ladies were greatly antagonised by the refusal of
working women to accept posts as domestic servants in the early 1920s;
the payment of the dole to women whose husbands were employed was
pronounced an evil.[28] Nor were they generally very sympathetic
towards social reforms which were sometimes denounced as 'grand-
motherly legislation'. They voted overwhelmingly against family allowances in 1926, rejected proposals for supplying birth control information as late as 1931, and on several occasions threw out Astor's
resolution in favour of raising the school leaving age to 16. Indeed they
were more in favour of reducing compulsory schooling by a year and
cutting teachers' salaries! This reflected an abiding suspicion about the
unsettling effects of education upon the minds of the young which was
strengthened by the influence believed to be exerted by socialists within
the educational system.[29] The effect of all this was to leave Conservative women such as Dame Helen Gwynne Vaughan, Nancy Astor,
Lady Selborne and Lady Maureen Stanley, who advocated both
women's measures and a number of social welfare reforms, in a
somewhat isolated position within the women's organisation. In the
event, however, the Conservative women found themselves marginalised politically because the Baldwin–Chamberlain leadership saw
the broad strategic question in similar terms to Astor and Selborne.
They judged that they had to 'play the socialist game', as their critics
put it, in order to stay in touch with the average woman voter; hence a
judicious and timely programme of social reform. By the 1930s the
party's strategy for coping with the influx of women into the political
system had settled down to a simple formula; politics must now reflect
'the viewpoint of the homemaker as well as that of the breadwinner'.[30]
This could be accomplished in the 1930s by reducing duties on food,
improving access to empire food, subsidies to agriculture, extending
the electricity system, promoting the construction of cheap houses for
sale, and the maintenance of the local network of maternal welfare
schemes and clinics.

Labour Housewives and Socialist Feminists

The relationship between women and the British Labour movement has
attracted a good deal of attention in recent years but has led to widely

differing interpretations. Some have been influenced by contemporary connections between Socialism and feminism and extrapolated backwards to earlier periods. Thus some writers regard an alliance between women and Labour as a natural phenomenon even to the extent of seeing Conservative women's reforms as distinctive to Labour. Others have emphasised the negative aspects of the relationship in terms of sharp divisions over specific issues and the social class gulf which often separated Labour from feminism.[31] It is in fact difficult to place Labour women in true perspective if one looks at Labour alone. The most important point is that Labour's experience in accommodating women and in containing feminism was broadly similar to that of the Conservatives; the difference lay in the fact that as Labour included both more *active* feminists and more voluble anti-feminists the debate grew fiercer and more public.

After 1918 Labour had a good deal of ground to make up in the mobilisation of women. The pre-war Women's Labour League, founded in 1906, had only 6000 members, precarious finances, and was barely tolerated in many working-class constituencies. Candidates like Margaret Bondfield who were a little disappointed in their by-election performances in the early 1920s speculated that the older women now on the electoral register were pro-Conservative in their views.[32] On the other hand there were grounds for optimism that amongst the activists Labour was gaining strength. Both the pre-war pact with NUSEC and the anti-war movement seemed to have had the effect of detaching many politically aware middle-class women from their Liberal or non-party background and leading them to Labour. In addition the expansion of women's trade unionism and the Women's Co-operative Guild, which affiliated to the party in 1918, offered the prospect of extra working-class support. The emphasis on constituency organisation and individual membership in Labour's 1918 constitution laid the ground for building a substantial women's membership (Table 5.5).

The figures are interesting in several ways. Clearly, by the late 1920s Labour had achieved a major advance over the pre-war position, thereby narrowing the advantage hitherto enjoyed by the Conservatives. However, since Labour's female membership stuck at around a quarter of the Conservatives, it is unlikely that the advantage was ever eliminated. Much, of course, depends on what proportion of the members were active and on how far branches were distributed in the marginal constituencies. The chronological pattern for the two parties was similar, with a rapid growth in the 1920s, a peak towards the end of the decade, followed by some loss of membership and stabilisation in

Table 5.5 Labour Party Women's Sections

1919	1922	1923	1924	1925	1927	1928
271	802	1000+	1250	1450	1728	1845

1929	1930	1932	1934	1935	1937
1828	1949	1704	1604	1580	1631

Membership of the Women's Sections[a]

1922	1924	1925	1927	1928	1930	1931
'Nearly' 100,000	150,000	200,000	300,000	250–300,000	250,000	Under 250,000

[a] These are estimates only.

Source: Annual Reports of the Labour Party Women's Organisation.

the 1930s. Labour's loss appears to have been more prolonged in that decade, and this is corroborated by the dwindling attendance at annual conferences. Moreover the reluctance of the national organisation to reveal the figures during the 1930s suggests a serious decline. There is clear evidence that, as with the Conservatives, women comprised a majority of Labour's *individual* membership especially in the 1920s. Where we have a run of figures in such constituencies as Woolwich and Wansbeck they underline how damaging was the effect of the crisis of 1930–1 on the women's membership. Despite some recovery by the mid-1930s the women never returned to the high membership levels of the late 1920s, and lost their position as the majority.

After 1918 women had some reason to feel confident of playing a significant role in Labour politics. They enjoyed an impressive hierarchy and an able leadership corps headed by the Chief Woman Officer, Dr Marion Phillips, who was succeeded by Mary Sutherland on her death in 1932. The women held their own annual conference in May, and four of their members were elected to the party's National Executive committee – in 1919 Ethel Snowden, Ethel Bentham, Mary Macarthur and Susan Lawrence. In 1930 Susan Lawrence became chairman of the party when the Countess of Iveagh – in some ways the equivalent figure – was occupying the same position amongst the Conservatives. The Labour Party also struck an early blow in the propaganda war with its Women's Emancipation Bill in 1919 which forced the Coalition government to come up with its own Sex Disqualification (Removal) Act. During the early 1920s Labour candidates were not only more inclined to make a specific appeal for women's votes than their rivals, they even took to describing their party as the Women's Party.

But what did they mean by this bold claim? In fact the chief thrust of the party's approach to women lay in the area of standards of living and state social welfare policies. This had been foreshadowed many years before by suffragists like Keir Hardie who had argued that women would eventually help to mould national politics by pushing the motherhood element to the fore. Mary Macarthur seemed to echo this in 1918 when she suggested that:

> Women were going to be very conservative – they were going to see that life was conserved. ... Women were going to bring a new idea into politics – the idea of the family.[33]

Within this framework Labour's women activists enjoyed a wide scope between the wars. For example, on the subject of the nation's food supply Labour attacked the abolition of the Ministry of Food in 1921 and advocated a greater role for co-operative and municipal authorities in undercutting the private producers and distributors. In particular it was suggested that national and local government might control the supply of milk, ensuring that cheap and pure milk reached mothers and children. Philip Snowden's reductions in the duties on tea and sugar in 1924 were seen as proof of the party's good intent. Interestingly enough, while Conservatives could not endorse violation of private enterprise, they found themselves echoing Labour's claims in terms of lower food prices and improved milk supply under the Milk Marketing Board in the 1930s. By 1929 Baldwin had set up the Food Council to which Labour responded by proposing a Consumer Council to investigate and report to the Board of Trade on excessive prices.

Another characteristic theme was improvement in the quality and design of houses. Again both parties worked in the same direction, assuming that this was of great concern to women; they simply differed in that one placed the emphasis on municipal and the other on private building. During the 1920s Labour took some trouble by means of questionnaires to ascertain in detail women's own priorities in terms of larger kitchens, extra bedrooms, proper bathrooms, hot water supplies and a preference for houses with gardens rather than flats.[34] Female aspirations to the private family home were of no little importance in modifying Labour's emphasis upon the collective approach to social problems in favour of a more individualist one. In addition Labour women keenly advocated social reforms such as widows' pensions, higher expenditure on maternity clinics with a view to reducing maternal mortality rates, and the adoption of the Washington Maternity Convention which involved providing maintenance for a mother and her child for six weeks before birth and for six weeks after. These policies clearly sat very comfortably within Labour's overall commitment to improving the standard of life for working-class families. But the women activists also played a much appreciated role in connection with great events like the General Strike by creating local networks of support for the families most affected by industrial action. Such work went a long way towards integrating women into the Labour movement and its priorities, in much the same way as the issue of empire trade facilitated the integration of Conservative women into their party.

However, any generalisation about the attitude of the Labour movement towards women is complicated by the variation between the different levels: constituency supporters, women's conference, national party organisation and the parliamentary party. This is obvious in connection with issues such as equal pay and the bar on the employment of married women. At the level of the national conferences it was possible for women and sympathetic men to marshal support for a feminist policy on these questions. But a major gulf separated them from the attitude and practice of the party's followers at the grass roots. Labour local authorities were prominent in imposing a marriage bar out of extreme anxiety to maximise jobs for men and even the women's sections were divided. One women delegate in 1935 declared that the 'employment of married women ... was definitely opposed to the principle of the Labour movement'.[35] This is by no means an extraordinary claim when seen in the context of some local Labour parties. In Preston, for example, Dr Savage has shown that the driving force behind the constituency party was certain trade unions, such as the AEU, which felt most threatened by female labour during the early 1920s.[36] In Preston Labour was very much the men's party, and its supporters looked to it to restore women to the home. Nor did they look in vain. Labour MPs strongly backed the Restoration of Pre-War Practices Bill in 1919; and one of the very few measures for women drawn up by the first Labour government in 1924 was a Factory Bill designed to 'protect', or exclude, women from certain jobs from which men were deemed not to require protection. The result of this bias, in Preston at any rate, was a loss of women's votes to the Conservatives. Preston may well have been an extreme case, though until we have more studies of the Labour movement at the grass roots in this period it will be hazardous to make firm generalisations based simply on the views of a few leading men and women within the national party. To

some extent most local parties were handicapped in their appeal to
women by the failure of the MacDonald government to live up to the
extravagant claims made before 1924. In particular Snowden's financial
caution dashed expectations of introducing a widows' pensions bill,
and thereby presented an opportunity which Neville Chamberlain took
in 1925. It has been cogently argued that MacDonald's second administration in 1929–31 alienated some women by its modifications to the
system of unemployment insurance and the added pressure on women
to accept domestic service on losing their regular employment.[37]

Essentially Labour was attempting to effect a judicious adjustment to
the women's role in politics, but as with the Conservatives, this was to
take the form of adapting women to the party's existing ideology and
programme rather than altering the latter to accommodate women.
'There is no fundamental difference of view between men and women
on political issues or any conflict of ideals in the field of social reform',
declared Arthur Henderson in 1918.[38] This, of course, was an expression of hope rather than a statement of fact. Any movement attempting
to base itself on the mobilisation of the working-class majority was
bound to have reservations, to put it no higher, about the independent
organisation of women. Nor was this simply a male fear. Mary
Macarthur and Beatrice Webb felt some alarm by the end of the war
over the growing assertiveness, as they saw it, of some women workers,
and the animosity between them and the men.[39] Ideally any rivalries
between the two sexes should have been subsumed under the heading of
social class. But some workingmen retained an abiding suspicion of *all*
women's organisations as inherently middle-class and divisive. Thus
Labour women were warned throughout the 1920s against being drawn
into educational work with the Women's Citizens Association, or even
the Women's Institutes: 'separate sex organisations are fundamentally
undemocratic and wholly reactionary', wrote Henderson.[40] In 1920
Marion Phillips formally condemned any dissipation of women's
energies in the non-party organisations; and in 1927 she refused to co-
operate with NUSEC in pressing for an equal suffrage bill.[41] Most
indicative of the party's attitude was a decision by the 1923 Labour
Conference that a woman who held membership of NUSEC or an
affiliated body was not eligible to become a conference delegate.[42] This
desire to inoculate Labour against the contagion of feminism was rather
counter-productive in that it merely had the effect of gradually reducing
the traffic between the two movements which had been to the party's
advantage during the war and post-war years. Feminist organisations
were one of the many half-way houses that brought fresh recruits to

Labour. Labour women also enjoyed considerable scope for propaganda within a number of non-party organisations for women. In any case the orthodox party regulars could never effectively disentangle Labour women from the wider contacts in, for example, the peace movement, nor could they ignore the work of the Women's Co-operative Guild which persistently involved Labour women in feminist causes as well as regular party issues. However, the grudging and suspicious attitude naturally made life awkward for many women activists who wished to promote both feminism and socialism; they were forever having aspersions cast upon their loyalty to the Labour movement because of their role in NUSEC or the WCA. Inevitably they tended to take refuge within the Fabian Women's Group and increasingly the ILP. Indeed between the wars the latter seems to have become the most important centre for feminists within the Labour Party.

As a result inter-war Labour was essentially two parties in women's politics. In the one hand stood the party loyalists, entrenched in the official hierarchy, who adopted the orthodox line that everything must be subordinated to the over-riding cause of the working-class movement. Marion Phillips, Margaret Bondfield, Susan Lawrence and Mary Sutherland are classic examples. On the other hand the feminists included Dorothy Jewson, Helena Swanwick, Dora Russell, Monica Whately, Mrs H. Laski and Mrs J. Adamson who continually crossed the lines between the Labour movement and the women's organisations. Occupying the boundary between the two were figures like Ellen Wilkinson who managed to advocate women's claims on a number of occasions both at conferences and in parliament, but also maintained her standing amongst the party leadership. It is significant that her feminist interventions were characteristic of the 1920s, while after 1930 she more often defended the official position on women's issues: Wilkinson's reputation for radicalism belies a shrewd and calculating politician.

The feminists in the Labour Party waged an ultimately losing battle on two broad fronts: the organisational and the programmatic. First, they attempted to assert and extend the role of women within the party itself. As early as 1921 Wilkinson proposed that the four women's representatives on the NEC should be chosen by the women's conference and not by the party conference where the trade union vote ensured that only acceptable loyal figures were selected.[43] The women turned this down by a 4 to 3 margin on the grounds that women would have less weight if they represented only fellow women, and that such a system would inevitably produce women representatives who were

primarily interested in women's issues. The failure of the party to
nominate women candidates in winnable seats came up for debate in
1927, 1928 and 1932 (see pages 168–9). Henderson squashed the idea of
creating special funds to support women by saying that 'the methods
suggested were in conflict with the established practice of the party' –
a claim which scarcely seems consistent with the trade unions' use of
funds to promote men.[44] Nor were all the women happy with the status
of their conference as a purely advisory body; their resolutions and
decisions, like those of the Conservative women, had no official status
and indeed made no progress unless the Joint Standing Committee of
Industrial Women's Organisations passed them up to the NEC itself.
Unable to influence the party conference, they also complained that
their own conference was increasingly stage managed by a combination
of a handful of leading women and the 'Big Man' who was wheeled in
to deflect unwelcome proposals from time to time.[45] In 1929 it was
actually proposed that male speakers should be excluded from the
women's conference – a reflection of the antagonism aroused over the
birth control issue. To make matters worse the party's rules were
modified in 1930 so as to make it more difficult to send women
delegates to the annual conference by increasing the required constituency membership from 500 to 2500 women members. Dr Phillips
defended this by explaining that the rule adopted in 1918 which
allowed for one woman delegate for 500 members had been intended as
a spur to recruitment; it remained open to constituencies to include
women amongst their ordinary delegates.[46] In spite of the protests,
however, none of these disputes over organisation were resolved
satisfactorily for the women.

Among the policy issues the most controversial was the proposal to
allow doctors to provide information on birth control to married women
at the local authority maternity centres. This was raised by Dora Russell
and Mrs Laski from 1925 onwards, and emphatically endorsed by the
women's conference. As Laski pointed out, birth control was already
available to the wealthy, yet the working-class women who badly
needed it were often denied help.[47] Two counter-arguments were
advanced. Catholics pronounced it to be impure and contrary to God's
will. Others saw birth control as a distraction from the chief purpose of
the Labour movement which was to overthrow capitalism; one proud
mother of thirteen claimed that large families would not be a problem
under socialism because they would receive state support. On one
occasion Marion Phillips rebuked Dora Russell on the grounds that 'sex
should not be dragged into politics, you will split the Party from top to

bottom'.[48] However, Phillips and Henderson were quite out of touch with the rank and file of Labour women on this question. The women's conference had voted for birth control three times by 1927; the problem was to persuade the party, in the shape of the National Executive Committee, to take some notice of them. Although a deputation was sent to the NEC it continued to prevaricate, and eventually agreed to put the matter to party conference in the form of a resolution stating that:

> the subject of birth control is in its nature not one which should be made a party political issue, but should remain a matter upon which members of the Party should be free to hold and promote their individual convictions.[49]

This was approved by 1.8 million votes to 1.0 million. When Russell raised the subject again at the 1928 women's conference Henderson, supported now by Ellen Wilkinson, argued that Labour could not be expected to legislate in advance of public opinion or, indeed, of the other political parties, a view which was narrowly endorsed.[50] However, the concessions by the minister for health in 1930 relieved the friction on this question.

Employment inevitably created division even amongst the ranks of the Labour women. On the one hand they condemned the marriage bar and those Labour local authorities who operated it. On the other hand the conference urged the introduction of a ban on overtime for women and a maximum working week of 48 hours for women.[51] In 1932 when Margaret Bondfield's Anomalies Act was attacked for undermining the claims of married women to umemployment benefit, she asserted that it was designed to meet *Labour* objections that too many women drew benefit after marriage.[52] The principle of equal pay had been adopted by the party conference in 1918, but there was little intention of putting this into practice. As several women observed, there was some inconsistency between advocating equal pay and extending protective legislation at the same time. The speakers in a women's conference debate on equal pay in 1930 clearly expected it to be achieved by the spread of trade union membership to women, not by government legislation.[53] According to Ellen Wilkinson equal pay was 'not a sex question, but emphatically it was a class question'.[54] By this she meant that the objective behind equal pay was to deter employers from using women to undercut men's wages; boosting the man's 'family wage' was the priority, not promoting equality for women.

The same perspective coloured the party's view of family allowances. Although the idea was backed by the WCG, the ILP and many Labour

Party women, the trade unions claimed that such payments would have the effect of depressing wages.[55] In 1930 Bessie Braddock opposed family allowances on the very Conservative grounds that people ought to control their own families and not rely upon state aid![56] In recognition of the strength of feeling the party and the TUC set up a committee to investigate family allowances in 1927, but when Dorothy Jewson raised it at the 1930 party conference she was defeated by the opposition of Ernest Bevin, of the Transport and General Workers Union. There the matter rested until revived by the Second World War. In view of Labour's deep commitment to raising the living standards of poor families by means of state intervention the strength of resistance to family allowances is a telling indication of the movement's anti-feminism; anything that ruffled the pride of the workingman, as Eleanor Rathbone's arguments clearly did, was hopelessly compromised.

The friction between men and women was more obvious in the inter-war Labour Party than among the Conservatives. But this reflects the fact that it was comparatively safe for Conservatives to be generous in incorporating women into the official party because fewer demands, in terms of policy, were made upon them. Many Labour women clearly devised an acceptable strategy for coping with the situation. They adopted the tactic already used by the WCG of attempting to push the issues associated with the home and the family further up the political agenda. Hence the focus on the health of mothers and children, housing conditions, food prices and supplies as well as wider concerns such as peace and family allowances. These approaches had the obvious advantage of keeping close to the party's own programme in the 1930s. In addition they facilitated friendly relations at least with those sections of the women's movement associated with the New Feminism which accepted the primacy of marriage and motherhood in women's lives. Thus by the end of the 1930s the Labour women's movement had settled firmly into domesticity. In 1938 a major campaign on the rising cost of living was being prepared in expectation of a general election.[57] Together with the emphasis on health and welfare reforms this gave Labour extra credibility amongst women during the war years and brought dividends in the era of the welfare state.

However, there was a price to be paid for the absorption of women into the party establishment. After the expansion and optimism of the 1920s many women felt they had reached a position of deadlock with the Labour Party. Feminist demands, both over the programme and party organisation, had been frustrated by the orthodox leaders of both sexes. Some activists concluded that the women's conference had become a waste of time because too little notice was taken of its ideas. The official response to this was that the women's conference was only ever intended as a nursery to bring women into party politics. By 1930 they had outgrown the nursery stage and would be better advised to participate fully in the national party organisation.[58] The generation of women that rose to prominence after 1945 largely accepted this view, seeing separate women's sections as a cul-de-sac. However, the result of this thinking during the 1930s was a loss of the vigour and élan of the early 1920s. By 1933 women's questions, as distinct from social welfare policies, were slipping off the agenda, attendance at the women's conference dwindled, and the organisation merely echoed the priorities of the party itself. At the time none of this seemed to matter very much. There was little point in being tied to a feminist cause which was apparently in decline. In a way this outcome had been implicit in the party's 1918 constitution, for the new system had been designed to consolidate the control of the trade unions. Their entrenched position checked feminism at least as effectively as it checked socialism during the inter-war period. Thus the feminists, who had an obvious interest in extending the role of the constituency parties where their strength lay, naturally concentrated in affiliated organisations like the ILP. However, the headlong decline of the ILP following its withdrawal from the party in 1932 served only to detach the feminists further from the mainstream of the movement.

Liberal Feminism and the Liberal Party

In some ways the radical Liberal tradition enjoyed a close affinity with equal rights feminism. Victorian Liberal politicians had often been promoters of women's causes in parliament; and this connection resurfaced briefly at the 1918 election when a number of Liberal candidates distinguished themselves by advocating equal pay. Thereafter, however, such radicals either disappeared from politics altogether, or joined Labour. It was to be decades before equal pay would return to prominence, and one is inclined to feel that the check administered to feminism between the wars was not unconnected with the long-term demise of radical Liberalism. Although MPs like Isaac Foot, Frank Briant and Sir John Simon upheld the equal rights philosophy, the party as a whole conspicuously failed to capitalise upon this theme. To a considerable extent Liberals followed the other parties in regarding women through the distorting lens of their own programme and priorities. Thus they saw women as especially interested in temperance, free trade, cheap food and peace. They may well have been right in this, but on several of these issues the Liberals were increasingly outbid by Labour. Of course, it was widely claimed that Asquith had achieved his political comeback at Paisley in 1920 on the strength of the women's vote. According to his daughter, Violet, the women showed themselves keen on his views on prices and temperance, and appreciated the fact that he never talked down to them.[59] However, this was a euphemism for saying that Asquith refused to adapt his standard speeches to the women voters for whom he actually had little respect. Lloyd George might have done more in the early 1920s, but by 1926, when he won the party leadership, he had other priorities in mind.

Nor did the Women's National Liberal Federation (WNLF) do much to help the party seize its opportunity to appeal to women. After being split for many years over women's suffrage the organisation had reunited in the Edwardian period and flourished for a time before going into a decline as a result of exasperation amongst its members over Asquith's obduracy before 1914. The official women's membership in 1920 was surprisingly high in relation both to the WNLF's own earlier membership and to that of the Labour women at that time. However, in complete contrast to the other parties the figures show a sharp decline in the early 1920s and only a limited recovery later in the decade. The relatively small size of its female membership provides a major explanation for Liberal weakness throughout the inter-war period, for none of the revivals, engineered at the national level, was ever firmly based upon organisation at the grass roots.

Table 5.6 Women's National Liberal Federation Membership

	1920	1922	1923	1924	1925	1926
Branches	723		788	746	820	919
Members	95,217	67,145	71,040	66,200	75,000	88,000

Sources: *Liberal Women's News*; *Annual Reports*, WNLF.

Like their male colleagues the Liberal women activists were essentially two parties where women's politics were concerned. On the one hand they included several leading feminists such as Margaret Wintringham, MP and Margery Corbett Ashby, although much of their effort was diverted into non-party women's pressure groups (see page 241). On the other hand there were the professional party loyalists such as Hilda Runciman, Violet Bonham Carter and Megan Lloyd

George who showed relatively little appetite for women's politics. During the 1920s the Council of the WNLF recorded its support for widows' pensions, equal pay, divorce law reform, separate taxation for married women, equal guardianship, improved arrangements for separation and maintenance, and family endowment. In 1923 the Council particularly requested the Liberal MPs to support divorce reform, equal franchise and women police. Yet this pressure was but faintly reflected in the party's election programmes. The 1922 manifesto contained a single sentence advocating political and legal equality for the sexes, which was widely incorporated into candidates' own leaflets without amplification. In 1923 the manifesto dwelt on women and free trade and mentioned equal guardianship, while in 1924 the only item referred to was widows' pension. From 1929 to 1935 nothing of specific concern to women appeared in the national manifestoes at all; even the special leaflet in 1929 entitled 'A Word to Women', simply argued that women had an interest in regular employment for their husbands. This emphasis was not simply the result of the influence of the party leaders, it was reflected in the concentration upon unemployment and peace by the women's organisation too. The absence of any real strategy for capturing the new women's vote was obvious in the addresses of Liberal candidates in 1929 who were less likely to make a direct appeal to women than candidates of either of the other parties.

Women as Voters Between the Wars

The enfranchisement of 1918 naturally provoked a good deal of speculation about what women would actually do with their votes.[60] Even in 1922 *Punch*, affecting to find the whole thing as much a mystery as ever, printed a cartoon of a woman as the Sphinx dropping her ballot into the box. Politicians had long pondered whether a female electorate would tip the balance in favour of one political party. But by 1918 there was a worse possibility – that women might vote for feminist candidates and their policies even to the extent of promoting their own party. They *believed* that they had drawn the women's electorate sufficiently wide to swamp the feminist minority. If this proved to be correct then the extra votes would simply amplify the predispositions of the existing male electorate. But only experience would tell. The peculiar and confused circumstances of the 1918 election thoroughly obscured the picture.

Is there any evidence that the new voters favoured feminist issues or candidates, or that they reacted against anti-feminists in post-war elections? The likely victims of such feelings were the 57 members of parliament who had voted against enfranchising women in 1917. In fact, amongst the 45 Conservative anti-suffragists 17 did not stand in 1918, 29 were re-elected (7 unopposed), and none defeated. Of the 12 Liberals, 6 stood down, 3 were re-elected and 3 defeated. This is not a particularly gruesome record; it contains little to suggest that the opponents of women's suffrage performed any differently from the other members of their parties, except perhaps for the humiliatingly low polls of Sir Charles Hobhouse at Bristol East and Sir W. Priestley at Bradford East. However, electors were not always aware of their MP's record unless his rivals saw fit to make an issue of it. At Bow and Bromley the victorious Conservative, Sir Reginald Blair, had already won a famous by-election in 1912 on an anti-suffragist platform; yet he did not suffer for his views in 1918. Perhaps the most significant feature was the high proportion of anti-suffragists who did not stand in 1918, though this was to some extent the result of boundary changes and the long period that had elapsed since the last election. It is likely that MPs who had already decided to stand down felt less inhibited about voting against women's suffrage in 1917.

After 1920 the Six Point Group deliberately attempted to pressurise unsympathetic MPs by mobilising the women's vote. Using their platform in *Time and Tide* they publicised a Blacklist of members who were judged to have an outstandingly bad record of opposition to women's causes, and a Whitelist of those who had been particularly supportive (Table 5.7).[61] Electors were urged to vote and work against the former group and support the latter. This stratagem was adopted during the general elections of 1922, 1923, and 1924. How much response did this initiative elicit? Among the members under attack from the Six Point Group a satisfying large proportion met defeat in 1922 and 1923, though since these were nearly all Conservatives this was hardly unexpected. Several had won their seats in the extraordinary circumstances of 1918 and the loss in 1922 of Glasgow Springburn, Wallsend, West Leicester, Gateshead and Linlithgow seems to require no special explanation. Several other Blacklisted Conservatives lost their seats in 1923 when tariff reform was the dominating issue, notably at Devizes, Newbury and Wycombe. These were much safer Conservative constituencies, and it seems likely that the women's vote played a part in the result. However, with the partial exception of Wycombe, there is no reason to think that this was the result of the anti-feminism of the sitting members rather than the national reaction in favour of free trade (see page 149). Because of the complicated arrangements over candidates in 1918 it is difficult to draw comparisons between the relative performance of the Blacklisted candidates in that year and 1922. However, the two subsequent contests make for more straightforward comparison. In 1923 those Blacklisted Conservatives who were opposed saw their share of the poll diminish by 8.6 per cent on average, against 6.0 per cent on average for opposed Conservatives as a whole. In 1924 the Blacklisted Conservatives improved their share of the poll by 8.5 per cent on average compared with 9.3 per cent for their party as a whole. This clearly suggests that they suffered slightly for their reputation as anti-feminists, though this was not sufficient to affect the result except in close contests such as Newbury and Devizes.

If the general impact was slight this may simply reflect the fact that in many of the constituencies targeted by the Six Point Group there was no noticeable effort at arousing the women voters. Feminist activists tended to be concentrated in, or attracted to, middle-class, residential seats in the south-east where Conservative members were difficult to dislodge. Only three constituencies saw a sustained effort. At Rich-

Table 5.7   MPs on the Blacklist and the Whitelist 1922–1924

		Blacklist		
Election	Total	Stood down	Re-elected	Defeated
1922	23 (20 Con.,1 Co.Lib., 1 NDP, 1 Ind.)	2	12	9
1923	16 (15 Con., 1 Lib.)	1	10	5
1924	8 (8 Con.)	1	7	0

		Whitelist		
Election	Total	Stood down	Re-elected	Defeated
1922	22 (10 Con.,7 Lib., 5 Lab.)	0	13	9
1923	21 (8 Con., 6 Lib., 6 Lab., 1 Ind.)	0	19	2
1924	19 (4 Con., 8 Lib., 7 Lab.)	1	11	7

mond Mr C.B. Edgar drew the fire of Lady Rhondda and the Women's Citizens Association for helping to wreck the Criminal Law Amendment Bill in 1922. Although the Liberal feminist Margery Corbett Ashby stood against him she came third in the poll. Edgar owed his defeat to the intervention of an independent Conservative who was able to charge the MP with going abroad and neglecting his constituents, especially the ex-servicemen.[62] In Brentford and Chiswick another Blacklisted Tory, Colonel Grant Morden, faced the noted feminist Mrs Ray Strachey who stood as an independent in 1918, 1922 and 1923. Again the member's opposition to the Criminal Law Amendment Bill had attracted the hostility of the women's organisations. Strachey enjoyed emphatic support from NUSEC, endorsement from two women MPs, Astor and Wintringham, platform speeches by Lord Robert Cecil and Sir Oswald Mosley (who featured on the 1924 Whitelist), and backing by the local Liberal and Labour parties who withdrew their candidates in her support in 1922. Strachey's public campaign concentrated on the League of Nations. However, she conducted many drawing room meetings for women and organised creches on polling day to help mothers who wished to vote; local Conservative opinion held that she polled large numbers of women voters during the afternoon in this way.[63] Nevertheless, in a straight fight in 1922 Strachey won only 43 per cent to Morden's 56 per cent, and this was largely due to the absence of Liberal and Labour candidates. Morden was in fact returned at every election from 1918 to 1929 when he saw off a challenge from the Labour feminist Dr Stella Churchill.

An equally persistent offender, Mr Dennis Herbert, also had little difficulty in retaining the rather less safe seat of Watford. In 1923 the Six Point Group brought in speakers including Lady Rhondda and Vera Brittain, mobilised local churchmen, and organised meetings to draw the voters' attention to Herbert's record of opposition on divorce reform and the Criminal Law Amendment Bill. In 1924 Mrs Corbett Ashby also stood in Watford as a Liberal. Faced with this Herbert resorted to a mixture of aggression and conciliation. He variously lampooned his critics as 'some ladies from London', as socialists, and as very clever women who wished to start a women's party.[64] But he also claimed to represent the average woman, and when presented with seven questions by the National Council of Women he managed to reply positively to five of them. This clearly took the sting out of the feminists' campaign, because, although his opponents supported all seven of the NCW issues they never made major issues of them, preferring to concentrate on the national policies of their respective parties. Thus even in 1923 Herbert's loss of votes was very close to the average for opposed Conservatives, and he retained his seat comfortably at every election from 1918 to 1935.

On the other side the fate of those members who appeared on the Whitelists was not very encouraging. A high proportion lost their seats, particularly Conservatives in 1922 and Liberal and Labour members in 1924. National party fortunes, in other words, appear to have swamped what small advantage they derived from the Six Point Group's listing. It is also of some significance that very few of the women candidates chose to make an overtly feminist appeal in inter-war elections (see chapter 6). Ultimately the whole strategy seems to have been a failure in that it was only ever applied in a small and dwindling number of constituencies, and it was abandoned altogether after 1924. Of course, it could be argued that the very possibility of being Blacklisted had a beneficial effect if only in deterring some anti-feminist MPs from drawing attention to themselves by voting in critical divisions. However, the dropping of the scheme after 1924 when so many women's issues remained unresolved suggests that there was not a sufficiently strong feeling amongst women in the country to make politicians vulnerable to pressure of this kind.

If the women amongst the inter-war electorate did not noticeably respond to feminism, the question arises whether they made an impact by favouring any of the political parties in different proportions from men. In recent years a good deal of empirical work by political scientists has tended to substantiate the view that women as a group support the Conservative Party in Britain rather more strongly than men, though the variation between the sexes is only modest.[65] The explanation for this takes several forms. Some writers have suggested that women are characterised by a lower level of interest in politics, a more deferential attitude which expresses itself in acceptance of the views of either husbands or authority figures, or simply by a greater prevalence of right-wing sentiments. The phenomenon has also been linked to certain social characteristics, notably the greater age of the female electorate, and to the stronger involvement with organised religion. The age factor is essentially a matter of different political generations; as women live longer than men they tend to be more representative of certain generations amongst which Conservatives enjoy an advantage over Labour. However, age does not fully account for the phenomenon, for some surveys have found that in *every* age group women are more inclined to be Conservative.[66]

It is important to remember that neither survey findings nor historical evidence should be interpreted as meaning that women are *inherently* more Conservative than men. During the 1980s, for example, there were some indications that in Britain and the United States women had shifted away from their traditional right-wing leanings. What we are concerned to do is to consider whether and why Conservatives in Britain have historically proved more successful in mobilising their support among women than have their rivals. In view of the impossibility of separating male and female voters and the absence of opinion polling in our period no one can pronounce *precisely* on this question. However, it is possible to make use of both statistical and impressionistic evidence, and to analyse the historical circumstances surrounding each election in order to arrive at an informed assessment.

There is some advantage in beginning at the beginning with the Coupon Election of 1918 in which women comprised four out of ten voters. The inclusion of the wives of workingmen – the bulk of the 8.4 million women – largely satisfied the non-Conservative politicians that there would be no additional advantage for the propertied classes. But the new electorate of women displayed an obvious bias towards age. Only the youngest of the women had been born in the late 1880s and thus reached an impressionable political age in the Edwardian period when Liberal–Labour reformism was at its height. The great majority of women voters are likely to have formed political loyalties in a period when the choice was between Conservative and Liberal, though we must allow for the realignment of some of the most politically active women as a result of the suffrage controversies prior to the war. Although most women electors had not voted even in a local government election before, the low turnout of 58.9 per cent in 1918 should almost certainly *not* be attributed to female abstention since the 12.9 million males included 3.9 million naval and military voters of whom it was reported that two-thirds failed to take the chance of voting by post or by proxy.[67] Modern studies confirm that *young* voters are consistently the least likely to participate, and it thus seems very likely that abstention in 1918 was due to male behaviour rather than to the more mature female electorate. This is corroborated by many contemporary accounts which refer to the women as undemonstrative but determined in turning out to vote.

Dr John Turner has approached the 1918 election by using the evidence provided by the electoral register of 1915 and the number of men included in the 1918 register to estimate the total number of *new* male electors.[68] He then examined the performance of the Labour Party's candidates and found that there was an *inverse* relationship between the size of the Labour poll and the proportion of new voters. In fact the greater the proportion of new male voters the less well Labour did; and the greater the proportion of women voters the less well Labour did. Yet a statistical relationship is one thing: explaining it is another. This can be done at two levels. From a long-term perspective the emergence of an organised Labour Party can be seen to have been linked to the relatively prosperous, unionised and politically aware working-class communities who were already enfranchised to a large extent. Consequently the incorporation of the whole of the male working class weakened Labour's position *in the short run*. Similarly women as a group were as yet relatively uninvolved in the social and institutional networks that fostered support for Labour, and their enfranchisement was unlikely, without further changes, to prove advantageous.

More immediately women appear to have reacted to the 1918 campaign in a rather striking way, as contemporaries observed. It is easy to be misled by the prominence of a small group of women activists in the anti-war cause. To those politicians who had hoped or feared that women would want to vote for international peace and conciliation the Coupon Election came as a shock. Anti-war candidates such as Ramsay MacDonald experienced heavy defeats in their constituencies, in his case at West Leicester where the women voters were reported to be 'bloodthirsty, cursing their hate', and as posing a physical threat to pacifist politicians.[69] Emmeline Pethwick-Lawrence first became aware of this in 1917 when helping a peace-by-negotiation candidate at Aberdeen; the women there 'were even more embittered than the men', she wrote. Subsequently as a Labour candidate herself in Manchester in 1918 she commented:

> I realised at once that my supporters were not the women – this election was their chance of 'doing their bit' and they were all for 'going over the top' to avenge their husbands and their sons. My supporters were the soldiers themselves.[70]

Similarly many Liberals attributed their defeat in part to women's determination to make Germany pay for the cost of the war; Asquith's own sensational defeat at East Fife was blamed by the local press and by his party at least partly on the women.[71] Of course, defeated politicians have a habit of reaching for easy explanations after the event, and one should therefore beware of accepting these diagnoses; the outcome of several inter-war elections was to be attributed to the women's vote by the losing side. However, in the case of 1918 we also have some telling impressions of women's behaviour during the course of the campaign. For example, Lloyd George addressed a big meeting of women on 9 December, organised by Mrs Fawcett. There he launched into a speech about peace and the League of Nations, trying, as usual, to adapt to his audience's predilections. But for once Lloyd George had misjudged. Dozens of women angrily interrupted, intent on pressing him about the expulsion of enemy aliens, and whether Germany would be made to pay for the war.[72] It also seems clear from the correspondence that other Liberals were initially misled about the women voters, but woke up to the fact of their hostility as time passed. In Eccles the Asquithian Liberal prophesied: 'I am afraid I am beaten – mainly by the women's vote which came up freely and I feel sure was hostile.' A colleague of his in nearby Manchester commented: 'the working-class vote, and especially the women amongst them, have been all out for the Kaiser's head, and I am not particularly hopeful about the result.'[73] These premonitions of defeat proved to be correct and the explanations are much more plausible than usual because they were made well *before* the votes had been counted. The key to the explanation lies less in gender than in the *civilian* experience of both sexes. A gulf had developed between soldiers and civilians during the course of the war which manifested itself in mutual incomprehension by 1918. Men who stayed at home felt vaguely guilty and attempted to compensate by an extravagant show of patriotism and hostility towards Germany. Voting for the Coalition in the Coupon Election was an easy way of proving one's credentials. Few women were prepared to put their contribution to the war effort on a level with that of men; they were therefore especially vulnerable to simple cries about hanging the Kaiser and making Germany pay at the end of the war.

Of course, the circumstances of December 1918 were very special to say the least, and one cannot assume that the right-wing leanings of female voters continued to be a feature of peacetime. The three general elections from 1922 to 1924 presented politicians with a better opportunity for assessing the reaction of the new electors. It was widely considered that the new electorate was volatile, a characteristic widely attributed to the women. For example the anti-waste campaign which sprang up and led to Conservative defeats in by-elections at Dover and Hertford seems to have been seen even by feminist organisations as a reflection of women's opposition to the government over high expenditure, taxation and rising food prices.[74] However, concessions by Lloyd George's Coalition took the wind out of the sails of the anti-waste campaigners and in the 1922 election its candidates found themselves squeezed out by the conventional parties. Yet the idea of women as a volatile element gained credence from the 1923 election which was called unexpectedly by Stanley Baldwin, ostensibly in order to obtain a mandate for the introduction of tariffs. As a result the election turned into something like a referendum in which the Liberal and Labour parties upheld free trade against the disconcerted Conservatives. In the event the Conservatives lost 87 seats net, and saw their average vote per opposed candidate drop from 48.6 to 42.6 per cent. Sir Samuel Hoare blamed this setback on 'the ignorant opposition and credulity of the women', while the party chairman, Sir George Younger, accepted that women had revolted out of fears that protectionism would lead to dearer food.[75] Certainly Baldwin's opponents had done their best to focus debate on the sheer uncertainty that now affected the cost of living. Conservative losses to Liberals at this election occurred in surprising places some of which were represented by MPs identified by the Six Point Group as anti-feminists – Devizes, Newbury and Wycombe. In Wycombe, where Lady Vera Terrington scored a spectacular victory, it is likely that the women's vote proved vital. As the Liberal candidate in 1922 Lady Terrington had established herself in the constituency, improved the organisation and maintained her activity between elections. Rather unusually for a woman candidate she upheld the full programme of the Six Point Group including equal divorce, guardianship and improved maintenance rights for women, in both elections. However, it is less clear whether this was a significant asset for her. What was different in 1923 was her capacity to make effective play with Baldwin's policy: 'under tariff reform the housewife would not know from one week to another what things would cost'.[76] Moreover, the Liberal gains at the expense of Conservative anti-feminists seem to have occurred regardless of whether the candidate attacked on women's issues or not. Thus the Liberal poll of 51 per cent in Devizes was exactly in line with that in nearby constituencies like Salisbury and Chippenham; the Newbury poll was almost identical to that in the adjacent Abingdon division; while the Wycombe result was close to that at Aylesbury. Indeed the whole stretch of country from the Chilterns to the Wiltshire Downs appears to have moved in the same way at this election. The next year, when the tariff issue had been removed from the agenda, the Conservative share of the poll in seats where the party was opposed rose sharply to an average of 51.9 per cent. This was slightly better than the 1922 figure and it reassured Conservatives that, barring mistakes such as that made in 1923, there was nothing for them to fear from the women voters.

Yet even in 1924 the full extent of women's impact as voters had not been felt, for it was not until 1928 that the special restrictions on them – the age limit and their husbands' local government qualification – were finally abolished. From that time a woman qualified in respect of her normal residence; consequently women comprised 52.7 per cent of the total electorate in 1929. Since, as in 1923, this influx coincided with a defeat for the Conservatives, contemporaries succumbed to the temptation to attribute the result to flappers. But several political scientists, including J.S. Rasmussen and David Butler and Donald Stokes, have drawn quite different conclusions about the parties' ability to mobilise the new electors.[77] As always it is difficult to separate the effect of structural change from the impact of the historical circumstances surrounding each election. As we have already noted, there are now major doubts about attributing Labour's modest gain in popular support in 1918 to structural changes in the composition of the electorate. But during the 1920s the party was in a position to benefit from several developments: its emergence as the most effective alternative to the Conservatives, its experience in holding office independently, its organisational expansion, and the growth of trade unionism. Until 1931 Labour's rise did seem steady and even inexorable. Even in the defeat of 1924 it had consolidated its position as the second party with 33 per cent of the national poll and an average of 38 per cent per opposed candidate. From this position the party seemed poised to make the final leap to majority status, for each additional percentage point would bring in many additional seats. This is why the electoral reforms of 1928 aroused so much hope and apprehension in the Labour and Conservative parties respectively. By raising its overall share of the poll to 37 per cent Labour managed to increase its victories from 151 in 1924 to 288, not far short of an overall majority.

Yet how far did this reflect the structural changes in the electorate? Press speculation about the 'flappers' obscures the fact that young women represented only a minority of the new voters in 1929 (Table 5.8). There were two further categories, first nearly 2 million young men, and second nearly 2 million women over 30 years but excluded under the terms of the 1918 reforms. They included resident domestic servants, unmarried women living with relations, widows residing with married children, and women occupying furnished rented accommodation. It cannot be assumed that each of these categories of new electors leant in the same political direction.

Although a majority of Conservative constituency associations attribute their defeat in 1929 partly to the 'flappers', later scholars have found grounds for thinking that the new women electors proved to be

Table 5.8   The New Electorate 1929

Electors in 1928	21.7 million
Electors in 1929	28.85 million

Women over 30 years not enfranchised until 1929	1.95 million
Women aged 21–29 years enfranchised in 1929	3.29 million
Men aged 21 years or more enfranchised in 1929	1.9 million

disadvantageous to the Labour Party, both in 1929 and, indeed, in the two subsequent general elections.[78] In their survey of voters' political histories Butler and Stokes charted the loyalties of successive generations of the electorate: those who came of age before 1918, the inter-war generation, those who first voted in 1945, and the post-1951 generation. They found that the behaviour of women was distinctive in that in both the pre-1918 and inter-war generations they were markedly more Conservative than men; this feature, however, declined sharply in the third political generation. Secondly, Rasmussen examined the actual voting record by showing the correlation between the level of the Labour vote and the level of the female share of the total electorate.[79] As with the 1918 study this indicated that Labour did less well the higher the women's electorate; but the correlation for 1929 was so close to that for the 1924 election that Rasmussen concluded that the influx of new voters had not significantly altered Labour's position. A third means of focusing on the impact of the new electorate's behaviour involves a comparison of results of nine by-elections which took place during January to March 1929 with the voting in the general election in May. These were three-cornered contests with one exception where Labour did not stand. They largely involved the same candidates and issues, for the by-elections were conducted in an atmosphere in which all parties expected a dissolution of parliament quite soon. The key change between by-election and general election was that the former was fought on the old register.[80] The pattern that emerges is a fairly consistent one. In every constituency in which the two main parties were involved there was a swing from Labour to Conservative ranging from a maximum of 8.5 per cent to a minimum of 0.5 per cent between the two elections. Of course the obvious explanation for this is not in terms of the new voters but rather in terms of a by-election protest against the government being reduced at the subsequent general election. This, however, seems unlikely to be a sufficient explanation because Labour was one of two opposition parties involved. The Liberals also were enjoying a revival during the late 1920s. One might well expect the improvement in Liberal fortunes engineered by Lloyd George and fostered by the lacklustre Baldwin administration to evaporate in the circumstances of a general election. Indeed that is the commonly held view, for the 1929 results, in terms of seats won, were undoubtedly disappointing for the Liberals. But in terms of popular support this is clearly a misconception. In most cases the Liberals *improved* their share of the poll at the general election even where they had run *third* in the by-election. In the comparable three-cornered contests Labour's share fell by an average of 2.9 per cent, while the Liberals' rose by an average of 1.5 per cent and the Conservatives' share by 3.7 per cent. This tends to highlight Labour as the party that was disadvantaged by the electoral reforms of 1928.

Of course, each of these three approaches to the new voters has shortcomings, but it is significant that they all point in the same direction. We must ask how far their message is consistent with other historical evidence. By comparison with 1924 the Labour Party clearly improved its position in 1929. It may well be that amongst the new voters the males gave a further boost to the party's support. They were relatively young, experiencing at first hand the problems of unemployment, many had been swept into the trade union movement just after the war and had participated enthusiastically in the general strike of 1926. For them self-interest and the institutional pressures associated with their employment pointed towards supporting Labour. These considerations cannot apply to the women voters with anything like the same force. Women were less likely to be involved in the industrial side of the Labour movement and, even where they did belong to trade unions, were often passive members. Conversely the Conservatives had capitalised on their pre-1914 position by mobilising approximately four times as many women members as Labour by the late 1920s. This does not mean that Labour was not narrowing the gap; its individual membership among women was many times greater than before the war, as was the level of trade unionism amongst women workers. But the Conservatives' advantage in absolute terms appears to have remained intact by 1929, and the leaders were able to bolster their position by flourishing the legislative achievements for women won during the 1920s. Therefore the extension of the female electorate at that stage seems almost certain to have had the effect of reducing the gains Labour was making by its attack upon the inadequacies of the Baldwin government over the economy and unemployment. The women were more likely than the men to stay loyal to conservatism, or to express their protests by voting Liberal rather than Labour. Had Labour done as well amongst the women as amongst the men a number of the seats where Conservatives held on by under 500 votes would have fallen, and the party's advance towards winning an outright majority would have been significantly faster.

Finally there are some grounds in Rasmussen's work for thinking that the 1929 tendencies were exaggerated by the political crisis of 1931. In that year Labour's share of the national vote fell from 37.1 to 30.6 per cent, and its vote per opposed candidate from 39.3 to 33.0 per cent. The traditional view that the overwhelming defeat was a consequence of the united front presented by the national government rather than to a loss of votes does seem consistent with the loyalty of male voters wedded to the movement via their trade unions. But Rasmussen's work shows that in 1931 the seats with a higher proportion of women voters became *more* anti-Labour than they had been in 1929.[81] It seems likely, therefore, that many women whose allegiance to Labour was relatively recent and fragile were more vulnerable to the appeal of the national government. Support for Labour was not yet a matter of firm habit and was easily undermined by the traumatic events of August 1931. The lasting effects upon a generation of women who retained a greater propensity to vote Conservative were detected by Butler and Stokes 30 years later.

Chapter 6   The Political Containment of Women 1918–1939

Up to the present day many talented women have found the search for a secure seat in the House of Commons a frustrating experience. One study of parliamentary candidates found that in the 1950s and 1960s it was still common for Conservative selection committees to ask married women why they were prepared to neglect their husbands and children, while also interrogating single women on their marriage plans![1] Each of the party organisations has invariably excused its discrimination against female aspirants by pointing to the prejudice amongst the electorate. However, there is reason to think that such prejudice has dwindled to negligible proportions, and that the heart of the problem has always been the constituency selection committees.[2] Consequently one tends to start from the assumption that women's parliamentary ambitions have always been thwarted by male obstructionism. But how far can we be certain about this? It would be surprising if attitudes among both politicians and voters had not fluctuated since the 1920s when women candidates were obviously a novelty. Nor would it be wise to assume that the aspirations of today's women are the same as those of the inter-war generation.

The Competition for Candidatures

Unfortunately, even the 36 women who became MPs between the wars have left relatively few papers; hardly any have adequate biographies, and their memoirs often paper over the problems they encountered within their parties. In any case they were the *successful* women. Those who were never nominated, or who failed to win an election, tend to be much more obscure. There are exceptions. We know that such women as Selina Cooper and Hannah Mitchell failed to become Labour candidates in the 1920s largely because they were too independently feminist, and too pacifist, for a party that placed a premium on loyalty and discipline.[3] The outstanding example of a Conservative who failed to get into parliament is Dame Helen Gwynne-Vaughan, an academic scientist with a distinguished war record in the WAAC and the WRAF. Handicapped by both her intelligence and her feminism, she had a reputation for being overbearing in her dealings with men, and declined to charm the Tory selection committees. In 1922 Sir George Younger, the party chairman, reminded the women's conference that constituency parties were usually shocked if asked to consider adopting a woman. But the problem also lay in Conservative Central Office which Ray Strachey reported as 'violently opposed to women MPs'. Younger himself was scarcely enthusiastic about Nancy Astor's adoption in 1919: 'the worst of it is the woman is sure to get in'.[4]

However, attitudes soon began to soften. In 1923 the young Miss Irene Ward was chosen by the Conservatives of Wansbeck in Northumberland, but was obliged to withdraw as a result of opposition from the rank and file.[5] Yet she contested the neighbouring seat of Morpeth in 1924 and Wansbeck itself selected another woman in that election. During the 1920s it was frequently argued that since women in their twenties were ineligible to vote they would not be taken seriously as candidates. This, however, did not stop youthful politicians such as Jennie Lee and Megan Lloyd George winning nominations. At this stage female candidates encountered a certain amount of heckling and rowdyism especially in mining constituencies, but once they had given proof of their competence and spirit on the platform they usually suffered rather less than men at the hands of their opponents.

Another favourite excuse of the 1920s was the claim that rural districts would be especially hostile to women candidates. Yet the claim was no sooner made than it was exploded by the voters themselves. When Margaret Wintringham stood at Louth in Lincolnshire in 1921 one local newspaper solemnly pronounced:

> The question arises, however, as to whether it is possible for a lady to adequately represent this large and important agricultural division. [Mrs Wintringham] cannot claim to fully and clearly understand the great agricultural industry which is the mainstay of the division. Neither do we think she can claim a knowledge of the intricacies of business and commercial life.[6]

In the event she scored a notable victory; the hostile comment was simply an attempt by her opponents to put doubts into the voters' minds. Similarly the Duchess of Atholl was advised by the Scottish Unionist chairman to seek an urban seat; but none was found and she won a remote rural one in 1923. Hilda Runciman was said to face prejudice against women in the Devonshire seat of Tavistock in 1929, but she almost gained the seat from the Conservatives and moreover had previously gained the equally rural seat of St Ives in Cornwall.

What one learns from such cases is that while male prejudice against women was obviously a factor between the wars it is far from being a *sufficient* explanation for the paucity of women's candidatures. Women's own attitudes and aspirations must also be taken into account. There are good grounds for thinking that in 1918 for example, few even among the politically active women seriously contemplated becoming members of parliament. This is partly because they had been concentrating on the war and on winning the vote. They assumed it would require a *further* struggle to persuade parliament to allow them to sit in the Commons. The bill to admit them, which was rushed through in the summer of 1918, genuinely surprised them. This helps to explain why only 17 women stood at the Coupon Election. An opportunity was thus missed, especially amongst Labour women, for during 1917–18 their party embarked upon a major expansion which involved over 300 additional candidates.

Some women, however, simply regarded parliamentary work as an unattractive form of political involvement. The best known example is Ruth Dalton who was able to compare her role on the London County Council with a brief spell as MP for Bishop Auckland: 'there we do things, here it seems to be all talk'. Yet this should not be exaggerated. Many male members also find it tedious to act as docile lobby-fodder for the whips. However, during the twentieth century backbenchers have increasingly found the most satisfying part of their work in dealing with constituents' personal problems. These are often housing and welfare matters which women, with their local government background, are often well qualified to handle.

It must be emphasised that the women who contested inter-war elections had often been sought out and invited by male colleagues; they did not take the initiative themselves. For example, Isabella Ford declined to stand for Labour in 1918, while Margery Corbett Ashby explained her own decision to accept an offer precisely on the grounds that so many women had refused nomination that she felt bound, as a dedicated suffragist, to take it on.[7] She was typical of a large number of women for whom parliament would have been a natural extension of their work in philanthropy, local government and women's causes. For Corbett Ashby the decimation of fellow Liberals in 1918 opened up extensive opportunities in the 1920s. However, this potential was never fully realised. Many Liberal women had grown disillusioned with their party during the suffrage struggle, withdrawn from membership during or after the war, or simply lost touch as a result of wartime disruption. Although Asquith was largely blind to the possibilities, Lloyd George showed a lively appreciation of the need to promote women candidates. He secured a seat for his daughter, but also played a role in setting Conservative women such as the Duchess of Atholl and Thelma Cazalet on the road to parliament.[8]

The Liberals' greatest failure was their inability to get Violet Bonham Carter into parliament. Asquith's daughter attracted immensely flattering comments in the early 1920s. In particular her public speaking for her father at the Paisley by-election of 1920 was widely regarded as the key to his impressive comeback at that point. Lady Violet, however, declined offers on the grounds that her first duty was to her young children. But she was by no means the only Liberal woman to receive invitations to stand. Mrs Runciman refused offers until 1928 when she stood out of duty to her husband (see page 178). Megan Lloyd George, who like Lady Violet was considered to have inherited a good deal of her father's political talent, turned down invitations to contest such seats as Pontypool in 1927, preferring to take on the safe seat of Anglesey later.

It is significant that none of these Liberal ladies was notably feminist; their primary duty and loyalty, after family, was towards the party. Those Liberal women who placed a higher priority upon women's politics either abstained, stood as Independents or undertook merely propagandist candidatures. Corbett Ashby is a good example of a woman who kept her feminism and her liberalism afloat for a long period – but without ever becoming an MP. Having agreed to stand in the hopeless seat of Birmingham Ladywood in 1918, she went on to tackle Richmond in 1922 and 1923, Watford in 1924, Hendon in 1929, Hemel Hempstead in 1935 and 1937, and Bury St Edmunds in 1944. Even for a Liberal this record scarcely looks like a serious attempt to get elected. Rather Mrs Corbett Ashby was waging her lifelong crusade, showing the flag for women, and attacking the citadels of notorious anti-feminist MPs as at Richmond and Watford. Ray Strachey did the same as an Independent at Brentford in 1922 and 1923. The only success for Independent feminism was that of Eleanor Rathbone who was elected for a university seat in 1929. Clearly the exclusion of Liberal women from parliament cannot be attributed in any great degree to hostility within the party. But was the same true of Labour and the Conservatives? Both the national party organisations professed to be keen to see women adopted. However, they appear to have been unwilling or unable to use their influence with the local parties. There is scant evidence of women being placed in winnable seats through central party direction. In 1918 Mary Macarthur, who was probably

Labour's leading woman at the time, stood in Stourbridge which might have been won; and in 1929 Arthur Henderson gave Leah Manning a promise of the next vacancy in a Labour constituency (see page 166). But it seems to have been more common for local parties to approach women: Emmeline Pethwick-Lawrence, Edith Picton-Turbervill, Edith Summerskill and Jean Mann were all beneficiaries of such initiatives.

On the Conservative side the traditional view that an MP ought to have connections with the chief commercial or industrial interests of his constituency militated against women. On the other hand since their candidates were drawn from a narrower field than Labour's, it seems that social class and personal influence often overrode objections based on sex. Several well-connected Tory women capitalised on this most successfully. Under Stanley Baldwin's leadership the local associations came under some pressure to reduce their financial dependence on the candidate or a wealthy patron, and thereby widen the choice of candidate. Certainly by the 1930s some local parties took pride in their ability to raise the money they required without extorting large sums from one or two individuals.[9] However, it is very doubtful whether this limited democratisation was at all helpful to female aspirants. The growing concentration on constituency fund raising had the effect of increasing the importance attached to a candidate who could produce a presentable and co-operative *wife*. She was assumed to have the time on her hands to be able to attend innumerable local functions and to deputise for her husband whenever necessary. Hence the reputed hostility of Conservative women towards female candidates, married or single.

To some extent this problem troubled women politicians of all parties. 'What I need is a wife', Ellen Wilkinson once exclaimed. However, a variety of expedients were found for tackling the wife problem in this period. It is often forgotten, for example, that several of the early women MPs enjoyed the advantage of a wife-substitute in the form of husbands and other companions. The best example was Nancy Astor whose husband, Waldorf, subordinated his own political career to hers, put in a good deal of the spade work on speeches and legislation, and was generally available to support and substitute for her. Similar remarks apply to the Duchess of Atholl whose husband supported her both by acting as president of her constituency association (where it was necessary to defend her position), and by handling the social side as a better 'hostess' than his wife. Eleanor Rathbone lived for many years with a close companion, Elizabeth Macadam, who provided both practical, political and emotional support. Jennie Lee, who was first elected in 1929 but not married until 1934, simply brought her parents down from Scotland. Her mother subsequently kept house for her and Nye Bevan so that they could pursue their political careers on an equal basis. While the impressionistic evidence is a valuable corrective to the assumption that male prejudice alone was responsible for excluding women from parliament, it is also necessary to consider how far one may generalise about women's experience on the basis of the relevant statistical evidence. In particular it is important to ascertain whether the numbers of women candidates increased significantly over time, whether they were fairly distributed between winnable and unwinnable constituencies, and whether the practice varied significantly between the parties. As the figures in Table 6.1 show, the total of women candidates rose remarkably slowly in the 1920s; the repeated general elections of 1922, 1923 and 1924, combined with the continued expansion of Labour candidatures, might have been expected to make a more emphatic impact on women's role. By the 1929–35 period women provided around 60–70 candidates or 5 per cent of the national total; but at this point they seem to have reached a plateau and remained stuck at the same level right down to the 1970s.

As to the distribution of women in the constituencies the inter-war period reveals a clear and not unexpected pattern. Over four-fifths of women candidates were placed in hopeless seats. The only qualification

Table 6.1   Women in British Parliamentary Elections 1918–1970

	Women candidates	As % of candidates	Total MPs	Women MPs	Women as % of MPs
1918	17	1	707	1[a]	0.1
1922	33	2.3	615	2	0.3
1923	34	2.4	615	8	1.3
1924	41	2.9	615	4	0.7
1929	69	4.0	615	14	2.3
1931	62	4.8	615	15	2.4
1935	67	5.0	615	9	1.5
1945	87	5.2	640	24	3.8
1950	126	6.7	625	21	3.4
1951	74	5.4	625	17	2.7
1955	89	6.3	630	24	3.8
1959	81	5.3	630	25	4.0
1964	90	5.1	630	28	4.4
1966	80	4.7	630	26	4.1
1970	99	5.4	630	26	4.1

[a]   The Countess Markievicz was elected as a Sinn Fein candidate in Dublin but did not take her seat in parliament.

here is that different definitions of a 'hopeless' seat could modify the picture a little and on the criteria adopted in Table 6.2 it was in fact possible for a number of women to be elected for such seats in special circumstances such as those prevailing in 1931 when several Conservative women found themselves swept into parliament on the strength of the national government's appeal. On the other hand less than 7 per cent of all the women were nominated in constituencies already held by their party and which they could therefore be expected to win, and half of these were only marginals. To some extent this pronounced bias in favour of unwinnable seats for women may be explained by the variation in practice between the political parties. Labour and the Liberals nominated a markedly higher proportion of women than the Conservatives but the overwhelming majority of them were in hopeless seats. This reflects the fact that these parties simply had far fewer safe seats to offer than their rivals. The Conservative

Table 6.2   The Distribution of Women's Candidatures at General Elections 1922–1935[a]

	Conservative	Labour	Liberal	Total	
In seats held safely by own party[b]	5	0	2	7	
In seats held marginally by own party	1	4	1	6	6.6%
In seats held marginally by another party	6	8	5	19	9.8%
In seats held safely by another party	28	80	56	164	83.6%
Party total	40	92	64	196[c]	

a   The elections of 1918 and 1945 have been excluded because extensive boundary changes make assessment of safe and hopeless seats difficult.

b   A constituency has been rated safely held if the candidate's own party beat its nearest rival by a margin of 10% or more of the poll in the previous general election. It is marginal if under 10%. Similarly seats held by opponents have been rated hopeless if the candidate's own party was beaten by 10% or more of the poll in the previous general election. It is marginal if the party was beaten by less than 10%.

c   This is not the total number of occasions on which women stood. Each woman candidate is counted once for her first contest; she is counted again only where she stood in a different constituency.

picture is the reverse. They produced only one-fifth of all women's candidatures but a relatively high proportion of them (15 per cent) occurred in seats already held by the party compared with only 4 to 5 per cent for the other two parties.

Of course the party difference also reflects the fact that there was rather less pressure from Conservative women partly because of the narrower social range from which the party recruited. One thus has something of a paradox, in that although Labour found nearly half of all the women's candidatures from 1922 to 1935 the controversy over women's nominations was to a considerable extent conducted with the Labour Party. If the opportunities were relatively great, the expecta-tions were higher. The situation is apparent in the painful progress of several of the party's leading women between the wars. Throughout the 1920s they invariably found themselves placed in tight three-way marginals. For example, Margaret Bondfield fought Northampton, then held by a Coalition Liberal minister, at a 1920 by-election, again in 1922 when she polled 37.9 per cent, and in 1923 when she was elected with 40.5 per cent; in 1924 with 37.2 per cent she was defeated. Susan Lawrence stood in East Ham North in 1922, won the seat in 1923 with only 35.7 per cent of the poll, lost in 1924 but was returned at a by-election in 1926 with 40.7 per cent and again in 1929, still with only 42 per cent. Ethel Bentham first contested East Islington in 1922 when she won 22 per cent of the votes, went on to stand again in 1923 and 1924, and was finally elected in 1929 with just 38 per cent. Ellen Wilkinson, after a three-cornered contest at Ashton-under-Lyne in 1923, fought Middlesbrough East in 1924 where she ion with 38.5 per cent of the poll and held the seat in 1929 with 41.3 per cent. In spite of their ability none of these women managed to win much more than a third of the vote and would never have been elected at all had they not persisted – which most women candidates did not do. Needless to say, almost any turn in the fortunes of their party was likely to bring them immediate defeat. The only qualification to this picture is that subsequently Bondfield obtained a much better seat at Wallsend in 1926 and Wilkinson at Jarrow in 1935. Lawrence, however, got only a losing contest with Harold Macmillan at Stockton in 1935, and even Bondfield ended up as candidate for Reading in the 1930s – a seat no better than her original Northampton.

Turning to the positive side of the question one must consider what routes women used in order to secure nomination by their parties. Here one may distinguish the structural and electoral conditions on the one hand from the personal qualities and experience of the candidates on the other. To take the structural-electoral first, three main conditions seem significant. The first simply relates to the timing. A woman who obtained a hopeless seat without too much difficulty might find herself elected if this coincided with an extraordinary swing of political fortunes, as in 1931. On that occasion at least eight Conservative women were returned for constituencies which their party had never anticipated winning: Mrs I. Copeland (Stoke on Trent), Miss F.M. Graves (S. Hackney), the Hon. Mary Pickford (N. Hammersmith), Mrs N.C. Runge (Rotherhithe), Mrs H.B. Shaw (Bothwell), Mrs M. Tate (W. Willsden), Miss I. Ward (Wallsend) and Mrs S.A. Ward (Cannock). The same pleasant fate awaited several Labour women in 1945.

A second helpful route for women was the by-election. Between 1918 and 1939 31 women contested by-elections for the three main parties, a tactic apparently favoured by Labour which provided 18 of them. Of the total of 36 women who became MPs between the wars no fewer than 10 first entered parliament through by-elections: Lady Astor (1919), Mrs Wintringham (1921), Mrs Philipson (1923), Mrs Runciman (1928), Mrs Dalton (1929), the Countess of Iveagh (1927), Lady Noel-Buxton (1930), Mrs Manning (1931), Mrs Hardie (1937) and Dr Summerskill (1938). Two others, Miss Bondfield (1926) and Miss Lawrence (1926), also re-entered at by-elections. The explanation for this is that for the parties rather less was at stake at a by-election than at a general election. The by-election was also a useful test of electors' reactions since it was tempting to focus attention upon the individual candidates, especially if they were women. That women polled very well on these occasions when placed under the limelight makes the parties' reservations about them seem irrational even in this period.

The third electoral-structural feature which was utilised by some women was the two-member borough. Before 1918 when a comparatively large number of these traditional constituencies still survived the Liberal and Labour parties had found them a valuable expedient for maintaining an electoral alliance and maximising their appeal. The reduced number of such seats remaining after 1918 presented each party with the opportunity to run a male and female candidate in tandem thereby helping to satisfy women's pressure for candidacies and enabling the local party to tap both the men and the women in the electorate. Yet it cannot be said that the parties exploited this option as fully as they might have done. In five of the two-member boroughs (Bolton, the City of London, Preston, Southampton and Stockport) no party included a woman at any inter-war election. But women candidates did make an appearance in the other seven boroughs: Blackburn (Labour), Brighton (Labour), Derby (Conservative), Norwich (Labour)

Oldham (Liberal), Sunderland (Labour and Liberal), and also Dundee where the Conservatives ran a woman as their sole candidate but in loose alliance with a male National Liberal in 1931. Clearly women occupied a higher profile in the elections of these towns than in the general run of constituencies, but only Labour seems to have made a deliberate tactic of the two-member seat as is suggested by the party's *repeated* use of women at Blackburn where Mary Agnes Hamilton (1924–31) was followed by Barbara Castle in 1945, Norwich where Dorothy Jewson (1923–31) was followed by Lady Noel-Buxton (1945) and Sunderland where Marion Phillips (1929–31) was followed by Leah Manning in 1935.

In this period multi-member constituencies also existed in four of the seven university seats. This provided an opportunity for Eleanor Rathbone who was elected as an Independent member for the Combined English Universities seat from 1929 until her death in 1946. But here there was an additional factor: the system used was the single transferable vote method of proportional representation. While this did not break the stranglehold of the parties it certainly made it easier for an Independent to succeed. Women already had reason to regard a multi-member electoral system as advantageous for them. For example from the 1870s they had done particularly well in elections to the school boards which used the cumulative vote in a multi-member constituency. This enabled supporters of a minority candidate who would never have been elected in a single-member seat to pile up their votes for a single candidate. Even as Independents women had found it comparatively easy to be returned under this system. The inclusion of proposals for proportional representation (PR) in the 1917 parliamentary reform bill reminded the women's leaders of its attractions especially for those who disliked party politics. In Britain PR had traditionally been seen as a means of enabling independently minded politicians to defy party discipline by appealing to the voters in multi-member constituencies. Not surprisingly, NUSEC and several other women's organisations advocated PR between the wars, and the experience of other European countries strongly suggests that such a system would have increased very significantly the number of women nominated and elected. However, PR never became a live question in interwar Britain except briefly during 1929–31; the majority of Labour and Conservative women followed the prevailing view in their parties, and it was thus left to a later generation of women to rediscover the importance of electoral reform.

For most of the inter-war women MPs personal circumstances appear to have been more central than structural ones in their route to parliament. It is notable, for example, that a high proportion owed their election to family connections, especially among the Conservatives. Several ladies stepped forward following the elevation of their husbands to the peerage: Nancy Astor for Plymouth Sutton in 1919, the Countess of Iveagh for Southend in 1927, and Lady Davidson for Hemel Hempstead in 1937. In 1923 the Duchess of Atholl stood in West Perth and Kinross which her husband had represented during 1910–17. Mrs Hilton Philipson contested her husband's Berwick constituency when he was unseated after an election petition in 1923. Lady Cooper stood unsuccessfully in Walsall when Sir Richard Cooper withdrew through ill-health in 1922, while Mrs B.F. Rathbone (Bodmin, 1941) and Lady Apsley (Bristol Central, 1943) entered parliament following the deaths of their husbands. Although this reliance on male relations was characteristic of Conservatives it was by no means exclusive to them. For the Liberals Margaret Wintringham succeeded at Louth after her husband's death in 1921, while Megan Lloyd George owed her nomination for Anglesey in 1928 to the influence of her father in North Wales. For Labour Lady Noel-Buxton won North Norfolk when her husband was elevated to the House of Lords in 1930, and Mrs Agnes Hardie became member for Glasgow Springburn after her husband's death in 1937.

In addition a very special marital link was employed by two women MPs who did not succeed their husbands but prepared the way for them. Mrs Hilda Runciman (St Ives, 1928) and Ruth Dalton (Bishop Auckland, 1929) both contested seats at by-elections on behalf of husbands who had already arranged to be adopted but could not actually stand until released from their existing constituencies by a general election. Both ladies won, and vacated their seats respectively for Walter Runciman (ex-Swansea) and Hugh Dalton (ex-Peckham) in 1929.

In all some 21 of the 36 women MPs were married or widowed at the time of their election, against 15 who were single, though 3 of the latter, Jennie Lee, Dorothy Jewson and Thelma Cazalet, did marry later. Marriage tends to be more characteristic of the Conservative and Liberal women. As middle- and upper-class ladies they enjoyed the support of servants to enable them to manage the home and a parliamentary career. Conversely Labour's ladies were married only to the party: Bondfield, Lawrence, Jewson, Wilkinson, Bentham, Phillips, Picton-Turbervill, Lee. In time more of Labour's women members were wives but they seem mostly to have come from wealthier families, such as Cynthia Mosley, Ruth Dalton, Lady Noel Buxton and Edith Summerskill; Mrs Hardie, however, was a working-class woman. It is noticeable that both single and married women MPs were fairly advanced in age when first elected. Two-thirds were in their forties and fifties, and the oldest, Ethel Bentham, was 68. Only two, Jennie Lee and Megan Lloyd George, were elected in their twenties, and a handful including Cynthia Mosley, Irene Ward, Thelma Cazalet and Edith Summerskill, were in their thirties. The explanation is that the un-married women had first to establish a career and a place in the party hierarchy, and the married women rarely even considered a parlia-mentary career until family circumstances had changed and children had grown up.

However, it would be a misrepresentation to suggest that the wives amongst the MPs were just wives. A number of other qualifications, achievements and connections gave them a claim on their parties' candidacies. For example, virtually all the women could point to various forms of war service; this was important in itself in giving them a feeling of involvement in the nation's affairs, and useful as a reminder that they had matched the male contribution to the war effort. Local government was also an apprenticeship for several women, especially the London County Council and the London Boroughs. Lawrence, Bentham, Hamilton, Rathbone, Phillips, Wilkinson, Dalton, Cazalet, Runciman and Summerskill all had such experience, and others like Atholl had been co-opted to County Council committees. It is doubtful, however, whether local government experience was a major reason for the women's adoption, rather it gave some of them the self-confidence and motivation to contemplate taking a greater role in public life. Just occasionally it proved critical. Thelma Cazalet represented East Isling-ton on the LCC from 1924. When a parliamentary by-election arose in the constituency in 1931 the candidate withdrew and, as 'no man could be found', she was adopted.[10] Though defeated she was in place for the subsequent general election which swept her into parliament until 1945.

A more direct route for a minority of women lay through paid, professional employment for their party; the expansion of such posts was a consequence of the enfranchisement of women in 1918 when the need for permanent women organisers was freely accepted. Marion Phillips became Labour's Chief Woman Officer and Agnes Hardie had worked as a party organiser in Scotland since 1919. Amongst Con-servatives Irene Ward and Florence Horsbrugh rose up through the organisation; Horsbrugh in particular made her political career by building up a reputation as an effective and professional public speaker. Of course a number of the Conservative women (Miss Graves, Mary

Pickford) and the Liberals (Mrs Runciman and Megan Lloyd George) were well known for their voluntary work as speakers and organisers for the party.

Very few of the women MPs seem to have used their position in women's organisations as a prop to their parliamentary careers. Eleanor Rathbone, president of NUSEC, is the obvious exception to this, and Mrs Wintringham gained advantage from her involvement in the Women's Institutes, as did Margaret Bondfield from her work for women's trade unionism. It has often been remarked, however, that on the whole the feminists who had campaigned for the franchise failed to capitalise on their work by becoming MPs. This is not quite true. In addition to Rathbone, Wintringham, Wilkinson, Bentham, Phillips and Picton-Turbervill all had some active experience in the suffragist movement, while Jewson and Cazalet had been involved with the militant campaign. However, there was no particular credit to be won with the electorate from such a record, and no woman seems to have wanted to remind the voters of her suffragism. At the most, some of the suffragists (and several non-suffragists) received some assistance from NUSEC in their election campaigns, but as we have already seen, this seems to have died out by the 1930s.

In many ways the Labour Party was the cockpit of the women's struggle for parliamentary representation between the wars. Although the party provided the lion's share of candidates, it required very stringent, if informal, qualifications. Proven loyalty to the movement was of paramount importance, especially for those who fished in the small pool of safe seats. In addition the question of funds loomed large since few constituencies felt able to bear the costs of election campaigns and of maintaining the organisation in between times. Since the late Victorian period money had dogged the steps of workingmen in pursuit of nomination as Liberals. The chief solution had been found in sponsorship by trade unions. During the 1920s as Labour extended its reach to virtually every constituency in the country, the male trade unionist who had a promise of regular financial support enjoyed a great advantage over most women who were either not union members or received no sponsorship from their unions. There were exceptions. Wilkinson enjoyed support from NUDAW, and Bondfield from the TGWU. Leah Manning's rise to the presidency of the NUT enabled her to seek a safe seat at East Bristol in 1929. However, the national party in the form of Arthur Henderson suddenly intervened and persuaded her to surrender the seat to Stafford Cripps. In compensation she was returned at a by-election in East Islington following Ethel Bentham's death in 1931. However, she was shortly to be defeated at the general election, and was obliged to give up the constituency when the NUT withdrew its financial contribution.[11] She did not return to parliament until 1945, a heavy price to pay for the advancement of Cripps.

There were other ways up the party hierarchy for a few. Marion Phillips emerged via local government and the Women's Labour League before 1914, the War Emergency Workers National Committee during wartime, and her status as the party's Chief Woman Officer from 1918. Even so, she faced financial problems with her Sunderland constituency. Phillips brought only £70 a year contributed by the Durham Labour women, plus the £50 that she donated towards her agent's salary. Susan Lawrence, on the other hand, had both her Conservative background and a middle-class accent to overcome. She, too, made her mark in local government, on the LCC, worked for the Women's Trade Union League, served on the WEWNC, and from 1918 sat on the party's National Executive Committee of which she was chairman in 1929 to 1930. But the key to her parliamentary success, apart from her undoubted ability, was that she was wealthy enough to be, in effect, a full-time but unpaid worker for the movement; thus Lawrence toiled away at the East Ham constituency until eventually elected.

Occasionally a Labour woman managed to circumvent the prescribed institutional route to a good, working-class seat. Jennie Lee accomplished it when she was adopted for North Lanark at the age of 23. A schoolteacher with a growing reputation as an orator for the ILP, Lee's selection in preference to several trade unionists backed by money was remarkable. Later she suggested that the local party was impressed by her university degrees, but she was probably nearer the mark when she wrote, 'just as important, I came out of the right stable'.[12] Her father was a miner and her grandfather had been an official of the Fife Miners' Union.

If trade union support was not generally available to women, there were alternative institutional resources for them. The ILP certainly assisted many women by utilising them as speakers extensively between the wars. For a middle-class professional woman like Mary Agnes Hamilton it was a natural point of entry, leading to a place on the national party's list of candidates in the early 1920s.[13] However, the ILP suffered from two disadvantages. It was never rich enough to promote many candidates. Moreover, by virtue of its role as left-wing critic of Labour Party policy it tended to marginalise the many women who belonged to it. Dorothy Jewson, Monica Whately and Kate Spurrell, all members, found that the National Executive was reluctant to endorse their candidacies because they were considered to have divided loyalties.[14]

The Women's Co-operative Guild, which was affiliated to the party from 1918, strenuously tried to promote its leading members as Labour candidates. But the WCG felt aggrieved because the best it could do for its general secretary, Mrs Eleanor Barton, was the nomination at King's Norton in Birmingham. Worse, she was badly defeated in two elections, which the WCG blamed on the failure of the local Labour Party to give her active support.[15] It is certainly significant that when she was replaced by a man in 1924 King's Norton was gained from the Conservatives quite against the national trend. Subsequently Mrs Barton was outbid by male trade unionist candidates in spite of the backing of the WCG, and failed to become an MP.[16]

Potentially the best institutional support for women lay in the Labour Party Women's Organisation itself. The defeat of the first three women MPs, Bondfield, Jewson and Lawrence, in 1924 prompted Ellen Wilkinson to launch an attack on the party for leaving women to fight the difficult seats. She quoted a senior party organiser's view: 'There is about a hundred-to-one chance in that division, but it might be won. It is just the sort of seat a woman ought to fight.'[17] In spite of Wilkinson's efforts the women's conference did not tackle the question seriously until 1927. Delegates identified four factors which deterred constituency parties from selecting women: there was still prejudice against them in the country; very few women were sufficiently well-known to have much appeal; domestic ties hindered their attendance in parliament; and they lacked trade union money. This last disadvantage was tackled by the women in County Durham. Since Labour was steadily winning most of the seats in the county the Women's Advisory Committee felt entitled to claim one constituency for a woman. To this end it persuaded the local women's sections to contribute to a fund to pay the expenses of a woman. They themselves selected Marion Phillips, and eventually secured her adoption in Sunderland in 1929. As we have already noticed this initiative by no means resolved the financial difficulties at Sunderland. But at least it produced an additional woman MP, and the Conference agreed in 1927 to investigate the possibility of extending the Durham scheme.[18] Unfortunately, by 1928 the party itself had launched a new 'Bid for Power' Fund in preparation for the next general election; this was seen as particularly necessary in view of the anticipated reduction in party income, arising out of the 1927 Trades Disputes Act which introduced the contracting-out system for union members' political levy. The new fund involved imposing financial quotas on each of the women's sections and a national target for the women's organisation as a whole. In this way the Durham scheme was neatly overtaken and lost in a national one.

Thereafter the party's attitude towards women candidates deteriorated because of the perceived links between feminists and the ILP. In 1932 Wilkinson again complained that women were being denied a fair share of nominations for lack of finance, but the women's conference remained surprisingly unmoved. The explanation was that the leading figures – Bondfield, Lawrence, Phillips and her successor as Chief Woman Officer, Mary Sutherland – had little sympathy for attempts to win special terms or concessions for women. They believed women should work their way up through the mainstream of the movement rather than construct artificial schemes designed to by-pass it. The traumatic events surrounding the fall of Macdonald's government in 1931 almost certainly strengthened the suspicion among party loyalists that special expedients to secure candidatures for women might be taken advantage of by feminists and the ILP or other left-wing organisations, thereby exacerbating the divisions within the party.

Such suspicions gained further force from the belief that women candidates would not bring any great strength to the party in the constituencies. In the solid working-class seats a woman was superfluous, and the men looked upon such seats as their reward for a lifetime's work for the movement. There was, however, a flaw in this thinking which presented a loophole for women. Though Labour's support grew fairly steadily between the wars it never exceeded the modest total of 37–38 per cent of the national vote. This was enough to make Labour the second party; but it was not going to win a majority in parliament on the basis of the safe working-class seats alone. What brought the party within reach of an overall majority in 1929 was a capacity to seize a number of constituencies in which industrial and rural districts, or working-class and middle-class communities were mixed up together. In such places Labour often went outside the ranks of trade unionism for its candidates. This provided opportunities for middle-class women such as Edith Picton-Turbervill to make their way into parliament. Although she joined the party in 1919 Picton-Turbervill had no real base in the movement and no solid record of support. Her public career developed from philanthropic and missionary work before the war which led her to the YMCA and to a wartime interest in the cause of peace and the advancement of women in the Church. She was invited to contest North Islington in 1922 and Stroud in 1924. In the following year she was selected as candidate in the

Wrekin in preference to a trade union official. She herself felt surprised at this, but there was logic behind the decision. The Wrekin, with its mixture of mining votes and agriculture, was winnable for Labour – but not very easily. As a staunch middle-class churchwoman, and an enthusiast for peace and moral reform Picton-Turbervill was ideally placed to attract the extra middle-class votes, especially those of former Liberals, which would give Labour the edge. No such claims could be made for the orthodox male trade unionist. Her emphatic victory in 1929 underlined the point. Similarly Mary Agnes Hamilton, a middle-class journalist and intellectual, added strength to Labour's ticket at Blackburn. Edith Summerskill was another who enjoyed no significant base in the party, but brought her known qualities as a practising doctor, local councillor and formidable intellect to the suburban seat of West Fulham which she won in 1938. The success scored by such women underlined how much both the women and the Labour Party stood to gain from fuller co-operation.

Women's Strategies as Parliamentary Candidates

Since the 1950s a number of studies have found that hostility by voters towards women candidates is very limited. A number of both men and women show a preference for a male candidate, but this hardly ever leads them to withhold their vote from a woman.[19] The fact is that misgivings about individual candidates, which are, of course, very widespread, pale into insignificance beside the loyalty to a national party. This is borne out by investigations of the performance of women in the general elections of 1966, 1970 and 1974 when there was actually very little difference between the votes polled by them and those of their male colleagues.[20] Even in by-elections, when interest often does focus upon individual candidates, electors do not generally appear to regard women candidates differently from men.[21]

Of course, these are comparatively recent findings. Things may well have been different in the 1920s when a woman parliamentarian was a great novelty. It might be expected that the backlash against feminists and flappers in this decade would have been reflected in parliamentary elections. But at this distance how are we to ascertain whether this was so? It is helpful in the first instance to consider what positive strategies women adopted in order to win votes and to deflect the anticipated criticism. In 1918, for example, female candidates, clearly apprehensive about men's emotional mood in the aftermath of war, made a point of drawing attention to the role of their male relatives in the armed forces, even to the extent of producing photographs of them in uniform. Even in 1922 Nancy Astor continued to emphasise her own war work in hospitals for servicemen.

However, this soon passed, though many women continued to be on the defensive. It evidently seemed wise to deny political ambition: 'I am not in public life for a career', announced Astor in 1919, 'I have six children and many interests.' Mrs Mabel Philipson frankly declared her intention of giving up her seat as soon as her husband was free to stand again, though in the event she remained an MP from 1923 to 1929 while he fought other seats.[22] Lady Cynthia Mosley employed a line of argument that was characteristic of Labour women:

> People said women's place was in the home and she quite agreed. That was the very reason why we should take an interest in politics ... politics were just the bread and butter of life.[23]

The practised woman orator – and there were many – also employed humour to disarm opposition before it got going. Thus Hilda Runciman:

> It is right and proper that women should agree with their husbands on all questions, but if you have Conservative husbands I implore you to think for yourselves.[24]

Ready humour was especially useful for the single woman who was all the more likely to be suspected of feminism. Thus Florence Horsbrugh found herself asked in 1931 whether she would be prepared to marry a man with only 15 shillings a week to live on:

> 'Ladies and gentlemen, I am sorry no one has asked me' [laughter]. There was a whispered message from a man in the front row and Miss Horsbrugh announced – 'I have just had a proposal of marriage. I think I am going to be rather cautious and ask [for] his proposal in writing in case there is any chance of breach of promise' [laughter].[25]

However, beneath the jocularity women candidates had to walk a tightrope; it was desirable to stimulate the interest of the women electors in coming out to vote for them, but not to the extent of frightening or alienating the men. A favourite method of dealing with this was simply to hold women-only meetings in addition to the normal 'public' ones. Mrs Runciman demonstrated her skill when addressing the men of the Newcastle Rotary Club in 1928. First she got them on her side by professing not to know what women's questions were, thereby establishing herself as a non-feminist. But she went on in her speech to argue that if it was intolerable for a young man to be *idle* (a good choice of word), so it was also for a young woman: tactically a judicious way of propagating the case for working women amongst men.[26]

Apart from Independents like Ray Strachey, hardly any women expounded feminist policies in their constituency campaigns: even the convinced feminists amongst them preferred to save their fire for parliament. For example, Ellen Wilkinson made no mention of equal pay in Jarrow in 1935, although in the following year she actually defeated the government on the issue in the Commons. The dangers are well illustrated by the early career of Edith Summerskill. As a young doctor she strongly supported birth control, and apparently found her views no particular drawback in local and parliamentary elections in London. But when she stood in Bury in 1935 she encountered formidable opposition from Catholic priests who presented an ultimatum: they would advise Catholics to vote against her unless she agreed to desist from giving birth control instruction to her patients.[27] She refused and suffered a heavy defeat. It is significant that Summerskill had not even raised the issue at Bury; one can easily appreciate how less determined candidates could be deterred.

Several of the early women candidates showed a degree of solidarity with their fellow women. For example, after Astor's election Labour women like Ethel Snowden and Edith Picton-Turbervill refused to stand against her on the grounds that she was doing good work for women and children. Astor and Mrs Wintringham, a Liberal and the second woman MP, exchanged telegrams of mutual support at elections. Both women supported Ray Strachey when she stood against a Tory anti-feminist MP in 1922. However, these signs of sex solidarity were typical of middle-class women only. Labour women who showed their feelings risked exposing themselves to charges of betraying the movement and the working class for middle-class feminism. By 1931 female solidarity had dwindled, in public at least, and party feelings ran too high for most women to risk stepping outside their party, though this was still easier within parliament than in the constituencies. The career of Irene Ward who defeated *two* women Labour MPs, Margaret Bondfield in 1931 and Grace Colman in 1950, gives a good indication of the priorities.

Successful women candidates employed three distinct strategies in this period. First there were those who played the traditional role as grand lady; only a handful could carry it off, but the careers of two Conservatives, Astor and Mrs Philipson, and the Labour recruit Lady Cynthia Mosley, are a reminder of the life that still remained in such an appeal. In her epic contest at Plymouth Sutton in 1919 Astor invoked a

whole series of expedients to avoid a defeat that might have set back the
political prospects of women very seriously. When Waldorf Astor's
succession to his father's viscountcy first became known it was
reported 'on good authority' that his brother Captain J. J. Astor would
be the new candidate. From the start it was understood that if Waldorf
could divest himself of the unwanted title he would stand again.[28] Thus
Nancy was put up as a stop-gap. This could be turned to advantage, for
Plymouth would be represented in *both* houses of parliament for a time.
For Nancy it was clearly important to establish the temporary nature of
her candidature because her hectoring style on the hustings could easily
have antagonised the male voters of Plymouth. She tempered her
assertiveness with humility, presenting herself as a wife doing her duty
for her husband; even in 1922, when she was not so obviously a mere
stop-gap, she continued to claim that she was carrying on her husband's
work. At the same time she put a distance between herself and
feminism. 'I am not standing before you as a sex candidate. I do not
believe in sexes or in classes.'[29] In this she was helped by a sympathetic
press which reminded voters that she had never been associated with
the campaign to win votes for women.[30]

Although the constituency had returned Waldorf with 66 per cent of
the poll in 1918 it was really only a marginal seat which he had won
back from the Liberals in 1910. Nancy was well known as a result of
her campaigns in the previous elections, and she followed Waldorf, as
a supporter of the Unionist Social Reform Committee, in making a
positive appeal to the working-class electors. Thus she could say with
some truth 'I stand as no party candidate', while yet enjoying the
official backing of the Lloyd George Coalition. She was a little lucky in
that the shine had not yet worn off the government in 1919, and
although Labour's vote increased sharply in 1919 the three-cornered
contest kept the anti-Tory vote divided. Her achievement in winning
with 51 per cent of the poll was, nonetheless, very impressive. The key
lay in her willingness to take the bull by the horns and allow her
personality to become the dominant issue. This was easier in a by-
election. The press focused their attention upon her. Hecklers gathered
in Plymouth expecting to force the lady candidate onto the defensive.
But this played into Astor's hands. Finding a long serious speech
irksome she enjoyed and benefited from frequent interruptions. They
enabled her to show her natural wit and sense of humour, thereby to win
a favourable press and put herself on the right side of the working-class
voters. As an experienced Primrose Leaguer herself Astor knew perfectly well that her wealth and title were no drawback in the con-

stituency provided she was frank and good humoured about it. The combination of wealth and title on the one hand with the common touch on the other proved irresistibly attractive to voters. Her appeal was not altogether unlike that of members of the royal family. She let people see clearly how grand a lady she was, offering them a figure about whose life they could romanticise; but at the same time she flattered them by putting herself in their hands, relying on her humanity and lack of pomposity to see her through. George Bernard Shaw summed up the strategy in 1929:

> In short, Nancy dear, let yourself rip and wear all your pearls: prudence is not your game; and if you ride hard for a fall you won't get it.[31]

Although this formula brought Astor success in seven elections it was not one that many women were able to emulate. Even in 1919 her election was seen as having only a limited significance; she and the circumstances were so extraordinary that no one could yet be sure about the acceptability of women candidates in general. 1919 was for Astor both the start and the climax of her career. By 1922 her efforts at controlling the drink trade had provoked an independent Conservative to stand against her. Thus her majority was quickly reduced, and if a Liberal had stood she might have lost the seat. In 1929 Labour ran her to within 200 votes of defeat. On the other hand it is most unlikely that Waldorf would have done better in Plymouth. Her combination of personality and political independence helped her to retain a seat which would have been beyond the grasp of an orthodox Conservative by 1929.

A variation on the theme of the grand lady was provided by Mrs Hilton Philipson who followed her husband as member for Berwick from 1923 to 1929. As Mabel Russell, a musical comedy star of the London stage before her marriage, she was very well known. She was seen as even more of a lightweight politician than Astor. 'Her speeches contain little of the reasoning power of the party politician', commented the *Berwick Advertiser* patronisingly, 'but after all how many of the women voters bother with the why and wherefore after they have made up their minds?'[32] Like Astor, Mrs Philipson boldly tackled the most deprived parts of her constituency, canvassing the Berwick slums enthusiastically; here she played her role as a real professional, throwing kisses to the crowds, winning photographs in the national press, and flattering the obscure inhabitants by drawing them into the limelight with her. She, too, scored a by-election triumph with 55 per cent of the poll in a three-cornered contest, but went on to see her majority slashed later; here too one suspects that the seat would have been lost by a more orthodox Conservative in the 1920s.

Labour also had its grand ladies such as the Countess of Warwick who fought the hopelessly Tory seat of Warwick and Leamington in 1923. The most conspicuous success was Lady Cynthia Mosley, daughter of Lord Curzon and wife of Sir Oswald Mosley, who gained a seat at Stoke-on-Trent in 1929. Even the *Woman's Leader* could not suppress a gasp at her adoption in 1925: 'we have seldom contemplated a more whimsical turn of the social and political wheel than that which is signified by this interesting candidature'. Titled and rich, Lady Cynthia might have felt obliged to sink herself totally in her new party. But she wisely rejected the temptation to be anything other than herself. In photographs of the Labour women MPs she stands out as elegant, fashionable and smartly dressed – rivalled only by Mary Agnes Hamilton – with a large fox fur draped around her shoulders. Naturally her opponents in Stoke played to what they assumed to be her weakness. She was derided as a 'Dollar Princess' on account of the wealth inherited from her American maternal grandfather. Both she and Sir Oswald were easily ridiculed: What did they have to do with labour? Were they really socialists?[33] But Lady Cynthia was articulate and capable on the platform; she had already assisted her husband in his Birmingham campaigns. To her critics she replied that she took all the money she could get hold of out of the United States and either invested it in Britain or gave it to the Labour Party. 'I am one of the most lucky ones in the country and I am not satisfied with things as they are. Surely to goodness if I am not satisfied, then the millions who live in squalid and miserable conditions are not.'[34] As in Astor's case the working-class audiences took to her, and as the campaign wore on it was her opponent who found himself struggling to cope with hostile heckling. In the event Lady Cynthia scored what is probably the most impressive victory by any woman between the wars. She increased the Labour vote from 13,000 to 26,000, raised the turnout from 75 to 81 per cent, and was elected with a majority of nearly 8000. Moreover she enjoyed none of the advantages of other women MPs. Far from stepping into her husband's seat, she faced a well-entrenched sitting member, in a general election rather than a by-election. One local newspaper specu-lated that 'many of the flappers were doubtless flattered by the oppor-tunity of voting for a lady of title and wealth', which may well have been the case, though the size of the victory suggests that the men must have been equally keen. The traditional fondness for a rich and influential MP who might somehow be able to help a town's industry was by no means dead. Nor were the Mosleys quite as exotic in the 1920s as some comment suggests. At this time Labour was acquiring many wealthy, upper middle-class supporters with an impeccable Establishment background. Amongst Ponsonbys, Trevelyans and Stracheys, Cynthia and Oswald were hardly out of place, and their popularity with the rank and file of the party was immense as the election of Mosley and Trevelyan to the National Executive shows.

Clearly the special qualifications of social status and personality which helped the Astors and Mosleys were not available to the majority of women. We must therefore turn to a second strategy which was much more typical of this period. By basing themselves squarely on the conventional role of women as wives and mothers many women candidates sought effectively to deflect criticism from men and also to evoke some mingled sympathy and pride from fellow women. The wife who came forward as a candidate in order to continue her husband's work as a result of his death, illness, ennoblement or unseating could be represented as admirable because she was acting out of a sense of duty and loyalty, not political ambition. There is some evidence that Mrs Wintringham, Mrs Philipson and Mrs Runciman all derived some sympathy from such emotions. Clearly most women adopted something of the wife-and-mother stance. Even, or perhaps especially, those who were actually unmarried invariably interested themselves in housing, slum clearance, milk and food, infant mortality and education questions. This was true of single Labour women who were numerous in the 1920s, and also of the single Conservatives such as Horsbrugh, Ward and Cazalet.

Several candidates, however, seem to have exploited the wifely role with particular effect, two of whom, Margaret Wintringham and Hilda Runciman, will be considered here. Wintringham, the second woman MP, fought a by-election in Louth in 1921 following the death of her husband who had himself gained the seat as a Liberal only the previous year at a by-election. She faced a difficult task, being opposed for the first time by a Labour candidate who was bound to split her husband's vote; her Conservative opponent posed as an Anti-Waste candidate and she was criticised as unsuitable to represent an agricultural seat. In the event she held most of the Liberal vote and retained the seat with a reduced majority. Her success was widely regarded as more significant than that of Astor because she was a more typical party figure, with no special advantages, coping with a tight three-cornered contest in an area which was rather remote from the world of feminism. If she could win, so could others; there was now 'an optimistic feeling that the Louth election establishes a custom'.[35]

The key to Mrs Wintringham's success lay in the fact that she was a feminist who could not easily be attacked for feminism. Before her marriage she had had a career as a schoolteacher; she was an active member of NUSEC and became president of the Louth Women's Citizens Association. This connection brought her several leading NUSEC speakers for the by-election and a body of 25 extra canvassers.[36] But she was also well known locally and enjoyed access to two important local networks. In 1920 she had been co-opted onto the County Agricultural Committee by the farmers, and she also enjoyed a prominent position as secretary to the Lindsey Federation of Women's Institutes. In fact Mrs Wintringham epitomised the WI image of the motherly woman, though she had no children herself. Reporters who covered the campaign clearly felt that the rapid spread of the WIs had quickened women's interest in politics, a development which Mrs Wintringham was perfectly placed to exploit and the unexpectedly large turnout by women voters in the villages was noted as a sign of her success.[37] In complete contrast to Astor she kept a low profile during the campaign. Partly because of her recent bereavement, and also because of poor health, she made no public speeches until a week before the poll. This, however, served only to underline her position as a faithful upholder of her husband's cause. She retained Louth in 1922 and 1923, losing in 1924 and only narrowly failing to regain it in 1929. As a reassuringly motherly figure Mrs Wintringham clearly contributed to breaking down prejudice and promoting the idea that women could be an asset to their party.

A different but more striking case was that of Hilda Runciman, wife of the former cabinet minister, Walter Runciman, who fought a by-election at St Ives in Cornwall in 1928. She faced a complicated situation. Walter had been elected at Swansea in 1924 but, anticipating defeat, he arranged to be adopted by the Liberals of St Ives for the next election. Obligation to his constituency and to the national party, however, dictated that he should not resign and cause a by-election in Swansea. This careful plan was nearly upset by the elevation of the sitting Conservative member for St Ives as a judge. Thereupon Hilda Runciman was adopted on the clear understanding that, if elected, she would stand down in her husband's favour at the general election which was expected within a year. Although the seat had been Liberal as recently as 1923, it had been lost to the Tories in 1924 in a straight fight; in the by-election the appearance of a Labour candidate threatened a further loss of votes. Then there was the additional complication of Walter Runciman's bad relations with the party leader, Lloyd George.

The latter was not even invited to speak at the by-election, and opponents naturally played on this in order to divide the Liberal vote. Above all it could not escape notice that the St Ives constituency was, in a sense, being made a convenience of by the Runciman family.

Yet Hilda Runciman gained the seat for her party. This feat was accomplished by deliberately seizing upon the unusual family situation which lay at the back of her candidature and turning it from a liability into an advantage. Naturally she could be presented as a loyal wife helping to rescue her husband from an invidious position. But the domestic strategy went beyond this. Walter, already a familiar speaker in the constituency, was so much in evidence on the platform expressing views identical to those of his wife, that the electors were, in effect, invited to vote for a husband-and-wife ticket. After the victory one local newspaper observed that 'husband and wife are virtually joint members for this part of West Cornwall'. But the campaign also featured Sir Walter Runciman, an ex-MP and the father-in-law of the candidate, and no fewer than four of her five children, including the future historian Steven Runciman. This invasion by seven family members spanning three generations of Runcimans was of immense practical help in handling the huge number of meetings required in a constituency where voters were scattered in innumerable villages and hamlets. But, as photographs in the local press show, it also enabled Mrs Runciman's candidature to be transformed from a mere manoeuvre into a great moral good: a united, loyal family dedicated to a cause and a constituency.[38] As a result she escaped criticism either as a stop-gap or as a woman candidate. It should be added that Hilda Runciman never hid behind her family. On the contrary she actively dispelled any doubts by her skill and confidence as a speaker and canvasser. She was, in fact, an experienced performer on temperance platforms and as president of the Women's Liberal Federation, and proved more adept than her Tory opponent at handling questions from the floor.[39] She had won a first class degree in history at Cambridge, been elected to the Newcastle School Board and been appointed a JP. Thus, despite her professed lack of political ambition, Mrs Runciman was a true professional, and in the by-election she clearly managed the trick of reassuring the men while also stimulating the women to turn out to vote in large numbers.[40] Though urged by the women Liberals of St Ives to stand again, she honoured her promise to withdraw; in 1929 she almost gained a seat at Tavistock while Walter was returned safely in St Ives.

The third strategy commonly resorted to by women candidates was the most obvious one of all: to immerse themselves so deeply in the orthodox appeal and policies of their party that their gender was reduced to insignificant proportions in the eyes of the electors. This was characteristically, though by no means exclusively, the tactics adopted by Labour candidates. This was partly because, as we have noticed, many of their candidates in the 1920s were single women and therefore more vulnerable in male, and indeed female, eyes to accusations of feminism; they could not so easily cover themselves in a defensive blanket of motherhood or wifely devotion. In addition the Labour women were more completely professional politicians whose life was bound up with the Labour movement to a degree that was unusual amongst Conservative or Liberal candidates. They tended to have a more carefully worked out ideological position, which sometimes left little room for feminism and, moreover, had enough political nous and single-mindedness to know that they would only jeopardise their prospects of ultimate success in the party if they indulged too much in women's politics. Margaret Bondfield, Susan Lawrence and Marion Phillips are, in spite of their personality differences, all classic examples of this approach.

Bondfield had risen by years of painstaking effort through the trade union movement, and by 1918 had reached the point where male union leaders were prepared to accept her as an honorary man. She was so deeply imbued with the ideology of the movement that she posed no threat; indeed her own modesty took the form of self-abasement: 'I am merely the product of the work of hundreds of thousands of unknown names' she declared. This sense of priorities was consistently reflected in Bondfield's campaigns. At Northampton in 1923 and 1924 she concentrated on the two standard issues – tariffs and the capital levy. At Wallsend in 1926 she immersed herself in the coal industry, a necessary precaution in view of the recent strike and the fact that a majority of voters had connections with the industry.[41] But in her later campaigns at Wallsend from 1926 to 1935 she neither drew attention to her gender nor took up any of the women's issues; everything was subordinated to the orthodox party line.

Such remarks apply with even greater force to Marion Phillips, the member for Sunderland in 1929, for she had a more distinct personality than Bondfield. As a full-time employee of the party from 1918 it was no doubt inevitable that she should reflect the official policies and priorities closely. As a candidate she came nearest to making an appeal to women with her speeches on housing and infant death rates. Rather unusually Phillips' feminism was tested at a public meeting organised by the National Union of Teachers at the 1929 election. This would not have posed a great problem but for the fact that there was another woman candidate, a Liberal who made a distinctly feminist appeal on the question of equal pay and employment for married women. Yet Phillips remained unmoved at the danger of being outflanked. In spite of the interest of women teachers in the marriage bar, she ignored the whole question of married women's work and simply reiterated the party programme.[42]

In some ways Susan Lawrence was the most striking of the early Labour women MPs. Very tall, with short, cropped hair, severe dress and a monocle, her appearance had stunned her first working-class audiences, while her upper-class accent reduced them to laughter. Yet in the course of six elections in East Ham she became a familiar figure ('Our Susan') and was so much a part of the national party establishment that she effectively lost what distinctive appeal, or weakness, she might have had as a woman. Like any national leader she concentrated on the major questions of the day: in 1923 this meant the capital levy and the Chanak crisis. She even boasted after her victory in that year: 'I did not make any direct appeal to the electorate as a woman!'[43] In 1924 she focused on the controversy over the Russian Treaties, and although she advocated widows' pensions and equal franchise she did this because they were now part of the official programme; they received no special prominence.

Several women of the other parties showed themselves equally adept at mastering the questions of the day. Megan Lloyd George, for example, eschewed women's politics and stood as a faithful disciple of her father. Among the Conservatives Lady Iveagh took over the Guinness family seat at Southend in 1927 as a loyal Baldwinite and remained the classic inconspicuous backbencher during her parliamentary career. In her first contest in 1923 the Duchess of Atholl took up the official Baldwinite line on tariff reform, though it nearly cost her the seat. In 1924 she concentrated on the Russian Treaties, the Campbell Case, imperial preference and unemployment like any male Tory. In both 1924 and 1929 she made no reference to women's questions except those which Baldwin himself had taken up or promised to tackle in the future.[44] Her consistent position during the 1920s was that the chief issues – trade and unemployment – affected the sexes equally. As with Bondfield, Lawrence and Phillips the duchess's orthodoxy was in part a reflection of her membership of the government. But it is also clear that her neglect of most women's questions was, like theirs, a sign of her own lack of sympathy both with feminist issues in particular and with women's politics in general. Like Lawrence she was chiefly interested in the central political topics of the day and, with her command of detail and argument, felt no inhibition in tackling them. Although supported by the duke she did not inherit his seat – he had ceased to be the member in 1917. Moreover the duchess was more intelligent, better educated and more interested in politics than he; she emerged as an independent person in her own right.

Of course, in identifying three strategies adopted by women one is simplifying the situation. Clearly many of the women combined a variety of tactics in their campaigns in order to maximise their appeal. While Atholl and Iveagh, for example, have been characterised here as orthodox party figures, they inevitably had something of the grand lady about them; nonetheless, neither had the flamboyance and personality of an Astor or a Philipson. Astor, for her part, while playing her grand lady's role also devoted much attention to the mother-and-child politics that came naturally to less socially elevated candidates. Bondfield, though well versed in party orthodoxy, and unmarried, nonetheless came across to some as a typical married woman, a person of 'homely common sense', and this won sympathy from both sexes.[45] Conversely Hilda Runciman, while capitalising on her role as the family woman, proved to be a highly orthodox – in a Gladstonian sense – advocate of free trade, temperance, retrenchment and peace.

Finally there is little evidence that constituencies lost sympathy with their women MPs because they were women. A few attracted criticism for neglecting their local base. Jennie Lee, for example, was considered to be concentrating too much on becoming a national political figure. Megan Lloyd George was criticised for not buying a farm in Anglesey and for spending too much time in Surrey. And the Duchess of Atholl was attacked for making too many visits to Spain and central Europe, though this was during the 1930s when she had already become a rebel on foreign policy. While women may have been a little more vulnerable than men to this line of criticism, they nonetheless appear on the whole to have held onto their seats as effectively as men. Conservative women lost ground in 1923 and 1929, and Labour women in 1931, in line with their party's national performance. But the question must be asked whether there is evidence that the parties suffered defeats that might be attributable to the sex of their candidates.

The most likely area for this would be in constituencies held by men but subsequently lost to another party when they were succeeded by female candidates. In fact there were only four possibilities between the wars. The first was in 1922 when Lady Cooper narrowly failed to retain Walsall which her husband, Sir Richard Cooper, had won as a Conservative in 1918. At the time her prospects must have seemed good. Astor's success may have influenced the local party to believe that a wife who stepped into her husband's shoes – Sir Richard retired through ill health – would be regarded as admirable and loyal. Like Astor Lady Cooper disclaimed any personal ambition. She was well known for her charitable work and from previous election campaigns. She even echoed Astor in emphasising that if elected she would vote according to her conscience on social questions.[46] She was apparently regarded as a good candidate and not subject to criticism as a woman. However, Walsall was a marginal seat, won only narrowly by the Conservatives in 1910; their 1918 victory was a poor guide. What upset Lady Cooper in 1922 was the appearance of a strong local Liberal candidate who succeeded in drawing off much of the Labour vote and repeating this success in 1923. This rearrangement of the non-Tory vote rather than the candidate's sex accounts for Lady Cooper's defeat; the Conservative share of the poll remained virtually constant at 37–8 per cent at three consecutive elections from 1922 to 1924; Lady Cooper's male successors won no more support than she did.

The 1929 election produced two losses by women candidates. One occurred in South Hackney where a Miss M. Gibbon inherited a Liberal seat but was pushed into third place. However, this was not surprising. She had come up against the formidable Herbert Morrison. Moreover, the seat had been won by Labour in 1923 in a three-cornered contest; the Liberal gain in 1924 occurred only because the Conservatives withdrew and most of their vote went to the Liberals. The reappearance of a Conservative in 1929 sealed the Liberals' fate regardless of their candidate. Also in 1929 a Miss M. Beavan lost as a Conservative in Liverpool Everton. This too was not surprising. The survival of traditional sectarian loyalties had enabled the Conservatives to hold on in the post-war period. But from 1922 Labour steadily improved its share of the poll, coming within a few hundred votes of victory by 1924. It seems unlikely that a male Tory would have done better than Miss Beavan in 1929. The fourth example of a woman who lost a seat formerly held by a man of her party was Mrs Jean Mann who was defeated in Dr Robert Forgan's seat in West Renfrewshire in 1931. However, Labour had won the seat in 1929 by a small majority in a four-cornered contest. In 1931 Forgan stood again as a National government candidate and a Labour defeat was almost a foregone conclusion.

It is possible that some women failed to gain seats for their party in which a male candidate would have performed significantly better. However, any such claims would be rather speculative. The most likely

example is that of Mrs Barton as Labour candidate at King's Norton in
Birmingham (page 168). Beyond this the women MPs do not appear to
have been any more vulnerable once elected than the men of their party.
Those who enjoyed safe seats held on to them. Amongst the Liberals
the defeats in 1924 of Lady Terrington who had remarkably won High
Wycombe in 1923, and Mrs Wintringham who had been struggling with
the marginal Louth, were not unexpected. On the Labour side the
defeats suffered by women MPs in 1924 conformed to a pattern. Their
vote diminished only marginally, but in three-cornered contests a
redistribution of votes from Liberal to Conservative sealed their fate.
The loss of all the Labour women in 1931 simply reflected the fact that
none of them enjoyed the really safe seat that was necessary in order to
survive the landslide to the National government. For the Conservative
women the 1935 election provided the severest test. The defeat of Mrs
Runge at Rotherhithe, Mrs Copeland at Stoke, Mrs Shaw at Bothwell,
Miss Graves at South Hackney and Mrs Ward at Cannock was in line
with the experience of male colleagues in such difficult constituencies;
perhaps more significant was the success of Miss Ward in retaining
Wallsend, Miss Horsbrugh at Dundee and Miss Cazalet at East Islington in spite of the national trend against their party. In general there is
little sign that women MPs were unduly vulnerable.

In recent times there have been a few attempts to assess whether
female candidates as a group do better or worse than men at general
elections. For example a study of their performances in the 1955 and
1959 elections found that while there was an average national swing of
1.2 per cent in favour of the Conservatives, the swing in seats where a
woman Conservative replaced a male was only 0.4 per cent and where
a male Conservative replaced a woman it was 1.6 per cent on average.
For Labour and Liberal candidates no difference between candidates of
the two sexes was found.[47] This suggested that prejudice against
women existed only amongst Conservative supporters, and that even
there it was worth no more than around 300 votes to the party in each
constituency. Unfortunately the value of all such broad comparisons of
relative performance is questionable because the seats contested by
women are not representative of the seats contested by their parties as a
whole. In order to make a fair comparison it would be necessary to set
women candidates' performance alongside their male colleagues in
constituencies that were very similar in terms of the level of party
strength, social class, regional characteristics or other qualities. However, there is inevitably an element of arbitrary judgement in adopting
such criteria; moreover, the number of really comparable seats would

be very small, and the results therefore of rather limited significance.

However, during the inter-war period there existed one category of constituencies in which the major objections do not apply. This is the two-member borough in which a male and female candidate of the *same* party stood in tandem at the same election. In such a case all factors are controlled for with the exception of the gender of the candidate and the kind of appeal he or she made to the electors. Here we have the best basis for comparing the relative performance of the two sexes.

In the constituencies of Blackburn, Brighton, Derby, Dundee, Norwich, Oldham and Sunderland there was a total of 16 elections between the wars in which male and female candidates ran in harness. (Two of the cases were in Dundee where a Conservative woman, Florence Horsbrugh, ran in alliance with a National Liberal male, Dingle Foot.) In every case but two the male and female candidates were either both new to the constituency or both incumbents, therefore neither had an advantage as the better known figure. In the 16 cases male candidates performed better than their female colleagues on nine occasions and the women performed better on seven occasions. Two qualifications should be made, however. One is that four of the nine elections in which a man did better were in Norwich. The other is that the difference between the candidates was, in most cases, a slight one, usually a matter of a few hundred votes. The chief conclusion to be drawn from the voting figures is that party loyalty was overwhelmingly the most important factor and that the gender of the candidates was, at most, of only marginal significance. The point is underlined by a typical example from Sunderland in 1929 (see Table 6.3). As the final result shows, the election produced a rather tight win for Labour, and it was therefore of no little importance that the party should poll its full strength for *both* candidates. Clearly the overwhelming majority of Labour's 31,000 or so votes came from electors who split their votes between the party's two candidates. Any discontent with a woman among Labour supporters might have manifested itself in a substantial number 'plumping' for Smith alone; but only 370 did so, even fewer than those who 'plumped' for Phillips. Alternatively male Labour supporters might have split their vote with another party. Smith picked up a total of 1113 split votes, but of these 799 were with the two Liberals; this suggests a residual Lib–Lab sentiment rather than hostility towards women, especially as a majority of these splits were with the Liberal *woman* candidate. Marion Phillips led her Labour colleague because she acquired more split votes than he did – a total of 1781. Since 970 of these were splits with the other woman candidate,

Elizabeth Morgan, there is a suggestion of a distinct, if small, women's vote. However, Phillips also picked up a substantial number of splits with the male Liberal. In all 1589 of her 1781 split votes were with the two Liberals, and one is therefore inclined to see the electors' behaviour more in terms of the Lib–Lab tradition in Sunderland than in terms of feminism.

In contrast to the Sunderland elections there are several cases where there was a gap of some significance between the male and female candidates, notably in Dundee, Derby, Oldham, Blackburn and Norwich. On closer inspection Dundee appears the least significant. Although the woman Conservative and the male National Liberal represented the National government in 1931 they ran separate campaigns

Table 6.3   Voting in Sunderland, 1929 General Election

Result		
	Dr Marion Phillips (Lab.)	31,794
	A. Smith (Lab.)	31,085
	Sir W. Raine (Con.)	29,180
	L. Thompson (Con.)	28,937
	Dr Elizabeth Morgan (Lib.)	21,300
	Sir J. Pratt (Lib.)	21,142
Splits		
	Phillips and Smith	29,602
	Phillips and Pratt	619
	Phillips and Morgan	970
	Phillips and Thompson	59
	Phillips and Raine	133
	Smith and Morgan	427
	Smith and Pratt	372
	Smith and Raine	146
	Smith and Thompson	168
	Raine and Thompson	28,371
	Raine and Pratt	155
	Raine and Morgan	79
	Pratt and Morgan	19,525
	Pratt and Thompson	113
	Thompson and Morgan	59
Plumpers		
	Phillips	441
	Smith	370
	Raine	296
	Thompson	167
	Morgan	240
	Pratt	358

Electorate: 101,875
Turnout: 80.2%

and the male benefited from the residual Liberal strength in the town. In Oldham in 1922 one of the Liberals, Lady Emmott, ran 3626 votes behind her male colleague (7.0 per cent to his 11.1 per cent); this was the largest gap in any election. On the face of it she enjoyed the advantage of being well known locally and the wife of a former Liberal member for the town, Alfred Emmott. However, the key to Lady Emmott's relatively poor performance lies in the presence of Sir Edward Grigg, a National Liberal who supported the Lloyd George Coalition. He exploited the divided loyalties of Liberal voters. In the event a large minority of Liberals split their vote for the male Liberal and Grigg; this group was seven times as large as the group that split for Grigg and Lady Emmott. One cannot easily divine the thinking of the electors here. It is clear – from the fact that very few Liberals plumped for a single candidate – that many wanted to promote the reunion of the party still divided between Asquith and Lloyd George. To vote for a representative of each wing of liberalism was a practical way of expressing that. But why favour one Independent Liberal over the other? It seems that Lady Emmott was adopted shortly before the poll and after the male candidate; to some Liberals this may well have seemed an unnecessary extra candidature which would only have the effect of postponing party reunion. Moreover, Lady Emmott was not only a woman candidate but, up to a point, a feminist one. This is clear from her speeches to the local Women's Citizens Association and her willingness publicly to advocate the full NUSEC programme. Afterwards she herself concluded that Oldham did not want a woman.[48] A similar situation developed at Derby in 1924 where one Conservative, Mrs Hulse, came 3700 votes behind her male colleague (20.3 per cent to his 23.8 per cent). This appears significant in that Sir Richard Luce was elected for the Conservatives along with Labour's J.H. Thomas. The explanation is partly that Luce received 1000 'plumpers' whereas Mrs Hulse had fewer than 100 – surely a sign of some resistance to her candidature amongst Conservative supporters? 'I had a feeling that my own party were not keen on supporting a woman', she said afterwards.[49] In addition Mrs Hulse picked up few split votes whereas Luce won 3000 – mostly with the Liberals – which put him narrowly ahead of the second Labour candidate. However, since the Conservatives were clearly not the largest party in Derby it cannot be argued that they failed to win the second seat because they had a woman candidate; a second Conservative man might have polled more strongly but not well enough to have won. As with the Oldham Liberals there was a case for saying that the Derby Tories should have run a single candidate, especially as only one Liberal was standing; and as a result Mrs Hulse attracted some dissatisfaction as an unnecessary addition.

One turns to Blackburn as a constituency in which a woman did notably well. In 1924, 1929 and 1931 Mary Agnes Hamilton stood alongside T.H. Gill, the president of the National Railway Clerks Association. The original plan had been to adopt Sir Oswald Mosley, but as he withdrew to Birmingham Mary Hamilton was brought in as the second candidate. As a graduate of Newnham College, an author and journalist she broadened the party ticket effectively. In order to counter any working-class hostility it was emphasised in Blackburn that she was a 'working journalist' who supported herself after the death of her husband. The Labour Party's verdict on the experiment was that there was no prejudice against a woman.[50] This is borne out by the closeness of the two candidates' poll. Only 200 voters 'plumped' for either Hamilton or Gill, and they picked up a similar number of split votes. However, Hamilton ran consistently ahead of Gill, and in 1929 when both were elected, she out-polled him by 1500 votes. She had only a few more 'plumpers' than Gill, but did significantly better on the splits. Split voting was the more likely since the Conservatives and Liberals ran only one candidate each in 1929. In the Labour–Liberal splits she was ahead of Gill by 800, and in the Labour–Conservative splits ahead by 500 votes (see Table 6.4). Here is an indication of a distinct, if modest, women's vote. Certainly there was scope for it in

Table 6.4 Voting in Blackburn, 1929 General Election

Result				
	Mrs M.A. Hmilton (Lab.)	37,256		
	T.H. Gill (Lab.)	35,723		
	Sir S.H.H. Henn (Con.)	35,249		
	Viscount Erleigh (Lib.)	34,504		
Plumpers				
	Hamilton	479		
	Gill	290		
	Henn	5,440		
	Erleigh	2,719		
Splits				
	Hamilton and Gill	33,697	Electorate	86,354
	Hamilton and Erleigh	2,103	Turnout	82.6%
	Gill and Erleigh	1,293		
	Hamilton and Henn	977		
	Gill and Henn	443		
	Henn and Erleigh	28,389		

Blackburn where the female share of the electorate rose from 44.5 per cent in 1928 to 55.4 per cent in 1929, which was well above the national average. Since the women of these textile towns were, to an unusual degree, working women and accustomed to trade union and political involvement they seem likely to have responded positively to Mary Hamilton. She herself was clearly an able candidate. Well versed in economics and interested in international affairs, she freely tackled the main issues of the 1929 campaign – unemployment and peace. She also went out of her way to propagate Labour's ideas on matters of interest to women – slum clearance, rent restrictions, improvements in maternity benefits and grants to supply milk for nursing mothers.[51] In this way Mary Hamilton showed how a woman could be advantageous to the Labour Party. She succeeded in treading a careful line by making an appeal to women but remaining sufficiently orthodox to avoid antagonising men. As a middle-class professional she could extend the party's votes a little beyond that of the standard male candidate.

A very similar electoral situation existed in Norwich, but here the outcome was different. In four consecutive elections from 1923 to 1931 the Labour Party nominated W.R. Smith, an official of the Boot and Shoe Operatives Union, with Dorothy Jewson, a middle-class professional woman. Both were well known locally. By 1923 Labour appears to have been the largest single party in Norwich and therefore stood to win the two seats; but it was not the majority and could therefore only expect to make a clean sweep if it polled the full party strength behind each candidate. In this situation the Conservatives and Liberals wisely ran a single candidate each from 1924 onwards. In the event both Labour candidates were elected in their first contest in 1923 when facing two Liberals and two Conservatives. In every election, however, Dorothy Jewson polled fewer votes than Smith. In 1923 the gap was only 700, but it steadily widened to 1800 in 1924, when both were defeated, and to 2600 in 1929. In that year Smith was elected and Jewson defeated. This appears to be a result of some significance. Only a few hundred electors plumped for either Jewson or Smith, but the latter prospered greatly from split votes, especially with the Liberal. Now there are obviously two explanations for this feature. One is that the Labour–Liberal splits were essentially Liberals who preferred a male Labour candidate to either a Conservative or a female Labour candidate. However, even in 1923 the Independent Liberal vote in Norwich was not very high, and there must be a suspicion that much of the split vote was that of Labour supporters who felt reluctant to vote for Jewson. She was clearly not handicapped by the structure of the electorate, for Norwich was rather like Blackburn in that the female share of the electorate had risen from 45.0 to 54.8 per cent. Jewson, however, was a different candidate from Hamilton and this seems to have been reflected in the widening gap between her and the male Labour candidate. At this time a single woman, Dorothy Jewson emerges both as a more convinced feminist than most Labour women, and as one who was *seen* to be feminist. An active suffragette before 1914, she became president of the Worker's Birth Control Group during the inter-war period. During her brief term in parliament she raised the question of birth control, and at both the Labour Women's Conferences and the party conferences she played a leading role in urging the party to include the provision of information on birth control in its policy. As a result of her adherence to feminist views she was nominated in 1931 not as a Labour but as an ILP candidate in Norwich. There appears to be no way of explaining Dorothy Jewson's relatively poor, and deteriorating, performance at Norwich apart from her reputation as a feminist candidate. It would be an exaggeration to suggest that the second seat was lost to Labour because of her candidacy since the tactics of Labour's opponents made it very difficult for the party to pull off a double victory. Nonetheless she clearly did not represent an asset.

From the experience of women such as Dorothy Jewson and Edith Summerskill at Bury there seems some reason for thinking that a woman candidate was at a disadvantage if she appeared to be a

Table 6.5 Voting in Norwich 1929 General Election

Result				
	G.H. Shakespeare (Lib.)	33,974		
	W.R. Smith (Lab.)	33,690		
	Miss D. Jewson (Lab.)	31,040		
	J.G. Fairfax (Con.)	30,793		
Plumpers				
	Shakespeare	3,123		
	Fairfax	2,676		
	Smith	366		
	Jewson	280		
Splits				
	Smith and Jewson	30,028	Electorate	82,143
	Smith and Shakespeare	2,846	Turnout	78.8%
	Jewson and Shakespeare	535		
	Smith and Fairfax	450		
	Jewson and Fairfax	197		
	Shakespeare and Fairfax	27,470		

feminist. Since, however, most women either were not particularly feminist or, if they were, took adequate measures to avoid being so identified in their constituencies, this was not a general problem for women during the 1920s and 1930s. Outside the two-member boroughs where tactical considerations sometimes militated against a second candidate, there is very little evidence that women proved vote losers for their parties. On the whole they seem to have done as well as their male colleagues and a number of women scored notable successes, especially in by-elections when they came under close scrutiny. One is driven to the general conclusion that even in this early period the prejudice against women was more a feature of the local party committees than of the electorate at large.

Women's Careers as Backbench MPs

By 1987, when the number of women MPs reached a peak of 41, the House of Commons had made no significant modifications to take account of the female presence. Parliament remains a men's – rather than a gentlemen's – club, grossly deficient in proper working facilities; its hours of business are bizarre; and its year continues to be dictated by the urge to rise every August for the start of the shooting season. Between the wars it must have seemed an uncomfortable and unwelcoming place for many of the women members. Although 36 women were elected, there were never more than 15 in the House in any one parliament. Consequently it proved difficult to make a major impact among 615 MPs. The acclaim invariably given to each maiden speech by a woman was sometimes just a polite veneer with which the parliamentary misogynists covered their resentment. After Astor's first victory Neville Chamberlain reported (to his wife): 'the melancholy news was circulated that that was the last day on which Parliament would sit without a woman MP'. Even in 1924 the Conservatives' victory celebrations were dampened for members of the Carlton Club where 'Lady Astor's success was greeted with stony silence'. The Commons, so Edith Summerskill concluded, was rather like 'a boys' school that had decided to take a few girls'.[52] As late as 1946 the rowdy inmates wolf-whistled Lady Tweedsmuir when she took her seat. Not surprisingly, the first women members found it difficult to participate fully in the social life and gossip of the bars, the smoking rooms and the members' cloakroom. Women were not supposed to penetrate these sanctuaries, and in any case, some had no wish to do so. However, to be denied access to the club life had political implications, for this was the sphere in which the Parliamentary Private Secretary picked up information for his minister, and the PPS had his foot on the first rung of the ladder that led to office.

Finding the right balance between conformity and individualism proved difficult, as Nancy Astor's career shows. The hostility towards her brought out her aggression. She had to fight to establish a regular seat in the chamber, and in 1938 Summerskill was astounded to see her belabouring Winston Churchill, who was sitting in front of her, about the head with her order paper.[53] Yet she confined herself to the chamber and her own room. It was left to later members such as Ellen Wilkinson to roam the smoking rooms and dining rooms where the men congregated. The experience and the reaction clearly varied according to personality and temperament. Even after 1931 Thelma Cazalet thought, 'there was still something slightly freakish about a woman MP, and I frequently saw male colleagues pointing me out to their friends as though I were a sort of giant panda'.[54] Leah Manning, who also entered the House in 1931, got off to a bad start by delivering a controversial maiden speech, an unintended offence to parliamentary convention.[55] On the other hand a confident middle-class woman like Edith Summerskill declined to be intimidated, and found it easy to make friendly contacts around the House; she also won an early battle by insisting on taking her seat in her maiden name.[56] Similarly Cynthia Mosley operated freely, especially when building up support for her husband and his views on the economy: 'we should have written off "Tom" much sooner but for her', observed Mary Agnes Hamilton.[57]

At a purely practical level the Commons was not an easy place for women members to work in. However, the inadequate rooms and secretarial facilities afflicted most backbenchers, male or female. The ladies were allocated one room plus a dressing room; in the latter stood a wash stand, a tin basin, a jug of cold water and a bucket.[58] It must have been a shock for the working-class members to see the spartan conditions which the aristocracy endured at this time. When the Duchess of Atholl changed her dress she was obliged to 'present her back to the half-open door to enable her maid, standing in the corridor, to fasten numerous small buttons which only the maid's practised hand could manipulate'.[59]

Several of the ladies coped rather better because of the presence of male relations. Husband-and-wife teams included Sir Oswald and Lady Cynthia Mosley, Walter and Hilda Runciman, Hugh and Ruth Dalton and William and Jennie Adamson; the Adamsons travelled up daily from their south London home from 1938 onwards. From 1929 Megan Lloyd George worked closely with her father, while Victor and Thelma Cazalet formed a brother-and-sister team from 1931. The difficulties faced by a woman who wished to play the conventional role in her family no doubt deterred many from even seeking election at all. But in the 1920s and 1930s this was a less common problem than it has been for later generations. Nearly all the women then were either single, or childless wives, or had grown-up children. Cynthia Mosley was the main exception to this. Some of Astor's children were also young, and there were occasions when their ill-health took her away from the House. However, all these women enjoyed access to a large staff of servants, nannies and governesses. Edith Summerskill managed to sustain her professional career, her London home and her London constituency with the aid of a young Scots nanny who cared for the children; each evening she would ring up from the Commons to keep in touch with their progress.

Yet the most difficult aspect of parliamentary life for the early women members was not the practical problems so much as the patronising attitude of many men towards them. Male pride led some to cling to their belief in woman as a fragile flower ill-equipped for politics. During a 22½ hour sitting in December 1933, for example, the six Conservative women sat stoically throughout the night enfolded in their fur coats; but at 4.30 a.m. they had to endure a Labour member's proposal for adjournment on the grounds that they were like washed out rags and unable to continue any longer.[60] The press played its usual game of trivialising the women by its relentless concentration on their dress. Astor arrived in 1919 to find her room literally full of hats sent in by enterprising milliners, but she immediately killed the game by confining herself simply to black and white costumes on all occasions. Yet as late as 1936 when Florence Horsbrugh received the honour of becoming the first woman to reply to the Royal Address, the newspapers filled many columns with speculation about her clothing for the occasion: 'Will She Appear in Evening Dress?', 'Will She Wear Plumes?'[61]

Several scholars have seen the performance of the inter-war women members in parliamentary debates as a major problem. Elizabeth Vallance, for example, wrote:

> Politics is the articulate profession par excellence and oratory and debate are its very centre. Women are not generally articulate, nor are they normally encouraged to take pleasure in the cut and thrust of debate.[62]

Similarly Brian Harrison has argued that the assertive, adversarial style of the House of Commons makes it an unnatural forum for women.[63] However, when one looks at the women of the 1920s and 1930s these points seem to lose much of their force. Their maiden speeches were often an ordeal, but no more so than for the men. Few male members were models of eloquence; most showed themselves capable of reciting from memory or from notes the standard views of their party and the grievances of their constituency, but little more. Women actually benefited to the extent that their approach was usually less pompous and self-important, more natural and sincere. Many of them continued to be treated with some deference; Jean Mann, for example, pointed out that Labour MPs generally hesitated to attack a Tory lady however much they disagreed with her remarks.[64] It is well known that Nancy Astor went out of her way to provoke interruptions in the chamber, just as she did outside. This was simply her way of getting through a speech! As an *enfant terrible* she gained a good deal of attention but never became an effective parliamentary speaker. She intervened far too often, and after a few years the House ceased to listen sympathetically to her.

However, Astor is a misleading guide to women's experience. Women had faced the practical problems of public speaking decades earlier, and doubts as to whether the female voice was too high-pitched or had the power to carry had been laid to rest. Mary Agnes Hamilton followed Arthur Henderson's avuncular advice to avoid the temptation to shout at the start of a speech; better to address the front rows of the audience and allow the strength of one's voice to increase gradually.[65] It was not surprising that in the House the compliments flowed fast and free. Hilda Runciman was praised for her 'clear, dulcet tones and perfect enunciation' and her 'soft and musical' voice. Irene Ward boasted the clear, vigorous speech of one who had been trained in elocution. Florence Horsbrugh, a tall, striking figure with a voice to match, was noted for her 'resonant, well-modulated voice' which could be heard easily in the chamber. Members seem to have been enchanted by the clear, melodious speaking of Megan Lloyd George: 'when she made her maiden speech she seemed too girlish to be the centre of such an interested throng. She scored a real success from the first.'[66] It is no doubt true that members were most fond of the women who appeared most *feminine*. John Wheatley praised Mrs Runciman's maiden effort as a 'matronly' speech, which he evidently intended as a high compliment. MPs became quite sentimental over the affectionate relationship between Megan Lloyd George and her father, who engaged in a kind of duet; when she spoke he would sit on the bench below her, bursting with pleasure and pride, uttering 'hear-hears' to every sentence of the speech.[67] Yet the lady members were also tough. Susan Lawrence, Margaret Bondfield and Marion Phillips were accomplished platform orators, the veterans of a thousand election campaigns. So, too, were Liberals like Runciman and Lloyd George and Conservatives like Horsbrugh and Ward. Some of them achieved high reputations for the quality of their debating. Eleanor Rathbone was always well briefed and effective. Ellen Wilkinson and Jennie Lee were as combative as any man. Lawrence emerged as 'aggressively brainy', 'the real bluestocking of our age', a compelling speaker who could deploy wit and sarcasm as well as any male member.[68] Atholl, though more restrained, made an immediate impact as lawyer-like, thorough and fluent.[69]

The question arises as to what use the women members made of their time in parliament. Dr Harrison has carefully analysed their contributions to debate throughout the period 1919–45.[70] He has found that in 16 out of the 25 years each woman spoke more, in terms of columns in *Hansard*, than the average male member. This was partly a reflection of their small numbers. When a party had only two or three women it sometimes expected one of them to contribute to certain debates. Also the early MPs could not but be conscious of the pressure and expectations placed upon them by women in the country, especially in connection with questions such as widows' pensions. In the 1920s Astor often received 1500 to 2000 letters a week, largely from women. Nonetheless the figures for the average performance of women members mask a considerable range. The most frequent speakers were Astor, Rathbone, Atholl, Bondfield, Lawrence and Wilkinson. At the other extreme there were few interventions by the Countess of Iveagh, Mrs Mabel Phillipson and Lady Davidson, all significantly Conservatives; by contrast the Labour women were almost all professional politicians for whom the party and politics was the central purpose of life. Megan Lloyd George, too, spoke so infrequently that she was privately criticised by her father for neglecting to make the most of her opportunities during the 1930s.[71]

As one might expect the women members' contributions tended to be concentrated in areas where they could claim special knowledge and interests, that is where they expressed the views of mothers on housing, children, health and welfare. In his study Dr Harrison identified eight broad areas: welfare (including housing, health, education, unemployment and labour relations) which attracted 49 per cent, of all women's contributions; foreign affairs and defence which accounted for 14 per cent; women's questions (including equal pay, family allowances, family law reform, and equal franchise) which comprised 13 per cent; economic affairs (8 per cent) ; the Second World War (4 per cent); moral issues (including drink, sex, gambling, and religion) which accounted for 3 per cent; legal and constitutional topics (2 per cent); and libertarian and humanitarian issues (2 per cent).

At first sight this appears to prove that women were driven into a specially designated female sphere of politics. This could have come about simply because it was easier to catch the Speaker's eye on topics that were regarded as being of concern to women. Cazalet and Summerskill considered Captain Fitzroy, Speaker from 1931 to 1943, to be unsympathetic to women, but his successor, Colonel Clifton Brown, was seen as friendly and receptive. However, there is a danger of exaggerating the male influence here. Many women wanted to speak on welfare, housing and health; they were playing a role they themselves had chosen. Leah Manning, as president of the NUT, regarded education as a speciality of hers; Ethel Bentham and Edith Summerskill, both doctors, had a real contribution to make on health. In any case the health and welfare topics loomed large in the interests of *male* backbenchers in this period. One suspects that on the Labour side in particular the debating profile of the two sexes would not look very different. The Conservative women were on the whole more ready to concede foreign affairs and defence as male territory. However, this was qualified by the interest many women took in the subject of peace and disarmament. By the late 1930s several women members had become very active as opponents of fascism and as critics of the British government's pusillanimous policy towards the Spanish Civil War. Atholl, Rathbone, Wilkinson, Lloyd George, Cazalet and Ward all became active members of the committee of MPs formed to secure the evacuation of children from Spain in 1937–8.

It does seem surprising that moral questions occupied such a small part of the women's contribution. However, the statistics based on columns of Hansard may be a little misleading here, in that moral issues do loom large in the bills successfully piloted through the House by women members; these measures did not involve lengthy debate. In general, however, the absence of the moral questions reflects a certain caution on the part of the women themselves and a tendency amongst MPs as a whole to avoid this area. The trouble with moral questions was that they easily led to sex and thus to feminism. This was something few of the women members wished to become involved with; in particular they avoided birth control, which occupied 0.05 per cent of their debating time. Women's issues as a whole comprised only 13 per cent of their total contribution. This points to an unwillingness on their part to initiate debates or legislation in this area. Some simply opposed feminist ideas. Others, especially on the Labour side, sympathised up to a point, but calculated that women's politics represented a cul-de-sac. The route of advance lay in tackling the matters that were of central concern in the movement such as welfare or unemployment. In this connection it is perhaps surprising that only 8 per cent of their contribution was taken up by economic affairs, though this is partly a reflection of the definitions adopted for each category. One commentator writing in 1932 suggested that women had failed to do anything memorable in parliament because the old Victorian issues which suited women's emotional and moral approach had faded away and been replaced by economics; now it was the concerns of the businessman that occupied centre stage in politics. In the 1931–5 parliament one can understand how this came about, and the complete absence of Labour women members at this stage naturally reduced women's contribution to economics. The Conservative women were mostly novices, though in time they took to invading the men's sphere. Nonetheless taking the inter-war period as a whole it cannot be said that women felt obliged to concede the economy as male territory. Bondfield's command of unemployment and labour relations in the 1920s was acknowledged; Mary Agnes Hamilton had the advantage of a degree in economics; and Summerskill, in spite of her self-confessed ignorance, felt confident enough to make her maiden speech on the 1928 budget. Other women tackled those aspects of economic affairs which had a special relevance to their constituencies – as of course did many men: Lloyd George spoke on agriculture, Ward on coal and shipbuilding, Horsbrugh on jute, canning and fishing and Wilkinson on shipbuilding. Nor should it be forgotten that as with male MPs the speeches made in the Commons never give a true picture of the members' range. On public platforms Atholl, Lawrence, Runciman, Lloyd George, Hamilton, Horsbrugh, Wilkinson and others clearly displayed a readiness to plunge into the standard economic controversies of the day as much as the average male politician.

The other dimension to women's role in parliament concerns their relationship with their parties. On the whole they seem to have been loyal, if not inconspicuous, backbench lobby-fodder. But the evidence of rebelliousness and feminism is by no means lacking. Obviously Rathbone as the lone Independent and the most committed feminist stands out as the leading and most persistent champion of women's causes. Of the four Liberal women Mrs Wintringham was the most feminist though she was not very voluble during her four years in the House. Among the Conservatives Astor displayed a consistently independent role, though the type of women's questions she was prepared to raise was strictly limited. Atholl, after appearing highly orthodox in the 1920s, developed into a major critic of her party leaders, but not on women's issues. In due course several of the Tory ladies swept unexpectedly into parliament in 1931 adopted a very independent and, up to a point, feminist line. This is true of Mavis Tate, later a champion of equal pay, and of Irene Ward and Thelma Cazalet, both of whom were influenced by the poverty and unemployment suffered by their constituents in Wallsend and Islington respectively. Ward adopted the role of champion of the industrial communities of the North East of England, and became steadily more active on women's issues. Cazalet's experience on the London County Council had already turned her into a social reformer like Astor and therefore rather impatient with her party leaders. She also enjoyed close personal relations with both Megan Lloyd George and her father, and actually married a Liberal journalist after becoming an MP, all of which must have deepened her detachment from conservatism. None of these Conservative women had any reason to feel gratitude towards their party. By obeying the party line they had little to gain – and their seats to lose. That Ward, Cazalet and Tate remained in parliament after 1935 while other Conservative women did not probably owes something to their capacity to appeal beyond mere party lines. During the Second World War they became even more rebellious. Amongst the Labour women adherence to the party line was the dominating rule. Only four women can be said to have been prepared to press women's issues from time to time: Ethel Bentham, Ellen Wilkinson, Dorothy Jewson and Edith Summerskill; significantly the first three had been active in the pre-1914 suffrage movement.

Not surprisingly, perhaps, the evidence of solidarity and co-operation across party lines amongst the women members is limited. The woman who took most risks was Dorothy Jewson who spoke on birth control during her brief term in 1923–4. No other woman except Rathbone appears to have done so, and in fact the chief pressure for birth control came from male MPs such as Ernest Thurtle (Labour) and E.D. Simon (Liberal). When Thurtle introduced a bill under the ten minute rule in 1926 Wilkinson was the only woman MP to vote in favour of it while the other three (Atholl, Philipson and Astor) $abstained. In 1927 Sir John Newman's bill on married women's employment drew the support of three women in the lobby (Astor, Bondfield and Lawrence), while the other three abstained (Atholl, Wilkinson and Philipson). After 1929 Eleanor Rathbone took up several women's issues, in some of which she was joined, most unusually, by Atholl. Both women raised the question of the voting rights of women in India. Much more controversially Atholl became concerned, through her work for the Church of Scotland Mission, about the brutal practice of female circumcision among the Kikuyu people of Kenya. She used a debate on colonial affairs in December 1929 to raise the matter in the House. Male members, thinking the idea an impossibility, did not even want to hear her on such a subject, and James Maxton interrupted the duchess's account, saying it was irrelevant. Rathbone intervened to quell him and Atholl was able to finish making her case.[72] The incident is of some significance. On such an embarrassing issue only a staunch feminist like Rathbone was prepared to lend support. Earlier work over moral-sexual questions, such as Josephine Butler's campaign to repeal the Contagious Diseases Acts, showed just how persistent one had to be on matters that the average politician preferred to sweep under the carpet. The incident is also important for Atholl in that it provides an indication of how a very conventional woman was sometimes awakened to the condition of her sex when faced with the narrow-mindedness of her male colleagues. It did not make Atholl a feminist but it was a stage on her route to rebellion. During the 1930s several women's issues had a similar effect. In 1930 when the claim of married women to retain their nationality was raised in the House Astor joined with Wilkinson and other Labour members in supporting it. In 1932 no fewer than eleven of the Conservative women members voted against the National government's policy on unemployment benefit for married women. And in 1936 when Wilkinson raised the question of equal pay for women teachers she was supported by all the Conservative women except Atholl in a successful defiance of the government's line. From these tests of the women members' stance on women's issues one is bound to say that they frequently failed to capitalise upon their position by not standing together in the lobbies and attempting to speak for the women in the country. In mitigation, however, it must be said that many of the Labour women who sympathised with women's claims sat in parliament for only very short periods, largely during the two brief Labour governments when they felt an obligation not to rock an already precarious boat. Thus the greater opportunities were available to the Conservative women. Yet few of them took much interest in women's questions. During the

1930s, however, they adopted a more rebellious and feminist stance; this pattern culminated in the Second World War when women's efforts were better co-ordinated than before.

Throughout the 1930s criticisms were voiced about the alleged failure of the women members to make an impact in parliament. The women's organisations felt aggrieved that they never made a distinctive stand over women's interests.[73] An obvious target was Megan Lloyd George who countered by arguing that they could not be expected to concentrate on women's issues to the exclusion of all else. In 'The Riddle of the Women MPs' in December 1932 a *Sunday Chronicle* journalist claimed that women had really been submerged by the economic crisis. Conversely, other observers felt they had neglected the central questions of the day in order to concentrate on a minor sphere of their own. This point was clearly taken by Ellen Wilkinson in 'Have Women Failed in Parliament?' in which she defended women's record in passing legislation, but admitted they had been too involved in mere 'bill-fussing'.[74] It is true enough that the bills in question largely dealt with children and moral matters, and were very limited in scope. But this was true of backbenchers' legislation in general; nothing would pass unless it commanded cross-party support and gave no offence to the government of the day. Moreover, the women members calculated that by demonstrating their capacity to steer legislation through the House they would prove women's ability more effectively than by raising controversial bills that were most unlikely to pass merely as a propagandist device. Horsbrugh, for example, introduced two success-ful measures and did eventually become a cabinet minister.

However, much of the criticism of the women MPs misses the point. Their contributions did to a large extent reflect what were the central concerns of the day and not peripheral issues. Herein lay the heart of the problem. Participating in debates on unemployment, welfare

Table 6.6   Bills Introduced by Women and Successfully Enacted
1919–1939

1919	Sale of Intoxicating Liquor to Persons Under Eighteen Bill (Astor)
1927	Registration of Nursing Homes Bill (Philipson)
1931	Illegitimate Children (Scotland) Bill (Atholl)
1931	Abolition of the Death Sentence on Expectant Mothers Bill (Picton-Turbervill)
1937	Sale of Methylated Spirits Bill (Horsbrugh)
1938	Poor Law Amendment Bill (Ward)
1939	Hire Purchase Bill (Wilkinson)
1939	Adoption of Children Bill (Horsbrugh)

benefits, housing and health was, up to a point, a perfectly sound strategy; but having been drawn into areas regarded by male politicians as perfectly acceptable and of real importance, many of the women failed to capitalise on their opportunities by making a distinctive contribution as women. For example, it is conspicuous in Dr Harrison's survey that a mere 3 per cent of their total contribution went on *women's* unemployment, and 0.8 per cent on equal pay. Eleanor Rathbone demonstrated what could be done even as an Independent. She showed a great facility for introducing women's interests and issues such as family allowances into discussions on other topics. If her approach was untypical this was not simply because few had her keen tactical perception, it was also because only a minority of women MPs regarded feminism as a priority. Although Atholl was well known for her view that the women's organisations did not speak for women, she was actually fairly typical in this respect. Most of the Labour women shared her view of working-class women as essentially separate from middle-class feminists. Despite their political differences they largely followed the same line as, say, Horsbrugh, in wanting to be accepted as MPs, not as women's MPs. Most of the women seem to have reflected wider attitudes in wishing to put a considerable distance between themselves and a feminist reputation. Runciman declared she did not believe in feminist politics and that 'politics as a profession will never appeal to any great extent to women'.[75] The pressures behind such views were no doubt partly tactical – a fear of antagonising one's own electors and a desire to keep in line with one's party. But the women's attitude was also a reflection of their own conventional ideas. Marion Phillips, for example, was to be heard arguing that Britain's need was not birth control but arresting the dangerous fall in population. As late as 1943 Lady Davidson claimed that women of 45–50 years were disqualified from registering for war work by the menopause![76] All this left only a small group of seven women members who had been active in the earlier campaign for women's suffrage and therefore felt some commitment to the wider cause of the sex. Even amongst these, however, one notices the caution of Edith Picton-Turbervill who confessed 'I abominate the word "feminist" ' in spite of her continuing work on behalf of a number of women's causes.[77]

Against the background of these reservations it is not surprising that few even seriously considered the idea of welding the women into a coherent force for effective action within parliament. The prospects for such an approach, however, varied markedly over time. During the early 1920s there were clear signs of a nascent women's party based on

Astor (1919), Wintringham (1921), Dorothy Jewson (1923) and Lady Terrington (1923). However, this prospect rapidly faded when the last three members lost their seats in the 1924 general election; those who survived were the more orthodox party representatives. The increase in the number of women members to 14 in 1929 encouraged Astor to take a fresh initiative by summoning a meeting to consider organising a woman's party in the House of Commons. However, this never really got off the ground, partly because several women felt unhappy about Astor as the self-styled leader; even her fellow Tories thought she was too full of herself. In any case Atholl, Iveagh and Lloyd George were rather improbable members of a women's party. Rathbone, clearly the ablest and most appropriate in some ways, was too pronounced a feminist to be acceptable. Ultimately the whole idea broke down on party loyalty, for 9 of the 14 members were Labour. They felt that they had been elected to tackle unemployment and living standards, not feminist fads. Any collusion with Astor would have provoked immediate criticism in the constituencies and the organisation. Nor did Astor's scheme seem necessary. Mary Hamilton recalled that on the London County Council there was 'never any nonsense about a women's group', and she claimed that the Commons was equally free from sex distinctions.[78] The 1931 landslide reversed the situation by eliminating the Labour women members; now 13 of the 15 women sat as Conservatives. Mostly new to parliament and not especially feminist, they took some time to find their feet. Later in the decade they were reinforced by Wilkinson and Summerskill on the Labour benches. This helped to foster some corporate feeling amongst the women MPs if only because in the face of the large National government majority, they were all equally helpless.

The Role of Women in Government

The handicaps suffered by women politicians in the competition for office between the wars were greatly exacerbated by their precarious position on the backbenches. This is not simply a matter of numbers, though no prime minister had more than a handful of women to choose from. It is also a reflection of fact that few women members enjoyed a long experience in parliament between the wars. Most of the 36 sat for periods of one to three years. Those enjoying longer terms were Nancy Astor (1919–45), Ellen Wilkinson (1924–31 and 1935–47), Megan Lloyd George (1929–51), Eleanor Rathbone (1929–46), Florence Horsbrugh (1931–45), the Duchess of Atholl (1923–38), Irene Ward (1931–45), Mavis Tate (1931–45), Thelma Cazalet-Keir (1931–45) and Mrs Mabel Philipson (1923–9). In the event none of these except Wilkinson and Horsbrugh can be said to have followed the typical male career pattern as backbencher, PPS, junior minister, and finally cabinet member; Wilkinson attained cabinet in 1945, Horsbrugh in 1953. On the other hand, in this period long service was clearly less of a handicap on the Labour side since most of the men also found themselves relative novices. Many of the men appointed to high office in the absence of any conspicuous ability commanded a place on the basis that they represented certain ideological, social or regional interest groups within their party. The women, however, simply forfeited such claims by largely repudiating any suggestion that they spoke for the women electors. Most of them wished to be accepted as regular members of their party, and it is hardly surprising that those who were singled out for office were on the whole loyalists, or believed to be so. A number of the Conservatives in effect ruled themselves out by increasing rebelliousness. Whether the ambitious were tamed by parliamentary experience is rather doubtful. The most likely example is Ellen Wilkinson, of whom Beatrice Webb said that she began to tone down her speeches: 'she is becoming, unknown to herself, moulded for the Front Bench and eventually for office'.[79] This is however, a characteristic Webbian observation: perceptive but unfair. Wilkinson conspicuously managed to maintain her feminism, liveliness and independence, in sharp contrast to many of her colleagues who were party loyalists *before* entering parliament.

The circumstances of party politics between the wars proved unhelpful to women's promotion chances. Two periods – 1918–22 and 1931–9 – were times of coalition government when the competition for jobs inevitably became severe because several parties had to be represented. This is clearly part of the explanation for the exclusion of all the Conservative women members, except one, from the National governments. Baldwin, though apparently more sympathetic to women MPs than most of his colleagues, was never in a strong enough position to do much for them. When Labour briefly held office its leaders were constrained by several factors. Some posts had to be filled by men from outside the Labour movement or those who had only recently joined it, which limited the room to reward the many elderly figures who had devoted their lives to building up the party. Most of the women were regarded, unfairly, as newcomers to the movement and not as great assets. In 1924 especially Ramsay MacDonald's chief object was to create a government that would conform to expectations in the country and reassure voters about Labour's competence. This necessarily limited the room for women, not because they lacked ability but because too prominent a role for them would appear a novel and disturbing feature of the new administration. In any case MacDonald was not, in spite of his political partnership with his wife Margaret, especially comfortable with able and assertive women. Fond of their company, he saw them more as an aid to relaxation than as a part of business. Edith Picton-Turbervill was disappointed to discover that when the prime minister invited women members to lunch in Downing Street he had no inclination to talk to them about politics, preferring to stick to trivialities like the weather and his silver collection.[80]

On the other hand certain factors improved the women's chances. Most prime ministers show some concern for administrative competence at least in the lower reaches of government; in the past this has often enabled men from unfashionable social backgrounds to win office. While few women had the opportunity to demonstrate competence in parliament, those actually chosen were regarded as having already shown ability and relevant experience: Margaret Bondfield as parliamentary secretary at the Ministry of Labour in 1924 and as minister 1929–31; Susan Lawrence as parliamentary secretary at Education in 1924 and as parliamentary secretary at the Ministry of Health 1929–31; the Duchess of Atholl as parliamentary secretary at Education 1924–9; and Florence Horsbrugh as parliamentary secretary at Health 1935–9. In addition it was thought expedient to allow at least one woman into office in the 1920s, not as a representative of her sex, but as a token gesture to the women of the country. Once Labour had taken this step in 1924 there was a degree of pressure on succeeding Conservative administrations to do no less for fear of giving offence to women in the party. However, the strength of this pressure was clearly not very great since no women held office in 1931–5 and only one after 1935.

Since three of the four women office-holders found themselves at Education and Health it does appear that prime ministers subscribed to conventional ideas about women's domestic skills and interests. However, Bondfield's career in the Ministry of Labour constitutes an exception of some significance. As the first woman to gain election to the TUC's executive in 1918 Bondfield emerged not just as the most prominent Labour woman, especially after the death of Mary Macarthur, but as the one most comfortably ensconced within the establishment. Modest, unassertive and thoroughly steeped in the movement, she reassured male trade unionists. Her expertise in the field of labour relations also made her an attractive choice in 1924 for her minister

Tom Shaw. The remarkable thing about her appointment as a minister was that it coincided with her election as an MP; she therefore had to learn the rules of the House as well as her departmental brief. Inevitably her nine-month term was constrained by the cautious economic strategy pursued by the chancellor of the exchequer, Snowden. She also spent the latter part away on a visit to Canada as chairman of a Commission on Overseas Settlement which planned to reduce unemployment by promoting emigration.

Bondfield's experience in 1924 and her return to parliament for a safe seat at Wallsend in 1926 appeared to be signs that she would be favoured with future office rather than Ellen Wilkinson who, as a member from 1924 onwards, gained greater parliamentary experience and made a bigger impact. Wilkinson, however, suffered from being more independent and less predictable. Yet it is often forgotten that Bondfield's real rival was not Wilkinson but Susan Lawrence. Easily the ablest parliamentary performer among the Labour women MPs, Lawrence's command of information and arguments made her a natural frontbencher; as Beatrice Webb put it, she 'gets up a case exactly like a lawyer'. Shortly after Bondfield's appointment Lawrence became parliamentary secretary to Charles Trevelyan at the Board of Education; though defeated in 1924 she returned at a by-election in 1926 and subsequently made her reputation by a sustained attack on Neville Chamberlain's Local Government Bill in 1928–9. In this context MacDonald's tendency to choose male mediocrities for his 1929 cabinet, while confining Lawrence to another parliamentary secretaryship, was striking. Though conspicuously middle class and an ex-Conservative, Lawrence had worked loyally and effectively for Labour since 1913. After her defeats in 1931 and 1935 she never returned to the Commons.

Even Bondfield's elevation to the cabinet in 1929 was not a forgone conclusion; she herself attributed it to the influence of Arthur Henderson on the prime minister.[81] The Ministry of Labour was not, however, an office that enjoyed high status in the 1920s. It had only narrowly survived the post-war attack on the new interventionist departments and its ministers were always drawn from the ranks of minor figures. It survived because no prime minister wished to antagonise the trade unions unnecessarily, but according to the most authoritative study even the unions themselves placed little intrinsic importance on the ministry.[82]

It cannot be said that Margaret Bondfield's ministerial career constituted a great success. Things had already begun to go downhill for her in 1926 when she served on the Blanesborough Committee on the unemployment insurance scheme. She found herself being denounced in union circles for signing a report which proposed reductions in the scale of benefits. She defended herself by pointing out that in spite of its defects the report's chief principle, a guaranteed legal right to benefit based on 30 contributions during a two-year period, was very desirable. In 1927, however, the TUC specifically repudiated the principle of contributory insurance.

While her knowledge and expertise as a minister were freely acknow-ledged, Bondfield found herself inescapably trapped between Con-servative criticism of her for borrowing for the Unemployment Insur-ance Fund and left-wing attack over the steady increase in unemploy-ment which was beyond her control. The Labour government engaged in a risky attempt at educating its own supporters by appointing a Royal Commission on unemployment insurance in 1930; the TUC's aim of non-contributory insurance was expressly excluded from its report.[83] Bondfield risked further unpopularity by making it clear that she wanted to reduce the borrowing requirement of the Unemployed Insurance Fund by cutting benefit in line with the falling cost of living and by tightening up on the qualifications. Her 1931 Anomalies Act had the effect of excluding 180,000 married women who had made contribu-tions from benefit. In the end, however, the continued growth of employment frustrated her attempts to reduce borrowing. Thus she got the worst of both worlds; she failed to impose her policy and under-mined her political base.

Of course, few members of the 1929–31 administration emerged with enhanced reputations, so one should not exaggerate Margaret Bond-field's difficulties. Like most of her male colleagues she accepted Treasury opinion about the economy and, in particular, about the inadvisability of Keynesian policies. When the crisis came in August 1931 she initially voted in favour of the economies consequent upon the report of the May Committee, including the 10 per cent cut in unemployment benefit which the TUC rejected. Subsequently she joined Arthur Henderson in backtracking on this. Loyalty to the movement was always the guiding rule. As a result she lost her seat at Wallsend and failed to regain it in 1935. Adopted as candidate for Reading, a seat as difficult as Northampton, she withdrew from politics during the Second World War. Bondfield had proved her competence on the detailed questions of government, but lacked any flair or wider sense of political strategy. She was unlucky to have been placed in the firing line in 1929. Her career cannot be said to have promoted the cause of women ministers in the Labour Party, and it may be significant that in the future the ablest Labour women were to advance by routes outside trade unionism.

For the Conservatives Bondfield's elevation in 1924 had posed a dilemma. Competition between the parties for the sympathy of women electors seemed to some to dictate that Baldwin should follow Mac-Donald's example. But he had little material to choose from: Astor, Atholl and Mrs Mabel Philipson. The latter was regarded as too light-weight and lacking ambition. As the best known and most experienced woman MP Astor's claims were obvious. But her independent and cavalier attitude towards her own party made her unpopular as a recipient of favours. Also, for many Tories she was the personification of the unsuitable woman in politics: indiscreet, flippant, illogical and super-ficial. Would she readily submit to the tedious grind of a junior minister in an obscure department or accept the discipline that membership of a government entailed? It seemed more likely that she would provoke rows leading to a hasty resignation. Consequently she was deliberately passed over. It was unfortunate for Astor that she presented such a stark contrast with Atholl. For the duchess was serious, unemotional, industrious and reliable. As Harold Macmillan commented approvingly, she had 'a masculine mind'! Moreover she was a conventional woman from an aristocratic family and not a pushy American. No faddist or feminist, the duchess was most reassuringly found to be still opposed to equal franchise for women. She must have seemed the safest of safe bets. In any case, Baldwin liked her, and her appointment would add a diligent administrator to the lower ranks of government while not unduly offending the party. Neville Chamberlain, perhaps anxious to keep her out of Health, suggested she should go to the Board of Education in view of her experience on county education committees.

In the event the careful assessment of the Duchess of Atholl proved to be only partially accurate. Like a good many Conservative women she grew increasingly independent and critical when she saw at first hand the way in which the men of her party actually conducted government. Her minister, Lord Eustace Percy, was somewhat high-minded and pompous; and the duchess felt that he resented the way his department had been singled out for a woman. His habit of ignoring her views and trying to exclude her from decision-making undermined her confidence when answering for the department in the Commons.[84] Percy succeeded in getting her out of the office for a good deal of the time by sending her on weekly prize-giving visits to schools and by despatching her to educational conferences abroad; she was also a representative on the British delegation to the League of Nations in

1925. However, although dismayed, the duchess refused to be deflected from voicing her opposition to Percy's policies. The prevailing need to balance the budget meant economies of £2 million for the Board of Education in 1925–6, which led Percy to abandon promises about reducing the size of classes and raising the school-leaving age. But when he suggested reintroducing fees for elementary education and postponing school attendance to the age of 7 the duchess strongly opposed him.[85] Although she defended the Board in the Commons, by January 1927 her disagreement led her to go over Percy's head by voicing her disquiet directly to the prime minister. This behaviour was a sign of her social status as the equal of Lord Eustace, her personal friendship with Baldwin, and her practical grasp of her subject. But politically it was hardly a wise move, especially as her intervention seems to have resulted in some success; Percy cannot have been pleased at being forced to retreat from his policies.

Baldwin's defeat at the 1929 election effectively terminated the duchess's ministerial career. When Conservatives returned to office in 1931 there was little chance of a job; just to make sure Astor warned Baldwin and MacDonald against appointing her on the grounds that she was not a feminist![86] But the real problem was that her experience of office had released an element of independence in Atholl which her colleagues had failed to see in 1924. Her intelligence and her position as a member of an aristocratic family made her a far more independent person than the career politicians. She rapidly became a critic, indeed a rebel, over three major issues. The first of these was Indian constitutional reform on which the duchess largely supported Winston Churchill's campaign from 1929 onwards. This culminated in 1935 when she resigned the government whip and assisted Churchill's son in a by-election in Liverpool in opposition to the official Conservative candidate. In her Perthshire constituency many influential Tories agreed with her views on India but resented her self-indulgence and disloyalty to the government. Although she won a vote of confidence at a public meeting she acknowledged local feelings and reapplied for the whip before the 1935 election.[87] However, as India subsided she became embroiled in controversy over foreign and defence policy, especially in connection with the National government's handling of the Abyssinian question and the Spanish Civil War. As time went on she grew increasingly alarmed about the rise of fascism and dismayed at British appeasement. Her visits to Spain and her defence of the Republican cause in *Searchlight on Spain* attracted attacks especially from the Catholics in her constituency. They alleged that she supported a

Spanish government which was anarchist, communist and atheist: hence the epithet 'the Red Duchess'. Her critics charged her with wishing to involve Britain in a war over Spain, and in 1937 they circulated a pamphlet alleging that she had ceased to represent the principles of the Conservative Party. The constituency association refused to organise meetings for her and began to demand that she support government policy of non-intervention on Spain.[88] Things reached a climax in the summer of 1938 when the duchess rejected the association's resolution supporting government foreign policy and resigned the whip again. They decided to seek a new candidate. The duchess forced the pace by resigning her seat, while the duke felt obliged to give up his position as president of the local association. The result was a badly timed by-election shortly before Christmas 1938 in which the duchess, as an Independent, was opposed only by a local farmer for the Conservatives. She lost fairly narrowly in a low poll largely because she was labelled a warmonger, which tended to alienate the Liberal and Labour voters who might have supported her. Had she waited for public opinion to turn against Munich in the spring of 1939 she would probably have been successful.

Clearly the Duchess of Atholl's rather spectacular career after 1929 did little to help the prospects of women in government. After her no woman held office until 1935 when Florence Horsbrugh became parliamentary secretary at the Ministry of Health. Her rise shows how the Conservative Party's practice was drawing closer to that of Labour. Horsbrugh had emerged through the party organisation, rather than from her family or personal position, and was thus the kind of orthodox loyalist with whom the leaders felt comfortable. But nothing apparently could alter the party leaders' view of aspiring women: token representation was all they merited. During the wartime coalition, neither Churchill nor Attlee was particularly sympathetic towards women's claims, and they simply conceded two parliamentary secretaryships, one to Horsbrugh and one to Wilkinson. After her return to parliament in 1935 Wilkinson had emerged as Labour's new token woman, though she probably owed her elevation to the cabinet in 1945 to the patronage of Herbert Morrison. In his brief caretaker administration in 1945 Churchill included Thelma Cazalet as well as Horsbrugh. Cazalet's appointment appears to be the one clear case of a prime minister who deliberately used office to tame a woman politician. In 1944 Cazalet had upset the government with a motion on equal pay for teachers. 'Now Thelma', Churchill warned her when giving her the job, 'no more of that equal pay business.'[89]

Chapter 7 The Cult of Domesticity in the 1930s

'In another fifty years' time when social historians are writing deep books on the early twentieth century', commented *Woman* in its first edition in 1937, 'earnest hours will be spent in reconstructing the Woman of the Period. We ought to be able to tell them, since we are the living creature which they ... will be trying to reconstruct.' Even allowing for the hyperbole of an ambitious and optimistic editor, the writer has a point. Popular women's magazines constitute an important but rather neglected source for the ordinary British woman of the inter-war period. For both the campaigns of the feminists and the strategies of the politicians designed to confine women to domesticity have to be seen in the context of the much more pervasive social and commercial pressures which reached out to the mass of women in their daily lives. Whether they merely reflected women's ideas and behaviour or actively influenced them, they were too universal to be ignored.

The Rise and Rise of Women's Magazines

During the 1920s and 1930s the number of magazines catering to women increased to more than 50. Both those that offered a diet of pulp fiction and romantic marriage for the working-class market and those that specialised more in household management for a middle-class readership continued to prosper and expand. Papers such as *Home Chat* and *Woman's Weekly* flourished well after the Second World War, although by then they had begun to suffer from an ageing readership. Even in the 1930s the older papers were being overhauled by a new generation which took advantage of technical improvements in the form of printing by colour-gravure, and were more glamorous and attractive to younger women. They benefited from the rise in living standards which manifested itself in the increase in advertising of cheap consumer goods. This new wave was best represented by *Woman's Own* (1932), *Woman's Illustrated* (1936) and *Woman* (1937). The new mass weeklies soon enjoyed circulations running into millions rather than hundreds of thousands. *Woman*, which emerged as the leader of the pack, rose to three-quarters of a million between 1937 and 1939, reached a million in 1940 and 3.5 million by the late 1950s. By that time five out of every six women in Britain read at least one woman's magazine each week, and many read three or four.[1]

The male historian must resist the temptation to dismiss these papers as merely purveyors of lightweight entertainment or as bland confections of love stories, recipes and knitting patterns. In some degree all of them propagated an ideology of domesticity; perhaps surprisingly some of the new ones did so more blatantly than their older rivals. *Woman*, undoubtedly one of the blander productions, opened its career with a thoughtful manifesto by Margaret Lane which reflected the force of criticism emanating from some feminists:

> In the last ten years there has been a movement, a tendency, which the suffragist generation calls backward, retrogressive. That is neither entirely true nor entirely fair. We are trying to do something which is as difficult, in its way, as the things which they achieved. We are trying to blend our old world with our new. Trying to be citizens and women at the same time. Wage earners and sweethearts. Less aggressive feminists than independently feminine. It is a difficult balance to strike.[2]

What this seems to have meant was an acceptance that many women would work for their living up to their early twenties, but that they remained as anxious as ever for the pleasures of home and family life. Whether, in the event, the balance to which Lane referred was ever struck must be in some doubt. The staple ingredients of *Woman* were fiction, marriage and housecraft slightly leavened by contributions on outdoor activities, sports and gardening. This bias was clear from the outset when the paper announced its team of seven experts on Beauty, Fashion, Life, Baby Care, Cookery, Furnishing and Housekeeping. The nearest *Woman* came to tackling feminist issues was in the Evelyn Home page. By this time the agony aunt or problem page had become an established feature of most magazines. On the whole their authors took little notice of issues such as divorce reform and continued to urge faithfulness and forgiveness in marriage. They were, however, inclined to be less disapproving about sexual relations outside marriage than before the war. But when 'Evelyn Home' advised one unhappily married woman to spend a weekend with her lover her copy was promptly censored and she lost her column![3] On the employment front *Woman* showed its true colours by urging women to contemplate jobs which would serve as a preparation for married life because of the practical skills they fostered: catering, decorating, costing and laundry work.[4]

In so far as *Woman* was prepared to lift the horizons of its readers beyond the immediate domestic scene it is significant that it looked not to women who had become successful in the male world but rather to a sphere in which romantic fiction and the traditional woman were united in a particularly satisfying way: the royal family. Of course the appeal of the royal family for women's magazines pre-dates the First World War, but the association seems to have strengthened markedly between the wars. Several factors contributed to the general popularity of the monarchy in this period: the king's personification of the national cause during the Great War, the late flowering of imperial sentiment now dramatised by the royal tours, the innovation of the Christmas broadcast by George V in 1932, and the celebration of his Silver Jubilee in 1936. By the inter-war years, also, the monarchy had achieved the 'modern' status which had eluded Queen Victoria in the sense that it was seen to be above party politics, a point underlined by the promptness with which the king invited Ramsay MacDonald to form the first Labour government in 1924.

From the perspective of the women's press the person who best encapsulated its conception of royal womanhood was Lady Elizabeth Bowes Lyon, who became Duchess of York in 1923 and queen in 1937 on her husband's accession as King George VI. Presiding over her two-child family – now preferred by most of her subjects – Queen Elizabeth seemed to epitomise the magazines' idea of womanhood: petite, charming, motherly, grand-but-accessible, special-but-domestic, and above all, perhaps, she provided vital support for her husband in performing his difficult role.[5] In the year following the abdication of Edward VIII no fewer than 89 of the 101 newsreels produced by Movietone News included items about the royal family, a level of publicity not equalled before or since. Not surprisingly the glamour of the monarchy proved an irresistible source of copy for the popular magazines. *Woman* came in on the crest of the wave in 1937; one of its earliest issues carried a cover portrait of the queen and followed up with the first of many pictorial features about her. If there was a flaw in this it lay in the king's fondness for privacy which resulted in some rather dull material supplied to the magazines by the palace. However, they plugged away in the firm conviction that the royal family was an invaluable aid to circulation. So much so that in the 1950s Mary Grieve considered the biggest single issue for women's papers to be the revelations by the royal nanny, Marion Crawford, on 'The Little Princesses'; this story alone almost enabled *Woman's Own* to overtake the huge circulation lead enjoyed by *Woman*.[6]

However, the royal theme represented only the mildest expression of the domestic ideology propagated in the women's press. From 1932

onwards *Woman's Own campaigned* for domesticity as, say, the Beaverbrook press campaigned for empire free trade. This is by no means fully
apparent from a breakdown of the articles printed in the paper in 1935
which comprised: household tips etc. - (35 per cent); fiction -
(28 per cent); babies and children - (10 per cent); dress - (8 per cent);
cookery - (4 per cent); film and radio - (4 per cent); editorial/gossip -
(4 per cent); personal problems - (4 per cent). Each of these topics
reflected the paper's philosophy that 'any girl worth her salt wants to be
the best housewife ever - and then some'.[7]

The most innocuous feature was apt to be exploited to propagate the
cult of domesticity. If marriage was the best job for a woman, paid
employment could be acceptable as a prelude to marriage, not as in
Woman's view for relevant skills, but ideally as a *route* that led to
marriage. To this end writers helpfully drew attention to the occupations most likely to yield husbands: nurse, library assistant, private
secretary ('short cut to a prosperous marriage') and telephonist ('many
a man falls in love with a voice').[8] This was the positive case. On the
negative side *Woman's Own* liked to depict the fate of the woman
misguided enough to devote her life to a career as a lonely and neurotic
individual: 'You have only to go into a restaurant, and note the strained,
dissatisfied look on the face of a woman feeding alone.'[9] This message
was reinforced by articles from a number of wimpish men who
explained how easily they were alienated by the successful, career-
minded female. One pleaded that in spite of his admiration for 'the
modern girl' who achieved such feats as beating her husband at golf, 'I
would be terrified of marrying one of them ... what have I to give in
return to such a paragon?'[10] The nub of the matter was that success in a
wife was practically impossible for a husband to cope with unless he
were particularly dull, pathetic and unambitious himself. 'All the talk
in post-war years of equality in marriage, legal, social and financial, has
not made an atom of difference to the character of man.'[11] A real man
felt the need to support a woman for 'a marriage in which the wife is
also a breadwinner isn't a true marriage at all ... I like to think that I
alone am my wife's shield against the world .... Even now I can grow
cold at the thought of living on my wife's earnings if I fell out of
work.'[12]

Similarly, the subject of cosmetics and fashion was tackled on the
assumption that the over-riding purpose of a woman's life consisted in
acquiring and keeping a husband. Consequently the beauty page in
Woman's Own appeared under the leader 'Looks Do Count After
Marriage', and carried endless advice on the don't-let-yourself-go
theme:

He will notice – none quicker – if you cease to be the attractive alluring girl he married. Resolve – early in your married life – never to get slack about your appearance.[13]

This swiftly developed into a rather insidious attempt to thrust guilt upon women for failure to retain their physical appeal:

It's very bad policy to care for your furniture and neglect your face ... (if you do) you aren't being quite fair to that man. ... He never suspected, poor darling, that a day would come when you would care more for the brass candlesticks than those precious cheeks of yours.[14]

As the words of a popular 1930s song expressed it: 'Keep young and beautiful, it's your duty to be beautiful, keep young and beautiful if you want to be loved.' From this emphasis on a woman's responsibility it was of course a short step to the third great theme of *Woman's Own*, the campaign to shore up the institution of marriage by arming its readers against threats such as reforms in the divorce laws and flirtatious girls, referred to as 'vamps'. Thus Barbara Hedworth in a one of a succession of counter-blasts intoned: 'Dress for your husband. After all he pays the Bill, and he is the one to please! Read this bracing article.' She went on to suggest that when a husband was ensnared by a typist or shop assistant his wife should:

Stop to think how often these lapses on the part of a devoted husband are due to the fact that their wives refuse to dress up for them ... really it was your face, the physical charm of you which first made you attractive and winsome to the man.

She reached a climax with a diatribe against the practice of wearing bedroom slippers around the house, a practice which,

warns a man that the beginning of the end has come so far as his wife's personal appearance is concerned and in my opinion the wife who greets her spouse in this slovenly type of footwear deserves all she gets.[15]

A battalion of female writers specialised in instructing other women on the techniques they would need for maintaining their marriages. Barbara Cartland insisted that a wife should pander to her husband's selfishness. Laura Sayle explained how badly men needed their sense of freedom, and felt they should be encouraged to feel like bachelors: 'when you come to think about it the average man gets a fairly raw deal out of marriage in comparison to what he puts into it'.[16] Real women, so the argument ran, gladly surrendered their freedom for 'the spiritual security of some one to look after us'; they should therefore be prepared to put up with a good deal of difficulty in married life because 'a bad husband is better than no husband at all'.[17] Marital instability increasingly concerned the magazine columnists. For example, Barbara Hedworth tried to reassure readers that: 'the happily married man has no more inclination to have affairs with any other woman than his wife desires with other men'. The way to avoid affairs, apparently, was to encourage his flirtatiousness:

> there is no reason why married women should not be able to hold their own against these vamps ... you can vamp your own husband throughout your life if only you will take the trouble to understand him.[18]

If in spite of all this advice a wife found that her husband was unfaithful she might be tempted to seek a divorce, particularly in view of the legislation of 1923 and 1937 which put the two sexes on an equal footing. This was anathema to the magazines. *Woman's Own* repeatedly printed articles along the lines of 'I Wish I Hadn't Divorced My Husband', and 'Dragooned Into Divorce'. In every case the moral was that a hasty resort to the law as a way of punishing an errant male was unnecessary and counter-productive:

> Men get these attacks like kiddies get measles. ... Let him have his fling and he'll come back a thousand times more in love with you than ever.[19]

Thus the writers cautioned against accepting the advice of relations and friends who were chiefly anxious to pin the blame on the husband. In this perspective divorce seemed merely a form of self-indulgence for a wife, and one obtained at the expense of her children who must suffer from their father's absence.[20]

However, by the later 1930s even *Woman's Own* had lost some of its original stridency. Its features on beauty and fashion became less didactic. The emphasis shifted towards a more realistic consideration of marital problems, with less preaching and more practical help in home-making. Romantic fiction occupied an even larger proportion of the paper than before. This tendency towards blandness may have been a sign of the need to compete with the hugely successful *Woman* from 1937 onwards. Nonetheless, the message never changed, it simply became less blatant.

How much significance should be attached to the inter-war women's magazines? There are broadly three views of this question. They may be seen as the proprietors professed to see them as essentially a reflection of the interests and aspirations of British women. Alternatively, they may be considered as a formative influence on women; however, their highly prescriptive approach must be measured against the evidence of female behaviour in this period. Yet again, one might well dismiss the magazines on both counts; for it is quite possible that they were purchased simply as ephemeral entertainment regardless of the message they carried. It has also been suggested that they were really middle-class in orientation. This is true in the sense that middle-class women bought more copies per capita. However, since the late Victorian period there had existed a vigorous literature aimed at working-class girls and women; the only change between the wars was the rise of journals such as *Woman*, which exploited a market that crossed the class divide; it could scarcely have achieved such impressive sales and advertising revenue otherwise.

Perhaps the most obvious charge which must be considered is that the magazines represented an imposition upon women by male proprietors, editors and journalists concerned to propagate the domestic ideology. This, after all, was a common interest of men in other walks of life where they enjoyed positions of power. Clearly there is some basis for the criticism, in that, with rare exceptions like Lady Rhondda, women did not control the British press. Moreover, the regular contributors to the women's papers included men such as Godfrey Winn who wrote on topics like 'First Love' and 'What has happened to the Femme Fatale?', not to mention the blatantly misogynist Beverley Nicolls. His forte was the brisk and bracing piece designed to emphasise that the female sex still enjoyed no political influence and that all would be well if women applied themselves properly to polishing up their traditional skills. 'You may not be a "clever" woman, and indeed I hope you are not, for the women I most respect are wise rather than clever. They are wise in a hundred adorable, subtle ways', he opined by way of introduction to a characteristic rant on housewifely duties.[21] On the strength of a few days without his servant and housekeeper Nicholls decided to test his own ability to fend for himself. Inevitably came the triumphant report on how easy it all was:

> I had hours of leisure. ... And at the end of the first day, the slackest day I had ever spent in my life, I found myself asking the question, 'What do women do?'[22]

Needless to say he was full of excellent ideas designed to help women make constructive use of all their spare time.

However, such contributions scarcely seem sufficient to justify the view of women's magazines as a male conspiracy to check the progress towards female emancipation. Winn, Nicholls and their like were only the token males amongst the mass of women writers, and their message sat squarely within the prevailing ideology of the day. *Good House-*

keeping stood virtually alone in printing some articles by feminists, though in the 1930s these became rare. Moreover, editorial chairs were by now occupied by women such as Mary Grieve and Alice Head. They clearly thought of themselves as emancipated women, not as mere tools in the hands of the male power brokers. Like most of those involved with the women's press, they defended themselves by arguing that they followed the demands of the market for their product. Indeed, it would be foolish to ignore the sheer scale of their commercial success. At a time when the forces of traditional feminism appeared to be dwindling, domesticity evidently met with a ready response. Even Mary Grieve admitted she had been surprised to discover that the pressures of the battle for circulation obliged her to devote a good deal of her editorial work to topics like knitting and the royal family.[23] According to Grieve, no significant change took place in the interests of British women throughout the period from the 1920s to the 1950s; they cared little for careers or for feminism, and wanted magazines that reflected their domestic concerns. The first editorial director of *Woman*, John Dunbar, believed that the paper ought to 'deal with social problems as well as flower arrangements'; but when he experimented with more serious articles the only result was a 30 per cent fall in sales.[24] The message was clear: the magazines must keep in step with the majority of women in the country. Perhaps the nearest approach to controversial questions came in the problem pages, but as Grieve recalled, the appearance of the Evelyn Home column represented 'our chief source of danger'.[25] It was here that topics such as family planning threatened to antagonise some sections of the readership.

However, the example of birth control exposes the weakness in Grieve's general defence. Since the majority of British married women were deliberately choosing to limit their family size by the 1930s, her editorial caution seems excessive. In avoiding birth control *Woman* was not keeping in step but falling behind the trend of opinion. There are other issues which suggest that the paper was more inclined to defy than to follow change. For example, women were distinctly more willing to seek a divorce between the wars than they had been before 1914, although the total numbers involved were still very low (Table 7.1). There is also some evidence that in spite of the barrage of propaganda about the working wife, rather more married women were going out to work during the 1930s. The shift was slight, but it is arguable that it would have been greater but for the pressure on women not to neglect their home and family.

Finally there remains the question of the pressure on the women's

Table 7.1 Petitions for Divorce in England and Wales 1901–1985

| | Percentage sought by | |
	Husbands	Wives
1901–5	53	47
1906–10	48	52
1911–15	45	55
1916–20	67	33
1921–5	41	59
1926–30	41	59
1931–5	45	55
1936–40	47	53
1941–5	56	44
1946–50	55	45
1951–5	44	56
1956–60	45	55
1961–5	42	58
1966–70	37	63
1971–5	34	66
1976–80	28	72
1981–5	27	73

Source: A.H.Halsey (ed.), *British Social Trends since 1900* (1988), p.80.

press from the advertisers. Cynthia White has argued that commercial interests wanted features which would focus women's attention upon areas of high and growing expenditure such as fashion, cosmetics, furnishings and food.[26] It cannot be denied that advertising revenue played a central part in the profitability of the new magazines; it is visible in the swelling size of each issue in this period. However, it is fair to say that the domestic ideology was already the dominant feature of the magazines before advertising became of overriding importance, and the force behind that ideology was clearly more than commercial. There is also a complication in the argument, for by promoting domesticity the magazines were not always serving the obvious interests of manufacturers. Whereas the housewife often had to be a rather careful spender, it was, in contrast, the 'working woman' who found herself obliged to spend much of her wages on buying the goods and services she had no time to produce herself. Many of the time-consuming activities recommended in the magazines were intended to save money. However, Mary Grieve's defence on this point was rather careful and specific; she denied that space was ever sold on the understanding that certain products would receive editorial support, or that the advertising department ever had a powerful say in the editorial content of *Woman*.[27] This appears to leave unanswered the charge that magazines directed readers' attention towards certain types of product or new areas of expenditure.

Housework Expands to Fill the Time Available

Perhaps the most important point about the popular propaganda disseminated in the 1930s is that in certain respects the domestic ideal was becoming more attainable by British women. Since the 1870s when real wages had been boosted significantly by sustained reductions in prices, living standards had risen. Large numbers of working-class families began to enjoy a modest surplus of income with which to buy more interesting food, small luxuries, entertainment or pay the rent on a better house. The choice in these matters was generally exercised by the housewife. The greater the choice the more satisfying her role; if the spread of grocery chain stores, the explosion of advertising, or the fortunes made by purveyors of cheap consumer goods like William Lever's soap all depended upon the housewife, then she herself felt less of a victim and more an independent decision-maker.

While the growth of real wages was checked in the late 1890s and early Edwardian period, the expectations engendered by consumerism were not. During the First World War prise rises in combination with higher family earnings seem to have stimulated aspirations to better living standards, and this helps to explain the growth of organisations such as the Women's Co-operative Guild which took a great interest in housewives' concerns. By 1920 real wages were about 10 per cent higher than they had been on the outbreak of war. Thereafter prices fell, sharply from 1920 to 1923, and then gently right up to the late 1930s. Meanwhile average money wages also dropped back during 1920 to 1923, but then remained fairly static, showing only slight falls even in 1926 and 1931–3. The result was a marked improvement in real wages. Those in employment (the majority even at the depths of the depression) enjoyed a higher standard of living in the 1920s than in the Edwardian period, and a higher standard in the 1930s than in the 1920s. The working class also benefited from a steady if modest redistribution of income in their favour via direct taxation and greatly increased expenditure on social welfare. Moreover, as families shrank in size there was more to spend per capita in many homes. It has been estimated that between the Edwardian period and the late 1930s average consumer expenditure per head of population had risen in real terms by nearly a quarter. This was the very real and tangible basis for the consumerism which pervaded the pages of the inter-war women's magazines and which manifested itself in the development of advertising, sales of canned, packeted, processed and bottled foods, the mass market in cheap women's fashions, the rise of the cinema, and the housebuilding boom.

It was not just that a woman's resources enabled her to do more in this period; there are also grounds for thinking that the household was becoming a more attractive place for women. Increasingly women married younger and had fewer children which meant that on average they had completed their families by the age of 28 years. This opened up opportunities. A woman might decide to return to paid employment, but in the 1930s she was more likely to remain at home and concentrate on improving the quality of life for her family by her efforts in and around the house. This did not mean she had more free time or that she escaped the burden of housework but it did tend to create an air of optimism and improvement for many. One of the things women wanted, and from which they were the major beneficiaries, was improved housing standards. They spent much of their lives in the home and had to cope with its inconveniences, its unhealthiness and inadequate space. A total of just over 4 million new houses were constructed between the wars, of which 1.1 million were council houses and 2.9 million built by private contractors. This alone made the period a remarkable one for women. Moreover, some two-thirds of the houses were produced in the 1930s. Since most of the homes appeared on large estates, whether on 'garden city' sites or council estates outside the towns, they tended to weaken old ties of community and to reinforce the centrality of home-and-family in British society. Thus women who derived inspiration and interest from the domestic orientation of their magazines were by no means the victims of an illusion. New semi-detached houses could be purchased for as little as £250 to £300 in the provinces, with a deposit of £25 and an interest rate of 4½ per cent on the mortgage. This put them within reach of many working-class families. Moreover, inter-war housing, especially council housing, was built to standards markedly higher than those attained hitherto, or since for that matter. With the recommendations of the Tudor Walters Report of 1918 on desirable housing density, size and arrangement the state began to set high standards which in due course speculative builders also followed. Housing is one of the few areas of policy where the authorities took some trouble to find out what women wanted and to see that their views were reflected in policy. From the housewife's perspective the need was for a larger kitchen with proper light and ventilation, an indoor toilet, a bathroom, more bedrooms and a cheap electricity supply.

Clearly the very increase in the size of the home threatened more housework for women; but it is important to remember that this was seen as a genuine gain at the time. A journal like *The Labour Woman* waxed as enthusiastic about the advantages of electricity as any popular women's magazine.[28] This was another area where government was seen to play a beneficent part in women's lives. In 1919 the country was divided into districts each under a Joint Electricity Authority responsible for increasing the supply; the government allocated £20 million for investment in new plant. In 1926 the Central Electricity Generating Board and the National Grid were set up so that by 1939 two-thirds of all houses were wired for electricity. Many women, were, however, thought to be nervous of the new form of power and to overcome this a pressure group, the Electrical Association for Women, was formed by Caroline Haslett in 1924. It sponsored travelling exhibitions and cookery classes. This crusade inspired on the one hand such propagandist works as Wilfred Randall's *The Romance of Electricity* (1931), and on the other a determined if belated effort by manufacturers of electrical appliances to increase their output.

None of this, however, revolutionised the daily lives of housewives in Britain. The spread of electrical goods was slow and patchy; for example by 1931 there were 1.3 million cookers, 400,000 vacuum cleaners and only 60,000 washing machines in use. The introduction of protective tariffs stimulated British manufacture of certain items hitherto dominated by American producers, but adoption of the new equipment was determined by calculations which varied from family to family. For middle-class women much depended upon how difficult and how expensive they found it to employ servants. There were in fact still 1.3 million female domestics in Britain by 1930, though they were increasingly likely to come in to a home for a day or two rather than be full-time residents always on call. The significance of electrical appliances in this context is best understood as facilitating the gradual reduction of middle-class dependence on servants. With a washing machine one might require a servant to come in only one day each week. But for the other six days the housewife would herself have to cope with cooking, fires and cleaning carpets; while the equipment made this possible it could not stop housework filling up a woman's time. In a sense the appliances helped to turn many middle-class wives into domestic servants. For working-class women most of the new appliances were still too expensive. Even the new houses were frequently built with the traditional kitchen range, and so there was no escape from the heavy and dirty work of solid fuel fires. The chief gain here was the greater use of anthracite which was cleaner than coal and would burn through the night. Elizabeth Roberts' study of the housewives of this period underlines strongly how life continued to be a matter of heavy lifting and carrying, bending and stretching, scrubbing and sweeping; this was especially so with the washing of clothes which still necessitated heating up the water, rinsing and mangling as well as ironing.[29] The most common piece of machinery in working-class homes was the sewing machine which involved much time-consuming activity.[30] A woman might devote more to this if she managed to save time on other aspects of her work. Thus, there is clearly no case for the view that the burdens of housewives diminished as a result of 'laboursaving' equipment; at most they improved the quality and range of their work.

Betty Friedan has aptly summed up this dilemma in *The Feminine Mystique* (1963) when she says that housework expands to fill the time available. She places much of the blame for elevating domesticity as the highest form of fulfilment for a woman upon the women's magazines of the 1940s and 1950s in America. However, if this reached a climax after the Second World War it was very clearly a marked feature throughout the post-1918 period. It would be anachronistic to portray British women between the wars simply as passive victims of the prevailing ideology as Friedan does for her society. The cult of domesticity has to be seen in a context in which women were showing great determination, in the face of disapproval from most male, political, religious and commercial pressures, to have fewer children. The smaller family was all of a piece with the domestic ideology in that it, too, was a way of raising the standard provided by the wife for her family. Moreover the oral evidence shows how much women took pride in their skills as housewives. Their strategies changed a little in this period; they made less use of the pawnbroker and more of the Co-op; with fewer children they had less washing to do but more clothes per head and better; their meals might be more varied and adventurous; their family might wash more frequently. This was all part of an improving life style in which they themselves had a central role to play. Many younger women, who had seen the near impossibility for their mothers of having a clean, attractive and comfortable home, in spite of their efforts, could now see the ideal being realised in part in their own homes; the hard time-consuming work remained virtually unchanged, but the greater reward increased their self-respect as managerial figures.

Marriage: the 'Best Job of All'?

The traditional imbalance between the sexes in British society had long
meant that marriage was denied to large numbers of women however
much it was regarded as the only proper calling. At first sight one might
suppose that this situation continued after 1914. Male mortality in
infancy has remained higher than female throughout the twentieth
century. And the three-quarters of a million male losses in the First
World War seem to exacerbate the imbalance disastrously. The 1921
census showed a worsening of the sex ratio especially among those in
their twenties and thirties. However, in the 5 to 9 years age group
females were *outnumbered* by males; and in the 1931 census almost all
age groups showed a decline in women in relation to men, a trend which
has continued ever since. Plainly the gloomy prognostications about the
prospects for marriage were flawed.

There are two explanations for the demographic changes. The first
long-term one is simply that after 1918 the pattern of emigration which
had carried off so many marriageable British males began to change.
Far fewer people left the country than before 1914, and indeed after
1930 more were returning than leaving. In addition the traditional view
about the effect of the war is seriously flawed. If normal mortality rates
are taken into account it is estimated that the actual loss attributable to
war was around 610,000. But this has to be set against the fact that war
also checked the emigration which, before 1914, often ran at a quarter
of a million each year, of which six-tenths was male. The losses by
death were thus balanced by the gains from the interruption to
emigration; indeed it can be argued that more people were actually
resident in Britain as a result of the war. At the very least it seems clear
that the indelible impression created by writers such as Vera Brittain
about a whole generation of women suddenly deprived of husbands is a
gross distortion of the facts. In fact the rate of marriage among women,
which had been declining a little before 1914, was only slightly reduced
during the 1920s. Even then it is striking that amongst women in their
late teens and twenties it was already *higher* than in the Edwardian
period. Moreover, from 1930 a greater proportion of all women began
to marry, and the trend was particularly marked in the second half of the
decade. One can now see that the 1930s marked the start of a significant
long-term trend towards marriage which lasted for some 40 years
before it was checked, apart, that is, from an interruption caused by the
Second World War (see Table 7.2).

The growing popularity of marriage in British society is a major

Table 7.2 First Marriage Rates by Age Groups Among Women
1901–1975 (per thousand population)

	16–19 years	20–24 years	25–29 years	30–34 years	First marriage rate per thousand population over 16
1901–5	15.4	103.4	90.5		57.4
1906–10	14.2	100.8	91.1		55.8
1911–15	16.0	104.7	116.4	65.3	58.7
1916–20	15.8	107.4	113.6	66.0	57.4
1921–25	16.7	108.6	116.7	60.3	55.2
1926–30	18.6	107.2	117.7	57.8	54.8
1931–5	21.0	109.7	127.6	62.3	57.3
1936–40	33.1	154.4	171.3	78.7	73.3
1941–5	45.6	171.6	132.2	62.6	67.6
1946–50	47.6	205.2	153.5	81.4	75.7
1951–5	55.5	231.9	157.2	75.1	76.8
1956–60	72.7	261.6	164.4	75.9	82.6
1961–5	76.4	260.2	161.3	73.8	83.6
1966–70	85.0	260.9	159.4	72.7	94.2
1971–5	86.2	228.2	167.8	83.4	91.9

Source: A.H. Halsey (ed.), *British Social Trends Since 1900* (1988), p.73.

phenomenon which has not so far been adequately explained. In earlier periods economic hardship was usually associated with postponement of marriage. Yet the inter-war depression scarcely appears to have had such an impact. This may be partly because, as we have noted, the slump did not, in fact, depress living standards for most people. Even the young unemployed were optimistic enough to embark on marriage; this is the real message of the famous novel by Walter Greenwood, *Love on the Dole* (1933). Amongst men the marriage ratio was not quite the same as for women – it increased sharply in the early 1920s for example – but the long run pattern is similar. This underlines the fact that, notwithstanding contemporary propaganda about female dependence and male independence, it is men who, on the whole, need marriage particularly for the comfort, security and self-esteem it brings. The tendency for both sexes to marry at a younger age is a marked feature of the inter-war years; by 1931 the average age at marriage was 27 years for men and 25 for women, and this pattern was not interrupted until the 1960s.

Clearly the popularity of marriage amongst the inter-war generation was no mere contrivance of the women's magazines – feminists were often equally keen on marriage, as we shall see in the next chapter. This suggests that perceptions of marriage were changing in ways that made it more attractive to women. In her novel *Honourable Estate* (1936) Vera Brittain depicted the companionate marriage, a partnership of equals in which a woman combined career and marriage. However, this kind of relationship can scarcely have extended beyond a few middle-class couples. On the other hand, was the alternative ideal of the romantic marriage, so sedulously propagated by the women's press, gaining a hold? There exists a certain amount of evidence that the working-class marriage had traditionally been regarded as an un-emotional, down-to-earth contract, a recognition of the mutual support the two partners could bring each other.[31] This did not suddenly give way to a romantic, leisurely existence. Elizabeth Roberts has shown how women continued to play the key managerial role after the war. But they also enjoyed greater resources, a slightly wider choice and the possibility of a fuller relationship with their husbands than before. One indication of this was changing sexual behaviour. For example, whereas only 19 per cent of women married before 1904 had had pre-marital sexual relations, 39 per cent of those married during 1915–25 had.[32] At the same time a long-term decline in prostitution was taking place. Generalisation is difficult but one has here some indications of a breakdown of the old stereotyped views about women as either 'ladies' on the one hand or loose women on the other; men were increasingly likely to engage in sexual relations with the women they would subsequently marry. This necessarily involved a franker acceptance that sex could be desired and enjoyed by any respectable woman.

Consequently married life did tend to become a more equal and affectionate affair. For one thing it lasted longer as a result of the growing longevity of both sexes; moreover, the completion of the family by the age of 28, on average, meant that a couple enjoyed a longer period together without dependent children. There are grounds for thinking that this relative childlessness, combined with the rising standard of living, had the effect of drawing men into a more intimate relationship with their wives. This is sometimes described as the 'domestication' of men. However, this does not mean that they took on the burdens of housework, only that they became more involved in home and family life. This was more apparent on the newer housing estates where man and wife were less involved in the community and more likely to depend upon one another for companionship and support. In particular the steady decline in drinking proved to be a major gain for women; it became increasingly common for husband and wife to visit the public house together rather than in single sex groups. Many were also attracted away from the public house altogether by cheaper forms of entertainment such as the cinema, in which the whole family could participate. Moreover, the home itself became a more important focus for leisure activities in the form of gardening, interior decoration, home improvements and the entertainment of friends. Between 1923 and 1939 the number of wireless sets increased from 200,000 to almost 9 million. For women the wireless was of particular importance in making the home, in which they spent so much of their lives, a pleasanter place.

On the other hand, the law remained stacked against married women between the wars. In spite of the Victorian reforms concerning property rights a wife's financial stake in her marriage was scarcely recognised in law. Houses were usually purchased in the name of the husband. If a wife earned dividends at the Co-op or saved out of her housekeeping money this was still judged to be the property of her husband. Even if she gained an extra income by taking in lodgers she was deemed in law to be acting as her husband's agent by using his rooms and beds. In practice this situation rarely attracted attention since most wives continued to manage the finances themselves. It was only when a couple sought divorce that the wife's position was exposed.

It might be argued that the increase in divorce and especially in the proportion of divorces sought by women undermines the view of marriage as a more attractive relationship in this period. In 1923 the law on divorce was made more equal between the sexes in that a woman could now obtain a divorce for adultery alone, as could her husband. In 1937 desertion was added to the grounds for divorce, an important gain for women, who were usually the ones to be left with the family to support. However, while legal reforms had a stimulating effect on divorce they were by no means the chief factor. The two world wars generated a rise in divorce, each being followed by a decline in spite of the legal situation. It is worth remembering that only 2 per cent of the marriages of 1926 ended in divorce after 20 years, and only 6 per cent of the marriages of 1936.[33] Even if one allows for the likelihood that some unhappy wives were deterred by the problem of inadequate maintenance arrangements, this is still a low level which seems to justify A.H. Halsey's conclusion that in the 1930s and 1950s 'marriages enjoyed a stability without precedent in history'. In earlier periods marriages were invariably cut short after only a few years by the death of one partner; the longevity of twentieth-century men and women clearly exposed marriages to greater potential scope for breakdown. Thus, when the women's magazines propagated the ideal of marriage and domesticity between the wars they were clearly in touch with their audience. Social and economic change strengthened the appeal of family life in this period, and a steadily larger majority of people experienced it at first hand as wives and husbands. This prevailing domesticity obviously had implications for all women's organisations; but it would be a mistake to assume that it necessarily precluded wider horizons for inter-war women.

Citizenship for Homemakers: the WIs

As we have already noticed, for the older generation of feminists, such as Fawcett, Rathbone and Rhondda, the developments in women's lives between the wars were a matter for dismay and puzzlement. To focus attention upon the trivial gains of home and family or the superficial glitter of fashion and leisure could be seen as undermining their lifetime's work. Yet if the domestic ideal represented an alternative to that espoused by feminists, it by no means constituted an impenetrable barrier to the mobilisation of the female population. Several organisations proved it was possible to involve ordinary women in activities outside their homes without challenging the conventional wisdom about sex roles, and indeed by capitalising upon fashionable trends and beliefs. This meant treading a careful path between two opposite poles: feminism and citizenship on the one hand and femininity and domestication on the other. This was the balance that *Woman* proposed to strike. But unlike the magazines organisations such as the Women's Institutes and the Women's Co-operative Guild went some considerable way to achieving this goal. At first sight they may seem rather different organisations; clearly the WIs looked rather more towards the domestic ideal and the WCG in the direction of feminism. But this is a matter of degree only, and the differences between them are less important than the similarities. For our purposes the point is that both were *successful* attempts to mobilise ordinary women at a time when many feminist groups were dwindling; both bridged the gulf between the rival ideals for women, and both provided an example, even a stimulus, to the more overtly feminist groups. They help us to understand why the women's movement evolved in the direction it did during the twentieth century.

The origins of the Women's Institutes lay in the long-standing concern about the decay and apathy of rural life in late Victorian Britain. On several occasions during the Edwardian period voices had been raised in favour of emulating the Canadian system of village institutes, but it was the shortages of food and rural labour during the war that provided the eventual stimulus for the scheme. In spite of its size the WI movement has not attracted the attention of students of women's history which it deserves. Stuck with the jam-and Jerusalem tag, it is easily passed over as a joke or a mild embarrassment. But historians must rid themselves of contemporary assumptions. In the context of 1915 when the first WI was established on Anglesey, it represented a radical innovation. This was both because it involved the least organised group of women, and because of the democratic nature of WI structure. The equal voting rights for every member were interpreted as something of a challenge to feudal traditions in the countryside.[34] Moreover, its staunchly non-sectarian character provoked some suspicions from churches and chapels that the WI would be liable to irreligion. Finally, we have already noted how apprehensive the political parties were, with Conservatives seeing the WI as a radical, left-leaning pressure group, and Labour seeing it as an agent for bourgeois feminism. While such fears seem exaggerated, even ludicrous, they serve to underline how momentous the new organisation appeared in the early 1920s. The very speed of its growth suggests how large a gap it began to fill in the lives of many countrywomen.

The character and personnel of the Women's Institute movement became fairly firmly set as early as 1919. During the war years the Board of Agriculture showed much interest in absorbing the new organisation as a branch of its Food Production Department. Since the WI received a grant of £2000 from the Treasury the ministry clearly believed it enjoyed a commanding position. But the president, Lady

Table 7.3   The Growth of the Women's Institutes 1915–1951

	WIs	Membership (England and Wales)
1916	40	
1917		
1918	760	
1919	1,000	50,000 (approx.)
1920	1,400	
1922	2,580	160,000
1925	3,500	
1927	3,997	
1932		297,000
1937	5,534	318,000
1943		288,000
1951	7,700	446,000

Gertrude Denman, who had been invited to take on the leadership in 1916 partly owing to her known interest in small-holdings, dug in her heels and insisted on maintaining the independent and democratic character of her organisation. It was in order to fend off an official take over that a National Federation of WIs was hastily established in 1918. The WI was, however, obliged to accept the transfer of headquarters staff to the Board of Agriculture during the war.[35] By 1919 the government had agreed to withdraw from its role in promoting the work of the WIs. The annual meeting in October 1918 laid down the basis of the organisation as democratic, for women only, non-sectarian and non-party political. Members joined for a 2 shilling fee of which 6d. went to national headquarters. Local Institutes functioned by open vote of the members, and elected representatives to the County Federations which in turn could join the National Federation. The Central Committee representatives were elected annually by secret ballot, and official information was disseminated through the journal *Home and Country* from 1919.

The real philosophy of the WIs was encapsulated, and indeed personified, by Mrs Margaret Wintringham, MP, for whom participation in the movement represented something of a political asset. In an article in *Good Housekeeping* entitled 'What Makes a Home-Maker?' she commented:

> The whole tendency of the Women's Institute outlook is to present the work of the Housekeeper, the Home-Keeper, or better still, the Home-maker, in the light of a highly privileged, skilled and nationally important occupation.[36]

It was, in short, essentially for married women, rooted in their homes and families. This made for a certain amount of common ground with the 'New Feminism' of the inter-war period with its greater emphasis on the welfare of the mother and housewife. Yet at the same time, the organisation was clearly understood by many of its members in a different sense. Writing in 1933, Janet Courtney insisted that the WIs 'take no narrow feminist view'; she disapproved of earlier attempts by women to lobby for the vote, and condemned current efforts at using the vote over controversial issues which threatened to generate friction between men and women.[37]

These somewhat contradictory impulses were usually contained because the WI, like many organisations of women, operated rather differently at national and at local level. It seems fairly clear that at the grass roots the chief activities of the institutes were handicrafts and the revival of skills otherwise in danger of disappearing. But the motive behind this was increasingly to improve the quality of domestic work, not to attain industrial levels of output or restore rural industry. The second type of activity involved agricultural-horticultural work, notably jam and fruit bottling, breadmaking, bacon curing, and the production of cheese, chickens and vegetables. These provided the material for exhibitions and market stalls. The third type of activity involved music, drama and dancing; the practice of singing 'Jerusalem' at meetings dates from 1924.

However, women like Denman and Wintringham clearly saw the purpose of the WIs as broader than this. This is why the organisation's objects had been deliberately amended in 1918 in order to incorporate the non-party political. By this means it proved possible to satisfy the eagerness of the early members to undertake action on political questions closely affecting women, notably housing; the WIs were free to exert pressure on their local councils to put into effect the government's new policy of state-aided house building.[38] Within this interpretation the movement was able to interest itself in a large number of 'women's' questions including cheap electricity, village water supplies, bus services and rural telephones, the supply of milk for children and young mothers and the provision of midwives and infant welfare centres. They took a particular interest in educational facilities by acting as agents for the distribution of books under rural library schemes, and by forming networks of village evening classes in cooperation with the county councils, the Adult Education Council and the Workers Education Association. Finally they advocated the use of women police, censorship of the cinema and the election of women to parish, rural district and county councils. The National Federation, assuming the title of the Countrywomen's Parliament at its annual gatherings of up to 5000 delegates, passed resolutions on all these questions and made representations to ministers from time to time. For all that, the WI seems to have *represented* the concerns of women rather than to have *campaigned* actively for them. Moreover the need to define its political range rather tightly gave rise to some controversy. Hence for example, the National Federation's withdrawal from the Consultative Committee of Women's Organisations in 1926, and the arguments over 'peace' campaigns. The executive encouraged local WIs to affiliate to the League of Nations Union, which some 600 evidently did. But when they refused to allow speakers from the Navy League to address their meetings they exposed themselves to criticism as a pacifist organisation.[39] This underlines the fact that the WIs owed their success to concentration on home-making and entertainment; their political dimension was a burden which could be carried only if it excluded feminist and other controversial items. Even within these limitations they did help to politicise many women, but how far this was advantageous for the wider women's movement is questionable. While it can be argued that the WIs diverted the energies of feminists such as Denman, Wintringham, Mrs Auerbach and Miss Haddow away from feminist work, this must be balanced by the contacts and the standing such women won through the organisation. Lady Denman's role as chairman of the Family Planning Association for example, cannot be seen as helpful to the Women's Institutes; but her prestigious and respectable status as president of the National Federation of Women's Institutes undoubtedly constituted an asset to the FPA.

Politics for Consumers: the Women's Co-operative Guild

Founded back in 1883 the Women's Co-operative Guild was clearly an established fixture in the women's movement a generation before the Women's Institutes appeared on the scene. It was largely an urban-based organisation, and drew its membership from working-class women, though it had always enjoyed a number of middle-class leaders like Margaret Llewelyn Davies. Though considerably smaller than the WI movement it was always potentially as large because it recruited from the huge body of Co-operative Society members. It was also more overtly feminist and after 1918 formally linked to party politics. Above all the WCG is of interest because it constituted one of the most effective attempts to sustain a political organisation of women that was adapted to the mood of the inter-war period. This is true in two senses. First, the WCG placed great emphasis upon its role as a mouthpiece for married women; this helped to make it more reassuring and more likely to be treated sympathetically by politicians than many of the feminist groups who were associated with the spinster and antagonism to the male sex. Secondly, the WCG remained unapologetically and defiantly an organisation for consumers; it aspired to awaken the housewife to what was styled the 'basket power' she wielded by virtue of her role as the spender of the nation's wages.[40] In this sense it extended the Victorian suffragist case for the enfranchisement of woman as mother, wife and household manager.

The WCG also stood strategically at the centre of three overlapping spheres: Co-operation, feminism and the Labour movement. This position determined the role that it performed in the twentieth century.

Clearly as an integral element of the Co-operative Wholesale Society (CWS) it was pledged to the spread of the co-operative ideal as a means of organising society. This implied a socialist vision, but one of a distinctive kind. The WCG criticised male socialists for assuming that labour and production would be the basis for the new society as it had been in the existing one. Instead the WCG argued for *consumption* as the vital basis for society. Thus the humblest woman consumer might in her daily life raise the standard of living of her own family by the distribution of the profits of the CWS. But, more ambitiously, she knew that the more she dealt on a Co-operative basis in goods produced under conditions approved by trade unions, the more she undermined the capitalist system and prepared the way for a real change.[41] Further, the WCG dedicated itself to inculcating some training for citizenship in women. In its local classes and branch meetings working-class women learnt the techniques of public speaking, chairing meetings, taking minutes, tabling resolutions and agendas, keeping accounts and conducting correspondence. This frequently served as an apprenticeship for involvement in municipal elections. All activities were conducted within a democratic structure stretching from the branch to the district, the central committee and the annual conference. In this respect the WCG was often doing for working-class women what the Women's Citizens Association and the Women's Local Government Society tried to do for the middle classes.

Finally the WCG sought to articulate the needs of married women and to win reforms for them by parliamentary methods. From its original concern for the health and welfare of mothers and children it became more political around 1900 when it took up women's suffrage. During the Edwardian period the WCG's action in support of specific issues such as the medical inspection of schoolchildren and the payment of maternity benefits under the National Insurance Act made it one of the most effective pressure groups. This work continued during the war especially in connection with infant mortality rates; and from 1918 the WCG was formally connected, via the CWS and the Co-operative Party, to the Labour Party itself. At this stage around 100 local WCG branches affiliated to their local Labour parties.

Widespread concern amongst housewives over rising prices and profiteering during and after the war helps to account for the sharp expansion of the WCG during the period 1918 to 1920. This growth continued right into the 1930s when other organisations of women found that the economic depression was undermining their recruitment. It may well be that the rising standard of living in the south and south-east

Table 7.4   Women's Co-operative Guild Membership 1914–1931

	Membership
1914	31,658
1915	29,573
1919	32,908
1920	44,000
1922	51,291
1931	67,293

of England was responsible for the particularly large increase in membership in those regions (Table 7.4). The combination of successful political pressure and expanding support helps to explain why the WCG was so ready to assert its independence within the Labour and Co-operative movements. This was emphatically demonstrated by its willingness to do without an annual grant from the CWS during 1914–18 rather than be dictated to by the men over its policy on divorce reform. Less controversially the WCG faced a proposal not infrequently made by men to their successful women's organisations to institute 'mixed' Guilds incorporating both sexes. The women shrewdly accepted the idea in the knowledge that men were quite unable to sustain local branches and that the grass roots of the Co-operative movement depended upon women for its motive force.[42]

This inherent strength enabled the WCG to play a uniquely independent feminist role within the framework of the Labour movement between the wars. For example, it firmly backed the idea of family allowances when this was opposed by the trade unions. On the subject of divorce the WCG advocated that the law should be equal as between the sexes, and, almost as important, that the procedure should be cheap enough for working-class women to afford. But perhaps its most characteristic theme between the wars was the need to reduce maternal mortality rates and to improve women's health generally. It particularly urged the extension of maternity clinics, and the provision of home helps who could relieve mothers of their domestic burdens in the weeks before and after their confinement. It is in the context of maternal health that one must see the WCG's early support for two controversial proposals – birth control and the legalisation of abortion.

However, it seems probable that the WCG achieved its successes in mobilising working-class women in spite of its radicalism and not because of it. The 60,000 membership seems less impressive when put in the context of a total Co-operative Wholesale Society membership of some 5 million in 1925. While the WCG continued to expand, the doubts were not voiced, but after 1945 the leaders began to ask why they had never managed to recruit more than a fraction of their potential support. One sympathetic observer, Mary Stott, who worked professionally on the *Co-operative News* in the 1930s, felt that the organisation had simply become too set in its ways to develop further; the rigid system of training placed a premium on mediocrity and failed to bring forward the most able women into leading roles.[43] An ageing membership was certainly identified after 1945 as a central problem. Moreover, while influential amongst politicians, the WCG was still largely using methods carried over from the days when women had been outside the pale of the constitution. Its leading women found it extremely difficult to make a personal impression in spite of their position within the Labour Party, as the career of Eleanor Barton demonstrates. It was not until after 1945 that several Co-operative women at last won election to parliament. The difficulty lay in the fact that they had to run an obstacle course to get there. The Labour Party had to be persuaded by the Co-operative Party to adopt its candidates. Yet the women usually held only a token place on the various committees of the Co-operative Party and the CWS. Moreover, by 1936 they felt they were being squeezed out of even this toehold in the movement.

Thus in spite of its success as an organisation for married women in bridging the gap between the world of conventional party politics and the world of feminism, the Women's Co-operative Guild fell short of its potential. It seemed to be swimming with the tide both by its connection with Labour and by its emphasis upon the health and welfare questions on which it spoke authoritatively. Yet it never fully capitalised on this advantage after 1918; and the peripheral position it had won within the political system by the late 1930s suggests that it had reached its natural limits by this time. The winning of the vote for women does not appear to have effected a major improvement in its bargaining power.

In spite of their obvious differences the WCG and the Women's Institutes demonstrated a common capacity to organise ordinary women during a period when many women's groups were dwindling. Both achieved their success from within the prevailing ideology of domesticity. This clearly gave them a substantial appeal amongst women, respectability and a measure of influence in British society; but at the same time it imposed limitations upon them. In the wider context their experience helps us to understand both why feminists were attracted by their form of organisation, and also why, in emulating it, they failed to achieve their objectives.

Chapter 8 The New Feminism and the Decline of the Women's Movement in the 1930s

'Today the battle we thought won is going badly against us', commented Cicely Hamilton in 1935, 'we are retreating where once we advanced.'[1] Her younger colleague on *Time and Tide*, Winifred Holtby, got closer to an explanation when she posed the question: 'Why, in 1934, are women themselves often the first to repudiate the movements of the past hundred and fifty years, which gained for them at least the foundations of political, economic, educational and moral equality?'[2] Such remarks by contemporary feminists are a valuable corrective to the claims made by Dale Spender that the inter-war decline of the women's movement is no more than another male conspiracy to deny women their heritage![3] Indeed the theme of decline has exercised several scholars recently. Olive Banks has argued that the movement 'trapped women in the cult of domesticity' and failed to 'survive the combined assault of both the Depression and the Second World War'. Susan Kingsley Kent has pointed to the impact of the Great War on perceptions of gender, suggesting that as early as the 1920s 'feminism as a distinct political and social movement no longer existed'. And the most severe verdict comes from Sheila Jeffries, who has condemned the leading inter-war feminist Eleanor Rathbone for 'defeatism' and speaks of her 'betrayal' of the movement.[4]

Few would deny that by 1930 the women's movement had reached an awkward crossroads. Its cutting edge was blunted by the general climate engendered by the economic depression; the optimistic mood of reconstruction had long since evaporated in a society increasingly intolerant of any female aspirations except the purely domestic. Yet up to a point feminists were simply the victims of their own success in the shape of the catalogue of reforms from 1918 to 1928. The almost inevitable consequence was a certain loss of momentum and increasing difficulty in mobilising women for further campaigns. Eleanor Rathbone quickly recognised the danger of apathy amongst the wealthy and leisured women who had sustained the suffrage movement before 1914 but had now achieved what they wanted. Replacing them was not easy. Younger women often thought it enough to show their emancipation by a personal pursuit of employment rather than collective political work. Much of the personnel of inter-war feminism found itself attracted into either the peace movement or the political parties in the belief that such activity helped to promote the wider cause of women's emancipation. Yet there is more than one criterion for measuring success and failure; and what looks like decline from one perspective appears as an evolutionary development from another. Much of the pessimistic comment on the inter-war period reflects the reaction of the post-1960 generation against the welfare feminism that culminated in the years after 1945. In assessing the strategies and alternatives of the 1930s, therefore, it is necessary to explain how women embarked on the route that led towards that particular conclusion.

Equal Rights Versus the New Feminism

The first shots in the inter-war debate over the future of the women's movement were fired as early as 1918 by feminists like Maud Royden who argued that women had shown themselves in the war to be the equals of men; the next challenge meant facing the fundamental differences between the sexes, and the fact that women did some things better than men.[5] For some years, however, feminists occupied themselves with the tempting targets now beneath their electoral guns – the unfinished business of the Victorian movement. Yet the underlying problems of ideology and tactics already loomed large in the original mind of Eleanor Rathbone, who succeeded Mrs Fawcett as president of NUSEC in 1919. The major constructive force upon British feminism in this period, Rathbone combined the intellectual's facility for diagnosing problems with the politician's capacity for acting on her convictions. She showed a shrewd appreciation of the political process; thus even before the vote had been won Rathbone anticipated future needs by founding the first Women's Citizens Association. Its especial purpose was to mobilise the millions of women who had remained beyond the reach of the suffrage movement even at its height and to increase awareness of their political role. Although the WCA proved inadequate to its task, in that it largely recruited existing middle-class activists, Rathbone remained alive to the opportunities for extending the market for feminism.

Meanwhile she grew impatient with the tendency for women's organisations, including her own, to remain caught in pre-1914 postures. She noticed that even a new body, the Six Point Group, con-

centrated its fire on such issues as the right of peeresses to sit in the
House of Lords, the right of a woman to enter the diplomatic and
consular service, and the right of a married woman to retain her
nationality on marriage to a foreigner. These causes, however worthy,
seemed scarcely sufficient to generate the momentum for a major
campaign. As the 1920s wore on Rathbone grew more convinced that
'equal rights' was nearly played out as the principal theme for the
women's movement.

Her position as a feminist was analogous to that of the 'New
Liberals' of the 1890s in relation to Gladstonian Liberalism, and it is
surely significant that this was precisely the background from which
she came. The New Liberals, while by no means repudiating the
traditional quest for individual political and legal rights, regarded this
as an exhausted seam by the century's end. In a similar fashion
Rathbone sought to broaden the work of feminism. For her, political
and legal equalities were no longer the pressing need, and were in any
case not enough in themselves. Real emancipation for women involved
recognising the social-economic dimension to their lives. Now in spite
of the fierce debate between New and Equal Rights feminists it is fair to
say that the need to promote the employment of women was common to
all factions. Critics of Rathbone and the New Feminists sometimes
malign them by suggesting that they simply wanted women to be
housewives, not paid workers. Such a conclusion overlooks the fact
that outside the debates within NUSEC's Council much effort was
channelled into employment questions, notably by the former London
Society for Women's Suffrage which became the London Society for
Women's Service in 1919. Ray and Pippa Strachey were leading
figures in this work.

However, it would be fair to say that while Rathbone remained keen to
advance women's opportunities for employment she recognised that the
majority of women were unlikely to be *primarily* interested in a career –
rather, they would continue to be wives and mothers. Somehow feminists must come to terms with this uncomfortable fact or risk alienating
themselves from the ordinary British woman. That Rathbone was always
inclined in this direction is apparent from her early interest in the idea of
'family endowment'. Wartime experience in Liverpool, where she
became involved with the payment of allowances for dependants to the
wives of servicemen, influenced her thinking. By November 1917 she
had established the Family Endowment Committee with Maude Royden,
Kathleen Courtney, Mary Stocks and H.N. Brailsford to propagate the
case for what became known as family allowances.

Although as a practical social reformer Rathbone was impressed by the improvements in health and living standards which could be achieved by channelling comparatively modest sums directly to mothers, she always regarded family allowances as part of a wider emancipation for women; thus the arguments over this reform crystallised the broader debate within inter-war feminism. In Rathbone's view feminists were wasting energy in futile campaigns for equal pay. As things stood most women entered the labour market only when driven to supplement family income, or when free from domestic obligations; consequently they would continue to experience low pay, to be neglected by trade unions and to regard the issue of equal pay with indifference. Tactically feminists made an error in concentrating upon a male conception of what constituted 'work'. Their objective should be to ensure that motherhood was treated as an important occupation with a claim on the resources of the state; hence the need to pay family allowances direct to the mother. Rathbone believed that in this way it would be possible to circumvent the whole sterile struggle over equal pay and the 'living wage' – for any standard wage was inevitably irrelevant since it was unrelated to the size of the family it was supposed to support.[6]

By 1925 a public debate had been joined between the New Feminists and supporters of equal rights – dubbed the 'Me Too' feminists by Mary Stocks. In her presidential address of that year Rathbone articulated a view that still reverberates today:

> At last we have done with the boring business of measuring everything that women want, or that is offered them by men's standards. ... At last we can stop looking at all our problems through men's eyes. ... We can demand what we want for women, not because it is what men have got, but because it is what women need to fulfil the potentialities of their natures and to adjust to the circumstances of their own lives.[7]

The implication was that feminists must modify their agenda to give more prominence to matters which did not affect the two sexes equally: family allowances, birth control and housing. Improvement in the status of women was intimately connected with the priority society gave to such matters. From a political point of view Rathbone judged 1925 to be the right moment for a change. On the one hand immediate legislative objectives over guardianship, maintenance, illegitimacy and widows' pensions had been attained, leaving only relatively minor equal rights issues to be resolved. On the other hand the outstanding questions such as the equal moral standard and equal pay were highly intractable and not entirely susceptible to legislative remedy even with the advantage of a sympathetic government, which was by now increasingly unlikely.

In addition to Rathbone and Royden the chief advocates of the new course were Eva Hubback, Elizabeth Macadam, Mary Stocks, Margery Corbett Ashby and Kathleen Courtney; their leading opponents from the equal rights tradition included Mrs Fawcett, Elizabeth Abbott, Chrystal Macmillan, Monica Whately, Helen Fraser and Lady Balfour of Burleigh. However, the leadership of NUSEC had already passed into the hands of the New Feminists with Rathbone as president (1919), Hubback as parliamentary secretary (1920) and Macadam as secretary (1919), and editor of the *Woman's Leader* (1923). The issue came to a head in 1926 and was resolved by a formal split in 1927. At NUSEC's annual meeting it was decided to introduce both family allowances and birth control into the immediate programme. This initiative provoked a good deal of agonising among the affiliated societies, some of whom thought the new issues should be handled by separate pressure groups, while others simply disapproved of birth control. In the Cardiff WCA, for example, a move to disaffiliate was averted by an assurance that each autonomous society remained free to accept whatever it wished from the national programme, though this did not prevent some rank and file resignations.[8] A debate on protective legislation at the 1927 annual meeting proved decisive. Although resistance to protective legislation had always been a central feature of feminism it had proved increasingly troublesome in that it exacerbated conflict with the Labour movement, and forced many women activists to choose between their loyalty to feminism and their effective participation in Labour politics. Now NUSEC sought to resolve the dilemma by passing an amendment declaring that in future protective legislation should be accepted if it reflected the wishes of the workers immediately affected. Following this narrow but significant infringement of equal rights ideology the previous year's resolution on family allowances and birth control was carried by a large majority.[9] As a result eleven members of the executive council resigned from NUSEC, some of whom subsequently migrated to the Six Point Group, the Open Door Council and the Women's Freedom League which remained loyal to equal rights. Paradoxically the chief emphasis of NUSEC'S work during 1927 was on a classic equal rights issue – the franchise – and the commitment by Baldwin in the spring made it virtually a foregone conclusion that the matter would be triumphantly settled in 1928. Yet the imminence of this victory doubtless had the effect of exacerbating divisions, for it stimulated the New Feminists to seek a fresh cutting edge for the movement while deepening the traditionalists' fears that the ground was slipping from under their feet.

Despite the vigour of this debate, however, the division within feminism was never total. Most feminists agreed on the desirability of family allowances, but some refused to give them high priority while so many equal rights issues remained unresolved. Only a few such as Mrs Fawcett actually opposed family allowances; and this reflected her Victorian belief in thrift and parental responsibility, not to mention her anti-socialism, rather than her feminism.[10] Conversely feminists largely continued to seek equality of treatment between the sexes. Only an outspoken revisionist like Mary Stocks was ready to argue that equality actually became undesirable if carried to its logical conclusion; she suggested, for example, that women ought never to aspire to equal entry into the armed forces.

In the wake of the split and the passage of equal franchise in 1928 NUSEC's leaders pushed ahead with a reconstruction designed to promote expansion in the 1930s. Yet they betrayed a significant ambivalence at this critical juncture. On the one hand they professed confidence that the new priorities in NUSEC's programme would make a powerful appeal to women. On the other hand the reorganisation on which they embarked suggested an awareness of their limitations. NUSEC still considered itself, with some reason, as the 'Corps of Royal Engineers' for the whole of the women's movement on the grounds of its proven expertise in influencing politicians and amending and promoting legislation. It would therefore remain as a specialist, London-based organisation. The question was how to strengthen its connection with the mass of women in the country. The leaders evidently recognised that in the large towns and cities so many competing women's organisations now existed that many were ceasing to be viable.[11] Indeed amalgamations between SECs, WCAs and the National Council of Women had already gone some way during the 1920s. On the other hand, in the rural districts such opportunities as existed appeared to have been more than adequately filled by the Women's Institutes; at best NUSEC might exploit them by supplying more speakers for their meetings. This left smaller towns whose population was above 4000 which was the official limit for the WIs. Here, if anywhere, lay scope for expansion of women's organisation, which would incorporate the features of the WIs on the one hand, and some of the feminism of NUSEC on the other. In pursuit of this objective NUSEC decided to divide its work into two branches. A National Council for Equal Citizenship would continue the specialist work of a feminist pressure group, backed by local affiliated societies. But in addition there would be a new National Union of Guilds for Citizenship whose role would be to educate women as citizens, to foster social contact between them and to promote the skills and interests of women as housewives or 'home-makers'. It was anticipated that this new organisation would recruit women beyond the range of the older feminist societies, thereby capitalising on the obvious success of the WIs for the ultimate advantage of feminism. Thus began what, from 1932 onwards, was known as the National Union of Townswomen's Guilds (TGs). Its development, if less dramatic than that of the WIs, was certainly impressive, reaching 54,000 members by 1939. This, at least, represented some welcome expansion after a period of decline; whether, however, the qualitative significance of this advance was quite what NUSEC intended remains much more doubtful.

With hindsight it is not difficult to see why the NUSEC leaders took encouragement from the WI model; it represented a conspicuous example of rapid growth in a period when women's organisations were largely stagnating or declining. Moreover, at this time the WI appeared to have more potential than it did because of the prominent role played by known feminists, including Lady Denman, Helena Auerbach, Margaret Wintringham and Margery Corbett Ashby, in its national leadership. Thus it was to be anticipated that the Townswomen's Guilds, staffed by such NUSEC stalwarts as Corbett Ashby, Mary Stocks, Eva Hubback, Gertrude Horton and Edith Picton-Turbervill, would ensure that the feminist purposes were kept in mind. In practice the feminism of all large women's organisations was diluted at the grass roots, and the Guilds rapidly grew away from their origins. From the early 1930s local TG activities showed a concentration on handi-crafts, home-making and gardening while citizenship and the status of women scarcely figured in the programme. Eva Hubback frankly accepted this compromise: 'the time is past when "equality" can be the rallying cry for a powerful organisation'.[12] This does not mean that the TGs were devoid of political awareness. They shared with the WI a political programme limited to domestic and local concerns, usually uncontroversial. Essentially, however, both organisations catered to married women who felt some need for a wider range of social contacts but not for active participation in politics. In the 1940s the TG took steps to avoid affiliation to as moderate an organisation as the National Council of Women, fearful of hampering its own growth by association with feminism. Thus while some able women were drawn from NUSEC into the TG leadership, it is not clear that the parent body ever benefited by fresh recruits moving in the opposite direction. One must conclude that in the long run the Guilds represented less an extension of the NUSEC tradition into the ranks of ordinary women than a diversion and a departure from it.

This is underlined by the failure to arrest the long-term organisational decline in the existing feminist bodies. At its peak in 1914 NUSEC boasted 478 affiliated societies. The number fell to 220 by 1920, to 163 by 1924 and to 90 by 1929. The figure of 177 for 1930 suggests a revival, but this included 110 of the new Townswomen's Guilds and only 67 SECs. By 1935 NUSEC had 48 affiliated SECs and its strength remained at that level for the rest of the decade. In Glasgow another major society was wound up in 1933 after a period of falling income and membership. Its demise was attributed partly to the difficulties faced by most voluntary associations during the economic depression, but more fundamentally to the inability to recapture the former momentum and single-minded enthusiasm of the suffrage campaigns; amalgamation with the WCA in 1924 was thought to have exacerbated the diffuseness of the organisation.[13] At Cardiff the WCA continued to function during the 1930s but the attacking edge of its feminism was blunted. Work on behalf of the League of Nations Union and the Peace Ballot loomed large, and the only other issues taken up were such matters as road safety for pedestrians, the appointment of women JPs and the provision of public lavatories. WCAs in particular appear to have had a tendency to converge upon the pattern of activities characteristic of the Women's Institutes at this time.

Loss of local branches had inevitable effects upon NUSCEC's finances, which fell continuously after 1914 until 1930 when income dipped below £1000 and then stabilised. At this time the TG raised around £6000 a year and the WI around £10,000. One result was that the journal, the *Woman's Leader* (originally the suffrage paper *Common Cause*) folded and was absorbed by the *Townswoman* in 1933. The NUSEC tradition did, however, survive in one of its affiliates, the London Society for Women's Suffrage, which had already become the London Society for Women's Service and which subsequently gave rise to the Women's Employment Federation in 1934 and to the Fawcett Society. During the 1930s several leading figures in NUSEC also seem to have become active in the Women's Freedom League, the Six Point Group, the National Birth Control Association and the Family Endowment Society. However, none of the rival organisations from the equal rights tradition of feminism can be said to have found a more viable alternative. Indeed it is arguable that they became marginalised earlier than NUSEC. For example, the WFL had dwindled to 40 branches by the early 1920s and existed largely on the energy and financial generosity of a handful of women including Florence Underwood, Dr Elizabeth Knight, Helena Normanton and the aged Mrs Despard. The death of Dr Knight in 1937 resulted in the immediate collapse of *The Vote*, a journal whose title is indicative of the WFL's reluctance to adapt to change. Though under the leadership of Stella Newsome, Marion Reeves and Dorothy Evans the WFL managed to survive, by 1939 it was very much a London-based pressure group of about 3000 supporters. Similarly the Six Point Group hung on with an income during the 1930s of only a few hundred pounds a year; unable to afford either an office or a secretary it was obliged to operate from Monica Whately's flat from 1934 onwards. Remaining true to their principles, both the WFL and the Six Point Group survived until 1961 and 1981 respectively; but this was achieved only at the cost of gradual isolation from the mass of women for whom they wished to speak, and they were eventually overtaken by a new generation of feminists.

Finally, it is not surprising that during the 1930s the women's organisations made relatively little impression in terms of parliamentary legislation. Backbenchers enjoyed scattered successes such as Edith Picton-Turbervill's 1931 bill to prohibit the passing of the death sentence on expectant mothers, and the Inheritance (Family Provision) Act which was a revised version of Rathbone's bill to prevent a husband disinheriting his wife and children. 1937 brought A.P. Herbert's divorce reform which extended the grounds for divorce to include desertion for three years, cruelty, insanity, rape, bestiality and sodomy; it also permitted a marriage to be declared null and void for non-consummation, venereal disease and epilepsy. For its part the government was primarily concerned to build upon existing social legislation for women, as is shown by the 1936 Public Health Act and the Midwives Act. The major innovation came in 1930 in the form of a limited provision of information on birth control in local authority clinics. In 1938 the home secretary agreed to tackle the question of women who were obliged to surrender their nationality on marrying foreigners; but the legislation was interrupted by the outbreak of war and was not enacted until 1948. By comparison with the record of the early 1920s, and in the context of the demands being made by women's organisations, this was a meagre catalogue. NUSEC and Eleanor Rathbone were being steadily checked in the parliamentary sphere in which they claimed considerable expertise. Perhaps the one mitigating factor is that during the second half of the decade the leaders were increasingly absorbed by the deteriorating international situation. On the one hand Rathbone herself became increasingly angry and appalled by the National government's weakness over the invasion of Abyssinia and the Spanish War and the undermining of the League of Nations. On the other hand Nancy Astor and Vera Brittain were increasingly seized with the need to maintain relations with Germany and avoid a repetition of the horrors of the 1914–18 war. All seemed to feel that the scale of the approaching war dwarfed domestic concerns, and it was not until the crisis had actually broken that feminist issues received a fresh stimulus.

Nancy Astor and the Moral Reform Tradition

Whatever view one takes of the long-term impact of the New Feminism it must be remembered that in the context of the late 1920s and 1930s it seemed to make good sense. Especially when articulated in terms of practical welfare feminism it was working with the tide of British politics. Moreover, although new in one sense, it also reflected a satisfying continuity with past thinking within the women's movement. For, as Olive Banks has emphasised, the New Feminists' focus on the special experience of women as wives and mothers represented a reaffirmation of the evangelical strain in the nineteenth-century movement. Generations of women had been inspired to play a public role by a belief in their special contribution as the more civilised half of society. This had manifested itself in a moral reform movement working for temperance, peace, the abolition of the slave trade and the ending of the double standard in sexual conduct. Although this tradition was, perhaps, more prominent a feature of the women's movement in the United States, it remained an important element in Britain too.

In some ways the personification of moral reform feminism between the wars was Nancy Astor. Perhaps because she has been widely regarded as a 'character', accounts of her career as Britain's first woman MP tend to neglect her contribution to feminism. Certainly her unexpected emergence in 1919 dismayed some feminists:

> Not for this had we laboured so long and so hard ... here was an American millionairess, known to us only by reputation, since we did not move in those circles, as a society hostess, stepping into a safe seat vacated by her husband on his elevation to the peerage not by reason of her own qualifications but merely *qua* wife. We feared the worst.[14]

However, even left-wing feminists soon admitted that their misgivings had been exaggerated, and they came to see her as an asset. Astor's undoubted waywardness, her tactlessness and her shallow grasp of the issues was mitigated by the influence of Ray Strachey who, finding her 'lamentably ignorant of everything she ought to know' became her political adviser. NUSEC attempted to brief her on the major issues, though her spontaneous performances in the Commons must have made her a frustrating apprentice. Yet as a wealthy, titled lady Astor brought a large measure of social status and respectability to the women's cause; her role as a great hostess, her husband's connections with Lloyd George, and her easy familiarity with the world of high politics might be turned to advantage by a movement largely limited to middle-class professionals. If the more staid feminists felt uncomfortable at her receptions, many of them acknowledged the value of such occasions to them.

Yet the real significance of Nancy Astor lay in the simple fact that she was a *recruit* to feminism. Not apparently involved even with the suffrage campaign before the war, she now embodied the wider appeal that Rathbone was so keen to make. For although an exotic figure, in some ways Astor enjoyed an affinity with the ordinary women who had also remained outside the ranks of organised feminism. With her combination of class and populist style she was better placed to appeal to women at large than the worthy intellectuals like Rathbone who dominated the movement. Characteristically Astor once defined her aim in terms of articulating the views of 'the real women, not the sort that is neither male nor female; I mean the real old-fashioned, courageous, sensible, solid, cup-of-tea women.'[15] Certainly the size of her post-bag – up to 2000 letters a week – suggests that many women regarded her as their special representative. Thus, in spite of her intellectual shortcomings Astor enjoyed tremendous potential as the figurehead, and indeed as the real leader, of the women's movement between the wars.

That this potential was never fully realised was not simply a reflection of her defects of intellect and temperament; it was also the result of her particular brand of feminism. For as an American she brought that emphasis on morality which was so pronounced a feature of women's movements in the United States. Her rather puritanical upbringing in rural Virginia seems to have left her with a moral-religious approach to life, a predisposition much strengthened by her disastrous first marriage at the age of 18. Quickly repulsed by her husband's excessive drinking and his sexual demands, she was separated from him in 1901 and divorced in 1903. Characteristically Astor managed to joke about her distaste for physical relationships: 'I can't even tolerate seeing two birds mating without wanting to separate them.' Inevitably her puritanism subsequently imposed strict limitations on her feminism.

Guided by her NUSEC advisers Astor energetically campaigned on a wide range of issues associated with health and welfare feminism including widows' pensions, provision of nursery schools, maternal mortality, female unemployment and the raising of the school-leaving age. However, her priorities were never identical with theirs. It clearly went against the grain to take up all the feminist causes, and on such matters as divorce reform and birth control she showed herself essentially a Victorian woman. In 1922 she publicly opposed legislation designed to give women equal grounds for divorce with men, a stance which was believed to have encouraged some MPs to resist change.[16] Somewhat ineptly Astor argued that women had not really gained from easier divorce in the United States. Yet as the beneficiary of American law she merely exposed herself to charges of hypocrisy. Her position became all the more uncomfortable when women wrote to her seeking her help over divorcing their own unwanted husbands.[17] Such pressure perhaps helps to explain her reluctant decision to vote for equal divorce in 1923. But during the 1930s she continued to prevaricate over all further attempts designed to help women by a liberalisation of the divorce laws.[18]

Similarly Astor instinctively resisted the demand to provide information on birth control. She subscribed to the traditional view that birth control invited looser moral conduct, thereby lowering women to the standards of men, and in any case the whole subject seemed distasteful. In addition, as her parliamentary seat became precarious she risked losing it by antagonising the opponents of birth control. Eventually she was persuaded to support a strictly limited relaxation of the rules on grounds of health, and on the basis that birth control was for many poor women an alternative to the far worse evil of abortion.[19] But she continued to oppose any national policy on the subject: 'Please don't think that I am in favour of wholesale knowledge of the methods of birth control.'[20] Thus she rejected unrestricted sales of contraceptives as a threat to the morals of the young, declined to become a vice-president of the National Birth Control Council, and avoided visits to birth control centres. Legislation on the subject was simply pronounced premature: 'it is useless to bring in measures in Parliament which are ahead of the articulate desires of the electorate.'[21]

In contrast to her equivocal position on these questions Astor enthusiastically embraced the causes of temperance, women police, the protection of children, and reform of the law on soliciting and prostitution. By tradition temperance had played an important part in bringing ladies into the public sphere, and since women continued to be the major victims of male drunkenness, it remained a cause for concern. For Astor 1919 was not only the year of her election, but also the year when prohibition triumphed in America. While her personal experience naturally prompted her to take up the question, it is significant that she felt obliged to disavow any desire to introduce prohibition to Britain. Her efforts were confined to a modest bill designed to prevent sales of alcohol to persons under the age of 18 which was enacted in 1923. Whether the issue ever proved advantageous either for Astor personally or for the women's movement must be doubtful. Certainly the association with prohibition, however tenuous, exposed Astor to attack and undermined her position in Plymouth. The controversy also drew some rash pronouncements such as her claim that England had lost the Ashes because its team drank while the victorious Australians did not! Such interventions in male grief, and the sense that she was taking satisfaction from a British defeat, could only provoke antagonism towards women in public life. Above all, the game was scarcely worth the effort. Between the wars the level of concern over alcohol greatly declined, partly because stringent wartime controls had checked the worst excesses of drinking, and because changes in social habits were curtailing all-male leisure activities. The great days of the Local Veto crusades had clearly passed, and as a result Astor's association with temperance made her a more marginal and quixotic figure than she could have been.

There was more momentum behind campaigns against the double standard in sexual morality. Astor became a keen, and generous, supporter of the Association for Moral and Social Hygiene (AMSH), an organisation that descended from the Ladies National Association for the Abolition of State Regulation of Vice, founded by Josephine Butler to secure the repeal of the Contagious Diseases Acts. As feminists rightly pointed out, inter-war governments adopted much the same attitude as their mid-Victorian predecessors in this area. The AMSH demanded that the authorities compel soldiers to 'live clean and honourable lives' by abandoning the distribution of prophylactics, placing all brothels out of bounds, ceasing treatment for venereal disease, and dropping the compulsory medical examinations of women suspected of carrying infection. Instead the men must simply be continent. In the civilian context the AMSH campaigned for legislation to raise the age of consent to 18 years, and to abolish the legal defence available to a man who had engaged in sexual relations with a young girl that he had 'reasonable cause to believe' that she was over the age of 16. In 1925 Astor introduced a bill designed to repeal the law on prostitution and street soliciting which was blatantly rigged in favour of men. Each year around 300 women found themselves arrested on charges of solicitation or annoyance; they were presumed guilty on the basis of a statement by a single police officer, and then fined or sent to prison. The male customers escaped because prostitution itself was not an offence. Astor and the AMSH wanted to prohibit indecent behaviour in public places by both sexes, and to prevent anyone being taken into custody for causing annoyance except on complaint by the person actually annoyed. This explains why Astor and indeed most feminists placed so much importance on extending the appointment of women in the police force. No sooner had Astor been elected than she was obliged to battle to save women police from disappearing altogether (see page 118). Such issues provided the basis for cross-party co-operation with other women members, notably the Liberal Mrs Wintringham and, later, the Labour MP Edith Picton-Turbervill. The latter, though lacking Astor's flamboyance, was similarly motivated by morality and Christianity, being especially concerned to secure the admission of women to the ministry in the Church.

Undoubtedly the most efficacious cross-party cause for women activists was peace, disarmament and the League of Nations Union. It also had the advantage of bringing feminists into closer co-operation both with working-class women in the Women's Co-operative Guild, and with many who were on the margins of or outside the feminist movement. However, during the 1930s steady deterioration in the international situation diverted many activists from feminist causes and also began to divide them. Rathbone, for example, grew increasingly critical of government weakness in the face of fascist aggrandisement. For Astor questions of war and peace loomed larger during the 1930s, and she devoted much less of her time in parliament to women's issues. In fact her career reached a plateau around 1930. Her attempt to mould the women MPs into a distinct party had met with a rebuff. Her hold on her constituency had become distinctly precarious, though the special circumstances surrounding the birth of the National government saved her from defeat. Moreover she found herself increasingly isolated within the Conservative Party, whose leaders had decisively passed her over for government office. She was now overshadowed by abler women politicians committed to the party line. As the decade wore on Astor became increasingly absorbed on a personal level with Christian Science, and publicly with the pressing need to maintain good relations with the Nazi regime in Germany. This is not to give credence to the wilder allegations made against the 'Cliveden Set' from 1936 onwards. But her preoccupation with this issue inevitably deepened her detachment from the women's movement. More damagingly, the debate over appeasement eventually led to accusations that she had been a traitor, which clearly made her a political liability for a time. Even with her sterling work during the Second World War she was unlikely to have been a major asset for the women's movement again.

Although the concern of the moral feminists for such matters as cinema censorship, moral hygiene, women police, control of sales of alcohol and peace undoubtedly engendered a wide sympathy in the community, the significance of their work was rather mixed. Some of their interests were simply too marginal in the inter-war period. Others, notably their attitudes towards censorship and divorce reform, tended to cause friction with the more liberal feminists. The traditional concern over sexual double standards was clearly fading by the 1930s as a result of greater familiarity with birth control methods and freer attitudes towards sex. There was far less resort to prostitution than in the pre-war era. But moral feminists refused to see any progress in the replacement of professional with 'amateur' sex – both indicated a lowering of women to men's standards. Yet in looking back to Victorian moral reform for their inspiration such activists were only cutting themselves adrift from the chief currents of change in women's lives in the twentieth century.

Welfare Feminism and Birth Control

With the benefit of hindsight many critics of the New Feminism suggest that it degenerated into a mere programme of health and welfare measures and was ultimately responsible for the loss of a radical cutting edge by the women's movement between the 1930s and 1950s. At the same time, however, such a pessimistic outcome could not easily have been anticipated. After all, the alternatives to New Feminism were hardly flourishing. A health and welfare strategy seemed to offer the best means of working with the political tide. The rise of Labour inevitably kept such questions near the top of the agenda even after 1931 when the National government dominated politics.

The susceptibility of governments to a health and welfare approach is apparent in the steady rise in Ministry of Health grants to local authorities for child and maternal welfare from £218,000 annually in

1918–19 to £983,000 in 1927–8. The only flaw in this was that while infant mortality rates fell from over 150 per thousand births in the 1890s to 51 by 1939, relatively little of the investment in health appeared to have got through to mothers. Maternal mortality rates stand out as the one major indicator of health and living standards which did not show significant improvement between the wars. In 1923, for example, the maternal mortality rate stood at 4.83 for every thousand births; it increased to 5.94 in 1933 but fell back to 3.25 by 1939. In these circumstances it is hardly surprising that many women should have chosen to focus attention on their health; even the least sympathetic politicians could not deny that further reductions in infant mortality were now contingent upon improving the health of Britain's mothers. Neville Chamberlain, whose own mother had died in childbirth, clearly felt the force of the moral and statistical case, and in 1928 he appointed a committee to enquire into maternal mortality and the operation of the Midwives Act. After the 1929 Local Government Act which gave powers to counties and county boroughs to take over Poor Law Hospitals, there was a steady rise in the provision of maternity beds and in the proportion of births taking place in hospital. The Public Health Act and the Midwives Act of 1936 helped local authorities to improve provision of clinics, home visiting and midwives' services.

Nonetheless women obviously suffered from lack of political muscle in the grubby scramble for resources. In 1933, for example, health insurance benefits for married women were reduced from 12 to 10 shillings a week while men's remained at 15. The official justification for this was that married women made heavy demands upon the insurance fund, which if true, was further proof of their need, and that the new rates were the only ones that could be justified actuarially. Yet no one proposed to apply this principle to those groups of *men* receiving actuarially unsound benefits. In this context the initiative taken in establishing the Women's Health Committee Enquiry in 1933 was timely. Representing such organisations as NUSEC (Eva Hubback), the WGC (Eleanor Barton), the SJCIWO (Mrs Ayrton Gould) and the North Kensington Women's Welfare Centre (Margery Spring Rice), the enquiry investigated the health of some 1250 married working-class women, and published the results as *Working-Class Wives* in 1939. Of the sample, 31 per cent claimed to enjoy good health, 22 per cent indifferent health (which meant only one or two serious ailments), 15 per cent bad health in the form of numerous major and minor problems, and 31 per cent were in a grave condition, that is, they never felt fit and well.[22] In view of the average of 4.5 births (over twice the national average) the women in the sample were clearly not fully representative of the female population. On the other hand the health visitors who conducted the survey invariably found that the women understated the seriousness of their condition either out of ignorance or low expectations. For many 'good health' was simply 'any interval between illnesses, or at the best the absence of any incapacitating ailment'. Though in general depressing, the findings were also consistent with gradual improvement in that amongst those claiming good health younger women, who reported substantially fewer pregnancies, formed a high proportion.

What emerged from the survey was the state's neglect of women's health. Hardly any of the women enjoyed health insurance. A few used their husband's panel doctor, others contributed to local hospital schemes or consulted doctors privately. In practice many of the women received no professional medical treatment even for gynaecological problems. A number of them feared hospitals and disliked doctors. They lacked confidence in the doctors' expensive and impractical advice, and felt very reluctant to spare the time involved in going for consultations. Still less would they stay in bed while husbands and children clamoured for attention.

The Women's Health Enquiry reached three broad conclusions. First, health insurance ought to be available to all women regardless of status and occupation. Second, since poverty remained a major cause of ill health, family allowances were recommended as an efficacious method of targeting resources where most needed. Third, a reduction in the number of pregnancies would contribute greatly to improved health. This serves as a reminder that New Feminists were by no means as conservative as is sometimes suggested. They were keenly aware that family allowances and birth control complemented each other; together they would give women much more control and choice over how to combine a career with motherhood.

However, the relationship between the women's movement and birth control is a complicated one. Since the popular practice of deliberate limitation of family size predates its adoption by the main feminist organisations it is obvious that the women's leaders were reacting to change as much as promoting it. In Britain the shift towards smaller families had begun as long ago as the late 1870s. Whereas the mid-Victorian woman had experienced an average of 5–6 live births, by the late 1920s her counterpart had 2.2. However, this revolution in social behaviour remains difficult to explain satisfactorily both in terms of the motives behind it and the methods adopted. Since the pioneering work of J.A. Banks in the 1950s the starting point of the explanation has been the economic pressures upon late-Victorian middle-class families and the realisation that children were ceasing to be economic assets. However, Professor F.M.L. Thompson has pointed out that approximately half of the reduction in fertility between the 1870s and 1914 can be accounted for by later marriage; thus the change does not necessarily involve deliberate strategies to achieve smaller families in this period.[23]

Another objection to the traditional explanation is that it appears to point to smaller families as essentially a *male* objective. Now women in all classes had a compelling motive for avoiding pregnancy: ill health and even death. Advertisements in women's magazines indicate the existence of a considerable middle-class demand for contraception. Even within the working-class practice varied widely. Where a large proportion of women worked outside the home, as in Lancashire, family size was relatively low. Conversely it was high in mining districts and agricultural communities where women enjoyed fewer employment opportunities. It seems likely that 'working' wives felt more able to be assertive about pregnancies, and that in factories and mills they exchanged information about the methods of family limitation more readily than others. Traditionally women resorted to prolonged breast-feeding and a variety of sponges and pessaries in order to avoid pregnancy; when they were desperate many methods for securing an abortion were employed. Among the 'male' methods it is assumed that withdrawal was the most widely practised, followed by abstinence which often meant abstinence for the wife and resort to extra-marital sex for the husband. Sheaths were used more for protection against venereal disease than for contraception, though rubber condoms were increasingly available in the late nineteenth century.

Obviously historians are never likely to be in a position to pronounce firmly about exactly how couples restricted the size of their families, especially as all the expedients were unreliable. Several things do, however, seem clear. First, the decline in family size *preceded* major innovations in birth control; what we are considering therefore is a change in attitudes which prompted couples to use the traditional methods more widely than before. Second, it is probably fruitless to attempt to account for changes in family size in terms of either male or female motivation, since a measure of co-operation and mutual confidence is necessary to most strategies. Admittedly one can only see this from limited anecdotal evidence. H.H. Asquith and his second wife, Margot, provide a prominent example. As a struggling barrister trying to support two families and his wife's extravagant tastes Asquith was obviously susceptible to the financial pressure for birth control. But Margot herself was acutely conscious of the dangers of childbirth as a result of tragedies amongst her own relations. In the 1920s, long after her own family was complete, she was moved when she saw the effect of a first baby on Cynthia Mosley, and she impressed upon her the importance of avoiding pregnancy for a long period. She had no doubt as to how this was to be done: 'Henry always withdrew in time, such a noble man.' As usual Margot's praise for her husband seems a little exaggerated. Asquith actually had five children by his first wife, while Margot experienced two live births and three stillbirths. Evidently there were limits to Henry's nobility, or, perhaps, skill. But in this family it is clear that male and female objectives converged on the idea of family planning, albeit with rather limited success. One suspects that their experience was not untypical.

However, at the beginning of the twentieth century the obstacles to family planning still appeared formidable in many ways. Ignorance about conception remained widespread even amongst doctors. The idea that no man should be denied his conjugal rights commanded staunch support, notably from the judges. The hazards of pregnancy, however feared, continued to be accepted fatalistically by many women. And the traditional methods for avoiding pregnancy were unreliable, while the more novel ones such as condoms lacked respectability. Certainly millions of condoms were distributed free during the First World War to minimise venereal disease in the armed forces, and in the 1920s they provided a cheaper option than previously. Yet they continued to be associated in people's minds with illicit sex. Margery Spring Rice reported in the late 1930s that only a minority of the couples who practised birth control used condoms.[24] Another method increasingly favoured by women in the 1920s was the cervical cap, but since this had to be fitted by a doctor its spread was severely limited. One is driven to the conclusion that the trend towards smaller families owed less to innovation than to a wider adoption of abstinence, withdrawal and the safe period. Thus the key to inter-war developments really lies in a further spread of the attitudes and aspirations which had led some couples to limit family size in the 1870s. The life experiences of many of the young women of the 1920s and 1930s underline the point. Many had been lifted out of routine home life during the war; contacts with large numbers of other girls probably speeded up the flow of information about birth control; easier social relations doubtless concentrated minds on the avoidance of pregnancy; and higher income raised expectations for the future. Subsequently most of the young women married and set up home – but with aspirations to a higher quality of life than that experienced by their mothers. For many of them the inter-war period was a time of improved housing and living standards. Moreover, the realisation that babies now had a much greater chance of survival consolidated the idea that a small, planned family would enable one to derive the maximum advantage from a higher standard of life.

What makes the emergence of the small family all the more remarkable an achievement is that it was accomplished by millions of couples with little assistance from the medical profession, only minimal, late and grudging support from governments, and in the face of much discouragement from the mass media, the churches, politicians, doctors and others in authority. However, a central part of the explanation is the way in which birth control gained respectability after the war. Historically it had been handicapped by association with controversial episodes like the prosecution of Annie Besant and Charles Bradlaugh, known as advocates of atheism, republicanism and socialism. Nor was the sustained propaganda of the Malthusian League anything but counterproductive. The League adopted such a negative and censorious view of procreation that it merely alienated support, especially amongst the working classes who felt themselves to be under attack for irresponsible conduct. Even in the mid-1920s the Malthusians boasted a mere 1200 members, though they included some distinguished names such as Arnold Bennett, H.G. Wells, J.M. Keynes and Lord Buckmaster.

Fortunately the case for birth control got on to a quite different course after 1915 when the Women's Co-operative Guild published *Maternity: Letters from Working Women*, which focused attention on the appalling effects of repeated pregnancy on the health of the nation's mothers. The next stage came with Marie Stopes' well-timed book *Married Love*, in March 1918. 'It seems incredible now that this book was such an eye-opener', wrote Naomi Mitchison, one of its enthusiastic readers at the time.[25] Though in no sense a cause of the inter-war trend to smaller families, Stopes' work helped to accelerate the change by removing the stigma from the whole subject and seizing the moral high ground. First, as the title itself suggests, she was as much concerned about marriage as about children. *Married Love* held out the prospect of a more satisfying and loving relationship by removing the element of fear from sexual pleasure. This is underlined by the deluge of letters Stopes received from women anxious to enjoy physical relations with their husbands, but presently handicapped by ignorance and thus often driven to abstinence. Further, Stopes freely accepted that the production of healthy children was a central and praiseworthy objective, thereby disarming some of the criticism provoked by the Malthusians. She advanced a rational case, calculated to make some appeal to both doctors and politicians, for limiting the number of children by a careful spacing of pregnancies. Not only would the resulting offspring be more likely to be born healthy and thus survive, but the mothers would also retain their own fitness. By contrast the haphazard approach to conception hindered improvements in the quality of the population and inflicted appalling suffering and sheer waste of life upon British women. J.R. Clynes, the Labour politician, confessed that until he heard Stopes' arguments he had simply not grasped what was meant by 'constructive' birth control.

Sophisticated people like Bertrand and Dora Russell considered *Married Love* so sentimental as to verge on the comical, but this doubtless explains its popularity. Reprinted twenty-six times between 1918 and 1923 the book enjoyed sales of 400,000; by 1939 the total had risen to a million. The most serious criticism to be made was that while Stopes was strong on the moral arguments she had relatively little to say on the practical side of the question. This was not surprising since Stopes lacked medical qualifications and in view of her own disastrous, unconsummated marriage, she did not have much experience to fall back on. However, an equally successful sequel, *Wise Parenthood*, rapidly followed the first volume and provided answers to the many questions generated by *Married Love*.

It would, however, be an exaggeration to imply that prejudice collapsed in the face of Stopes' work; for some years she encountered stiff resistance from those in positions of authority. Some newspapers, including *The Times* and the *Morning Post*, refused to carry advertisements for her Queen's Hall rally in 1921, and others declined to report the event. During the early 1920s the home secretary came under pressure to impose a ban on the sale of birth control literature and on contraceptive advertisements. Governments took refuge in the view that it could safely be left to the police to prosecute under the existing laws on obscenity. The prosecution of Rose Witcop and Guy Aldred for circulating *Family Limitation*, a birth control pamphlet by Margaret Sanger, and the dismissal of a health visitor, E.S.Daniels, for giving birth control advice to her clients, underlined the dangers. Stopes took care to use only acceptable language to make her case. Yet she also needed publicity, which explains her decision to institute an action for libel against some Catholic doctors in 1923. By November 1924 the case had ended up in the House of Lords, who ruled against her, but it all helped to keep the issue in the public eye. 1923 also saw the appearance of the film *Maisie's Marriage*, effectively a screen version of *Married Love*, which was a vital means of getting the message across to a young, cinema-going audience. In this the superiority of the small, carefully planned family over the large,haphazard one was illustrated in a typically English parable about pruning roses in order to achieve perfect blooms. T.P. O'Connor, the Catholic president of the British Board of Film Censors, felt inclined to withhold approval for the film. However, there was little, in detail, to object to. The BBFC enjoyed only advisory powers, and neither the Home Office nor the local authorities shared O'Connor's misgivings.[26] After four viewings the film was granted an A Certificate. O'Connor's chief object was to eliminate the association between the film and Marie Stopes, hence the title – *Maisie's Marriage*. In practice Stopes' name was frequently used in promotional material.

This propaganda war had to be waged so long as governments declined to condone birth control policies. Their position, however, was gradually undermined by the establishment of voluntary clinics for women who required advice. In 1921 Stopes launched her own clinic in Holloway to be followed by the Malthusian League at Walworth in 1922, the Women's Welfare Centre at Kensington in 1924, and another clinic in Manchester in 1925. Of this latter Mary Stocks recorded that the protest meetings organised by local Catholics merely had the effect of prompting large numbers of Catholic women to seek help on birth control.[27] However, progress was slow. Fewer than twenty clinics were operating in the 1920s. Although the leaders of the medical profession continued to denounce birth control, some sympathetic doctors, handicapped by their own inadequate professional training, turned to the voluntary clinics for help in advising their own patients. Increasing fears that treatment of women was gradually passing out of their own hands eventually drove the British Medical Association to accept that the provision of information on birth control was justified for women whose health was threatened by further pregnancies.[28] This switch came in 1930, the year in which the Church of England, at its Lambeth Conference, also belatedly dropped its outright opposition. It also seems that after the 1929 Local Government Act some local authorities opened clinics or used existing hospitals to give advice to mothers in spite of the prohibition by the Ministry of Health. In short, by 1930 it began to look as though the effort required to stop the dissemination of information on family limitation was ceasing to be worthwhile.

What Arthur Greenwood, the minister for health, actually said in 1930 was that he did not, after all, have the power to prevent local authorities supplying information, which was a neat way of putting them into the firing line. For eight months the minister failed to circulate his memorandum incorporating this climbdown to the local bodies, but it was leaked and publicised by Marie Stopes. Thus in the 1930s local authorities were permitted – but not required – to provide birth control information either in their own clinics or through voluntary ones. However, many were slow to avail themselves of the opportunity. By 1937 only 95 out of 423 local authorities had actually authorised birth control advice in their own clinics, though another 70 voluntary ones now operated. In any case the advice was provided only to married women for whom pregnancy would be detrimental to health. This was relaxed in 1934 to include women suffering poor health for reasons not connected with childbirth. And in 1937 it was decided to give advice at the post-natal clinics, though only around 10 per cent of mothers attended anyway. Thus much of the burden continued to be borne by voluntary efforts organised under the National Birth Control Council which took the title of Family Planning Association in 1939. Having squeezed limited concessions out of the government, they never managed to win the resources that would have been justified by the needs of women. Too many politicians remained uneasily poised between appreciation of the case for 'constructive' birth control, their fears of a declining population, and the antagonism of the Catholic community.

The Two Generations of Feminism

The question arises whether the move in favour of birth control represented a victory on the part of British feminism. There can be no simple answer, partly because birth control itself is but one of a congeries of issues concerning marriage, men, women's sexuality and the double standard. Some scholars have minimised the connection between feminism and liberalisation in sexual behaviour, arguing that at least until the First World War traditional Victorian ideas still prevailed. One extreme variant on this view holds that those women who began to elevate heterosexual sex as a positive good for women can scarcely be considered feminists at all. At the opposite end of the spectrum many writers of the post-1960 generation contend that the women's movement had always espoused a radical critique of sex, marriage and the family which has simply been neglected as a result of the concentration on other themes such as the franchise.[29]

It is very easy here to fall into the trap of reading backwards from present day priorities, identifying the pioneers of current causes and exaggerating their historical role. In the late twentieth century women's emancipation appears inextricably bound up with sexual freedom, but the historian can scarcely assume that this has always been the case. In almost any period it is possible to identify women – and men – who adopted a radical view of sexual relationships. One thinks of women like Stella Browne before 1914 and Dora Russell between the wars. Russell summed up her approach in an eloquent passage:

> To me the important task of modern feminism is to accept and proclaim sex; to bury the lie ... that the body is a hindrance to the mind, and sex a necessary evil to be endured for the perpetuation of our race.[30]

However, Browne's view of women's sexuality and her bold endorsement of abortion as a matter of women's right put her well ahead of her time; during her life she remained peripheral to the women's movement. Russell was clearly closer to the inter-war mainstream, though her arguments were distinctly more radical than those of most of her contemporaries.

During the Victorian and Edwardian eras the ideas of both of these women were no more than marginal to a women's movement steeped in the ideology of moral reform. Generations of intelligent women regarded sexual promiscuity as all of a piece with excessive drinking, domestic violence and warfare – pre-eminently the male vices. Both ideology and empirical observation seemed to point to women as fundamentally different by reason of their greater self-control and relative lack of physical passion. Anything like birth control, designed to free sexual activity from the possibility of pregnancy, seemed calculated to promote excessive and irresponsible behaviour by men; many women would therefore take a lot of convincing that it was also in their interests. The alternative ideal for women meant minimising physical relations and attaining independence from men. Christabel Pankhurst's famous attack on the 'Great Scourge' was but a late and unusually vehement expression of this attitude. Even between the wars the traditional view continued to exercise its attraction for women who wanted their sex to take pride in itself. Witness Rebecca West's defiant, against-the-tide manifesto in 1924: 'I am an old fashioned feminist. I believe in the sex war.'[31] As a youthful victim of H.G. Wells – a typical example of a man who approved of sexual liberation for women because it suited his own predilections – West had good reason for sticking to her brand of feminism. Her life led her, via a successful career and independence, to a somewhat conventional middle-age marriage, thence to serene old age and this conclusion: 'If I were young again, I would deliberately (and against my nature) choose to be a lesbian.'[32]

It now seems that from the First World War onwards increasing numbers of fairly conventional feminists began to face up to what Dora Russell called 'the central issue of women's emancipation'. One catches the mood in the thoughts of Catherine Marshall, hitherto immersed in the franchise campaign, but by 1918 apprehensively considering 'the wisdom of having public discussion of things which are largely so intimate and personal'.[33] Maude Royden, another NUSEC activist, went further in a volume of essays on feminism's future in which she applauded women for recognising their passionate nature; modern woman, she wrote, 'does not elevate a defect into a quality, or think of sex as something alien and base'.[34]

For such women the rationale provided by Stopes proved timely. Eva Hubback and Edith How-Martyn, long sympathetic to the idea of birth control but unhappy about the cold authoritarianism of the Malthusian philosophy, now gladly adopted her arguments; the promotion of women's health and happiness through a satisfying marriage seemed to constitute a central part of the future advance towards emancipation for women. But this was not quite a move towards the radical modern view of sexual liberation. Naomi Mitchison, a young and enthusiastic advocate of birth control in the 1920s, recognised that for her generation the change meant neither population control on the one hand nor permissiveness on the other; it meant family spacing and happy marriages.[35] In this spirit a large part of the women's movement began to rally behind the new ideas about women's sexuality and, in particular, the cause of birth control. The Women's Co-operative Guild led the way in advocating birth control information; but it was followed in 1924 by NUSEC, the Labour Party Women's Organisation and the newly formed Workers Birth Control Group. Slightly more conventional organisations joined them, notably the Women's National Liberal Association in 1927 and the National Council of Women in 1929. But feminists were only coming into line with what ordinary women increasingly practised, not leading them. In any case several organisations such as the Six Point Group and the Women's Freedom League continued their opposition to the new thinking and, as we have seen, NUSEC itself suffered some loss of membership over the issue.

For many of these women the argument over birth control crystallised a broader division of views about the status of marriage and the meaning of emancipation. Stopes' romantic celebration of marriage as

a triumphant merging of two persons contrasted sharply with the
alternative ideal of independence and self-realisation for women which
characterised Cicely Hamilton's *Marriage as a Trade* published in
1908. To a considerable extent the division was between two generations. Many feminists of the pre-war generation disapproved of the
changes in women's lives: the increase in casual sex, the public display
of fashionable clothes, cosmetics and dancing, the growing pursuit of
marriage. These were all symptoms of what Helena Swanwick called
the 'boring obsession with sex' in a review of the novels of D.H.
Lawrence; looking back from the mid-1930s she saw the war as 'the
beginning of the sex craze as we have had it since'.[36] These sentiments
were frequently echoed in the writing of equal rights feminists in
particular. Lady Rhondda condemned 'that perpetual, unsatisfied sex-
hunger which is so marked a feature of this generation. A puzzling and
surely in part artificially induced thing.'[37] Even Winifred Holtby felt
moved to some acerbic comments on the subject:

> Today there is a far worse crime than promiscuity: it is chastity ... I think we
> shall one day get over this somewhat adolescent preoccupation with the
> human body.[38]

In the eyes of many of the pre-war generation much of the behaviour of
their successors looked like a retreat, or even a betrayal. For an able and
ambitious Edwardian girl life had appeared to present a *choice* between
a career and marriage, the latter being very much second best. Cicely
Hamilton, for example, had grown up rebelling against pressure to
conform to masculine expectations; thus for her the retention of her
spinsterhood and the ability to support herself gave her independence
and self-respect.[39] As she looked back nostalgically from the 1930s
candour compelled her to accept that her ideal was simply not shared by
most young women. As a feminist she felt vindicated by her own life,
but somewhat isolated. From the opposite side of this gulf Margaret
Lane, writing in 1937, commented: 'The fierce feminist is an old-
fashioned figure unsympathetically remembered by all but a few.'[40]

   Although the division of the women's movement between generations is more than simply a matter of age, it is significant that by the
inter-war period the leadership was still dominated by women who had
served their apprenticeship in the Victorian and Edwardian eras. Some,
like Mrs Fawcett and Charlotte Despard, had been born in the 1840s, or
like Ethel Smythe, in the 1850s. On the whole, however, they were the
children of the 1860s (Helena Swanwick, Emmeline Pethick-Lawrence,
Flora Drummond, Elizabeth Robins, Evelyn Sharp), of the 1870s

(Maude Royden, Eleanor Rathbone, Cicely Hamilton, Nancy Astor, Kathleen Courtney, Pippa Strachey), or of the 1880s (Margery Corbett Ashby, Catherine Marshall, Lady Rhondda, Ray Strachey, Eva Hubback). If feminism was to grow, or even survive, as a significant movement it had to recruit from the younger generations of women, educated in the Edwardian years and advancing into adult life in the 1920s and 1930s.

Two features of these younger women are of great significance. First, the extent to which their feminism called for sustained involvement in the women's movement varied considerably; they were at once more dilettante and more professional than their elders. Second, they often took a different view of what constituted progress and emancipation for women. A classic example is Mary Stott, born in 1907, who supported herself as a journalist from the age of 21 onwards. Too young to have participated in the Edwardian suffrage campaign, she only began to be conscious of herself as a feminist after reading Ray Strachey's history of the suffrage movement in the 1920s. Significantly Stott saw no inconsistency between her independence and feminism on the one hand and her marriage in 1937 on the other. Indeed, she put it rather emphatically: 'In marriage I was liberated.'[41] In taking so positive a view of the marital state Stott felt herself somewhat apart from earlier feminists and, subsequently, from the post-1960 generation too. It is also significant that although involved with the Women's Co-operative Guild as a professional journalist, and as an historian of the Townswomen's Guilds later in life, Stott seems not to have been actively drawn into women's causes during the greater part of her career.

There appears to be an important link between age and subsequent participation in women's politics. This emerges from the lives of two slightly older women, Mary Stocks and Naomi Mitchison. Born in 1891, Stocks was old enough to have participated in the suffrage campaign. Consequently the link with Rathbone and the New Feminism and her advocacy of family allowances and birth control led her to a lifelong involvement with the women's movement. But she exemplified the feminism of the younger generation in combining marriage and three children with a career as a lecturer which culminated in the principalship of Westfield College and a life peerage in 1966. Naomi Mitchison, born in 1897, had not been an active suffragist but became, in effect, a New Feminist. Her marriage in 1916 left her disappointed until the discovery of *Married Love* in 1918. Like Stocks and Stott, Mitchison combined her role as a wife and mother with a successful career (as a novelist) and also did some political work on behalf of the

Labour Party. She strongly believed that effective birth control and a franker and freer approach to sex both inside and outside marriage represented a major advance for women.[42] The real objective for her lay in finding ways of making the married woman's role compatible with an attractive career: 'Motherhood must be made into an honoured profession.'[43] Although a propagandist for her brand of feminism Mitchison seems to have been detached from the women's organisations.

Dora Russell took a similarly positive view of motherhood and sex, and denounced those feminists who sought to escape female biology: 'what a denial of our humanity'.[44] Born in 1894 she sacrificed her own first career and a fellowship at Girton College for marriage and motherhood. Subsequently, however, Russell rebuilt a career for herself, while taking up a number of causes including the Workers Birth Control Group, the National Council for Civil Liberties and the Campaign for Nuclear Disarmament. Taken together Stott, Stocks, Mitchison and Russell clearly share a common assumption that men, marriage and family are basically desirable for women; and each of them managed by one strategy or another to combine family with a career. Therein lay emancipation. Only Stocks, however, kept up a sustained involvement with the women's movement; the others, though no less feminist, reflect a more fitful and detached pattern of activity.

In some ways the dilemmas of balancing employment and motherhood are best illustrated by the life of Vera Brittain. Though a familiar figure she has been misunderstood in the context of feminism. Another child of the 1890s, she showed herself conventionally feminine and quite determined, Oxford notwithstanding, to get married. War interrupted this for a time and led her to attempt to carve out a career as writer and journalist with Winifred Holtby. Not until 1922 did Vera join the Six Point Group; but she was also, and inconsistently, a member of the Labour Party from 1924, and in addition worked for the League of Nations Union. However, it was not long before her earlier ideas reasserted themselves in the shape of marriage to George Catlin in 1925: 'One happily married wife and mother is worth more to feminism ... than a dozen gifted and eloquent spinsters.'[45] Thereafter her greatest contribution to feminism lay in what she later described as the 'semi-detached marriage'. She continued to use her own name, left her husband for some time in the United States, set up home in Britain with Winifred Holtby, produced two children and went on to a triumphant career as an author and propagandist. While celebrating the married state and motherhood Brittain insisted that women should never be trapped by domesticity. She once pointed to the gap between her generation and the older feminists. When the latter complained of the failure of younger women to participate in the women's movement they forgot that this was impractical for those who were trying to hold down a job and run a home at the same time. The pre-war generation had been full-time propagandists able to fill their normal working hours with endless committee meetings and lobbying.[46] Brittain herself clearly drifted away from organised feminism in the 1930s. She left the Six Point Group and concentrated more on her writing and on the cause of international peace which, after the Second World War, led her to take up the Campaign for Nuclear Disarmament.

For Vera Brittain, as for most of the younger feminists, women's emancipation clearly consisted in ordering one's life so as to enjoy what both employment on the one hand and domesticity on the other had to offer; it was no longer primarily a matter of formal work for a women's movement. However, it must be said that the line between feminism of this sort and anti-feminism becomes harder to draw as one moves along the spectrum of attitudes. Many of the women who established highly successful careers in women's magazines, such as Mary Grieve, Alice Head and Margaret Lane, regarded themselves as *emancipated* women, but yet avoided using the word 'feminist' to describe themselves. Lane defined the goal in terms of balance: 'trying to be citizens and women at the same time. Wage earners and sweethearts.'[47] But how much separates their position from that of a woman like Barbara Cartland, not generally known for her feminism? The romantic rhetoric which became her stock in trade stands in awkward and ambiguous relation to the empirical facts of her own life. Born in 1904, Cartland suffered the death of her father in 1918 which left the family in financial hardship. Yet she declined to deal with the problem in what her own writing suggests was the natural way: marriage. On the contrary she worked to support herself both by journalism and by writing novels. Though she succumbed to marriage in 1927 she had filed for divorce by 1932, remarried, and had her first child in 1937. In this light Cartland emerges as the very model of the modern, emancipated inter-war girl: a whimsical product, to say the least, of all the years of work on behalf of women by the feminist movement.

Chapter 9   Women in the Second World War

On the face of it the Second World War represented a more significant and formative phase for British women than the Great War. They entered it as citizens of their country for the first time, and as such could expect to be called upon to play a more equal part in the war effort than previously. Also the experience of the First World War meant that a number of policies relevant to women were adopted more quickly or applied more extensively: rationing, the provision of milk and school meals, the establishment of day nurseries and the emergency hospital service. Perhaps more importantly the political momentum behind such social measures ensured that some of them were sustained after the war. Finally, the military circumstances prevailing during 1939–45 were rather different. For much of the period the British effort was comparatively slight in quantitative terms – a consequence of Germany's dramatic successes and the reluctance of the allies to engage them again on the European mainland. Instead the war came home to the civilian population, which put women in the front line. Amongst the 130,000 civilians killed during the blitz there were no fewer than 63,000 women. Moreover, in industry Britain broke new ground as the first power to conscript its women for the war effort, a feat that neither Nazi Germany nor Stalinist Russia managed to emulate. It is reckoned that about twice as many women were mobilised for industry and the services as in the First World War.

On the other hand the war experience for women was to a considerable extent a repetition of the first war. Some of the advances turned out to be ephemeral or actually unpopular with women themselves. Nor was wartime change an uncomplicated matter of emancipation – in some respects it turned out to be distinctly conservative in character. Several writers have observed that despite the centrality of women's role no significant reforms or concessions were actually won by them which would stand comparison with those associated with the First World War. This is partly to be explained in terms of the different chronological pattern. By 1914 the women's movement had concentrated its efforts on a narrow front and was apparently reaching a peak. In 1939 it stood at a rather low ebb after a prolonged period of gradual decline; nor can the movement be said to have been clearly focused upon certain major objectives. It is, then, not surprising that it proved difficult to capitalise upon women's vital contribution to victory in the war. However, even if it is agreed that no significant policy changes emerged, it is still possible to argue that war made its impact upon the attitudes and aspirations of British women. Unhappily scepticism on this point is greatly strengthened by the availability of rather better evidence than that for the 1914–18 period in the shape of oral testimony and the Mass Observation reports from the late 1930s onwards. The results have had a dampening effect upon claims that the Second World War constituted another revolution in women's lives.

House and Home in Wartime

By 1943, when mobilisation for the war effort reached its peak, there were 7,250,000 women employed in industry, the armed forces and civil defence, many of them admittedly reluctant and dissatisfied recruits. However, it should not be forgotten that even more (8,770,000 in fact) remained full-time housewives. War impinged upon the domestic sphere in ways that nearly all of these women found disruptive and demoralising.

As a result of the prevailing assumption that 'the bomber will always get through' the British authorities anticipated that war would commence with huge numbers of casualties leading to a collapse of civilian morale and the crippling of industry in a fairly short time. Hence the swift imposition of a policy of evacuation to the less vulnerable parts of the country which was applied to some 3.75 million people, largely children, during the first three months. Over half the women subsequently questioned by Mass Observation either refused to part with their children in the first place or brought them home again after a short period. Of those whose children remained in the countryside the majority were unhappy about it.[1] This hardly requires explanation. Not only was the war taking husbands and sons, it was literally breaking up homes. The insecurity many women felt on parting from their children inevitably engendered a conservative reaction in favour of family, home and marriage. In the short term many women attempted to maintain something of a normal family life even though this meant that they bore a tremendous strain both physically and emotionally. As one housewife, uttering sentiments that recur endlessly, put it:

> It's getting on my nerves what with the overtime, shopping, doing a bit of housework here and there, and rushing my meals down, I am fair run down.[2]

Evacuation proved to be only the beginning of their worries as far as children were concerned. As the war progressed increasing numbers of women took on part-time or full-time employment. The consequent need to find ways of caring for their young children presented one of the great opportunities of the war. The majority of mothers declared themselves content to place children in nurseries, but for several years this facility was simply not available.[3] By 1944 some 1500 day nurseries, provided by local authorities, could cope with around 72,000 children at a not inconsiderable cost to their mothers of one shilling per head per day. Even so, three-quarters of children under 5 years old of working mothers were not catered for in the official schemes. Consequently women resorted to a variety of traditional expedients. However, it was not so easy to rely upon relations and neighbours as in peacetime, and mothers often found themselves driven to a succession of child-minders throughout the war.[4] Nonetheless, nursery provision did represent a major advance on the First World War and inter-war situation, and clearly went some way to meeting one of the demands voiced by feminists. Unfortunately it was not sustained after 1945 and Britain continued for decades to lag behind other European countries in the provision of nurseries. This experience was, however, significant in another way. Mothers of young children in particular felt regret at having missed so much of the early life and development of their offspring; one result was a sense of guilt later in life. This helps to explain why in the late 1940s and 1950s so many women were vulnerable to the propaganda emanating from medico-scientific sources which attributed the problems of British youth to early neglect by mothers. This was to be one of the most profound and conservative consequences of wartime experience.

Wartime surveys of morale showed women to be fairly consistently more dispirited and resigned than men. A combination of the blackout, loneliness through disruption of family and neighbourhood networks, rising prices and food queues, poor transport, tiredness and the loss of small luxuries all took a disproportionate toll on those whose life was dominated by domestic concerns.[5] For example, the normal problems of housekeeping were greatly exacerbated by the deterioration of the housing stock: half a million homes suffered serious damage. To this were added power cuts and shortages or even the disappearance of food items usually taken for granted. Authority was slow to comprehend the importance in most women's lives of an apparently lowly activity like shopping. The employed were obliged to sacrifice lunch times to join long queues for food, or to lose pay by taking time off. For a time women war workers received priority cards to enable them to jump the queues, but so much friction resulted that shopkeepers abandoned the scheme. One Ministry of Food official loftily dismissed the whole matter: 'It should not be beyond the ability of married women war workers to arrange for a neighbour or friend to purchase their food for them.'[6] Some did rely on older female relations or on their eldest daughters, but otherwise women were condemned to an unending and wearying scramble to keep their families supplied. As a result women were invariably found to be not only more depressed about the war than men, but to feel less involved and less interested in the progress of the war.[7] One qualification should, however, be made to this general point. Young and unattached women suffered much less from depression although they, too, were somewhat detached from the war by comparison with men.

As in the 1914–18 war women became the target of a prolonged bombardment by the government propaganda machine, particularly the ministries of Information, Food and Labour, anxious to avoid waste of food and fuel, to lure women into the labour force and to check the expected slump in morale. Rarely was so much effort expended on so many to so little obvious effect. For example, Mass Observation soon discovered that advertisements designed to educate housewives about nutrition failed to get the message across; even when official pamphlets were read they were largely ignored.[8] Even the BBC's five-minute talks by 'Gert and Daisy', though popular, were considered *entertainment* rather than practical instruction. Eventually the sheer volume of propaganda produced boredom and cynicism. Posters urging the necessity for avoiding gossip drew resentment among both sexes on the grounds that ordinary people had no secrets to give away. One of the most celebrated slogans of the war – 'Be Like Dad, Keep Mum' – was generally thought amusing, though some women failed to understand it.[9] Significantly no criticism was reported on the grounds of the sexism in the slogan. The flagging impact of official appeals to women presented an opportunity for the women's magazines. By 1941 the proprietors were virtually begging the Ministry of Information to allow them to assist its efforts to encourage women to be more co-operative. Eventually the government succumbed and gave the editors an official contact at the ministry; subsequently they used the magazines as an additional vehicle for propaganda on food and fuel, and also to sound out opinion over conscription.[10] This appears to have been a one-way process in that the magazine proprietors helped the authorities without ever trying to extract concessions for women in return. This was by no means a peculiar feature of the women's papers. In both world wars most of the press instinctively sought to win prestige by associating themselves with the national war effort.

The strain and drama of the war bore rather less heavily upon many middle-aged women especially those living in small towns and rural areas. For them, after all, the crisis provided a tremendous stimulus to voluntary activity similar to that undertaken in the First World War.[11] The chief difference was that the work was now more efficiently co-ordinated by the Women's Voluntary Service (WVS) which acted as a channel of communication between the various organisations and the government. Inevitably the outbreak of hostilities obliged the Women's Institutes and Townswomen's Guilds to suspend their meetings because halls had been commandeered by the authorities. But activity soon resumed. By the second week of war the WI had swung into action to utilise masses of fruit which was about to go to waste; sugar was made available for jam and bottled produce. This, after all, was precisely the kind of work for which the WI had been intended back in 1915.[12] By early 1940 the WVS had some 600,000 volunteers at its disposal, busily engaged in boosting food production by gardening and poultry-keeping, organising collections of scrap metal and other scarce materials, coping with evacuees and receiving servicemen who were often billeted with them at short notice. Such women were essentially playing their conventional domestic role on a grander scale; they received praise but little financial compensation for their efforts. In spite of the friction caused by the clash of town and country, not to mention of middle and working class, the women volunteers at least enjoyed the satisfaction of knowing that they were contributing to the national effort. In Lady Denman's words:

> Those of us who are not called upon to endure the hardships of actual warfare will be glad to feel that we have comfort to go without, difficulties to contend with in daily life, and that by meeting such troubles cheerfully and helping our neighbours to do so, we are taking our small share in winning the victory which we believe will come.[13]

In these measured and reassuring tones one senses the strong measure of continuity with the First World War for many middle-aged and middle-class women throughout Britain.

Family and Morality

A good deal of contemporary comment from the 1939–45 period focuses on the marked loosening of social behaviour and the drop in moral standards. Much of this is very similar to criticism made during and after the First World War. It is obviously impressionistic and exaggerated, and should not be taken as indicative of long-term social change. Rather predictably much of the male comment during the war tended to attribute declining morality to women. The Auxiliary Territorial Service, for example, was widely regarded by men as an opportunity for women to pursue sexual adventures. For its part the government found it desirable to distribute condoms to the servicemen in order to protect them from venereal disease, but left the women in the forces to face the dangers of becoming pregnant. In contrast to the traditional male view one notices that women's accounts during the war tend to suggest that they became the victims of excessive teasing, sexual harassment and violence, especially in isolated and exposed situations in the Land Army or when serving as conductresses on trams at night.

Yet wartime had its attractions for many young and unattached women. Their experience was often a much happier one than that of the housewives who loom so large in the Mass Observation reports. Freed from some of the usual restrictions of home life, earning more money, meeting daily with large numbers of people of both sexes, they found it all too easy to relieve the tedium of work with a lively social round. Male responses to this were distinctly mixed. For some, wartime presented unusual opportunities for promiscuity, but others clearly felt unsettled, even intimidated, by the large numbers of young women appearing in public places normally dominated by men.

One conspicuous manifestation was the growing tendency for women to visit public houses; in London Mass Observation found over 40 per cent of customers to be female. In fact this was no more than an acceleration of an inter-war trend. Some publicans still preferred to serve men only, often failed to provide ladies' toilets, and claimed that women got drunk more easily. But they admitted that women were extending the market, and were, in any case, entitled to brighten up their lives. Amongst the drinking classes one-third continued to disapprove of women's presence in public houses, especially if not accompanied by husbands. It was still claimed that the women were really there for immoral purposes. But basically men feared the invasion of their club: 'It kind of puts the damper on us blokes when there's women about.'[14] Nonetheless the critics grudgingly tolerated the phenomenon as another consequence of wartime: 'it's like every-thing else, they rule the roost now they have come in the place of men'.

It was often the older, married men who felt most threatened and voiced criticism of moral lapses, as this comment made towards the end of the war suggests:

> Sexual morality has decayed a great deal in recent years, and the war has spurred on a process already set in motion earlier. Promiscuity is no longer considered wicked. ... No one seems to see any value in fidelity to one and the same partner.[15]

Behind such views were the many wives separated from their husbands, who were lonely and keen to find wider social outlets. Many inevitably began relationships with servicemen, also bored and restless, whose numbers were swollen halfway through the war by an influx of American troops. The latter enjoyed notable advantages in the form of a higher income, access to scarce consumer goods, and greater self-confidence and maturity in their approach to women. Inevitably the widespread separation of married couples, the extra-marital affairs, and the growing number of marriages hastily contracted by young partners after fleeting affairs resulted in an unusually high level of marital breakdown. Whereas during the four years before the war an average of only 7500 people filed petitions for divorce each year, the average rose to almost 39,000 in the four years after the war; and 58 per cent of these emanated from *men*, a sharp reversal of usual practice. Some of this increase would, however, have occurred anyway as a result of a further liberalisation of the laws on divorce in 1937.

Angus Calder has suggested that the Second World War induced a kind of *wanderlust* in British women. But if so, this is not obviously demonstrated in their subsequent behaviour. Even those who left for Canada and the United States were going in order to marry and enjoy a more comfortable family life style. The war seems, in fact, to have done nothing in the long run to check the trend towards marriage. Certainly the marriage rate dropped sharply during 1941–5, but thereafter it rose above the pre-war level and continued to rise until 1972.[16] It was the popularity of marriage that helped to keep the birth rate in Britain surprisingly buoyant in this period. Naturally the immediate effect of war was to push the rate slightly below the level of the 1930s. But this turned out to be a brief phase. With the return of the troops from the continent in 1940 the birth rate rose again; it dipped rather low in 1941, then increased sharply in 1942, reaching a peak by 1944. This was followed by the famous baby-boom of 1946–8 after which a slight downward drift began.[17]

What provoked so much pessimistic comment from moralists at the time was the fact that a growing proportion of the children being born were illegitimate – 9.1 per cent of the total births by 1945, which represented a doubling of the pre-war rate. However, the figures are misleading. During the 1930s roughly one-third of all mothers first conceived when out of wedlock, but a high proportion of them married before giving birth. Wartime circumstances often delayed marriage and thereby inflated the official figures for illegitimate births. Illegitimacy was thus, in a sense, a phenomenon of wartime, but an ephemeral one.

Impressionistic evidence suggests that society was becoming more relaxed about both illegitimacy and divorce during the Second World War. But to some extent this was happening gradually during the 1920s and 1930s. The war may simply have accelerated the trend. One must also remember that if war weakened moral attitudes in the short run, it also generated a moral backlash which was still making itself felt in the 1950s. Barbara Cartland, who worked as a welfare officer in the RAF, had first-hand knowledge of the strains placed upon relationships. One suspects that the romantic ideal of love, fidelity and marriage that she advocated so strongly owed a good deal to the impression that broken marriages and illegitimacy had made on her during the war. This is corroborated by opinion surveys and the marriage rate. Men were keen to return to home and family life. Women were on the whole anxious to withdraw from war work to settle down and start families. In this respect the 1939–45 war seems to have been no more revolutionary than that of 1914–18.

The Mobilisation Of Women

For understandable reasons the extent of women's entry into the labour market during the Second World War has occupied a disproportionate amount of attention. By late 1943 46 per cent of all women aged 14–59 years were undertaking national service in one capacity or another. The basis for this was the introduction of conscription for women by the minister of labour, Ernest Bevin, in 1941. Bevin has gained a reputation as a master politician who always knew that conscription would be necessary but moved towards it carefully until the moment was right to launch so potentially controversial a policy.[18] However, such praise seems misplaced when the matter is seen from the point of view of women's attitudes and responses. In fact government policy was rather a mess, though Bevin was by no means to blame for it. During the first

year of war, as industry began to find labour in short supply, unemployment among women mounted steadily; by November 1940 it stood at
300,000. In the critical case of engineering women's share of the jobs
rose from 10.5 to only 13.2 per cent between June 1939 and June 1940.
In this situation Bevin's approach was a mixture of First World War
liberalism and trade unionism. As a staunch believer in the family wage
he had no desire to rely more than was absolutely necessary on women
workers. Thus he began simply by appealing for further volunteers to
come forward, an approach which failed. He also sought the agreement
of the unions to the admission of more women, especially in the
engineering industry and, by way of reassurance to them, the Restoration of Pre-War Practices Act, reminiscent of Lloyd George's pioneering efforts, was passed in 1942. However, by the beginning of 1941 it
had become apparent that the extra 2 million women workers, said by
the Manpower Requirements Committee to be essential, would not
materialise without more drastic measures. Thus with reluctance,
especially on the part of Churchill, the cabinet agreed to conscription.
This was carried out initially by requiring women to register by age
groups at their local labour exchanges; subsequently they would be
allocated jobs and, if necessary, directed to take them up. By 1951 this
had been extended to 51 year olds.

At the time the official view of women's war work consisted in the
comforting belief that they had been moved by patriotism and the spirit
of national unity. This has been echoed by those historians who regard
the experience as having had a positive and radicalising effect on the
position of women. Both interpretations suffer, however, by taking
insufficient notice of the evidence of women's own attitudes which
suggest that wartime work was both less significant and also more
negatively viewed by many participants. More recently Penny Summerfield has shown how the traditional prejudices surrounding women's
employment survived the new policy, while Harold Smith has pointed
out that for women war work was unlikely to appear as a form of
emancipation when it was forced upon them by the authorities.[19]

The first feature of women's experience is the way in which the
hesitancy of government policy in the early months dissipated much of
the original goodwill. After the first six months of war half of those who
had volunteered still lacked employment, women continued to be made
redundant, and middle-class women often spent much effort on finding
jobs only to be rebuffed. But beyond their ranks the demand for work
was not overwhelming. In December 1941, 52 per cent of women
questioned by Mass Observation indicated that they preferred the

voluntary system, and support for compulsion was usually expressed in terms of forcing idle rich girls to play their part.[20] The young women who were the first to encounter the new system displayed a light-hearted attitude to the whole thing; while not enthusiastic about it they were not worried because they did not expect it to affect them much.[21] Paid employment was, after all, already a fact of life for the majority of women. By 1943 it was found that only 28 per cent of women employed in industry had not already been working in September 1939. Clearly many of these were young women who would have entered the workforce by 1943 even in the absence of a war. Others were married women now re-entering the workforce as they had always done in response to fluctuations in family fortunes and changing economic opportunities. Some women, finding the allowances paid on behalf of their husbands in the armed forces to be inadequate, felt driven to take up jobs temporarily to tide them over. Thus from the perspective of many women wartime work was rather less a sharp discontinuity than it may appear from the government's side of the fence.

In spite of the obvious economic pressures forcing women into employment, it seems that many continued to be reluctant; in August 1941, for example, one-third of those who were apparently available for work indicated that they did not want it.[22] This is largely explained in terms of the mounting pressures upon housewives. Many of them sought only part-time work, and it was not until 1943–4 that the government accepted this preference. To work twelve hours a day for six days a week was intolerable for many and only resulted in many women taking Saturdays or Mondays off. Shopping was an obvious problem, though eventually employers granted leave of absence or adjusted their shifts so that housewives could cope. Similarly the hours adopted by most day nurseries – from 9 a.m. to 4 p.m. – were quite incompatible with industrial shifts, and it consequently took time for women to make arrangements to have young children looked after. None of these problems was insuperable, but even sustained public criticism on behalf of working mothers voiced by the eight women on Bevin's consultative committee produced only gradual modifications in official policies on the recruitment of women for the war effort.[23]

Those women who did venture into the services, industry and white-collar work still encountered a good deal of discouragement from men. This often began with their own fathers and husbands who opposed 'the conscription of our wives and sweethearts who are the very people we are fighting to protect'.[24] This seems to have been especially acute with regard to the 198,000 women in the Auxiliary Territorial Service. In the event the ATS provoked many complaints over poor living conditions, lack of useful work and bullying by officers which led many recruits to swallow their pride and apply for a transfer.[25] There was more contentment amongst the 30,000 girls who joined the Land Army at the beginning of war, though some of them also dropped out. And the 375,000 women enrolled in civil defence found a variety of challenging tasks connected with Air Raid Precaution, the Auxiliary Fire Service, driving ambulances and as nursing auxiliaries. The 470,000 women who joined the armed forces often experienced traditional prejudice probably because they were seen to represent a real threat. This was obvious in the RAF where the war revived the inter-war challenge posed by the intrepid lady pilots. In fact they were permitted to fly, though strictly in non-combatant work. But for many their work kept them far from the glamorous side of the war; as one woman summed it up: 'whatever one applies for, they always try to get one committed to working in a canteen'.[26]

In industry women quickly proved themselves adept at skilled work, especially in engineering, as they had done in the Great War. However, the trade unions blocked women's claims to apprenticeships, and the sexual division of labour was invariably maintained either by splitting a man's job or by modifying it by the introduction of new machinery. On the other hand the electrical and engineering unions did admit women to membership and their numbers rose from 970,000 to 1,870,000 by 1943. The unions could accept this so long as it was temporary and so long as the women were excluded from positions of responsibility. The war also had the effect of reviving the cause of equal pay for women. Indeed some feminists optimistically believed that conscription would eventually bring them a victory on this issue. Certainly the government, conscious of the 1936 vote for equal pay for civil servants in the House of Commons, anticipated renewed pressure. But it stubbornly refused to back down partly because of the sheer financial costs of paying women on an equal basis and, in Bevin's view, because any concession would provoke industrial unrest amongst men. In fact several unions did press for equal pay, but on the whole they connived with the employers to ensure the maintenance of differentials. Even where an official equal pay policy existed there were enough loopholes to make women ineligible.[27] In practice most women worked for something between 50 to 70 per cent of men's wages. The Woman Power Committee (WPC), the official advisory body headed by Irene Ward, continued to harass Bevin over the issue, and some of the women's organisations distributed leaflets to encourage women to demand equal pay when registering for war work, but the grievance does not seem to have been very strongly or widely felt at the time. Equal pay did become an issue in a major strike amongst the workers at the Rolls Royce aircraft engine plant near Glasgow in 1943, but the united resistance of Bevin and the union leaders beat off the threat. Frustration with the government, combined with a sense that Bevin's political position was not strong, led to the formation of the Equal Pay Campaign Committee towards the end of 1943. It decided to concentrate on the civil service and teaching as the weakest links in the government's defences. But the cabinet remained solid to the end, fortified both by the support of the union leaders and by the conviction that most women regarded their employment as temporary, as indeed it was; from the spring of 1944 the number of women working in engineering began to fall sharply.

In fact by 1944 fewer than a quarter of women were ready to continue in their present work according to a Mass Observation survey. Most appear to have anticipated a repetition of the post-1918 era in which war was followed by severe unemployment. In these circumstances they were resigned to their lot: 'It's not so much what's going to happen to us, as what's going to happen to the men who come home.'[28] To be sure, those who enjoyed professional occupations, as well as the widows and single women, were more inclined to remain in employment. The one manifestation of real change consisted in the 29 per cent of *married* women who indicated that they hoped to continue working. They tended to be middle-class or older women whose children were no longer dependent. But the majority of younger single women planned to stop work for marriage, while most of the young married women found the double burden of home and work excessive:

> You can't look on anything you do during the war as what you really mean to do; it's just filling in time till you can live your own life again.[29]

Women's Politics: Revivalism and Consensus

In complete contrast to the First World War, which interrupted the women's movement at its peak, the Second World War generated something of a revival. The various organisations found little difficulty in putting aside their differences and began to co-operate in pressing for equal treatment of women by the wartime coalition governments; in January 1940, for example, some 21 women's groups attended a conference convened by the Women's Freedom League to co-ordinate activities. Within a few months of the outbreak of war a multitude of grievances had arisen. Sir John Anderson, the home secretary, abruptly shelved the Married Women's Nationality Bill which had been so near to completion. Mrs Corbett Ashby, who had seen it all before in 1914– 18, attacked the government for excessive promotion of voluntary work which was contributing to the unemployment amongst skilled women, and for its reluctance to appoint women to positions of responsibility in industry and the administration.[30] Dorothy Evans of the Six Point Group took up with the Ministry of Health the inadequate level of payments made to foster mothers caring for evacuated children; in particular she demanded to know why this form of national service was deemed not to merit separate pay for the women themselves as opposed to merely allowances for the children.[31]

None of this effort would, however, have made much impact but for fresh initiatives amongst the women members of parliament who were quick to see that the war would not only multiply women's problems, but also present opportunities. Their position during the previous decade had been an uncomfortable one, subject as they were to the charge that they had failed to make an impact in parliament. Many of them, especially the Conservatives, had gradually become rebels, and few now had anything to lose by adopting an independent line towards the wartime governments. The emergence of the coalition in May 1940 made their task easier in that criticism could no longer be seen as disloyalty to party. Consequently, from early 1940 the lady members' room in the Commons – known derisively as The Boudoir – began to assume the character of a party headquarters.[32] Two women, Florence Horsbrugh, and later Ellen Wilkinson, enjoyed posts in the government and so could not be relied upon, and Lady Davidson was fairly inactive. But this still left an able group of nine including the Conservatives Astor, Ward, Tate and Cazalet-Keir, the Liberal Lloyd George and the Independent Rathbone. Additions to the Labour members as a result of by-elections in 1937–8 (Edith Summerskill, Agnes Hardie and Jennie Adamson) made for a politically balanced team. In their hands something approaching a women's party began to emerge 20 years after the politicians had first feared such a prospect, but it took the war to breathe life into this moribund concept.

Dissatisfaction had steadily built up during the 'phoney war' period under Neville Chamberlain. The British Federation of Business and Professional Women, under Caroline Haslett, inspired a number of meetings between women's groups and the women MPs with a view to persuading the authorities to involve women more in the war effort.

This resulted in a major deputation under Astor, Summerskill, Lloyd George, Ray Strachey and others to the financial secretary to the Treasury in February 1940. They demanded more civil service posts, especially senior posts in the Ministry of Labour, for women and the abandonment of the marriage bar. However, they made no progress until May when Chamberlain was replaced by the all-party administration under Winston Churchill. An early concession came from Herbert Morrison who seemed more alive than most to women's claims, perhaps due to the influence of Ellen Wilkinson. As minister of supply Morrison appointed the women MPs as members of an Advisory Committee on the Collection of Salvage under Megan Lloyd George's chairmanship. He accepted their recommendation that local authorities should be compelled to organise collections, a modest success which encouraged further co-operative action amongst the women members.

Their chief target, however, was Ernest Bevin as minister for labour, an altogether less sympathetic figure. He agreed to establish another advisory body, the Women Power Committee, but was hampered by hostility within the Labour movement; for example, the Standing Joint Committee of Working Women's Organisations declined to be represented, and Ellen Wilkinson damned it as a vehicle designed to enable middle-class women to secure supervisory jobs in factories. Bevin required little encouragement of that kind, and his unco-operative attitude led the committee to demand the appointment of a woman minister within his department to deal with the problems of female workers. Meanwhile the members maintained a steady pressure on the minister in the Commons which culminated in March 1941 in a manpower debate which Ward described as a 'milestone in British Parliamentary history'. Speakers included Ward, Summerskill, Lloyd George, Cazalet-Keir, Hardie, Tate, Davidson, Adamson, Horsbrugh and Rathbone. The atmosphere is reflected in a series of clashes between male and female members. When Summerskill complained about inequalities in pay Bevin interrupted to dispute her statements:

| Dr Summerskill: | Even he admits my figures are right. |
| Mr Bevin: | I think your figure's perfect.[33] |

Later Mavis Tate joined in:

Mrs Tate:	The minister is a man and he made a mistake.
Mr Grenville:	Do women never make mistakes?
Mrs Tate:	I should be the last woman in the world to pretend that women do not make mistakes, when I look around and see some of the men they bring into the world.

However, the men rapidly tired of this. Churchill enunciated a rule that major matters could be raised only in secret session, which had the effect of killing off debates on womanpower.

The women members were on their strongest ground on issues whose implications appeared to be relatively limited – for example the question of compensation for injuries sustained by civilians in bombing raids. It is a striking indication of the resilience of traditional male attitudes within government that women were considered to be worth only two-thirds of the rate payable to men. Nonetheless over 100 MPs signed Mavis Tate's motion in support of equal compensation, and when the issue was pressed to a vote in November 1942 the government suffered a sharp defeat by 229 votes to 95. Thereupon the government set up a select committee on the subject to cover its ignominious retreat. Successes of this kind fuelled speculation about the possible development of a women's party at the next election. No doubt the suspension of normal party warfare and the striking by-election successes gained by independents and the Commonwealth Party added credibility to the idea if only for a brief period.

However, the restlessness was rather greater in the Conservative ranks as is evident from the formation of the Tory Reform Committee whose 40 members were particularly concerned to persuade the government to implement the Beveridge Report. The fact that its membership overlapped with that of the Woman Power Committee added considerably to the effectiveness of the women's campaigns in the latter half of the war. The appearance of R.A. Butler's Education Bill in 1944 gave them the opportunity to press successfully for the abolition of the marriage bar in teaching. It also spurred the agitation for equal pay to fresh triumphs. During 1943 this issue had been gathering steam under the aegis of the Equal Pay Campaign Committee (EPCC) which, with Mrs Tate, Dr Summerskill and Pippa Strachey, was reasonably representative of political and feminist interests; indeed it claimed affiliation from 100 women's organisations altogether. The EPCC first tackled the civil service, but in the absence of support from the trade unions, it was rebuffed.[34] However, the Education Bill provided a golden opportunity for mobilising the sympathy amongst MPs which had already been shown in the 1930s. Thelma Cazalet-Keir was deputed to move the amendment to give equal pay to women teachers, and warned the chief whip that it would be pressed to a division, 'a threat which he received with a sort of pitying nonchalance natural enough when the odds seemed so heavily on the Government's winning'.[35] In the event the debate went in favour of the rebels, for this was just the kind of question which MPs could treat as a question of principle rather than as one in which the policy of the coalition government was at stake. The amendment was thus carried by 117 votes to 116. However, there followed a remarkable closing of the ranks by Tory and Labour politicians. Ernest Bevin apparently undertook to resign if Butler's bill were not relieved of the equal pay clause. Churchill insisted on a vote of confidence in his government, with the predictable result that equal pay was duly squashed. 'Sometimes when a genius has tantrums', wrote Cazalet-Keir, 'ordinary folk have to humour him.' She herself voted with the government.The only concession was the appointment of a Royal Commission with instructions to consider the effects of equal pay on women's employment, but with no powers to make recommendations! Faced with this classic delaying tactic – the Commission did not report until October 1946 – Tate and the EPCC angrily accepted the futility of persisting with the struggle in parliament.

In a sense educational reform had been intended to divert some of the momentum building up behind social welfare and the Beveridge Report. For feminists it was especially significant that the payments now made to the wives of servicemen brought the question of family allowances back onto the agenda during 1942. In May of that year a White Paper appeared on the subject, in September the TUC at last came out in support, and in December Beveridge put his seal of approval on the proposal. Thus when Rathbone took a deputation to the chancellor of the exchequer in February 1943 he was ready to concede official acceptance of family allowances. The bill, which provided a weekly payment of 5 shillings for each child after the first, was introduced in the spring of 1945 and passed before the coalition broke up. Though a great triumph for Rathbone this was of rather mixed importance for the wider women's movement. Parliament had not really accepted the feminist rationale for family allowances as is evident from the original proposal that the payments should be made to *fathers*. On this point the government was, however, forced to back down. Also much of the extra momentum behind family allowances clearly came from concern about the birth rate. Beveridge – no feminist – saw the reform as one way of boosting population by making motherhood more attractive. The measure fitted neatly into his wider scheme as a pragmatic, cost-effective means of directing resources where they were needed. This is why family allowances were not payable for the first child – a significant departure from Rathbone's principle that the state should recognise the value of the mother's work.

Family allowances were an important harbinger of the pattern of post-war politics for women; for the issue demonstrates the limited influence that the parliamentary feminists could expect to wield. While women at large welcomed the reforms, they could not be mobilised behind any distinctively feminist type of reform. As the political parties ranged themselves in varying ways behind Beveridge-inspired proposals, feminists became marginalised, even when women's interests were being tackled. For example, in the Conservative Party the women's organisation never even met for an annual conference between 1939 and 1946. At the election of 1945 the party adopted its, by now, customary approach by treating women's interests as a subdivision of social security. This meant flourishing the, not inconsiderable, record of the coalition on such measures as the National Milk Scheme of 1940 for expectant mothers and children under 5 as well as family allowances.[36]

The Labour women were more active, holding conferences in 1940, 1942, 1943 and 1945, but showed a similar tendency to lose women's interests in the broader programme of the party. This is understandable, for the effect of the war was to heighten Labour's fundamental concern to defend the living standards of working-class families. Indeed the war often provided practical demonstrations of how 'socialist' control could be used to promote women's interests – food rationing, for example. Thus many Labour activists felt that women's interests were rising up the agenda. But there was clearly a gap between the feminist issues taken up by middle-class Labour women in parliament and the priorities of the rank and file who concentrated on milk supplies, rent rises, post-war housing, evacuation and the Beveridge Report. Within the organisation, however, feminism made no recovery after its steady decline in the 1930s. On employment, for example, Mary Sutherland reiterated the official party line that married women should not be obliged to go out to work: the priority remained the 'Living Wage' for men, and only those married women who were free should volunteer for work.[37] More remarkable was the hostile reception given by the 1942 women's conference to a resolution urging the constituency selection committees to give sympathetic consideration to women parliamentary candidates. One delegate 'deplored the fact that they had any resolution on the agenda which had any suggestion of feminism or asked for special treatment for women.'[38] The rejection of the proposal was confirmation of the long-term evolution of the organisation away from feminism; it suggests how slight an impact the campaigns of the women parliamentarians were making.

The acid test for the women's movement and its wartime revival was to be the general election of 1945. As early as 1940 Edith Summerskill had urged the Six Point Group to seize the opportunity of wartime to launch an initiative to secure the return of 100 women MPs at the next election: 'she did not mind what party, for the women already in Parliament had found it possible to work together on feminist issues irrespective of party'.[39] In the event their efforts were co-ordinated by a new organisation, Women for Westminster, whose tactics were to encourage the women in each constituency party to nominate a woman candidate themselves and thus avoid the impression of outside interference by feminists which antagonised the party regulars.[40] However, since the local parties did not function normally for most of the war this was in practice not easy to organise, even assuming some sympathy from the members. When the election drew near hundreds of candidates were adopted rather hastily with little opportunity for the women to make their claim. Barbara Castle wrote later that she would not have been chosen at Blackburn had not the local women demanded their own representative; but the male-female ticket was already an established feature for Labour in Blackburn, and few other constituencies offered a similar opportunity.

In the event 1945 saw 87 women candidates, an increase of 20 over 1935; but as this amounted to only 5.2 per cent of the total, compared to 5.0 per cent, it made very little impact. Of the candidates nominated by the three main parties the overwhelming majority, some 70 per cent, stood in seats safely held by their opponents, though this was admittedly a slightly lower percentage than that for the 1920s and 1930s (see Table 9.1). Twelve women were defending seats already held by their party but these did not represent fresh gains for women; they were either Conservative seats won in 1931 or Labour seats gained at pre-war by-elections for the most part. In this sense the efforts of Women For Westminster must be counted largely a failure. Nor was the performance of the parties much changed with Labour fielding just over

Table 9.1 Women Candidates (Conservative, Labour and Liberal) in the General Election of 1945

	Total	Safely held by own party	Marginal	Marginally held by opponents	Safely held by opponents
Conservative	14	2	4	4	4
Labour	38	2	2	3	26
Liberal	18	1	1	1	15
Total	70	5	7	8	50

half the women and the Conservatives running third behind the Liberals. On the other hand the number of women elected rose sharply from 12 on the outbreak of war to 23, of whom 20 were Labour. It could not be foreseen in 1945 that the women MPs were to remain close to this level for the next 40 years. As in inter-war general elections the chief explanation for the results lay in the shifts in party fortunes. Thus all the Conservative women members who had not withdrawn before the election were defeated except for Lady Davidson at Hemel Hempstead. The impressive 20 victories for the Labour women were largely a consequence of quite unexpected success in hopeless constituencies rather than the result of any party strategy for women. The outcome also left women's parliamentary position looking rather unbalanced. Of the three non-Labour members Lady Davidson was inactive, Eleanor Rathbone was to die shortly, and Megan Lloyd George tended to co-operate with Labour anyway. In effect this put an end to the wartime experiment of a party for women which crossed the ideological divide of party politics.

The case for regarding the Second World War as having made a more significant impact on the lives of women than the First consists not so much in the extent of change but rather in the fact that changes were often *sustained* into the post-war period. This was partly the result of shifts in public opinion which culminated in the Labour landslide of 1945 – a political pattern quite different from that of 1914–18. Much of course, depends upon the significance one places upon key innovations such as family allowances and the post-1945 welfare state. While family allowances had started out as a feminist reform, by 1945 the momentum behind it was clearly very different. Similarly there is a case for saying that women were simply the incidental beneficiaries of the welfare state measures rather than being central to the ideology behind it. By 1945 the women's movement was too weak at the grass roots to be capable of influencing these innovations, and it is not clear that it was able to draw fresh inspiration from the post-war phase of reform.

It is, perhaps, on the employment front that the positive view of the war gains validity by comparison with the First World War. For example, the marriage bar was suspended in teaching and the civil service, and this turned out to be a permanent gain. On inspection the reason consists largely in official expectations of labour shortages after the war, and in an acceptance that the government could not consistently urge industry to take on married women if it failed to set an example.[41] Thus, although many women abandoned their jobs after the war, more seem to have survived within the labour force than in the post-1918 reaction. By 1948 there were 350,000 more insured women workers than in 1939. They were largely older, married women. It can be argued that the shift towards employment amongst married women was the most significant consequence of the war. However, some qualification must be made. The trend was already under way in the 1930s. To compare the proportion of married women at work in the censuses of 1931 and 1951 – up from 10 to 21 per cent – would be to exaggerate the effect of the war itself. In any case one must enquire why this happened. It is by no means clear that official ideas changed, simply that after 1945 the government wanted to boost output so desperately that it was even prepared to encourage married women to return to work. This economic opportunity was an indirect consequence of the war. Whether, however, the attitude of women themselves had changed is much less obvious, as is emphasised by the continued trend in favour of marriage and motherhood. If more women felt able to combine a domestic role with employment at some stage or stages in their lives this hardly indicates emancipation, but rather a variation in women's traditional strategies for family survival. And any change clearly depended crucially on the vagaries of the British economy rather than on wartime experience.

Chapter 10 The Nadir of British Feminism 1945–1959?

Whatever happened to British feminists and the women's movement during the period between the Labour landslide of 1945 and the revivalism associated with 'women's liberation' in the 1960s? The conventional assumption that feminism was a spent force that petered out in a decade of conservatism and materialism, though not without empirical foundation, is a considerable exaggeration. The post-war backlash against feminism flourished through the 1950s, especially in the pages of the women's magazines. Witness a typical attack on the working mother by Monica Dickens in 1956:

> Will her children love her more if she is an efficient career woman who pops in and out of the house at intervals, knows a lot of stimulating people, and can talk about everything, except pleasant, trivial, day-to-day matters that are the breath of family life? ... She is not cheating her children by staying at home. She is giving them the supreme gift – herself. Long after they have left home, they will be grateful to her.[1]

By 1956, however, this was more a defensive attempt to boost the morale of mothers who remained at home than a realistic effort at stemming the drift to work. In some ways a more characteristic expression of the mid-1950s was Alva Myrdal and Viola Klein's cautiously argued book, *Women's Two Roles* (1956), which suggested that paid employment and family responsibilities were compatible for women.

Yet the gulf between the mass of British women and the organised movement working on their behalf did yawn wide in this period. Stalwarts of the Edwardian generation of feminists such as Margery Corbett continued to be active in women's pressure groups. However, their ranks were now greatly thinned, they made few headlines and by comparison with the post-1918 era were relatively marginal in political terms. They were not, however, without some achievements, notably equal pay for civil servants and teachers. It was during the 1950s that the failure of inter-war feminism to recruit a large body of young leaders became apparent. The most notable feminist of that era was Edith Summerskill who fought for women's causes both in parliament and in the traditional non-party pressure groups throughout the 1950s. But a more telling symptom of the weakness of her generation is to be found in the career of another prominent inter-war woman, Vera Brittain. Fascism and war had turned her to pacifism, thence by the later 1950s towards involvement in the Campaign for Nuclear Disarmament. From her perspective this was not an abandonment of feminism, for its victories had largely been won. Brittain probably represented the views of many politically aware women after 1945 when she argued that the welfare state was 'a product of the women's revolution' because it 'embodied the change in social values which that revolution accomplished'.[2] Even in the 1940s some feminists regarded this enthusiasm for the welfare state as naïve, but the point is that for many women social reforms really did appear to be the culmination of women's campaigns since 1918. Consequently, for the younger generation of the 1950s the combination of welfare reform with economic opportunities and political rights seemed to deprive the women's movement of any really significant targets to aim at. Thus, for example, Marghanita Laski admitted:

> I was born too late for the battle. Older and nobler women struggled that I should be free, and did their work so well that I've never even bothered about being bound. Rights for women, so far as my generation is concerned, is a dead issue.[3]

This sense of historical detachment from the women who had struggled for reforms before the war was echoed especially by those women who were establishing political careers during the 1950s. 'I am too old for women's Liberation', commented Judith Hart, one of the most successful women politicians of the 1950s and 1960s. Similarly Shirley Williams, discussing her mother's views, admitted, 'I'm not a feminist either, but that's a matter of generations. I think, don't you?'[4] Of course, both Hart and Williams *were* feminists in that they supported certain women's causes; but their remarks signify that they could afford to take for granted the achievements of earlier generations of feminists, and that they themselves ventured onto their political careers from a position *within* the establishment, not as outsiders bent on changing the rules. The rise of this younger generation during the 1950s and 1960s inevitably left Summerskill, let alone Corbett Ashby, somewhat isolated and passé exponents of feminism. All of them were to be taken rather by surprise at the emergence of a new wave of feminism by the late 1960s.

The Working Woman in the Post-war Economy

For most women the process of demobilisation at the end of the Second World War was much less traumatic than had been the case after 1918. As we have seen, many greeted peacetime with a profound sense of relief; they both wanted and expected to return to normal family life.

For some the transition to peace was, in any case, more gradual than after the Great War. Women workers often remained in their industry or occupation but were squeezed out of their wartime roles into lower level jobs designated as 'women's' work. In banks, for example, women cashiers found themselves instructing young men recently out of the army:

> They took over the counter and we watched them for a week and stood by them for a week ... then we went back to the jolly old machines, the ledger machines, and the statement machines, and the shorthand and typing.[5]

In every sphere of employment the instinctive male assumption was, as in 1918, that women must be the first to move aside. Those women who approached their trade unions for support found themselves regarded as an embarrassment. Audrey Russell, the BBC's first woman reporter and accredited war correspondent, recalled that when she entered the tweedy male atmosphere of the BBC reporters' room at the end of the war she suddenly encountered a feeling of hostility towards her.[6] Neither was the new government under Clement Attlee disposed to take a more liberal view. Since the 1942 Restoration of Pre-War Practices Act it had been made clear that the cabinet intended to repeat First World War policy, which in the words of the minister responsible for reconstruction, meant 'putting back the man in his own preferential position'.[7] This was underlined when government subsidies for day nurseries were reduced by half in 1945 and withdrawn in 1946, thereby obliging local authorities to close them down.

In spite of the survival of traditional views in the establishment, it is apparent that women's position in the labour force did remain very extensive and, indeed, actually strengthened, during the decade after the war. The explanations are all closely connected with the performance of the British economy, rather than with attitudes towards women. In the first place the Labour government rapidly found itself driven to adopt a rather inconsistent policy on women's employment. By 1947, faced with a massive loss of earnings from foreign investments and visible exports, Britain had a balance of payments deficit of £443 million. The loan raised from the United States was beginning to run out, and the central social policies of the government were in jeopardy. It seemed essential to increase industrial output and thereby raise the earnings from British exports. The shortage of workers – put at 1.3 million in 1946 – was not helped by the maintenance of a large army of 1.2 million men and the continuation of National Service throughout the 1950s. Thus the cabinet reverted to wartime emergency strategies for incorporating more women into the labour force. Now women were required not for domestic service or clerical work but in 'productive' industry, in particular in cotton, rayon and nylon which were thought important for exports, and also in rubber, footwear, transport, and iron and steel. The Women's Land Army was also maintained until 1950. The official campaign ran from June 1947 and was pitched especially at women in the 35–50 age group, including married women who had worked during the war. It took the form of posters, newspaper advertisements, ministerial appeals, film trailers at cinemas, mobile recruitment vans and royal visits. These efforts did have a limited impact; by the end of 1947 there were 800,000 more women in employment than in 1939. But in spite of such slogans as 'Birmingham's bread hangs by Lancashire's thread' there is doubt as to whether women responded to the unglamorous image of working life now being proffered.[8] They were, after all, subject to a wholly different propaganda barrage from commerce and women's magazines. More importantly, many women were willing, after a break, to return to work temporarily, but not just on any terms. In particular they were resistant to the official pressure to accept work in industry, preferring the cleaner and higher status employment in offices. Consequently, in spite of government appeals women continued to leave the cotton mills.

The second helpful influence for women's employment was the long-term buoyancy of certain industries, concentrated in the Midlands and South East, including light engineering, aircraft and railways. Here employers who adapted quickly to peacetime demand often found it expedient to retain or re-engage women workers on repetitive, unskilled jobs because this helped to keep production costs down. For example, in engineering as a whole women had comprised 10 per cent of the labour force in 1939 but 22 per cent by 1951; this reflected expansion in sectors such as electrical engineering where they were used in producing light bulbs and batteries. As the consumer boom gathered pace during the 1950s such opportunities inevitably increased.

Finally the post-war era saw a continued shift of the British economy towards sectors in which women already held a large share of employment: broadly the clerical, administrative, commercial and lower professional areas. This was speeded up by the growth of government employment nationally and locally as a result of the welfare state, by the demand for schoolteachers and nurses, and by the boom enjoyed by building societies, estate agents, banks, solicitors and other service industries. Between 1931 and 1951, for example, the number of women clerks and typists rose from 657,000 to 1,408,000. And they continued

Table 10.1 Women as a Percentage of the Labour Force 1931–1981

1931	29.8
1951	30.8
1961	32.4
1971	36.0
1981	38.9

Source: A.H.Halsey(ed.), *British Social Trends* (1988), p.166.

to strengthen their position over succeeding decades, such that between 1951 and 1981 they increased from 49 to 70 per cent of all clerks, cashiers and office machine operators in the country.[9] This, of course, represented a continuation of the well-established trend in which women were leaving domestic service, cotton and clothing occupations for the service industries.

There are, of course, a number of qualifications to be made about the pattern of women's employment after 1945. They continued to be heavily concentrated in low-paid, unskilled occupations with no career structure. Much of their work was temporary and part-time. It is particularly noticeable that in the higher professions women's position improved from 5 per cent in 1921 to only 9 per cent by 1966. This was a reflection of their failure to significantly expand their access to higher education. Amongst university undergraduates, for example, women comprised 27 per cent in the 1920s, but remained stuck at around this level through to the late 1950s when a slight rise took place.

It is not, then, the qualitative but rather the quantitative, aspect of women's employment that is significant in this period. The figures for their share of the total workforce in Britain suggest how slight was the response to the post-war appeals for extra labour, but also how sustained was the long-term growth. On the other hand the negative effects of post-war demobilisation and the marriage-and-baby boom are evident in the 1951 figure for the proportion of women in employment. Thereafter, however, the gap between men and women narrowed steadily as more and more women went out to work (Table 10.2). Two social characteristics of the post-war female workforce are noteworthy. First, the age composition was changing. By 1951 only a third of the women workers were under 25 years, the rest being drawn fairly evenly from those in their thirties, forties and fifties; in contrast in 1931 half were under 25 and fewer in the older age groups. Second, the marital background of women workers changed drastically. Whereas in 1931 only 10 per cent of married women worked outside the home, 22 per cent did so by 1951, 30 per cent by 1961 and 47 per cent by 1981.

Table 10.2 Male and Female Participation Rates
in the Labour Force 1931–1981

	Women (%)	Men (%)
1931	34.2	90.5
1951	32.7	87.6
1961	37.5	86.3
1971	42.6	81.47
1981	45.5	77.8

Source: A.H.Halsey (ed.), *British Social Trends* (1988), p.168.

These developments point strongly to the collapse of the traditional ideal of the non-working wife amongst both middle-class and respectable working-class families in Britain. Increasingly the acceptable practice was for a woman to work before and in the early stages of marriage, but to return to the labour market while her children were still of school age and thus dependent upon their parents. For some of the older married women the return to employment may have been a sign of their need for extra female company and relief from the tedium of domestic life. But for many it was, as always, a response to economic opportunity. In the late 1940s the rising cost of living provided a spur. During the 1950s the temptation to help to raise the family's standard of living in terms of housing, holidays, motor cars and household goods often proved irresistible, especially as employers increasingly offered part-time jobs which could be seen as compatible with domestic responsibilities. Thus the expansion for the economy and the market for consumer goods and services was the key factor in the new pattern of women's work. Now equipped with Keynesian techniques of economic management, governments succeeded in maintaining full employment for an unusually prolonged period; indeed, unemployment did not exceed 2 per cent for 20 years after 1945. This proved very important for women, for it meant that the force of the traditional arguments about the iniquity of women who deprived men of jobs had largely been dissipated. Women's work could be seen as advantageous both for the economy at large and for the family in particular.

The Age of the Consumer

In many ways the characteristic manifestations of the modern consumer society arose in the 1930s; but the 1950s and 1960s saw a much more rapid growth in popular demand for goods and services which only the acute balance of payments difficulties managed to check. Four times as many people enjoyed foreign holidays in 1970 as in 1951. Whereas only one household in fifteen possessed a television set in 1951, ten out of fifteen did so by 1960. The number of motor cars on British roads increased from 1.5 million in 1945 to 3.5 million in 1955 and 5.5 million in 1960. But it was the craze for spending money on better housing that was most typical of this era. Even in the 1948–51 period around 200,000 houses were being built annually, and under Conservative governments the rate rose well beyond this. Increasingly the objective of families was to buy and not rent their homes; hence the inexorable trend towards owner occupation which before 1914 had accounted for only 10 per cent of the housing stock, but which rose to 35 per cent by 1939, and to 59 per cent by 1981.

The key to the improved standard of living which these trends indicate was the spread of the two-income family in an era of relatively high employment. The working wife thus became the central figure both because she earned the family's extra income, and because she was largely responsible for spending it. In retrospect the double burden of employment and domesticity may not appear to make the 1950s a liberating phase for British women, but at the time the widening of choice and availability of attractive consumer goods clearly helped to blunt the edge of discontent and make the decade one of conservatism.

During the course of the Second World War the time and effort that the Labour Party and its women's organisation had devoted to such questions as the design and construction of houses, the supply of milk for mothers and children, and the extension of gas and electricity supplies began to pay dividends. By 1945 Mass Observation surveys suggested strongly that women were both volatile in their political allegiance and particularly interested in the kinds of domestic issues on which Labour had built its case. After the victory of 1945 came a number of measures of especial value for women including the National Health Service and the implementation of family allowances from 1946. In spite of the prevailing financial stringency it was also decided to abolish purchase tax on a range of household equipment in 1946, and to fund subsidies on food which, by 1948, cost the exchequer £400 million annually. The effect of these was to reduce the price of tea by between one-fifth and a quarter, that of bread by a third and that of butter by nearly a half. Even in 1950 a Mass Observation survey for *Good Housekeeping* reported that 80 per cent of housewives felt food rationing was still necessary.[10]

Faced with this apparently successful formula the Conservatives simply endeavoured to turn Labour's domestic strategy to their own advantage by orchestrating a campaign through the sympathetic press and the Housewives League on the subject of food shortages and lack of choice in the shops, the poor supply of fuel, the inadequate house-building programme, and the low quality of clothing and household goods.[11] In 1949 R.A. Butler set up a special committee under Malcolm McCorquodale MP and Mrs E. Emmet to look into women's questions. It came up with a familiar set of proposals for building houses and improving gas, water and electricity supplies, dignified with the pledge that 'the strengthening of family life will continue to be of paramount concern to the Conservative Party'.[12] The party leaders' evident belief that women constituted the vulnerable part of Labour's support, and their decision to target the women voter, certainly flattered and stimulated the women's Conservative organisations in the years before the 1950 election. So much so that Labour found itself outflanked in domestic strategy. In a post-mortem debate after the 1951 election one woman expressed a widely held view that 'the last election was lost mainly in the queue at the butcher's or the grocer's'.[13]

After their return to office the Conservatives proceeded to cut food subsidies by £160 million in the first year. In order to offset this they introduced reductions in income tax, encouragement to the building industry, further easing of official restrictions on business and easier credit to enable purchases of the refrigerators, washing machines and vacuum cleaners which women increasingly desired.[14]

In this the Conservative governments of the 1950s enjoyed an important, if undeclared, ally in the shape of the women's magazine industry. Despite their wartime role as supporters of the political establishment, the magazine editors and proprietors declined to respond to post-war efforts to entice women back to work in the national interest. However, they were increasingly propagating a self-defeating message to their readers. On the one hand women were urged to be full-time wives, but on the other to take advantage of the range of consumer goods available to them. As we have seen, many women ignored the injunctions to stay at home, and doubtless rationalised their decision with the thought that part-time or temporary employment would enable them to help the family without depriving its members of proper care and attention. Clearly the magazines' own interests lay in effecting a rapid escape from post-war austerity; hampered by shortage of newsprint, rationing and lack of choice in the shops they could not expect to recover the advertising revenue on which their profits depended. The commercial interests for their part naturally saw women's magazines as an important vehicle for generating a demand for consumer goods and higher living standards after the privations imposed by war. Thus Mary Grieve of *Woman* waxed lyrical:

> After years of strictures, rations and restraints a whole new world of commodities flowed in on the flood-tide of the nineteen fifties. Younger women had never known such joys, few older women had been able to afford them pre-war. The women's magazines, with their close understanding of women, their sympathy with the situation, and their printing techniques, carried this new life straight into the homes and hearts of millions.[15]

The editors certainly seem to have judged correctly that a simple reversion to the narrow range of domestic interests spiced with romantic fiction and features about the royal family would restore their pre-war markets. Between 1946 and 1950 *Woman's* sales doubled, and those of *Woman's Own* trebled. As late as 1958 it proved possible to launch yet another traditional magazine, *Woman's Realm*, which soon sold 1.4 million copies. No fewer than five out of every six women read at least one magazine each week, and many saw several.[16]

The inevitable effect of this was not only to sustain popular aspirations to a wide range of consumer goods during the 1950s but also to help skew the terms of political debate in ways that favoured the Conservatives. The ideal propagated in the women's magazines – cosy, individualist, home-owning, materialist – was much closer to their brand of politics than to Labour's.

The widespread sense of growing material prosperity engendered by full employment and rising real wages produced a series of Conservative victories with increasing majorities at the elections of 1951, 1955 and 1959. This was unprecedented and it generated a prolonged debate over whether Labour was doomed never to win again. Flocks of researchers settled upon working-class communities in prosperous towns in the Midlands and the South with a view to testing the thesis that as manual workers improved their standard of living they gradually adopted middle-class aspirations and behaviour, including the habit of voting Conservative. They largely confirmed that working-class Tories were now less likely to vote out of deference and more inclined to regard Conservative rule as better for the economy and for their personal prosperity.[17] But they found little support for the view that Conservatives had gained support because of affluence and *embourgeoisement*. However, the investigations suffered from a tendency to assume that the evidence of this phenomenon would be found amongst *men* and in the work situation; as a result they neglected women and the

domestic situation. Yet women were much more directly and continuously exposed to the affluence of the 1950s. Moreover, even as
workers, their typical experience in the service industries brought them
more closely into association with middle-class values than did their
husbands. They were therefore much more likely to be politically
susceptible to the impact of affluence and *embourgeoisement* than most
men, as indeed, one study of Victorian domestic servants has
suggested.[18] Jean Mann, one of the Labour MPs who was herself a
working-class housewife, certainly felt that her fellow women were
inclined to identify with the middle class in the 1950s, and that
Labour's poor electoral record could be attributed to the party's failure
to attend to the women's vote as the Conservatives had done.[19] The
point is not that one party's strategy had proved more efficacious than
the other's. They had adopted much the same view of women as voters
who could best be reached through their domestic interests. It was
simply that during the 1950s one party was able to do this more
credibly.

Motherhood and the Welfare State

From the perspective of the 1980s feminists have often looked back in
exasperation to the 1950s and asked why women were so eager to return
to femininity and domesticity after enjoying their freedom during the
war.[20] This reflects a double misconception. Many women had not felt
any sense of freedom and welcomed the opportunity to establish a home
and family of their own. Moreover the domesticity they looked forward
to had changed in character. In 1945 a young woman on the verge of
marriage could reasonably anticipate that only a few years of life would
be occupied by the pregnancies and childbirth that had loomed so large
in the lives of her mother and grandmother. This meant that there would
be time and opportunity both to enjoy home life and to move out into
the labour market again. Now that couples could enjoy physical
relations without the perpetual fear of another pregnancy, the ideal of a
companionate marriage of equals appeared to be within reach.

At all events the institution of marriage continued to gain in
popularity in Britain. After the disruption of wartime there was a rush
to the altar and registry office, and the trend progressively increased
right up to 1972. At first the post-war marriage rate was reflected in the
birth rate. But the baby boom proved short-lived, and by the early
1950s births had receded to the level of the 1930s. A modest increase

Table 10.3   First Marriage Rates for Women (England and Wales)
per Thousand Population

1936–40	73.4	1956–60	82.6
1941–5	67.6	1961–5	83.6
1946–50	75.7	1966–70	94.2
1951–5	76.8		

Source: A.H. Halsey(ed.), *British Social Trends* (1988), p.73.

Table 10.4   Birth Rates per Thousand Population (England and Wales)
1931–1975

1931–5	15.0	1946–50	18.0	1961–5	18.1
1936–40	14.7	1951–5	15.3	1966–70	16.9
1941–5	15.9	1956–60	16.4	1971–5	14.0

Source: A.H.Halsey (ed.), *British Social Trends* (1988), p.40.

occurred again during the later 1950s and early 1960 followed by a return to the former low levels. This pattern of behaviour suggests that married couples were not easily manipulated by those in positions of authority who had appointed the Royal Commission on Population in 1944 because of their fears about national decline. Herbert Morrison spoke for many politicians when he declared that parents ought to achieve a *normal* family of three or four children, in which they would be assisted by government inducements in the form of cash, kind and care.[21] In the same spirit the archbishop of Canterbury told the Mothers' Union in 1952 that 'a family only truly begins with three children'. Even *Good Housekeeping* succumbed briefly to the mood with features entitled 'Hurrah for Large Families'.[22]

Fruitless as the propaganda may have been, it remains true that planning was a fashionable idea after 1945, and as Morrison's remarks suggest, the deliberate encouragement of family life became one of the central objectives of the welfare state. Its guiding spirit, after all, was an Edwardian social imperialist, William Beveridge. 'In the next thirty years', he wrote, 'housewives as Mothers have vital work to do in ensuring the adequate continuance of the British Race and of the British Ideal in the world.'[23] This left very little scope, apparently, for a wider role:

> The great majority of married women must be regarded as occupied on work which is vital but unpaid, without which their husbands could not do their paid work and without which the nation could not continue.[24]

Since the welfare system was to be based on the Victorian principle of benefits in return for contributions it followed that women would be disadvantaged. Yet because of the pressing need to encourage women to concentrate on their domestic role Beveridge favoured the introduction of family allowances and wished to pay them a much higher maternity benefit, which was in fact done between 1948 and 1953. He disapproved of benefits for divorced and separated wives unless they were innocent of responsibility for the breakdown of their marriage, and he proposed no provision for unsupported mothers who would have to rely on supplementary benefits.

Beveridge's moral-political view was to a considerable extent reflected in the post-war welfare system. Under the 1946 National Insurance Act the married woman was treated as the non-working and dependent part of a team; her entitlement to support rested on her husband's claim. Those married women who did work were expected to pay no contributions and thus enjoyed no claim to benefit themselves; if, however, such a woman did opt to contribute she would be entitled to a lower rate of benefit. The single working woman could be insured as a man, but her contributions were lower on the grounds that she did not have dependants to support. It subsequently transpired that the level for subsistence had been set rather low and was undermined by inflation; as a result there was an increasing resort to supplementary benefits. However, a married woman could not claim supplementary benefit for herself; her husband must claim for them both. This led to the notorious 'cohabitation ruling' which meant that a woman living with a man to whom she was not married was denied benefit and regarded as economically dependent upon him. It was felt that any more liberal treatment would tend to discourage marriage.

Some protests were voiced over the categorisation of woman as a mere dependant, notably by Elizabeth Abbott of the WFL, and by the National Council of Women. The Women's Co-operative Guild specifically asked that married women be made insured persons equally with 'productive workers' and thus entitled to benefit irrespective of their husbands' status. But ministers, calculating, perhaps, that most women would see a lot to be grateful for in the reforms, dismissed such claims as unreasonable. Indeed, any balanced view of the welfare state should recognise that it brought several notable gains to women. The family allowance, at a cost of £59 million, meant 5 shillings a week for second and subsequent children, an additional income greatly appreciated by millions of mothers. Also, in view of the relative neglect of their health in the past, women benefited disproportionately from the new National Health Service.

However, it seems very probable that most women regarded the welfare innovations primarily in the light of their effect on *other* members of the family, especially the children. In this respect they simply reflected the renewed emphasis on childcare and motherhood that became so pronounced a feature of the late 1940s and 1950s. This was not unlike the anti-feminist propaganda after 1918, though it was less shrill and enjoyed the endorsement of professional and scientific authorities. An early symptom was Dr Benjamin Spock's famous book *Baby and Child Care*, first published in Britain in 1947, in which the author declared, Beveridge-style: 'useful, well-adjusted citizens are the most valuable possession a country has, and good mother care during early childhood is the surest way to produce them.'[25] The message gained impact in 1951 from Dr John Bowlby's report, *Maternal Care and Mental Health*, produced for the World Health Organisation, which ran to nine impressions by 1960. Especially in the bowdlerised versions this material could readily be used to encourage married women to feel guilty if they undertook employment while their children were still at home. Where once the popular magazines had accused the working wife of destroying the pride of her husband, it now became fashionable to blame her for the social and psychological disorders of her children.

In fact Bowlby's work was by no means novel; essentially it gathered together a wide range of conventional opinions and surveys which emphasised the long-term effects of the kind of parental care received in early childhood, particularly the child's need for a 'warm, intimate and continuous relationship with his mother'.[26] He disparaged the Victorian-Edwardian preference for removing children from bad homes, and even criticised day nurseries which were said to have a disruptive effect on emotional development as well as being an uneconomic use of the state's resources.[27] A bad home was preferable to institutional care because of the measure of continuity and security bestowed on children even by neglectful parents. However, Bowlby listed working mothers as one of the causes of mental disorder in children.

The report suffered from several flaws. First, many of the symptoms of disturbed and neurotic behaviour observed were the product of wartime evacuation. It was surely this experience that made many parents susceptible to the arguments about mother care, but few saw how inappropriate it was to draw sweeping conclusions from extraordinary wartime circumstances. Second, the evidence was largely drawn from children in institutions, and even Bowlby accepted that this was not comparable with the position of the children of the working mother. Thirdly, no attempt was made to consider the significance of neglect of children on the part of fathers, but Bowlby pleaded lack of evidence.

During the 1950s *Maternal Care and Mental Health* helped to feed concern about unconventional behaviour, crime rates and juvenile delinquency. This was a favourite subject for discussion by women's organisations. For example, the Townswomen's Guild members readily accepted the fashionable view that juvenile delinquency was directly linked to the increase in the number of working mothers. Margery Corbett Ashby challenged this, but her voice was now a lonely echo of the feminist tradition in what had become a conventional women's organisation.[28] At least Corbett Ashby reminds us that the maternal care thesis did not go unquestioned, though the argument was conducted very much within the ranks of the middle class. One of the most reasoned defences of the working mother came from one of the less widely recognised feminists of the decade, Mrs Margaret Thatcher. In an article published in 1954 she asked:

> What is the effect on the family when the mother goes out to work each day? If she has a powerful and dominant personality her personal influence is there the whole time. ... Of course she still sees a good deal of the children. The time she spends away from them is a time which the average housewife spends in doing the housework and shopping, not in being with the children assiduously. From my own experience I feel there is much to be said for being away from the family for part of the day. When looking after them without a break, it is sometimes difficult not to get a little impatient. ... Whereas, having been out, every moment spent with them is a pleasure to anticipate. ... Later on there will not be that awful gap which many women find in their lives when their children go away to school.[29]

A 27-year-old housewife when this was written, Mrs Thatcher personified the evolution from inter-war feminism to post-war feminism. Its central feature consisted in challenging the assumption that a woman must choose between family life and a career. This was not entirely new. Vera Brittain had advocated semi-detached marriage, and urged women not to allow housework to dominate their days, a view that was to be echoed by Betty Friedan in the 1960s. But in the 1950s the cautious and limited case for the working mother was made in a book that is characteristic of the decade, *Women's Two Roles* (1956) by Alva Myrdal and Viola Klein. Their argument proceeded from the belief that the state needed women's contribution to the labour force, not from the view that women had a right to exercise their choice. But even this shifted the terms of the debate. The question was not whether married women should go out to work, as in the 1920s, but rather, whether the *working* woman should marry. Myrdal and Klein passed lightly over the implications of the two roles for women. There was no suggestion that husbands ought to share the domestic duties with their wives. Like Brittain and Thatcher they took a brisk, middle-class view that housework ought not to be very demanding if properly organised. Nor did they pose a direct challenge to the importance attached to child care by the young mother. Rather they saw married life in different stages. The first would be dominated by a woman's babies, but the subsequent decades would involve some combination of employment and domesticity. If this was a limited and understated defence of the working mother it was calculated to lend her respectability in a conservative era. Any guilt a woman might feel about neglecting the family would be outweighed by the pride to be derived from shouldering the double burden.

Political Strategies

In an era dominated by the Cold War, the welfare state and consumerism it was difficult for feminists to command the attention they had enjoyed after 1918. Women in politics no longer posed a threat, nor did they have novelty value. Consequently the remnants of the non-party women's movement had to work hard for relatively few gains. A few long-standing grievances were resolved. 1948 brought the long-promised Nationality Act for married women, and 1958 saw the admission of peeresses to the House of Lords. But the major success for feminism during the 1950s was equal pay in the government service. By the 1940s the principle of equality of pay commanded widespread support, but governments continued to prevaricate over the timing and the extent of their capitulation. The House of Commons had voted for equal pay for civil servants in 1920 and 1936, and for teachers in 1944. Opinion polls showed a large majority of the public in favour. In 1947 the Labour Party Conference defied its leaders by giving a 4:1 vote for equal pay. After the war the National Association of Local Government Officers negotiated through the Whitley Council for equal pay in the higher grades; and in 1952 London County Council introduced equal pay for its teachers.

After 1945 the Equal Pay Campaign Committee enjoyed a more balanced support than hitherto; successive chairmen were the former Tory MPs, Mavis Tate and Thelma Cazalet-Keir, while its parliamentary backers included the Labour members Dr Summerskill, Leah Manning and Barbara Ayrton Gould, joined in 1950 by Elaine Burton and Eirene White. Lord Pethick-Lawrence also helped by raising the issue in the Lords. They concentrated on equal pay in government service and avoided pressing the claim in industry where both employer and union reactions were mixed. However, some trade unions did promote an Equal Pay Co-ordinating Committee, and it has been suggested that this body was more influential than the patently middle-class EPCC, though in view of the rebuffs continually dealt out by the Labour government this seems unlikely.[30]

The immediate task of the EPCC was to raise the level of public interest in the issue, but they were hampered at first by the need to await the report of the Royal Commission set up in 1944. When it appeared in 1946 the report marked no advance on the official position around 1918. It largely followed its brief in ignoring the question of equal pay as a matter of justice for women, and concentrating on the practical effects in terms of reducing the number of women employed and levelling down the wages of men. It did, however, recommend equal pay in certain occupations where the sexes clearly performed the same work.[31] During its early years in office the Attlee government's priorities lay in financing the welfare measures, and by 1947 the room for additional and competing claims on resources had narrowed greatly. Successive chancellors – Cripps, Dalton and Gaitskell – argued that in the face of the economic crisis the inflationary effects of granting equal pay to civil servants could not be contemplated. They were backed up by by-election candidates and by Mary Sutherland, the party's Woman Officer, who insisted that the issue was in abeyance while the economic crisis lasted.[32] In spite of the polls, it was suggested, there was no great resentment among women at large.

Thus ensued a period of deadlock in which both Attlee and Churchill declined to receive deputations on the subject of equal pay. The EPCC attempted to embarrass the politicians by largely traditional expedients – cross-questioning of candidates at by-elections, mass rallies in London, leaflets and the spread of local branches.[33] The most novel weapon was the production of a film entitled *To Be A Woman* which was made by Jill Craigie at a cost of £4157.[34] The 20-minute film was circulated by film societies and through the Regent Film Distribution organisation. Local activities were, however, severely limited by short-age of funds and provincial members; the EPCC tended to rely on existing groups such as the Fawcett Society for secretarial services.

It was several years before the economic pressures against equal pay diminished; but meanwhile the political circumstances changed in ways that proved advantageous. In particular the 1950 general election removed the large Labour majority and put the two main parties on a fairly equal footing; expectations of a further election encouraged all three parties to include equal pay in their manifestoes. In the 1950 election the EPCC secured far more promises of active support from Conservative candidates but the closeness of the result put all parties on their mettle. There ensued a period of competition in the Commons in which each side attempted to establish its own credentials on the issue. In November 1950 Irene Ward mobilised Tory support for her amendment to the King's Speech regretting the omission of equal pay. After the 1951 election the EPCC ascertained the views of 184 of the new members; of these 118 were ready to give active support, including 48 Conservatives, 65 Labour and 5 Liberals.[35] In September Douglas Houghton (Labour) placed an equal pay motion on the order paper with 50 Labour, 17 Conservative and 8 Liberal signatures. But the momentum was not sufficient to drive the new Tory government into a speedy concession. Its main priority was to cut income tax which, in 1952, cost some £229 million compared to the £29 million required to finance equal pay for civil servants. However, there was a warmer response in the spring of 1954 when the two equal pay pressure groups presented petitions backed by 680,000 signatures to parliament. Ward and Houghton placed numerous questions on the order paper and the latter introduced a 10-minute bill before the budget. The chancellor, R.A. Butler, now indicated that he would finance the gradual introduction of equal pay in the civil service.[36] Although the easing of the economic crisis had helped, the key factor here was Conservative fears about the next election. They had won narrowly in 1951 with fewer votes than Labour, and saw equal pay as a means of outflanking the Opposition on women's matters at the 1955 election.

How much significance should be attributed to the victory over equal pay? Clearly the objective was a limited one which enabled the government to calculate the costs fairly precisely. There were no immediate implications for private and industrial employment. It is true that the concession to civil servants was followed in 1955 by a similar policy for teachers, and in 1956 it was decided to extend equal pay to the National Health Service, gas and electricity. But in December 1955 the EPCC debated a proposal to dissolve itself, and the group was wound up in the next year. Clearly the implication was that neither the momentum nor the resources existed for extending the campaign into commerce and industry. It looked as though middle-class women had got what they wanted. As a result the triumph over equal pay does not seem to have been used to raise the general profile of the women's movement. Nothing, in fact, arrested the declining fortunes of organised feminism during this decade.

The sudden death of Eleanor Rathbone in 1946 symbolised the waning of inter-war New Feminism in Britain. Admittedly several of Rathbone's colleagues, including Corbett Ashby and Eva Hubback, continued their public work. But Hubback in particular had moved far from her feminist origins; her books on population in the 1940s reflected a highly conventional concern with finding means of encouraging women to have more children. The umbrella organisations, including the Fawcett Society, the Women's Freedom League and the Six Point Group, continued in existence, and the Suffragette Fellowship kept alive memories of the earlier struggles over the franchise. Of these the liveliest was the Six Point Group, now led by some able women including Dr Summerskill, Monica Whately and Dorothy Evans. But it was dogged by arguments over whether it would be best to channel the limited effort into single-issue groups like the EPCC and Women for Westminster, or indeed to amalgamate with one of them. There was a move to wind up the group altogether which was supported by the aged Lady Pethick-Lawrence who felt that too many small societies were struggling for the same objects with inadequate resources, and that for women who wanted to influence political debate the party route was now the most realistic one.[37] However, Whately and Evans preferred to keep going as a separate organisation, partly because they valued the connection with international women's groups, and because they remained too sceptical of the political parties to be willing to dispense with the independent women's organisations altogether. 'I have over and over again been threatened with excommunication owing to my fight for the complete emancipation of women', observed Whately, who had several times stood as a Labour candidate.[38] However, even the relatively new groups relied upon the same limited pool of support. Women for Westminster, founded in 1942, depended upon the familiar names – Summerskill (Labour), Tate and Cazalet-Keir (Conservative) and Corbett Ashby (Liberal) – to maintain its claim to non-party status. With 32 branches and an income of only £1000 in 1946 Women for Westminster never made much impression on the women's share of parliamentary candidatures (see page 303). By 1949 the pressure to amalgamate with another organisation became irresistible, and it joined the National Women's Citizens Association which had itself recently merged with the National Council for Equal Citizenship.[39] The three

larger women's organisations from the inter-war period, the WI, the
Townswoman's Guild and the WCG, enjoyed mixed fortunes. Membership of the first two continued to be buoyant. But the political
quiescence of the TG was challenged in 1953 when critics proposed
that it should 'express its views on National Affairs, especially on
matters concerning women and children', and put pressure on government departments if necessary.[40] Though the mood was more favourable to political activity in the 1950s, the predominant views of the
members, as Corbett Ashby found, were by no means feminist. On the
other hand the Women's Co-operative Guild now began to show some
of the signs of an ageing membership common to the older feminist
groups. At 61,000 in 1947, the WCG membership remained stagnant
for several years, and in 1952 commenced a gradual decline down to
48,000 by 1959. This was ascribed to a failure to recruit younger
women who, it was suggested, either went out to work, or felt satisfied
with their rising standard of living, or succumbed to the superior
attractions of the less political women's organisations.[41] Also, it is
likely that the achievements of the Labour government, in terms of
social welfare, had gone some way to blunting the campaigning edge of
the WCG.

Against this background one might well expect to see women in the
post-war period giving a rather higher priority to the alternative method
of pressing their claims by working through the formal political system.
In order to assess whether this was so we must examine the evidence for
the extent and nature of their participation. A survey of candidatures in
the four general elections fought in the 1950s shows that the idea that
women are generally given marginal constituencies is a myth – only
19.7 per cent fall into that category. A massive 70 per cent were in
hopeless seats, almost exactly the same as the figure for 1945 and only
a modest improvement on the inter-war pattern. On the positive side
some 16.5 per cent of the women fought seats already held by their own
parties, almost the same as the 1945 figure and well above the 6.6 per
cent for 1922–35. This is reflected in the slightly stronger share of
representation in the House of Commons during the 1950s; at between
3 and 4 per cent, or two dozen at most, the women comprised a more
secure and stable minority than they had between the wars, but a
remarkably stagnant one in terms of numbers (see page 160). The party
political pattern changed a little in the post-war period in that the
Liberals gave a higher share of candidatures to women, but these were,
of course, almost entirely in unwinnable seats. Also, two-thirds of the
candidatures in seats held by the candidate's own party were Labour.

Table 10.5   The Distribution of Women's Candidatures at General
Elections 1950–1959

	Conservative	Labour	Liberal	Total
In seats safely held by own party	7	18	0	25
In seats marginally held by own party	4	9	1	14
In seats marginally held by another party	13	21	1	35
In seats safely held by another party	54	50	71	175

This shows itself in the markedly pro-Labour character of the women MPs. In the period from 1945 to 1959 29 women were elected for Labour but only 15 for the Conservatives and one for the Liberals. As this period encompasses two Labour election victories and three Conservative ones it appears that, for whatever reason, women now enjoyed a more advantageous position in the Labour Party than amongst the Conservatives.

Were there any changes in the type of woman elected after the war, or in the methods women employed to attain nominations? It is immediately obvious that the old practice of a woman stepping into her husband's shoes virtually died out. The exceptions were Lady Gamans (Conservative, Hornsey), Lena Jeger (Labour, Holborn and St Pancras), and a pre-war MP, Lady Davidson (Conservative, Hemel Hempstead). In 1945 a high proportion of the women members – 75 per cent – were married, but the figure declined to only 56 per cent by 1974.[42] This was not significantly different from the inter-war position except that on the Labour side the proportion of single women diminished; in fact only 4 of Labour's 29 post-war members were unmarried, against 7 of the 15 Conservatives. In occupational terms the post-1945 members were predominantly drawn from the professional middle classes; as Shirley Summerskill noted: 'Medical practice is rather like being an MP with surgeries and so on.'[43] A high proportion of these professionals, though married, had no children. For women politicians such as Edith Summerskill, Barbara Castle, Judith Hart, Bessie Braddock and Margaret Thatcher a supportive husband was clearly an important factor in their long public careers. Equally importantly it emerges that for many of the women elected in the 1950s the encouragement and example given by their fathers proved to have been responsible, in part, for the original decision to seek a political career; Eirene White, Alice Bacon, Margaret Thatcher and Barbara Castle are all examples.

The institutional routes used by women to make their way into parliament after 1945 were very similar to those used before the war. For Conservatives and Liberals it was even more necessary, in view of the abandonment of the practice of substituting a wife for her husband, to demonstrate loyalty to party by fighting some unwinnable constituencies and by working for the party machine. Many of the post-war members had already established their credentials by service between the wars. Local government experience figured prominently in the background of several women, including Joyce Butler, Miss Mervyn Pike, Bessie Braddock, Judith Hart and Mrs Castle. On the Labour side participation in the Women's Co-operative Guild strengthened the claims of Barbara Ayrton Gould, Joyce Butler and Harriet Slater to winnable seats. Women also became very prominent in both the national party organisations. Between 1945 and 1959 five women served as chairman of the National Union of Conservative and Unionist Associations, and one as president; however only one of these, Mrs E. Emmett, became an MP. The Labour Party chairmanship was held by Wilkinson, Bacon, Summerskill, Miss Margaret Herbison and Mrs Castle, and the same women, apart from Wilkinson, also acted as chairman of the National Executive Committee during the 1950s. However, these positions were won as a consequence of their parliamentary and political status, they did not lead to the original nomination by the party.

Many of the women MPs of this era have denied that anti-female prejudice was ever a serious obstacle to them. This, however, tells us only that they were the successful ones. While a woman's hopes of a career remain alive it is bad tactics ever to blame male prejudice, as this merely exacerbates the sense of defeatism and failure. In attempting to account for the failure to increase the number of women MPs significantly one has to take note of two factors: the attitudes of the parties towards women, and the extent of the pressure from women to become candidates. We do, in fact, have an approximate indication of the demand in the form of the national lists of approved candidates maintained by each party. It is not difficult to get one's name on these lists, and indeed, for many years both the main parties have been keen to increase the number of women on them. In the late 1970s just under 9 per cent of those on the Conservative list were women. On the Labour Party's 'B' List (the 'A' List comprises trade union sponsored candidates) women constituted 8.4 per cent.[44] At the general election of 1979, 6.8 per cent of candidates were actually women. This suggests that the *extent* of the discrimination against them had become quite minor, and it underlines the fact that the reluctance or inability of women to seek nominations is a major reason for their low profile in parliament.

Nonetheless, during the 1950s bias against women aspirants continued to be a factor, primarily at the level of the local constituency. Herbert Morrison has been singled out as a patron of aspiring female politicians at Labour headquarters, but in the best seats women continued to be disadvantaged by their inability to win union backing.[45] For a few working-class women like Jean Mann and Alice Bacon this presented no problem because their families were so deeply rooted in the Labour movement as to make them acceptable male surrogates. However, the more typical member was a middle-class 'working woman'. If she had built up a record of work for the party before 1945 she could, with luck, find herself elected in a 'hopeless' seat on the strength of the Labour landslide. However, most of the women MPs who lost their seats when the national tide turned towards the Conservatives never returned. One or two were favoured. When boundary changes undermined Alice Bacon's Leeds NE seat she was transferred to the safe Leeds SE. When Dr Summerskill's West Fulham seat was merged with East Fulham the nomination went to the male incumbent, but since she won a seat at Warrington her career was not interrupted. To set against the losses new Labour women members arrived throughout the decade: Elaine Burton and Eirene White in 1950, Harriet Slater and Lena Jeger in 1953, Joyce Butler in 1955, and Judith Hart in 1959.

The Conservatives suffered more embarrassment over their choice of candidates. Under the Maxwell Fyfe reforms in 1948 the party modified its selection methods with the object of involving more of the large membership in the process. The party conference also voted in favour of restricting donations made by each candidate to his local party to £25. Yet it is doubtful whether reforms of this kind actually helped aspiring women politicians. One vice-chairman of the party reminded the women's conference that although he always added women's names to lists of candidates they were usually unsuccessful because the women on the local committees preferred men.[46] There are several possible explanations for this often-made criticism. Some women simply resent the ambition and achievement of fellow women in the male sphere. Others consider it irresponsible for a married woman with children to attempt to take on a parliamentary constituency. Most feel that a woman candidate, married or single, is unlikely to bring the *additional* support to the constituency organisation that a married male would bring.[47] Even so, the chief influence on the selection continues to be that of men who tend to choose as candidates people very similar to themselves in class, occupation, education and interests.

One sees the result of this in the failure of nearly all the Conservative women MPs defeated in 1945 to get back to parliament. Cazalet-Keir never got closer than third place on a short-list of four in her local constituency: 'I was forced to the conclusion that the only effective qualification would be a change of sex.'[48] On the other hand Miss Ward and Miss Horsbrugh did return, but only by winning Labour seats once again. On the whole the lady members simply worked their passage in the classic fashion. Patricia Hornsby-Smith fought hopeless contests at Ebbow Vale, Glasgow Bovan and Pontypool before securing the winnable Chislehurst; Edith Pitt contested Birmingham Stechford and Small Heath before getting Edgbaston; Miss Pike stood in Pontefract and Leek before landing Melton Mowbray; and Miss Betty Harvie Anderson tried at West Stirling and Sowerby before her victory in East Renfrew. Only Mrs Emmet walked straight into a safe seat at East Grinstead. Perhaps the most remarkable triumph was Mrs Thatcher's nomination for Finchley in 1958 when she was a 32-year-old mother of 5-year-old twins. She had helped herself by contesting Dartford, a safe Labour seat, twice in 1950–1; as the youngest woman candidate she came to the attention of Central Office. Then in 1951 she married a wealthy husband who was keen to support her ambitions. But thereafter the path led uphill. She clearly resented advice to the effect that she should simply go home, have her babies and postpone politics. Her willingness to give talks to the Six Point Group and to defend the working mother in print during the early 1950s indicates at least a feminist phase in Mrs Thatcher's life. Not surprisingly she found herself rejected by plum Tory constituencies in the south-east, including Orpington, Beckenham, Maidstone and Oxford. Meanwhile she established a second career as a lawyer, and kept applying. There are no obvious lessons in her win at Finchley; hers was an isolated success and not part of a trend.

There is some slight evidence that women, once elected, occupied a more influential position, in terms of government office, after 1945 than between the wars. The post-war members enjoyed the advantage of a longer period in the House, on average, and thus produced more senior figures in their respective parties. Mrs Castle's term ran to 34 years, Mrs Hart's to 28, while Bacon, Braddock, Herbison and Lee all sat for

25 years. Because of the 1945 election the Conservatives' average was shorter, but several of the pre-war members like Ward and Davidson acquired long experience as did Hornsby-Smith and Joan Vickers. One may assess women's role in the light of three criteria: the number promoted to office, the type of post received, and the degree of success achieved.

Only two women reached the cabinet during 1945–59 – Ellen Wilkinson and Florence Horsbrugh, both at Education. In addition junior posts were awarded to Summerskill (Food and National Insurance), Herbison (Scottish Office) and Mrs J. Adamson (Pensions) under Attlee; while the Conservatives promoted Hornsby-Smith (Health, Pensions, Home Office), Edith Pitt (Health and Pensions) and Miss Pike (Assistant Postmaster General). Clearly the Conservative record was relatively poor, for after 1954 when Horsbrugh left office, Hornsby-Smith was the sole woman in government until 1959, and none sat in a cabinet until Mrs Thatcher in 1970. To some extent this can be explained by the different career patterns of the Conservative women. Among the experienced members only Horsbrugh wanted office; Davidson lacked ambition and Ward had perfected her role as an independent-minded backbencher. The rest entered parliament during the 1950s and were relatively junior. However, much the most important factor was the attitude of the prime ministers of the period. Neither Attlee, Churchill, Eden nor Macmillan felt much sympathy towards women in politics. Witness the contrast between them and the premiership of Harold Wilson from 1964 to 1970 which saw a concentration of 11 women in office despite the fact that there had been only a slight increase in the number of women MPs. Even then ideological preference was partly responsible in that Wilson promoted long-standing left-wing associates such as Mrs Castle, Mrs Hart and Miss Lee.

It is conspicuous that the posts given to women were confined to the 'domestic' sphere of politics – Education, Health, Pensions, Food. This was in spite of – or because of – Margaret Bondfield's pioneering role in an economic ministry. The performance of women in office is difficult to assess, especially for the junior ministers. Certainly none of the more prominent women of the period were regarded as notably successful at the time. Wilkinson suffered some criticism within her party for passively implementing the 1944 Education Act, though her death in 1947 curtailed what might easily have been a more illustrious ministerial career. Summerskill – at the Ministry of Food in years of shortages and queues – inevitably endured an uncomfortable time through a situation that was not of her making. She was an effective defender of the government's policy, to put it no higher. Horsbrugh's position as education minister from 1951 was undermined by her exclusion from cabinet until 1953. Unfortunately for her education was simply not a priority for the Churchill government, and like Atholl, Horsbrugh found herself deciding where to impose economies. But she did not fight the policy, and resigned in October 1954; it then fell to her successor to withdraw the expenditure cuts. Thus, although a popular member and an experienced legislator, Horsbrugh was seen as a weak minister.[49]

How far did women make an impact as parliamentary backbenchers? Although their numbers increased in the post-1945 period they largely failed to sustain the concerted pressure that had been such a feature of wartime politics. There are several reasons for this. In spite of the camaraderie of the ladies' room at the Commons the women were far from a united group. Though they included a number of closet feminists, only a small minority worked actively for women's causes. The Labour women were not unaffected by the ideological friction between right-wingers like Mrs Mann and Mrs Braddock and left-wingers like Mrs Castle and Mrs Hart. Above all the women were constrained by a political system that was now dominated by two great parties. The only independent, Rathbone, died in 1946; Megan Lloyd George, an increasingly independent Liberal, lost her seat in 1951, only to return in 1956 as a Labour member. According to Jean Mann the new Labour MPs of 1945 were instructed to avoid private members' bills, to keep quiet and vote the government's legislation through.[50] After 1951 they obviously enjoyed more scope. Conversely the Conservative women had been all but eliminated in 1945, and although six returned in 1951 the small size of Churchill's majority increased the pressure not to rock the boat until 1955.

By and large, however, the women MPs seem to have been *willing* to place party first in their priorities. They fall into to three main types in this period: first, those who aspired to the status of national party politicians like Castle, Hart, Horsbrugh and Lady Tweedsmuir; second, the relatively unambitious 'housewife' members like Mrs Mann, Agnes Hardie, Mrs E. Hill and Lady Davidson for whom a seat in parliament was the end rather than the beginning of their public careers; third, the handful who, like Miss Ward and Dr Summerskill, were prepared to take the risk of pushing for women's issues. The problem was that these two senior feminists were reinforced by only a few new members such as Elaine Burton, Eirene White and Joan Vickers. They tackled three main issues: equal pay, divorce reform and the rights of married women. The newly elected Mrs White won fifth place in the private members' ballot in 1950 and took up a bill to liberalise the divorce laws. However, she immediately came under pressure from the party leaders to drop it for fear of antagonising Catholic voters; when the bill reached committee stage the government offered a Royal Commission on divorce and the measure was withdrawn. Questions involving the legal rights of married women clearly commanded support across party lines in the 1950s. For example, the Conservative Joan Vickers introduced a bill to help deserted wives to win maintenance by means of obligatory deductions from the wages of defaulting husbands. Edith Summerskill fought for many years to secure for the housewife the right to her housekeeping money and the dividends she earned from the Co-operative Society. It was not until 1963 that she achieved a success with a bill that gave a woman half of her savings in recognition of the value of her contribution to the family. However, none of the seven bills promoted by women members which actually became law during the 1950s involved feminist issues. To some extent members were constrained by tactical considerations, as were the men. Those who obtained a high place in the ballot felt tempted to use it on an uncontroversial measure likely to pass. A classic example of this was Mrs Thatcher. Newly elected in 1959 she enjoyed an opportunity of delivering her maiden speech on a bill dealing with the admission of the public to local authority meetings. To steer a piece of legislation through the house was a notable coup for a new member anxious to gain the sympathetic attention of the front bench.

A recent study of women MPs has noted that those who were elected in the 1940s and 1950s were generally much less likely to regard themselves as *women's* representatives than those returned in the 1960s and 1970s. Typical of the post-war generation was Barbara Castle who frankly confessed:

> I never had any conscious determination not to take up women's issues – I have just not been particularly interested in them. I always thought of myself as an MP not as a woman MP.[51]

Women politicians often rationalised their position by saying that it was all too easy to become immersed in women's questions with the result that they were typecast and marginalised. The alternative strategy involved deliberately seeking to establish a reputation in 'male' topics on the assumption that this would do more to promote women's cause in the long run. For example, Mrs Castle and Mrs Hart interested themselves in colonial affairs and defence. Since they eventually obtained jobs in overseas development, transport and employment this approach may well be considered to have been justified. In the 1950s, however, Summerskill took the opposite view, arguing that women should carve out distinct spheres of government related to their domestic interests.

To a large extent the approach and the priorities of the women in parliament were a natural reflection of the character of the wider party base from which they emerged. Those women members who did take up feminist issues were obliged to rely more upon the non-party women's organisations for backing than upon support from their own parties. For example, Eirene White's divorce law bill was not supported by the Labour Women's Organisation. As in the past the Conservatives experienced less internal controversy over the role of women than their rivals. Both sexes seem to have been largely content with the status quo. With over a million members the Tory women continued to enjoy a strong presence in the party. They could not help being flattered by the high priority which the party's new committee on women seemed to give them. And although largely oriented towards the family and domesticity the policy did include proposals for paying women 'the rate for the job' in government employment, for admitting women to the House of Lords and for obliging husbands to pay maintenance to their wives. The only other women's questions in which the Conservative women took any interest in the 1950s were the separate taxation of married couples and the right of a working woman to claim her housekeeper's allowance against tax. On the whole, however, the women's organisation was highly conformist and right-wing in character. Only once did it rebel against government policy – when it dissented from a Criminal Justice Bill which reduced the number of crimes punishable by corporal punishment.

After 1945 the Labour Party Women's Organisation continued its gradual evolution towards party orthodoxy. Alice Bacon disparaged women's politics in a typical speech in 1946:

> Our Labour Women's movement has never been a merely feminist one, shouting shrilly for the rights of women. Our scope is much wider and covers a much wider variety of activities and subjects where women's experience is particularly useful.[52]

However, the result of this approach was that the organisation was steadily reduced to simply organising women in the country and gathering annually to hear addresses from their leaders and perfunctory speeches from Mr Attlee. Like the Conservative women they had no more than an advisory role in policy, and by the late 1950s the National Executive Committee took little notice of their deliberations. As the attendance at the women's conference dwindled steadily to under 500 by 1959 this is not entirely surprising. Neither the feminists nor the national party loyalists saw the women's conference as an important occasion. It is noticeable that even after 1945 when Labour had 20 women MPs very few of them, apart from Summerskill and Bacon, even spoke at the conferences. As a result the question was again raised whether there was any need to maintain a separate conference for women.[53] By implication the failure to generate distinctive policies meant that the separate organisation for women had become redundant. Traditionally the case for the women's conference had been that it gave a forum to women who would not otherwise be heard and would be denied the experience of political participation. But by the 1950s women like Barbara Castle clearly believed this argument had lost its original force. As the first woman to be elected to the National Executive in the constituency section, as opposed to the reserved women's section, she had at least proved the strength of her convictions. Yet her case was a weak one, for the women who rose high up in the party's hierarchy failed to use their position to promote either women's issues or other women. It is only fair to record that by the end of her career in the Commons, when she was herself replaced by a male candidate in Blackburn, Mrs Castle concluded that she had been in error during the 1950s in neglecting the separate women's organisations.[54] She thus provides an epitaph on the decade, but also a positive link with the new world of feminism ushered in by the 1960s.

Chapter 11   Women's Liberation

By the 1960s the women's movement had reached a critical stage in the cycle that affects all radical causes. This, of course, is not to suggest that the movement had disappeared during the 1950s. Activists including Marjory Corbett Ashby, Dora Russell and Rebecca West provided a living link with the campaigns of the early part of the century, while organisations such as the Fawcett Society and the Women's Freedom League maintained direct continuity with the equal rights tradition stretching back to the late-Victorian period. However, the winding up of the WFL in 1961 symbolised the gradual decline of the earlier generation of feminists. When Dale Spender researched the lives of women active in previous decades she began with the assumption characteristic of younger feminists that the movement had virtually died out at some stage since the inter-war period, and was corrected by her respondents.[1] The realisation that the movement enjoyed a longer history than they had supposed was a great stimulus for 1970s feminists, but the very fact that they had to rediscover it speaks volumes for the dwindling impact of the cause on the consciousness of post-war women.

The emergence of what came to be called 'women's liberation' was, of course, much more than a British phenomenon, for it embraced North America, Western Europe, Australasia and Japan. Yet the resurgence of feminism in Britain also reflected circumstances special to Britain and the movement exhibited some national characteristics, as we shall see in this chapter. The commemoration in 1968 of the fiftieth anniversary of the winning of the vote by eight million British women was a sobering occasion, for it highlighted the fact that so many feminist goals still remained to be achieved. Women's access to careers continued to be restricted, equal pay was a long way off, and only one in four university students was female; women's lives were largely circumscribed by role stereotyping imposed by men, they lacked freedom of choice in sexuality, and they were often the victims of rape and violence.

All of which pointed inexorably to the conclusion that the formal political structure, to which previous generations of women had devoted so much attention, was not the chief obstacle to equality; the problem consisted in a more disparate collection of factors   including cultural attitudes, the institution of marriage and the family, and economic conditions. This was the starting point for 1960s feminists. In Britain their outlook was also conditioned by the surge of interest and hope aroused by the ending of the thirteen-year Conservative rule and its replacement by a Labour government under Harold Wilson in 1964 – and by the subsequent disillusionment. In this decade the women's organisations, including the Fawcett Society, the Status of Women Group, the TUC Women's Congress, the National Council of Labour Women and the Child Poverty Action Group, attempted to put pressure on the government but with only limited success. In a sense this represented a final application of traditional tactics and was the prelude to women's liberation.

Not that the 1960s was a barren experience in terms of legislation; it brought major bills on equal pay, divorce and abortion for example. But reform fed the growing expectations of women without satisfying them; and the new prime minister, who won power as a moderniser, appeared to be more receptive to women's influence than was really the case. Wilson appointed more women than was usual to his cabinets , including Barbara Castle, Judith Hart, Shirley Williams, Peggy Herbison and Alice Bacon. However, none of these was actively feminist at the time; they tended to assume that women would gradually achieve their goals almost as a by-product of other social and economic changes.[2] Castle's rise to prominence was perhaps the most significant for women because she broke new ground by occupying economic ministries at Transport and Employment. But Wilson was motivated more by a wish to reward his own supporters and party stalwarts than to advance the cause of women in politics. The Labour Party remained very much a party of elderly male politicians and trade unionists whose conservative social views and belief in male superiority had scarcely been dented. The deputy leader, George Brown, had compelled his wife to abandon both her employment and her political work on marriage in order to be a supportive housewife for the rest of her life; her only escape lay in eventual divorce.[3] In short, for all the superficial impression of change and modernisation, the attitudes of the 1920s remained very lively amongst the politicians of the 1960s. Consequently the achievement of so much social reform by the Wilson governments must be attributed more to the accidental influence of certain individuals than to any wider female pressure within the system or the party. The 1964 general election had produced a mere twenty-eight women MP's – 4.4 per cent of the total – compared with twenty-five in 1959; the number remained at twenty-six in 1970 and twenty-five in February 1974. When Wilson was eventually succeeded by James Callaghan in 1976 he promptly sacked Castle; and as the promising career of Shirley Williams dwindled in the later 1970s the absence of major female figures in Labour politics became all too obvious. The effect of all this was to encourage the anti-party sentiments in the reviving feminist movement; women's liberation was on the whole inclined to seek solutions outside the male-dominated institutions of British politics.

Origins of the Revival

In explaining why the movement for women's liberation emerged during the late 1960s and early 1970s one has to take account of certain underlying conditions which facilitated it, as well as the short-to-medium-term factors which stimulated fresh initiatives. It is obvious that the chief engine of women's liberation lay in the recruitment of a younger generation of women who were the products of the post-war baby boom and the beneficiaries of social change in the twenty years since 1945. They were a healthier and more affluent generation which could take for granted full employment and which expected to enjoy opportunities to develop its talents. On the one hand parental authority seemed to weaken , while on the other, extra money offered access to a wider choice of lifestyle and social behaviour. During the 1960s a higher proportion of qualified girls began to apply for university entrance, thereby gradually narrowing the gap between the sexes; whereas in 1965 one in four students was female, by 1981 it was one in three. The availability of student grants helped overcome the reluctance of parents to support their daughters' education, and the creation of new universities by the Wilson governments further accelerated the process of recruiting women.

It has usually been assumed that the experience of full employment and affluence made the 1960s generation radical in that by removing the fear of poverty it encouraged the young to repudiate the pursuit of mere consumerism. But for women there was a further twist in the explanation. For it was precisely during the early 1960s that concern over rising unemployment and the deterioration of the British economy began to pose a threat to rising expectations. This intensified the competition for jobs between men and women, threatened the expectations of the well-educated women now emerging from universities, and heightened their awareness that control over entry into careers still lay in the hands of men.

Another general precondition for women's liberation lay in changing attitudes towards marriage.[4] Admittedly the links are complex. Later critics of feminism frequently blamed it as the *cause* of the increase in divorce and the collapse of marriage and the traditional family. But it is arguable that women's liberation was as much a *response* to changes already underway during the later 1950s and the 1960s. In many ways that period saw the culmination of the inter-war ideal of marriage in terms of high expectations of romance, security and sexual fulfilment. But the reality fell short of the expectation; women increasingly felt forced to look further for personal happiness. Even under the existing law, which worked by making one partner the guilty party, divorce was on the increase. Eventually in 1969 the government reformed the law so as to facilitate divorce when marriage had irretrievably broken down. This clearly represented a response to wide disquiet about the status quo; yet it is unwise to interpret this as a sign of the permissiveness of that period. Although feminists severely criticised marriage as currently practised, they can hardly be made responsible for what was widespread social behaviour during the 1960s. Whatever dissatisfaction there may have been about the institution of marriage, the ideal retained its attraction for some time to come. In the early to mid-1960s 81 per cent of women aged 21–39 were married, and 96 per cent were married by the age of 45. As a result of affluence and earlier puberty marriage was still occurring at a younger age, which meant that a higher proportion of women became mothers. This was the context from which women's liberation emerged. Britain was hardly a society in the grip of permissiveness, as the critics sometimes claimed. The marriage rate continued to rise towards its peak in the early 1970s. However, many women who had become disillusioned by their experience of early marriage ,looked for alternatives and were thus more receptive to a feminist critique. In effect the conventional ideal of marriage was tested to destruction during this period, was subject to reform in 1969 and only subsequently went into a decline during the heyday of women's liberation.

The proximate cause of the revival of feminism lay rather in the impact of a series of radical movements which swept the United States and Britain during the 1960s, in particular the campaigns over civil rights, nuclear weapons and American policy in the Vietnam War. During the 1950s the Campaign for Nuclear Disarmament had mobilised large numbers of men and women, but after 1960 the prospects of a disastrous nuclear confrontation between the Soviet Union and the United States seemed more imminent as a result of the Cuban Missile crisis, the threat to West Berlin and the extension of Soviet influence in Africa, the Indian Ocean and the Middle East. Finally, the determination of Presidents Kennedy and Johnson to esca-

late the war in South East Asia in order to check what they regarded as
the spread of Chinese Communist influence aroused a massive opposition among young, politically aware people. Although Britain was a
minor player in these events, her government's supportive stance
towards American policy attracted widespread condemnation. Despite
his association with the left wing of his party, Harold Wilson never
intended to adopt unilateral nuclear disarmament, and in office he continued Conservative policy on the subject. Over Vietnam he resisted
American pressure to give direct support, but consistently refused
demands to criticise the large-scale bombing of the country by US
forces. In effect he acquiesced in American policy in return for support
for sterling.

The prolonged deadlock over these issues throughout the decade had
the effect of radicalising a whole generation of men and women and
alienating many of them from the Labour Party in particular and the
political process in general. To many people the party system seemed
wholly impervious to moral considerations and to public opinion. In
effect, then, the radical campaigns of this period provided a training
ground for many of those who later became active in women's liberation; it made them more conscious of their own status and underlined
their capacity for independent political action.

During the mid-1960s and early 1970s CND's membership began to
dwindle. This was partly an indication of a relaxation in East–West
relations and the signing of the Non-Proliferation Treaty. As the belief
in détente took root, so the work of the peace organisations seemed less
urgent. The result was a diversion of activists, some towards Green
issues and others into women's liberation.

It was, however, the United States that triggered women's liberation
and generated the pioneering manifesto for the movement. In *The
Feminine Mystique* (1963) Betty Friedan popularised the issue by
attacking the American ideal of the happy and fulfilled housewife and
mother as a myth. Friedan condemned the myth as pernicious for
encouraging women to be passive and superficial, dedicated to the
empty pursuit of consumerism, and absorbed by producing babies and
supporting men: 'Where is the world of thought and ideas, the life of
the mind and spirit?'[5] For her, the worst of this empty ideal was that
many women who felt their role to be stultifying were made to feel
guilty by the domestic propaganda which surrounded them throughout
their lives. What Friedan wrote was not especially novel, but her book
attracted a huge response and it sold a million copies in the USA and
Britain by 1970. She became one of the founders of the National

Organisation for Women (NOW) in October 1966, an organisation which grew out of the tradition of liberal feminism and was committed to obtaining equal rights for women by co-operation with sympathetic men, by educating public opinion and by bringing pressure to bear on the legislature. It seems that the recent struggles over civil rights for blacks had made Americans more receptive to feminist pressure of this kind, and the President and Congress quickly accepted several of the demands made by NOW. However, some feminists felt that NOW was too closely attached to the political system to be really effective and that it was too focussed on well-educated, middle-class women to become a popular movement. Consequently liberal feminism was overtaken by radicals who placed more importance on sexual liberation and on a broader rejection of conventional gender roles. In 1967 the first radical feminist groups began to meet, initially as a result of their treatment by men in the New Left conferences who largely marginalised the women. It was from this time that the phrase 'women's liberation' began to be used. It achieved a rapid notoriety in September 1968 when women demonstrated outside the annual Miss America Contest in Atlantic City. The protesters were incorrectly reported in the press as having 'burned their bras', which was subsequently regarded as damaging to the movement. However, this symbolic non-act at least forced the message into the consciousness of millions of people throughout the western world.

The Character and Organisation of the Movement in Britain

In Britain, women's liberation emerged during 1968–70 from a mixture of initiatives, including local industrial action by low-paid women workers supported by middle-class feminists, which embarrassed trade unionists and the Labour government. This was followed up by the International Marxist Group, the Revolutionary Socialist Student Federation, the International Socialists and the Communist Party which created several journals including *Socialist Woman* and *Women's Voice* with a view to analysing the sexual oppression of women within the framework of capitalist society. From 1969, organisations such as the London Women's Liberation Workshop spread into the provinces. Finally six hundred delegates held the first national conference of the women's liberation movement in February 1970 at Ruskin College, Oxford.

While the movement in Britain shared a good deal with women's lib-

eration in America in terms of issues, aims and texts, it differed significantly. In the first place the British movement owed much more to
women's experience in the peace movement. The campaign over
Vietnam in the United States had been fuelled very much by men's
opposition to the draft for military service. In Britain, women such as
Vera Brittain, Diana Collins and Edith Summerskill had been prominent
in the protests over the testing of the H-bomb in the 1950s, and women
often formed a majority of local activists. Following the foundation of
CND in January 1958, Peggy Duff, Jacquetta Hawkes and Dora Russell
enjoyed high-profile roles.[6] In spite of this, however, the women felt
they were being marginalised, and by 1960 the CND Women's Group
had ceased functioning as a separate body. Subsequently it was revived
by women who became involved in the mass sit-ins and pram-pushing
demonstrations outside foreign embassies in 1961; this in turn led to the
formation of Voice of Women and the Liaison Committee for Women's
Peace Groups. But as CND itself dwindled during 1963–5 female
activists began to leave; the emphasis of the older peace organisations
on maternalist peace campaigns now looked somewhat dated and inadequate to younger and more radical women. The Partial Test Ban Treaty
in 1963 also accelerated the process by reducing fears about international conflict. For women who had experience of the peace movement
women's liberation addressed their concerns by redefining the question
of violence; it changed the emphasis from the great global issues of
nuclear weapons to the personal experience of women as the victims of
male violence in the domestic and sexual context. Violence, in short,
took on a gender dimension that it had not had hitherto. Consequently,
for some years a separate women's peace movement disappeared as the
activists transferred their energies to women's liberation.

The British and American movements also differed in that the central
influence of the civil rights campaign was obviously lacking in Britain.
British feminists responded less to issues of race and more to those of
social class than their American counterparts. Liberal feminism was
weaker in Britain especially amongst feminists in their twenties and
thirties; nor did any figure equivalent to Betty Friedan emerge to articulate liberal feminism. Thus it was the New Left in the shape of a variety
of Socialist and Marxist groups which took the initiative. Many feminists had long been inclined to Socialism but had often been alienated
by Marxist analysis and by the heavily masculine ambience of the
Labour Movement. However, during the 1960s the New Left analysis of
capitalism put much more emphasis on the role of ideas and culture as
the means by which the ruling class maintained its control, which

seemed more congenial to a feminist outlook. As a result, women's liberation was at first less divided ideologically than the American movement, being more focussed on a socialist-revolutionary approach.

On the other hand the *methods* adopted showed a good deal of continuity with traditional liberal practice; the emphasis was on debates, conferences, journals and marches designed to educate public opinion and influence the politicians. Some Socialists who regarded this as naïve and optimistic spoke about organising for revolution. However, since this implied the unification of the working class, it proved an ambitious and elusive gaol. In practice, Socialist feminists largely used methods similar to those of liberal feminists despite their reservations. Expressions of direct action usually took the form of strikes by women workers. But civil disobedience was far from typical of women's liberation. One exception occurred in November 1970 when a hundred women demonstrated against the Miss World Contest at the Albert Hall; five of them were arrested for trying to disrupt the proceedings. Later in the campaign there was also some picketing of sex shops and cinemas showing pornographic films. But these were only mild echoes of the militancy and confrontational tactics used by the Edwardian suffragettes.

In fact, whereas the suffragettes had taken politics as their prime target, 1970s feminists, especially Radical feminists, were more inclined to by-pass the entire political system. This no doubt reflected the disillusion engendered by decades during which women, though part of the system, had been marginalised by it. Consequently the hallmark of women's liberation consisted in avoiding the formal, hierarchical structures typical of male politics. The alternative took the form of communes which were self-contained, all-female units. Since communes proved difficult to sustain, a more common expedient was to create small groups from which men were excluded and in which women felt less intimidated; with their democratic and co-operative approach and absence of formal leadership, these groups sometimes verged on anarchism. But they offered an ideal means of allowing women to share their experiences of sexism, a technique known as 'consciousness raising' which became a central part of the movement.

Thus, women's liberation operated as a loose, decentralised affair relying on local initiatives and focussed on the development of alternative societies as much as on direct attempts to reform the male-dominated system. It is true that some semblance of central organisation existed in the national conferences which met annually from 1970 onwards and laid down the four immediate goals of the movement:

1. equal pay for equal work; 2. equal opportunities and equal education; 3. free contraception and abortion on demand; 4. free twenty-four-hour child care. Over several years the original four demands became seven. Even so, they never quite amounted to a national programme, for local groups remained free to improvise and take up their own priorities as they wished. Significantly the Women's National Co-ordinating Committee, established in 1970, lasted for only a year. Consequently the movement never enjoyed a national leadership or strategy. This, however, did not prevent national initiatives. The first conference was followed by a march from Hyde Park to Trafalgar Square in March 1971 to publicise the movement's demands by presenting a petition to the prime minister. But thereafter the campaign became largely local or regional. It spread spontaneously across the country without co-ordination from the centre. Typically the local organisation took the form of women's centres, workshops, play groups and refuges, sometimes backed by local authority grants, but often enjoying a precarious existence by operating in private homes or in abandoned properties . The most famous example of local initiative was Erin Pizzy's Women's Aid Centre, formed in Chiswick in 1971, which effectively highlighted the issue of male violence and inspired the formation of many similar groups.

This is a reminder that the devolved character of women's liberation should not be seen simply as a weakness, for it gave full scope to the energy, enthusiasm and originality of a wide range of women who effectively adapted the broad principle of women's liberation to the needs and ideas of their own communities. Above all the experience was empowering in that it showed what could be accomplished outside the formal structures of male-controlled politics.

One characteristic expression of this fast-expanding movement was its interest in recording the history of British women. This activity was pursued at both amateur and professional levels; indeed the two gradually merged, partly because history as an academic discipline was already focussed on social history and made use of the oral sources so plentifully available to women researching in their local communities. Historical research proved to be significant in several ways. Most political movements feel the need to know their own history and benefit from the sense of purpose and ultimate triumph which that imparts. One of the indirect effects was to draw together different generations of feminists. One young woman wrote with real surprise and pleasure about the women of the 1920s who 'said things about sexual freedom and the right to abortion that we twenties somethings believed we had invented.

I had never dreamed that older women had once wanted what I wanted: the right to work, to make love and to control their own bodies.'[7]

The development of women's history had other implications. The publication of such pioneering books as Sheila Rowbotham's *Hidden From History* (1973) stimulated a vast range of research, and for some women the very work of research became an important expression of their feminism. Hitherto many had been deterred, perhaps assuming that the material for a history of women did not exist. Books such as Deidrie Beddoe's *Discovering Women's History: A Practical Manual* (1983) helped to show the way forward. The next step – to promote the academic study of women in universities – came up against a lack of women academics and inadequate resources. During the 1970s, however, courses began to appear in history, English and the social sciences. They provided opportunities for women who had sometimes pursued their studies informally to enter or re-enter higher education to take an M.A. in women's studies. In the process a generation of women acquired the qualifications that would enable them to find employment in the field later on. Despite institutional reluctance, universities felt obliged to respond to the evident demand for women's studies courses and by the 1990s few university history courses could afford to neglect women's history. This was backed by the growth of a range of academic journals including *History Workshop Journal, Women's History Review, Gender and History, Feminist Review, Quest* and *Signs*. Initially the academic study of women took the form of separate courses or modules which made it appear esoteric and also left it vulnerable to financial cutbacks. The real object therefore was the gradual modification of conventional courses so as to take full cognisance of women's role in society. Already by the 1990s women's studies had evolved into 'gender studies' in some institutions, a recognition of the need to encompass *masculinity* as well as femininity. The effect of these developments was to render the women's movement to some extent immune to the fluctuating fortunes of politics and campaigns; for the recognition of the study of women as a legitimate field of work represented a lasting shift in society's perceptions and values.

These changes in the academic sphere were complemented by a commercial dimension. The enthusiasm of an educated, middle-class constituency put a good deal of money behind the idealism of women's liberation. One symptom of this was the huge expansion of women's publishing in which the leader was Virago Press (1975), followed by The Women's Press, Sheba and Onlywoman Press. Moreover, most existing publishing houses felt obliged to follow suit in deference to the demand for books about women in the past, present and future; academic publishers such as Routledge and Blackwell soon developed large catalogues of women's books and trade publishers made substantial profits from the writing of well-known feminists.

However, this commercial success was not something actively sought by the movement. On the contrary, at the start of the campaign feminists had often refused to speak to the press on the grounds that editors and journalists simply wished to use them for their newsworthiness and to represent them as extremist, emotional and irrational. Yet there were obvious advantages for women's liberation in being dragged into the mainstream of political debate, not least in attracting recruits and building momentum quickly. In 1970 Women in Media was formed with a view to improving the way in which women's issues were reported. As a result several of the quality newspapers dropped the traditional women's pages full of trivia in favour of a more issue-based approach.

In spite of this, many feminists preferred to by-pass the male-controlled press altogether by launching their own magazines for women. Early examples were *Shrew* (1969–74) which sold five thousand copies, and *Socialist Woman* which began in 1970. By far the most influential was *Spare Rib* (1972), an immediate success whose sales reached 30,000 by the mid-1970s. *Spare Rib* was deliberately less sectarian than other feminist journals and initially it retained some of the features of conventional women's magazines in order to extend its appeal to the less committed. Other new journals in this period included *Woman's Voice* (1972), *Red Rag* (1972–80), *Women's Report* (1972–9), *Link* (1973) and *Sappho* (1972–81).

Taken as a whole, women's writing, including journalism, polemics and works of fiction, constituted one of the foremost vehicles for women's liberation. Though in some sense a precondition or even a cause of the movement, women's writing was also very much symptomatic of its success as well as being an important means of sustaining the cause over several decades regardless of the fluctuating fortunes of specific campaigns and issues. In this connection one should not overlook the role of post-war novelists such as Iris Murdoch, Margaret Drabble and Doris Lessing for their depiction of the dilemmas faced by women as a result of marriage, dependency and sexuality. The publicity attracted by the trial over D.H.Lawrence's *Lady Chatterley's Lover* in 1960 also made its contribution in the sense that Lawrence effectively highlighted the point that women had as much right as men to sexual satisfaction. The indirect impact of these novelists may have been as important in preparing the way for women's liberation as the more obvious feminist tracts and manifestos. Simon de Beauvoir's analysis of the origins of female oppression in *The Second Sex* had first been published in 1952 without making much impact, though it became available in paperback in 1961. It was probably less widely read than Betty Friedan's *The Feminine Mystique* (1963) which articulated the issues in women's lives in a more accessible way. By the 1970s a succession of feminist analyses had appeared, including Germaine Greer's *The Female Eunuch* (1971), Kate Millett's *Sexual Politics* (1971), Betty Friedan's *It Changed My Life* (1976), and Shulamith Firestone's *The Dialectic of Sex* (1980). As with all historical movements, however, it is difficult to measure the influence of any book or writer. *The Female Eunuch*, for example, sold over a million copies and clearly reached beyond the existing body of activists to a wider public. However, many feminists were never really happy with Greer's focus on sexuality and the body; it seems likely that the book's success was symptomatic of the frisson already created by women's liberation rather than a cause or a formative influence on it.

Nonetheless, the famous feminist authors helped to raise the profile of women's liberation and keep the idea in the news, especially as some were turned into celebrities by the media, though the other side of the coin was that they made the movement appear schismatic. The divisions were, however, easily overstated. All feminists, including male supporters, started from a common belief in the equal worth of all human beings and in opposing unequal treatment of women on the basis of their sex. In practice, therefore, there was little difficulty in uniting to campaign against specific forms of discrimination regardless of different ideological perspectives. However, the priority given to the different issues varied considerably and this reflected the underlying interpretations adopted by feminists. Liberal feminists, not as prominent in Britain as in the United States, retained their confidence in reform achieved through the democratic process, which was tacitly shared by many Socialist feminists who accepted the need for male allies. Especially in the early years Socialist feminists played a more dominant role in the movement. They took their starting point from Engels's original analysis of bourgeois marriage as the first form of class oppression and of wives as the original powerless class in society. In so far as they focussed on the damaging effects of domesticity on modern women the Socialist feminists shared much common ground with Radical feminists. However, there was a crucial difference. Radicals were unconvinced that the exploitation of women could be attributed simply to capitalism; even a revolutionary change in the economic system would fail to end the oppression of women in their view.[8] For Radical feminists the cause lay with men, or the system of patriarchy maintained by male violence. Consequently they focussed much more on the biological basis of the female condition and on the nuclear family as the key institution for maintaining male control. Ultimately they believed that only the ending of the tyranny of the family role would achieve real freedom.[9] This implied that women must control their own sexuality, emancipate themselves from traditional assumptions about female passivity and begin to make choices about their sexuality; they argued that it was equally legitimate for a woman to be celibate, heterosexual, bi-sexual or lesbian. Since most feminists came to share this belief in choice for women, the Radical critique was less divisive than it might appear, though in time their increasing emphasis on lesbianism as the most desirable expression of feminism did create friction within the movement.

Issues and Campaigns

In view of the devolved character of women's liberation it was inevitable that the activists would focus on a wide range of issues and that the priorities would change over time. For the sake of simplicity this account will consider these campaigns in three groups dealing with marriage, divorce and violence, sexuality, and economic grievances.

As we have seen, by the 1960s the traditional institutions of marriage, the family and motherhood had attracted a good deal of criticism among women generally; and for feminists of all kinds they appeared to be the key to female subordination and the chief expression of women's exploitation. For younger women the immediate solution lay in postponing or rejecting marriage and maternity in favour of either a career or some alternative personal relationship. Yet marriage continued to gain in popularity until 1972 when the peak was reached. Moreover, it was even more common amongst women than men; whereas up to the 1940s 15 per cent of women remained lifelong spinsters, and 8 per cent of men, by the 1970s only 5 per cent of women and 7 per cent of men did so.[10] Subsequently as marriage lost popularity it was to a large extent simply replaced by cohabitation. By 1983 some 12 per cent of unmarried women aged 18–49 were cohabiting, for some of whom this offered an alternative to and for others a route towards marriage.[11] For those who did marry the marital state lost a good deal of its permanency

Table 11. 1   Petitions Filed for Divorce in England and Wales
1956–1985

1956-60	137,400
1961-65	188,200
1966-70	284,400
1971-75	608,800
1976-80	812,400
1981-85	884,800

Source: A.H. Halsey, *British Social Trends* (1988), p. 80

at this time in view of the rising divorce rate. However, not all feminists welcomed this, for it still seemed likely that easier divorce would offer men a Casanova's Charter. In fact, large numbers of women availed themselves of the 1969 divorce reform which enabled them to escape after three years from a marriage that had irretrievably broken down. In enacting this measure parliament was almost certainly motivated primarily by a belief that the existing law actually undermined the whole institution of marriage by prolonging unhappy marriages and thereby causing distress for all concerned. Reform certainly unleashed a wave of petitions from those previously trapped in unsatisfactory relationships.[12] As a result, by the early 1970s about 10 per cent of couples were divorcing compared with 7 per cent in the 1950s; by 1974 19 per cent of marriages ended in divorce after ten years. (See Table 11.1.) Nonetheless, marriage remained popular, and almost half of divorced people had remarried within five years. This adherence to traditional relationships indicated the limits of the influence of Radical feminism amongst the female population; moreover, the more that women could count on escape if things went wrong, the less likely they were to reject the whole idea of marriage. Nonetheless, the availability of divorce must be counted a major liberating factor for women in the last three decades of the twentieth century.

In spite of this, many women continued to be the victims of male violence inside and outside marriage, and this increasingly formed a key campaigning issue for feminists. After Erin Pizzy set up the first centre for battered women in 1971 some ninety such centres were created by 1976, and the attention attracted by the problem led to the Domestic Violence and Matrimonial Proceedings Act of that year which offered women some protection against husbands and partners. However, the reform scarcely diminished the need for refuges, and feminists extended the campaign against male violence in several ways. Recognising that women often failed to report cases of rape, they opened the first rape crisis centre in London in 1976, and the Sexual Offences (Amendment) Act of that year helped to make it less traumatic for victims to approach the police in order to bring charges. This in turn highlighted the unsympathetic attitude of the courts, hence the campaigns run by Women Against Rape to expose examples in which guilty men were let off or lightly treated on the grounds that their careers ought not to be damaged by their actions. Finally, feminists identified pornography as effectively responsible for encouraging violence against women and argued that it was a form of violence in itself; this led to the organisation of street protests in Soho, Leeds, Manchester, Bristol and elsewhere to expose the commercial exploitation of sex by shops and cinemas.

For many feminists the major single advance in this period was the greater availability and acceptance of contraception in the form of the contraceptive pill which was on sale from 1961 onwards; it could be obtained on the National Health Service from 1963. In 1969 the Family Planning Act allowed local authorities to give women advice on birth control and contraceptive supplies, and the Family Planning Association went further in 1970 when it began to offer contraceptive advice to anyone over sixteen years regardless of marital status. As a result , by the end of the 1960s birth control had become the general practice among younger couples. There are, however, two qualifications

Table 11.2 Contraceptive Methods in Current Use Among Ever-Married Women Aged 16–40 Years 1970–1983 (percentage)

	1970	1975	1976	1983
Pill	19	30	32	29
IUD	4	6	8	9
Condom	28	18	16	15
Cap	4	2	2	2
Withdrawal	14	5	5	4
Safe period	5	1	1	1
Abstinence	3	1	0	1
Total at least one	75	76	77	81
Not using any	25	24	23	19

Source: A.H. Halsey, *British Social Trends* (1988), p. 59.

Table 11.3 Birth Rates per 1000 Population in England and Wales
1960–1977

1960–65	18.1
1966–70	16.9
1971–75	14.0
1976	11.9
1977	11.6

Source: A.H. Halsey, *British Social Trends* (1988), p. 40

to be made here. As Table 11.2 shows, women still used a wide variety
of methods, among which the pill, though the most common, was far
from being typical. Fears about its effects upon health after 1977 also
diminished its use slightly. It may well be that the availability of the pill
during the 1960s had the effect of promoting the use of all forms of
contraception in the long term, especially condoms.

The trend towards contraception had important implications. Initially
it seems to have checked the birth rate, which had been buoyant in the
1950s but fell steadily down to the late 1970s before rising slightly
again (Table 11.3). More fundamentally the use of contraception was
widely regarded as the most significant form of empowerment for
women in that it gave them the control of their own bodies that feminists desired. Pregnancy was not the inevitable consequence of marriage; it could be postponed until later in a woman's life; and
pre-marital sex was now seen as desirable because it would enhance sex
within marriage. Not surprisingly many feminists celebrated the new
freedom from passivity and subordination which this gave them. On the
other hand, sexual permissiveness reawakened misgivings among those
who felt that freedom imposed new pressures upon women to conform
to a heterosexual feminism. Was female sexuality, after all, not fundamentally different from that of men?[13] If it was, then greater freedom
for women could not be a solution for everyone. This encouraged feminists to consider whether satisfying emotional relationships were not
more easily attainable with other women. This line of thought was complemented by the growth of the Gay Liberation Front after 1971 and by
the increasing acceptance of same-sex relations among men. As a
result, in 1974 women's liberation agreed to incorporate a sixth demand
in the original programme, seeking an end to discrimination against lesbians and the right to define one's own sexuality. In the process many
lesbians were drawn into the women's movement, but heterosexual

feminists expressed strong reservations about their prominence which they believed would alienate many women from the cause. Tactics pointed to a separation of the economic-political campaigns from questions involving sexual orientation. Nonetheless, it proved impossible to exclude lesbian issues from the agenda of the movement.

Despite the wide acceptance of contraception, feminists continued to believe that the control of women's bodies would remain incomplete without access to abortion. Ever since 1936 an Abortion Law Reform Association (ALRS) had existed in Britain, but the legalisation of abortion enjoyed little public support from women's pressure groups apart from the Women's Co-operative Guild. Despite this, abortion was so widely practised that by the 1960s public concern over the dangers to the health of women who resorted to illegal backstreet abortionists paved the way for reform. Eventually David Steel introduced a backbench bill in 1967 with the tacit support of the Home Secretary, Roy Jenkins, which allowed women to have abortions under the NHS within twenty-eight days of conception and with the consent of two doctors. There was no question at this time of conceding abortion on demand, partly for fear of undermining parliamentary support for the bill and partly because the scheme depended upon the co-operation of the medical profession which could not be taken for granted. As a result, in 1967, 9,700 NHS abortions took place, in addition to 10,000 private ones and an unknown number of illegal operations. The total rose to 22,000 in 1968, 75,000 in 1970 and 128,000 by 1980. However, the steep rise cannot be seen simply as an increase since thousands of abortions which hitherto took place illegally now came under the NHS.

The abortion law is an example of a reform which effectively predated women's liberation; consequently the chief task for feminists subsequently was to *defend* the status quo rather than extend it. Hence in 1972 the old ALRS gave way to the National Women's Abortion and Contraception Campaign which in turn became the National Abortion Campaign (NAC) in 1975; it organised public demonstrations under the slogan 'A Woman's Right To Choose'. The campaign also highlighted the uneven implementation of the legislation; it was, for example, more difficult to get an abortion in the north than in the south of England. Above all the NAC had to fight off hostile bills in 1976, 1977, 1978, 1980 and 1982 introduced in order to undermine the 1967 Act. By the late 1970s the number of abortions had stabilised, and opinion polls showed that a large majority accepted the new status quo, though only 18 per cent of people supported abortion on demand. The defence of the law against the backlash from a vocal minority of anti-abortionists, especially after a change in the political climate, was one of the lasting achievements of women's liberation.

By contrast, the results of campaigns over economic issues were less dramatic in the short term, though here feminists were undoubtedly working with the grain of events and opinion. Significantly, when Benjamin Spock revised his manual on baby and child care in 1973 he removed the original bias against working mothers – a good illustration of the tendency for influential books to reflect changing attitudes rather than to initiate them. Feminists adopted a wide range of tactics including direct action, strikes, co-operation with trade unions and legislation. At this stage they were beginning to take advantage of the opportunities created by structural changes in the British economy; this is best illustrated by female participation in the labour force which increased from 37.5 per cent of women in 1961 to 42.6 per cent in 1971 and to 45.5 per cent by the 1981 census.

However, feminists were largely absorbed by the terms and conditions of women's employment rather than by its extent. The enactment of the Equal Pay Act in 1970, which was implemented from 1975 onwards, proved to be disillusioning. In the first three years the wages of female workers rose from 50 to only 52 per cent of men's. Some feminists drew the conclusion that they were unlikely to achieve much through a trade union movement still dominated by men and lacking interest in women's grievances and aspirations. They found an alternative in focussing on the remuneration of women who worked unpaid in the home, arguably the most exploited and numerous group. This line of argument echoed the campaign waged for the 'endowment of motherhood' in the 1920s by Eleanor Rathbone who had also regarded equal pay as a very distant and elusive goal. During the 1970s the Campaign for Wages for Housework attracted great enthusiasm and also the support of the press; however, it was rejected by Socialist and Radical feminists who considered that it pandered to traditional notions of women as essentially domestic. As a result, Wages for Housework remained a rather separate and marginal part of the movement.

However, this issue forced Socialist feminists to address the charge that it was futile for women to rely upon trade unions to promote their interests. In fact these years were marked by a series of attempts to engineer greater co-operation between female workers and the unions. During 1970–2 Socialist and Marxist groups promoted campaigns to improve the wages of very low-paid women and to encourage them to join unions. At first this was undermined by the hostility of union officials and hampered by the inability of manual workers to share the broader ideological objectives of the middle-class feminists. Nonetheless, dozens of strikes occurred among low-paid women during 1973–4. As this was a period of general militancy provoked by opposition to the government's trade union legislation, the prospects for closer collaboration across gender lines were good. The big general unions such as the TGWU, the AUEW and the GMWU recruited large numbers of women, as did white collar unions including NALGO, NUPE and COHSE. Moreover, in 1981 the Trades Union Congress belatedly recognised the importance of women by increasing its female delegates from two to five, admittedly out of a total of forty-one! In 1974 it also produced the Working Women's Charter campaign, a ten-point programme which covered wages, conditions, promotion, training, child care, maternity leave, family allowances and contraception. In 1978 the TUC even gave its support to the demand for easier abortion.

This rapprochement between feminism and the trade union movement had important long-term political implications, though during the 1970s the gains were not striking even under a Labour government. Meanwhile, women's liberation added a fifth item to its programme in 1974 – the Financial and Legal Independence of Women. This was intended to overturn the various regulations and laws which effectively made women the dependants of men in respect of taxation, pensions, national insurance, supplementary benefits and mortgages. Despite minor modifications to social security, however, discrimination in these areas largely continued into the 1980s. Frustration over women's employment and economic status stimulated pressure for another extra demand in the women's liberation programme – the provision of twenty-four-hour child care. This appeared more radical than it was, the aim being to make limited child care available to facilitate women's employment even during inconvenient hours, not, as critics alleged, to encourage women to abandon altogether their responsibilities as mothers. Despite the clearly recognised need, the politicians continued to take refuge in the plea that a national policy would be expensive. As a result many women's groups took matters into their own hands by organising voluntary creches and nurseries run by local collectives. But the issue underlined the failure of the movement to command real political influence.

The Turning Point?

It has been argued that by the later 1970s women's liberation had lost some of its momentum and was suffering from dwindling support. This pessimistic view does, however, reflect the short-term difficulties arising out of the deterioration of the economy and the change in the political climate around 1979.[14] It was not yet apparent that the economic turmoil of the next few years would in fact leave women the beneficiaries in many ways; nor did it appear that either legislation or alliances with the unions were really delivering concrete gains. As we shall see in the next chapter, from a longer perspective this looks unduly pessimistic.

However, it is fair to say that by the end of the 1970s the movement was increasingly divided between economic causes on the one hand and the issues of sexual politics on the other. In these circumstances the absence of overall leadership appeared a major weakness, and women's liberation showed some signs of turning inwards in order to debate its strategy and purpose. In many ways this was comparable to the dilemmas of feminism during the 1920s; following major legislation and disillusionment, some loss of momentum was almost inevitable. The problem lay precisely in the fact that the government was not completely resistant to women's demands; it managed to some extent to defuse the issue by making what appeared to be major concessions but which only went a limited way to satisfying the reformers' grievances. The nub of dissatisfaction lay in the Equal Pay Act and the Sex Discrimination Act of 1975. The latter was condemned by many feminists as a fraud both because it contained loopholes and because the means of enforcement appeared wholly inadequate. Responsibility lay with the Equal Opportunities Commission, the Advisory, Conciliation and Arbitration Service, and with industrial tribunals. But the officials who ran these bodies were widely felt to have been insufficiently energetic in pursuing cases of discrimination; the courts were often unsympathetic, and in any case many women remained reluctant to come forward to press their claims. For example, during 1976 only five out of twenty sex discrimination cases were successful; and of the one hundred and ten equal pay cases taken to tribunals only thirty-one succeeded.

It was therefore particularly frustrating that, according to the opinion polls, the public believed that the legislation had largely resolved women's grievances. Inevitably the government concluded that it could now afford to ignore pressure for further change from feminists. Women's liberation was in the classic dilemma of a pressure group when dealing with politicians. Having become almost fashionable the cause was in some danger of being tamed by closer association with the system. A succession of propagandist initiatives such as International Women's Year in 1975 and International Women's Day underlined the problem.

This situation crystallised the choices facing the movement. Feminism could indeed become part of mainstream politics and in the process expect to lose some of its revolutionary potential, or it could keep its distance and preserve its integrity; certainly some feminists reacted by becoming more suspicious of conventional politics and by seeking a more radical agenda. In effect this implied placing less emphasis on the economic-social reforms and giving a higher priority to sexual politics, the latter being less susceptible to incorporation by the politicians. This shift was encouraged by the deepening disillusionment with the Labour government in its declining years, by the deterioration in the economy and by cuts in public spending which heralded a wider attack on the welfare state.

One effect of this was to accentuate the anarchic tendencies in women's liberation. It ceased to function as a co-ordinated national movement and became increasingly a series of campaigns linked loosely by feminist journals and common personnel. When national conferences were held, sharp divisions emerged between Socialist and Radical feminists, with the result that the movement to some extent turned its energies inwards and away from the general public. The debate also produced a polarisation between heterosexual feminists and lesbian feminists in which the latter were more aligned with the Radicals. Radicals and lesbians shared a desire to complete women's liberation by excluding male influence and by seeking direct confrontations with male authority. By 1978 several of their demands had been incorporated as a seventh item in the movement's programme, in particular the demand for freedom from violence, intimidation and sexual coercion by men. But the critics felt that this threatened to make all men the enemy rather than simply male institutions. Similarly the assertion of the right of every woman to self-defined sexuality was seen as giving precedence to lesbianism. The most extreme formulation of this view argued that to engage in heterosexuality was to maintain male supremacy.[15] The implication was that a real feminist ought to be lesbian and thus achieve a revolutionary change by withdrawing all forms of co-operation with men. However, this left many feminists feeling that they were being forced to defend relationships with men because of their heterosexuality. 'Until women stop attacking all men, branding them as rapists and batterers', wrote Erin Pizzy, 'we will never have a women's movement which truly represents all women. Believe it or not, most of us like men.'[16] However, two qualifications must be made about what appears to have been a dangerous polarisation of views. Many women continued to work at local level on practical self-help schemes without being distracted by theoretical debates about feminism. Secondly, the changes in the external political climate around and after 1979 went a long way towards suppressing the disagreements by realigning feminist forces along a more structured and politically-orientated strategy.

Chapter 12 Feminism in the Era of Thatcherism, 1979–1999

Like all successful radical movements Women's Liberation had eventually to confront the problem of maintaining its momentum. By the later 1970s the growing contrast between women's advances on the socioeconomic front on the one hand and the static political situation on the other raised the old question as to whether a change of tactics would now be appropriate. While many Radical feminists, alienated by the political process, preferred to pursue their aims by organising an alternative feminist culture within patriarchal society, others began to conclude that the achievement of further reforms would require greater support within the male-controlled system; as a result, attention switched to potential alliances with the trade unions and the Labour Party.

In addition, the expansion of the movement inevitably led to ideological division and the dissipation of energy on internal disputes. During the 1980s and 1990s the press regularly promoted feminist writers whenever they attacked one another in their books and lectures. This, however, gave a misleading and exaggerated impression. At the grass roots a younger generation of women were devising their own ways of expressing their feminism even if that included children and marriage; the hallmark of these decades was the search for expedients designed to combine independence with femininity. Some women simply postponed motherhood until later in life so as to avoid having to abandon promising careers too early. Others coped as lone mothers. The idea of lesbian motherhood also gained currency. But the overall tendency was to give a more positive status to the maternal role among feminists and to advance the idea of maternity free from male domination even if this involved no more than a greater sharing of the responsibilities of domesticity and employment between men and women. The sheer force of economic pressures worked to accelerate this trend by multiplying the number of dual-income families.

The other problem for feminism was its relationship with the broader political climate. The 1990s saw a gathering moral crisis, not unlike those of the 1890s and 1920s, which appeared at least superficially unhelpful to the women's cause. Moreover, since the late 1970s left-wing politics had waned significantly, culminating in a series of defeats for the Labour Party and a profound and lasting intellectual demoralisation among its leading figures; this persisted to the end of the 1990s

334

notwithstanding Labour's return to office in 1997. Meanwhile the domination of politics by Conservatives and Conservatism, particularly by the doctrine of Thatcherism, after 1979 changed the whole climate and agenda, in the process forcing feminism on to the defensive and strengthening its enemies. As a result, during the 1980s and 1990s it became fashionable to treat feminists as scapegoats for all kinds of social change and moral decline. In these circumstances, it was not clear whether the political system should be regarded as hopeless, or whether the trend made it all the more necessary for feminists to re-enter the political mainstream in order to defend their earlier gains

'One Prime Minister doesn't Make a Matriarchy'

In fact the connections between Thatcherism and feminism were complex, negative in some obvious ways, but positive in others. On the face of it Mrs Thatcher's emergence as party leader in 1976 and as prime minister in 1979 represented the climax of female advance in twentieth-century Britain. Thatcher herself was a beneficiary of the gains and reforms achieved by earlier generations of women. She enjoyed the vote and access to higher education; she became pregnant only once and was not seriously handicapped by motherhood; she pursued careers in industry, the law and politics. Yet she steadfastly refused to acknowledge any debt or wider responsibility. Like many women successful in public life Mrs Thatcher chose to believe that she owed her success solely to her own talents and hard work; women, in her view, should stop complaining and capitalise on the opportunities open to them already. When in a position of power she behaved like a male executive and tended to avoid association with other women;[1] no woman, except briefly Lady Young, entered her cabinet, and the careers of a number of able Tory women suffered a check under her leadership. In short, Thatcher used her sex but refused to champion the cause of women. In addition to her personal stance, the policies of Mrs Thatcher's governments appeared unfavourable to women's interests. The introduction of separate taxation for women by the Chancellor, Nigel Lawson, represented the only obvious gain. Much criticism focussed upon the freezing of child benefits which threatened to kill off what had been one of the most beneficial measures for women; the government also resisted pressure to improve the provision for maternity leave in which Britain lagged far behind other western countries. In short, 'one prime minister doesn't make a matriarchy', as *Spare Rib* appositely commented in 1979.

However, this is a very limited perspective on the phenomenon of Thatcherism. In many ways – and especially in terms of morality and social behaviour – the political conformation of the 1980s proved to be an irrelevancy. The government underlined the point in 1989 when it vetoed a survey of British sexual lifestyles, signifying thereby its disapproval of changes which it remained largely powerless to check. Moreover, the government stimulated a great deal of *unintended* change especially on the economic front. The expansion of the service industries, for example, greatly accelerated the growth of female employment; also its *laissez-faire* approach, though disadvantageous for employees in general, encouraged employers to take on much more part-time labour, a trend from which women proved to be the overwhelming beneficiaries.

Nor should one ignore the political-psychological significance of the Thatcher premiership. By the 1990s younger feminists such as Natasha Walters, a little removed from the direct blast of Thatcherite rhetoric and policy, regarded her almost as an unsung heroine. Clearly one needs to distinguish the impact of Mrs Thatcher at several different levels and from different perspectives.

At the general election of 1979 Mrs Thatcher had not, contrary to expectations, been an electoral drawback to her party, though she was less popular than her rival James Callaghan. Studies by political scientists in the aftermath, though admittedly not very extensive, indicated that her gender had made little if any impact on the result.[2] Though hardly a dramatic conclusion, it was important in laying to rest one of the last myths about women in politics. Mrs Thatcher went on to win elections in 1983 and 1987, admittedly without actually increasing her party's vote, but she continued to be regarded by the Conservative rank and file as their greatest asset. If never exactly popular in the country, she did finally kill off the idea that women had no aptitude for politics.

The impact of Mrs Thatcher's long premiership on younger women and girls, many of whom grew up in the knowledge that their country was dominated by a woman, was intangible but surely profound and lasting:

> Above all she normalised female power. She made us realise that women can do the things that men once thought were all their own. These things include being powerful and confident. They may also, less comfortably, include being cruel, megalomaniac, and war-mongering.[3]

In short, by the 1990s a generation of women had emerged who took it for granted that women could play leadership roles. If the prime minister had done nothing directly to promote women in politics, the 1980s and 1990s were to be marked by the appearance of female role models in a variety of occupations in which they had not hitherto been prominent. For example, Stella Rimington led the Crown Prosecution Service, Betty Boothroyd presided over the House of Commons, Rosie Boycott became editor of *The Independent* and the *Daily Express*, Elizabeth Butler Sloss was appointed Lord Justice of Appeal, and in the City of London Nicola Horlick attracted widespread attention as a successful and highly paid executive who also ran a large family.

In spite of herself, then, Mrs Thatcher was almost certainly a radicalising force for British women; but her success inevitably posed a dilemma for many feminists whose own inclinations were towards socialism. If they loathed her opinions and policies, many felt some admiration for her, they refused to lend support to 'Ditch the Bitch' campaigns by fellow left-wingers, and they experienced a certain *schadenfreude* over the summary fashion in which the prime minister treated her hapless male colleagues in the Tory Party. Ironically, in the long run Thatcher had a galvanising effect, not so much on the women of her own party, but on *Labour* women, the effects of which were not to be fully appreciated until the mid-1990s when many of them sought a power base within the political mainstream.

Feminism and Anti-Militarism

Perhaps the most striking and successful response of the women's movement to the Thatcher era lay in the return to issues of war and peace. During the 1970s the women's peace movement had dwindled as the activists focussed on violence in the domestic context. But during 1980–1 a new and revitalised movement sprang up centred around the Greenham Common peace camp at Newbury in Berkshire.[4] There are several explanations for this revival. Some women came to feel that women's liberation was perpetuating the male value system in respect to violence. They were also unhappy about the campaign, especially in the United States, for equality for women within the armed forces. Above all, the growing awareness of the dangers posed by nuclear accidents, both abroad in the Soviet Union and in America, and at home at Windscale in Cumbria, wholly undermined official claims that nuclear power was safe. The Thatcher government's obstinate insistence that nuclear power stations were both desirable and economically viable, which was eventually shown to be untrue, was a further provocation. By the end of the decade awareness of the link between plutonium production in nuclear reactors and the manufacture of nuclear weapons presented opponents of the nuclear industry with an argument which attracted wide public sympathy. Consequently, the news in October 1979 that 140 Cruise Missiles with nuclear warheads were to be stationed in Britain gave a focus for a new campaign fuelled by the knowledge that the policy was a NATO decision on which parliament had not been consulted. When the Ministry of Defence announced that ninety-six Cruise Missiles would be stationed at Greenham Common a campaign was launched by Joan Ruddock, then a local Labour Party activist and Citizens Advice Bureau worker.

Whether the anti-nuclear campaign that emerged from these circumstances was a *feminist* cause aroused some disagreement. The women-only groups were seen as divisive within the peace movement, and at first organised feminism was slow to take up the issue. But from 1980 onwards local groups sprang up spontaneously; and the Cruise issue was effectively articulated by *Spare Rib* when it wrote about it under the heading 'Take the Toys from the Boys'.[5] Then in the summer of 1981 a group of women organised a march from Cardiff to Greenham Common under the banner 'Women for Life on Earth', an expression which captured the wider concerns over the way in which male-led science and technology was steadily destroying the earth – a kind of eco-feminism. 'Women for Life on Earth' was thus a spontaneous movement which welled up from the grass roots and was not closely involved in the ideological debates of the women's movement; but it effectively accelerated the momentum of women's liberation during the 1980s. One of the most striking aspects of the campaign was the way in which it recaptured – for the only time in the twentieth century – something of the élan and the tactics of the Edwardian suffragettes. By chaining themselves to the perimeter fence at Greenham Common, by fixing hundreds of domestic artefacts to it, by encircling the whole base as a human chain, by cutting the wire and entering land from which they were banned, and by continuing to camp on the Common in the face of eviction orders, the women brilliantly symbolised the issue and offered a challenge to male space and male authority. Like the suffragettes they argued that a woman-only campaign would maximise non-violence in confrontations with the police or troops. As a result, by 1982 the peace camp had achieved a high profile which was maintained by a series of court cases leading to sentences in Holloway for some of the women involved.

In spite of this success, Greenham Common continued to generate some dissension within the wider movement; some feminists regarded it as little more feminist than Women's Institutes, as too biased towards maternalism, and as a symptom of the decline of women's liberation rather than of its revitalisation. Nonetheless the peace camps continued through the 1980s; and though the government stubbornly maintained its policy, the women's message gradually got through to the country at large. Polls showed that a higher proportion of women than men opposed both nuclear weapons and the nuclear industry, and this helped to bring about a broader change in the political stance of women as a whole which became evident during the 1990s. The campaign also left its mark on the women's movement in that it accelerated the shift away from Socialist feminism towards an emphasis on gender difference and on the positive celebration of a woman-centred culture.

The Revolution Continues

However unfavourable the political configuration of the 1980s and 1990s may have been, an empirical approach to the period suggests that the changes that had occurred in women's lives in the previous decade were by no means checked; if anything they accelerated. Nowhere was this more apparent than in marriage and motherhood. The marriage rate, which had reached its peak in Britain in the early 1970s, fell by about half between 1971 and 1991. To a large extent marriage was being replaced by cohabitation which increased ninefold – from 3 to 26 per cent – among single women aged twenty to forty-nine years between 1978 and 1993; in this period it became almost usual to cohabit prior to marriage. In the process the old double standard in sexual relations greatly diminished. On the other hand women continued to be the victims of violence within and outside marriage. In 1981 a conference of eight hundred women organised by Women Against Violence Against Women helped to focus the debate on this issue, and feminists regularly attacked judges who treated offences involving rape too lightly. The House of Lords ruling on marital rape in 1981 marked an important victory in this struggle.

Increasingly in this period women succeeded in limiting the effects of child-bearing on their lives. By 1990 the average age for giving birth had risen to twenty-seven years, and to twenty-five for the first child. Moreover, it was estimated that 21 per cent of all women born in 1965 would remain childless. As a result, statisticians expected the population of Britain to begin to fall for the first time since the Black Death.

The postponement or avoidance of motherhood enabled more women to establish their careers during their twenties and thirties as well as boosting their standard of living. Nor was the move away from child-rearing necessarily to be interpreted simply as a feminist victory over men, for male partners were often equally ready for a childless relationship.

Much the most controversial change was the growing instability of the institution of marriage. By the 1990s over 150,000 couples divorced each year, and nearly four in ten marriages were expected to end in divorce. In the public debate this was often linked with the phenomenon of the single-parent family and the alleged collapse of parenting skills.[6] Just as in the 1950s women were made to bear the responsibility for delinquency and criminality amongst the young. In fact, the traditional two-parent family continued to be the norm, though the trend away from it was certainly marked. Whereas as in 1971 7 per cent of families with dependent children had been headed by a lone mother, by 1994 the figure had risen to 20 per cent. Of these cases only two-fifths actually arose out of divorce; the rest were largely the result of the growing number of births taking place outside marriage; between 1978 and 1993 there was a threefold increase in births outside marriage to 30 per cent of the total. Amidst the fashionable criticism over births and lone parenthood it was easy to overlook the more positive side of the phenomenon. The National Council for One Parent Families argued that women were quite capable of exercising enough authority to bring up children successfully themselves; the problems they experienced had more to do with poverty than with parenting skills as such. Moreover, politicians who attempted to exploit the issue invariably found that there were few votes in attacking single mothers. This was because the phenomenon went far beyond feminism. Several famous women including Madonna, Sharon Stone and Koo Stark let it be known that they wished to become mothers; consequently they required a man, but once he had given them a child they intended to bring it up alone.[7] It is difficult to know what significance to attribute to such examples. Obviously they enjoyed unusual material advantages as single mothers; but they were surely symptomatic of a wider feeling of confidence among women in their capacities both as home-makers *and* as breadwinners.

Economic considerations certainly loomed much larger in feminism during the 1980s and 1990s, no doubt partly because underlying changes in the British economy continued to work in favour of women. It is now clear that between 1979 and 1994 three million, largely male, jobs disappeared in British industry. As a result the official unemployment rate which stood at 10.3 per cent in February 1994, for example, concealed a male rate of 13.2 per cent and a female rate of only 5.4 per cent. Whereas in 1971 44 per cent of all women had been in paid employment, by 1994 the proportion had risen to 53 per cent. This was especially marked among younger women; amongst those aged 25–44 years 52 per cent had worked in 1971 but 68 per cent did so by 1987. In effect the 2.3 million increase in the labour force between 1971 and 1987 was almost wholly accounted for by women. As a result, by the late 1990s women exceeded men in the British labour force for the first time. This was no short-term blip but the product of a gradual trend since the 1930s, though undoubtedly it had been accelerated by the dramatic collapse of manufacturing and the expansion of the service industries since the 1970s. By the end of the 1990s the Department of Employment expected nine out of ten new jobs to be filled by women, thereby sustaining the phenomenon of a predominantly female labour force well into the new century.

It would, however, be simplistic to interpret this trend as an automatic consequence of structural developments in the economy. It also reflected changes in attitudes and aspirations amongst women themselves. Since the 1960s a growing proportion of qualified girls had made applications for university places, thereby steadily narrowing the gap with boys. They benefited from the overall expansion in student numbers which was concentrated in arts and social sciences, though women also markedly increased their representation in areas such as biological sciences and mathematics. Moreover, on graduation young women began to demonstrate a more positive approach to employment; for example, they were less willing to accept jobs for which they were over-qualified and showed more determination than their male competitors. In 1994 the Association of Graduate Careers Advisory Services reported that women were displaying a better attitude at interviews, were more flexible and superior communicators, and devoted more time to career planning than men.[8]

The other shift of attitudes among both men and women involved working mothers. In this period it became generally accepted that a woman was justified in going out to work even when she had children of school age, something traditionally frowned upon. By 1990 41 per cent of mothers whose children were under five years had paid employment, compared with 23 per cent as recently as 1983. Even the post-1997 Labour Government put pressure on single mothers to take up paid work, though this was inconsistent with its rhetoric about the family.

On the other hand, feminists identified some serious weaknesses and drawbacks in this general pattern of advance into the world of employment in terms of the status, the quality and the pay of the jobs women held. In spite of the legislation on equal pay, for example, the gap between the sexes remained substantial. By 1990, women earned 71 per cent of male income in manual occupations and 63 per cent in non-manual ones. The overall figure of 68 per cent compared unfavourably with that in other European countries, such as France and Germany with 80 per cent and Denmark and Italy with 85 per cent.[9]

The more women advanced into the labour market the more attention became focussed on the existence of a 'glass ceiling' which prevented their rise into the highest levels in most occupations. To some extent this reflected women's concentration in part-time employment – they comprised four out of five workers in this category – and also their different age structure by comparison with the men in most professions. However, this was far from being a complete explanation; stubborn prejudice and male control continued to hamper women's advance in both business and the professions. By 1990 women comprised barely 8 per cent of architects, 10 per cent of chartered accountants, 23 per cent of dentists, 21 per cent of solicitors and 26 per cent of vets for example. This of course represented an improvement, and a notable one in some areas. By 1995 women outnumbered men among solicitors aged under thirty years, and more women than men were being admitted as vets.[10] But it remained extremely difficult for women to reach the highest positions in the law and in medicine. Although almost half of all medical students were female by 1990, many dropped out, often because of the excessively long hours, but also because of the discrimination against women who were married and had children on the part of the men who controlled appointments and promotion. The hospital authorities largely refused to meet the needs of women by offering part-time employment and in effect excluded them from promotion. As a result, women comprised only 22 per cent of GPs, barely 15 per cent of hospital consultants and only 12 per cent of consultants even in obstetrics and gynaecology; in 1986 only six out of 957 consultant posts in surgery in England and Wales were held by women. Such a high proportion of trained women doctors ceased to practise that special schemes had to be launched to encourage them to re-enter medicine especially in areas where GPs were in short supply.

This pattern of limited advance for women underlined how dependent they were on unguided economic opportunities; neither legislation nor feminist pressure availed much in the face of entrenched institutional prejudice. In 1991 the prime minister, John Major, launched 'Opportunity 2000', a scheme to improve women's position in senior public appointments, though as he had no women in his cabinet at the time his support carried little credibility. The policy was pioneered by 'Business in the Community', whose backers included major companies such as ICI and British Airways. Yet as these were precisely the kind of businesses in which men were obliged to work excessively long hours in order to reach the higher rungs of the hierarchy, it was obvious that they had not begun to accept the implications of promoting more women. Corporate business mentality remained a major obstacle to change. Perhaps the most promising sign was the growing realisation that men and women shared a common interest in reducing Britain's relatively long working hours and thereby achieving a better balance between family responsibilities and careers for both.

One result of the debate about the 'glass ceiling' was the increasing priority attached to child care facilties; many feminists argued that the neglect of such provision remained the major factor limiting women's employment.[11] Yet despite regular promises from politicians, provision of local authority places remained extremely limited, and as a result most women were obliged to pay for child care, which deterred those in low-paid occupations from seeking work. As a result, by the 1990s the central dilemma for women lay in balancing employment opportunities against their domestic role. For while many women spent extra time in employment, they also continued to bear the brunt of domesticity. 'New Man', though widely discussed, was regarded by feminists as a figment of the progressive imagination. One survey in the late 1980s suggested that in 72 per cent of households domestic tasks were done mainly by women and were shared equally in 22 per cent of cases. Another in 1993, based on people born in 1958, found that women did 66 per cent of the shopping, 75 per cent of the cleaning and 77 per cent of the cooking.[12] However, the pessimistic view of such investigations missed the point; the findings reflected significant *reductions* in the extent to which women carried the burden of domesticity on their own shoulders. Though not yet typical, 'New Man' was on the increase.

Anti-Feminism and Male Reactions

Despite its undeniable success the women's movement remained vulnerable to counter-attack during the 1980s. It has been estimated that the movement consisted of around three hundred feminist organisations including some 10,000 regularly active members, though it was of course capable of mobilising far larger numbers of supporters on specific issues.[13] It fell short of being a mass movement, for while many women sympathised with feminist causes, large numbers remained indifferent or hostile. Older women often saw feminism as irrelevant to their lives or even as a threat. Some may have been susceptible to suggestions from the press which blamed feminism for undermining the family or giving young men the excuse to neglect their responsibilities. Others found the prominence of lesbians within feminism uncomfortable, especially when they appeared to criticise heterosexuality. However, the strength of such hostile reactions is easily exaggerated. Although lesbians had remained largely hidden from public attention during the 1960s and 1970s, they became the subject of discussion as a result of the publicity attracted by prominent women such as Martina Navratilova and the MP Maureen Colquhoun. Popular entertainment probably played a useful role in building tolerance; certainly by the 1990s gays and lesbians had begun to figure regularly in television 'soaps' which removed the novelty from the issue and allowed a more relaxed view to emerge. As a result during this decade a number of male and female politicians, voluntarily or involuntarily, declared their sexuality; when the M.P. Angela Eagle 'came out' in September 1997 she attracted relatively little publicity and virtually no criticism.

Much the most sustained and strongly supported expression of female anti-feminism was the campaign against the law on abortion. Enlisting support from MPs such as John Corrie, David Alton and Anne Widdecombe, the Society for the Protection of the Unborn Child repeatedly attempted to amend the 1967 Act. Although Corrie's 1979 Bill was defeated, even in a Conservative House of Commons, in 1981 the Department of Health and Social Security modified the grounds on which a doctor could perform an abortion; the decision was to be based on medical grounds alone, not on social. Since a million abortions had been performed since 1967 on social grounds, this appeared to pose a major threat. However, the ruling was not generally put into practice. Both the medical profession and members of parliament had largely come to accept the existing law, and it was the anti-feminists who now represented a vocal minority.

The example of abortion reflected a more general shift of attitudes towards the feminist position. It has been argued that the media was both negative and highly influential in its treatment of women's issues in this period.[14] Certainly the *Daily Mail*, *The Daily Telegraph* and *The Sun* mounted regular and vituperative attacks on feminism which they held responsible for moral decline and for undermining the family. On the other hand, the *effect* of their efforts was insubstantial. The strength of anti-feminism is perhaps best evaluated by comparison with the United States where campaigns for the restoration of traditional moral values and social behaviour were far more intimidating and more representative of public opinion. In Britain the churches were far less militant and less politically involved than in America. Above all, attempts by politicians to capitalise on moral questions proved counter-productive, as John Major's calamitous 'Back to Basics' campaign demonstrated. In many ways the British Establishment, including the Royal Family, the churches and the politicians, had become too discredited by the 1990s to be capable of exercising any real influence in moral and social affairs. Consequently, the public showed little sign of responding to the views advanced in the newspapers they read. Indeed influence may have been in the opposite direction on some issues; for example, *The Sun* bowed to opinion in 1999 when it abandoned its hostility towards gays. Such a pattern was by no means entirely new. In interwar Britain large numbers of ordinary people had persisted in practising birth control in the face of disapproval by the media and most of the Establishment until the latter eventually came into line. Similarly by the 1990s abortion and one-parent families came to be taken for granted by most people regardless of the views expressed by the self-appointed leaders of opinion. In this sense the atmosphere in which feminists operated at the end of the century was less hostile than might have been supposed.

On the other hand one has to take some account of the reaction amongst men for whom women's liberation was ostensibly a threat to status and power. This manifested itself in a multitude of symptoms and grievances during the 1980s and 1990s. Men were widely thought to be losing their role as breadwinners; male suicide rates soared; boys were 'underperforming' in schools; there was a shortage of male teachers in primary schools; the Child Support Agency was turning men into taxpayers without rights; health resources were being concentrated on female problems like breast cancer while prostate cancer went neglected; husbands were being criminalised by the House of Lords ruling on marital rape. Behind this catalogue of complaints a new thesis took shape. The Establishment, so the argument ran, had fallen under the thumb of the feminist lobby, and women's liberation had gone too far; it was destroying the family, marriage and men's role in society. In short, men, not women, had now become the victims. Fuelled by this sense of grievance a 'Men's Movement' emerged during the 1980s and

1990s comprising such pressure groups as Families Need Fathers, Dads After Divorce, and the Campaign for Justice in Divorce , as well as a quarterly magazine, *Male View*, a 'Men In Crisis' helpline, and Neil Lyndon's book, *No More Sex War* (1992).

This might have been treated simply as an absurd over-reaction to change but for the readiness of some prominent *women* to corroborate the thesis behind it. For example, the novelist Fay Weldon accepted that feminism had gone too far and blamed it for the disheartened and under-achieving men in British society.[15] The journalist Melanie Phillips, writing about government pressure on single women to take employment, argued that men needed paid work more urgently than mothers:

> This desire to eradicate sexual and gender differences in order to re-engineer men arises from a kind of feminism that has flowed into Britain from America to become the orthodoxy among social science researchers, public sector professionals and much of the chattering classes.[16]

Phillips condemned 'female supremacism' for despising men and treating them as superfluous to family life; the result of taking the goal of independence too far, she argued, was to lead thousands of women into the trap of poverty or forcing them into employment they did not really want.

Of course, the belief that feminism emasculates men and leaves them unable to play their role in society is one that has surfaced regularly, most obviously during the 1920s as a result of the disruptions of wartime. It is hardly surprising that it should have re-emerged in the 1990s partly as a result of *fin de siècle* alarmism and partly as a result of economic changes over several decades. Employment was, and still is, widely seen as the key means of integrating men into family life by giving them status and by providing some justification for their limited contribution to domesticity. Mass unemployment, which became a continuous feature of British society from the 1970s onwards, inevitably posed a threat to the self-confidence of millions of British males. Two sections of male society appeared especially vulnerable: the young and the middle-aged. A fashionable view held that boys were 'underperforming' in schools, which meant that they had been overtaken by girls in examinations results. By 1997 government surveys suggested that whereas two-thirds of fourteen-year-old girls attained the expected levels, only half of boys did so; and where once boys had overtaken girls at 'O' level stage, now 48 per cent of girls achieved five good GCSE passes compared with only 39 per cent of boys. The result was a group of young men who, for lack of qualifications, were likely to become almost unemployable after leaving school; this in turn led to high crime rates and to a soaring suicide rate amongst young men. The other aspect of the male employment crisis concerned those in middle age who were increasingly likely to face redundancy or to take early retirement. Between the 1970s and the 1990s a major change of expectations occurred as millions of men in their fifties and sixties became resigned to an early end to their careers. Four out of ten men over the age of fifty-five but below retirement age had given up work and, moreover, had no expectations of further employment.[17] In addition, by 1995, 20 per cent of men had female partners who were the main breadwinners in the household – three times as many as in 1980.

However, the significance of these trends was not as obvious as the leader-writers and pundits believed. They assumed, perhaps mistakenly, that any gain for women automatically implied a corresponding loss for men. In fact, many middle-aged men were happy to take early retirement and even planned for it as a release from the treadmill; their wives often developed their own careers more fully at the same time, as their children had now grown up. In addition many younger married men were keen to place limits on their role as family breadwinners in order to develop their role as fathers. In the process, gender relations were being *re-adjusted*, rather than completely overthrown, to the benefit of both partners. This is a reminder that hostile male reactions to women's liberation have to be kept in perspective. The surprising thing, in the long run, may well be not how strong the reaction against feminism was, but how limited and how ineffective.

Back to Politics

One of the most conspicuous changes of tactics in the women's movement during the last years of the twentieth century was the adoption of a much more positive stance towards the political system. Previously, activists in women's liberation had, rightly, regarded formal, institutional power with suspicion, assuming that hierarchical structures were almost calculated to preserve the dominance of men despite nominal concessions to female representation.

Initially the Thatcher era seemed likely to confirm this view. Yet the striking contrast between a female prime minister and the meagre total of nineteen women MPs elected in 1979 – a lower total than any since 1951 – was highly provoking. The contrast between the social and economic advances made by women and the static political system seemed both anomalous and an obstacle to further progress. In 1980 the Fawcett Society and Women in Media organised a Women's Day of Action to focus on the need for more women to get into positions of power. This led to the formation of the '300 Group' which aimed to prepare women of all parties as parliamentary candidates with a view to occupying half the seats in the House of Commons.

However, the position scarcely improved in 1983 when only 23 women were elected. The number did begin to edge upwards thereafter, to 41 in 1987 and to 60 (of whom 37 were Labour) in the 1992 general election. This was symptomatic of a growing feeling amongst younger women that the time had come to suspend suspicions and to work within the party organisations in order to gain access to power. There were negative and positive reasons for this. On the one hand the blatantly anti-feminist attitudes and policies of the Conservative administrations threatened women's interests; on the other hand the more traditional Labour Party politics became discredited, the greater the opportunities that existed for women to replace a generation of men whose political careers had ended. Prolonged electoral defeat also ushered in what became known as 'New Labour'. If not explicitly pro-feminist the New Labour agenda seemed to make the party more accessible to women if only by its frank repudiation of the traditions of the movement and the domination of the trade unions.

Yet it was plain that no significant improvement in female representation was likely without a more deliberate and centralised strategy. Women proved to be the beneficiaries of the weakening of the Labour Party's grass-roots organisation at the expense of the national party which was now dedicated to sweeping innovations in ideology and personnel. The 1993 party conference adopted a radical policy of positive discrimination with the object of returning eighty to ninety women Labour MPs at the next election. To this end each region was required to identify the constituencies in which a sitting Labour member was due to retire, and the winnable marginals, defined as seats where a 6 per cent swing to Labour would bring victory. In these two categories _half_ the constituencies were to draw up shortlists comprised entirely of female candidates. Initially the scheme relied upon voluntary co-operation by the local parties to reach the quota for their region. Not surprisingly a backlash developed especially among male members in the party's heartlands in the midlands and the north. When the MPs were required to vote for four women in the elections for the shadow cabinet in 1993 many retaliated by using their votes for a large number of women, thereby spreading the women's poll so thinly as to exclude most of them from the successful candidates. By May 1995 only eighteen constituencies had adopted all-women shortlists voluntarily. However, the National Executive Committee made clear its readiness to impose the policy if necessary. In July 1996, by which time 34 women had been adopted under the policy, two disgruntled male aspirants successfully posed a legal challenge to the scheme. An industrial tribunal in Leeds ruled the party's policy to be contrary to the 1975 Sex Discrimination Act. Though apparently a serious setback, this case came too late. There was no attempt to reopen candidatures already decided, and the female candidates already going through the process of adoption were not stopped. In fact many of these were in constituencies not regarded as winnable, but the women were swept into parliament in 1997 by the size of the national swing against the Conservatives. Labour comfortably exceeded its target by returning 101 women members who, with the thirteen Conservatives, three Liberal Democrats and two Scottish Nationalist members, made a total of 119; this rose to 120 following an early by-election. 'A line has been drawn in history and we'll never go back', declared Dawn Primarolo, one of the Labour members.[18]

This verdict certainly appeared to be justified. The 1997 general election cannot be dismissed either as a freak result or as an isolated breakthrough. In the first place it was part of a wider expansion and a qualitative change in the political role of women in Britain. Ever since 1918 the Conservatives had benefited from the gender gap at general elections. For example, as recently as 1992 Labour support among women stood at 34 per cent compared with 44 per cent for the Conservatives; but at the same election the Conservative lead amongst male voters was only 4 per cent. However, a generational shift had already manifested itself in that the Conservative lead was concentrated among older women, while in the 18–24 age group Labour enjoyed the advantage. At the 1997 election Labour's lead over the Conservatives was 14 per cent among men and 13 per cent among women. The historic gender gap had finally disappeared.

This heralded fundamental problems for the Conservatives whose superiority in local organisation ever since the 1880s had rested largely on the voluntary efforts of women. By the 1990s the party's membership had become alarmingly elderly – with an average age of sixty-six. Whereas earlier generations of middle-class women had had the time and inclination to do the painstaking work for the party, by the end of the century they were more likely to be absorbed by their careers and families, and, possibly, alienated by the party's unsympathetic stance on women's questions during the Thatcher era. This acute weakness among women voters and activists was a paradoxical outcome to the first female premiership, though it was probably more a reflection of long-term social change than of short-term reactions to government policies. As a result the Conservative Party came under severe pressure to compete with the high profile enjoyed by women in the parliamentary Labour Party; it had to recover lost female activists and persuade local constituencies to abandon their resistance to women candidates.[19] The advantage in these developments from the point of view of the women's movement was that they made the female electorate and women's interests more central to politics than they had been for a long time.

The other reason for regarding 1997 as a lasting breakthrough lay in subsequent developments. The adoption of proportional representation systems for other British elections was calculated to promote women's representation even if that was not the motive behind it. In the 1999 elections to the new Scottish Parliament, for example, no fewer than 48 women were returned in a total of 129 members of whom 29 won in constituencies and 19 in the top-up seats. European Assembly elections had already provided an alternative route into politics for women. Some became Euro-members before entering the House of Commons, while others moved to Europe as an escape from a failing Westminster career. In 1999 twenty of the 86 United Kingdom representatives were women.

On the other hand, this picture may be over-optimistic. Although many of the newly elected Labour women were widely regarded as close supporters of the new prime minister and were well represented in government, the fortunes of women politicians were mixed after 1997. In the cabinet Margaret Beckett's promising career stalled, Clare Short was sidelined and Harriet Harman was soon sacked. To some extent these setbacks were balanced by the rise of Mo Mowlam in popularity and the prominence of several junior ministers including Tessa Jowell, Glenda Jackson and Helen Liddell as well as Baronesses Jay, Blackstone and Hollis in the Lords. Yet it was by no means obvious that the new government placed women's grievances very high on its agenda, especially as the much-promised minister for women disappeared without trace. On the contrary, an early decision to reduce the cost of benefits for lone mothers suggested that the new government was no different from its predecessor and provoked severe disillusionment in the country. This was all the worse in view of the failure of the large number of women members to use their influence on the issue.

Only nine women were among the 101 MPs who signed an early-day motion in protest at the cuts. And subsequently only eight defied the whips by voting against the government. To some extent this reflected the fact that rebellion was easier for more experienced members; the women were largely newly-elected members anxious not to mar their chances of promotion. But their apparently uncritical loyalty to the Blair government seemed to justify the scepticism of radical feminists who had never been fully convinced of the validity of the parliamentary strategy. Nor was it clear whether the women's presence would improve either the atmosphere or the conduct of House of Commons business. It was hoped that the traditional rowdyism would diminish and that the pattern of late-afternoon-to-midnight debates would give way to more normal working hours as a result of the female role; but little changed during the first two years of the new parliament.

These reservations underlined the fact that the relationship between Tony Blair and feminism had always been an unstable one. Well before the election he had made clear that the party's experiment with women-only shortlists would not be repeated; consequently a deterioration in the party's fortunes threatened a major fall in female representation at the next election. The prime minister and his advisers were sympathetic to the extent that they had grasped that the *zeitgeist* of the 1990s was female; his opportunistic association with 'Blair's Babes', as the press called the new members, and his shrewd exploitation of the national mood after the death of Princess Diana were indications of this. But beneath the surface Blair was a socially *conservative* figure whose emphasis on the traditional family sat awkward with the views of many feminists. In any case his actions were strongly influenced by electoral opportunism which dictated maintaining his hold on right-wing opinion; he signalled this by pandering to prejudice against single mothers.[20] As long as he was not seriously challenged by the Conservatives, Blair's hold on female support was unlikely to be seriously threatened, but within two years of his victory major doubts had emerged about the efficacy of the parliamentary strategy for feminism.

New Directions?

By the end of the 1990s it had become fashionable to portray the women's movement as confused and uncertain as to its direction; the emergence of 'New' and 'Old' feminists gave some substance to this view, though the differences between them were often a matter of emphasis and priorities rather than about fundamentals . Certain questions, such as free contraception, abortion on demand, educational reform, legal and financial independence for women and discrimination against lesbians probably stood somewhat lower down the agenda of the movement by this time, while the key issues now centred around equal opportunities in employment, equal pay, provision for child care and women's health. It was natural for feminists to focus increasingly on the dilemmas posed by women's steady entry into the labour market, and especially on the family, which appeared to be the chief remaining source of women's subordination and inequality. Consequently child care provision became a major goal.

To some extent the shift of priorities within the women's movement reflected the views of a new generation. In 1999 when Germaine Greer published a sequel to *The Female Eunuch*, entitled *The Whole Woman*, she betrayed her disappointment with the fruits of women's liberation and her doubts about the New Feminism which she saw as rather conservative. By contrast, Natasha Walters, author of *The New Feminism*, regarded feminists such as Greer as having been obsessed with sex and the body. For younger women, feminism had become essentially materialist, more pragmatic and politically focussed by the 1990s. Their reaction echoed that of the younger feminists of the 1920s who had frankly accepted that women's position had improved greatly and who, as a result, had attracted criticism from older women for their desire for marriage and motherhood. Without minimising the obstacles Walters and others were inclined to believe that it was now within women's grasp to attain economic and political equality by adopting a positive and focussed approach.

Of course, some critics thought this naïve. After all, by the end of the decade it had become apparent that the process of slowly narrowing the pay gap between men and women had stalled. Worse, the government, for all its professed sympathy, refused any legislative remedy, preferring to rely on mere exhortation to employers to achieve equal pay; it was apparently more concerned to avoid offending business than to appease women. Yet despite such gloomy signs, much feminist comment continued to exude a confident, even triumphalist, tone. An interesting symptom of the mood was a book entitled *Sacred Cows: Is Feminism Relevant to the New Millennium?* (1999), written by Ros Coward. She argued that during the previous twenty years the overarching system of male oppression had largely been dismantled and that gender stereotypes had changed so that in many respects men had become the victims; the disparagement of male flaws and the celebration of female values had given rise to 'Womanism'. This view was certainly widely reflected in the advertising and films of the 1990s which increasingly portrayed women as 'on top' and sanctified female assertiveness as 'empowerment'. It is difficult to know how much significance to attribute to such expressions. In a way they corroborated the claims of the men's movement and underlined the ineffectiveness of the backlash against feminism. The intriguing aspect of all this was that it suggested that the ancient gender stereotypes – the one aspect of male dominance that was not susceptible to legislative or political remedy – really were becoming obsolete. If real equality remained some way off, the last twenty years of the century appeared to have brought the final steps in that direction appreciably closer.

Notes

PREFACE TO THE SECOND EDITION

1. *Suffrage and Power: The Women's Movement 1918–1929* (1997), p. 226.

1 WOMEN AND THE WOMEN'S MOVEMENT BEFORE 1914

1. See Pat Thane, 'Late Victorian Women', in T. R. Gourvish and A. O'Day (eds), *Later Victorian Britain* (1988), p. 181.
2. Susan Kingsley Kent, *Sex and Suffrage in Britain 1860–1914* (1987).
3. Joan Perkin, *Women and Marriage in Nineteenth-Century England* (1989); Pat Jalland, *Women, Marriage and Politics 1890–1914* (1986).
4. Elizabeth Roberts, *A Woman's Place: an Oral History of Working-class Women 1890–1940* (1984).
5. F. Prochaska, 'A Mother's Country: Mothers' Meetings and Family Welfare in Britain, 1850–1950', *History*, 74, 242 (1989); Brian Harrison, 'For Church, Queen and Family: the Girls' Friendly Society 1874–1920', *Past and Present*, 61 (1973); Martin Pugh, *The Tories and the People 1880–1935* (1985).
6. Anna Davin, 'Imperialism and Motherhood', *History Workshop Journal*, 5 (1978).
7. Millicent Garrett Fawcett, 'Female Suffrage: a Reply', *The Nineteenth Century* (July, 1889).
8. Patricia Hollis, *Ladies Elect: Women in English Local Government, 1865–1914* (1987).
9. Andrew Rosen, *Rise Up Women!* (1974).
10. Jill Liddington and Jill Norris, *One Hand Tied Behind Us* (1978).
11. Leslie P. Hume, *The National Union of Women's Suffrage Societies* (1982); Sandra Holton, *Feminism and Democracy* (1986); Martin Pugh, *Women's Sulfrage in Britain 1867–1928* (1980), and 'Labour and Women's Suffrage', in K. D. Brown (ed.), *The First Labour Party 1906–14* (1985).
12. Jill Liddington, *The Life and Times of a Respectable Rebel: Selina Cooper 1864–1946* (1984); June Hannam, *Isabella Ford* (1989).
13. Holton, *Feminism and Democracy*, pp. 124–5.

2 THE IMPACT OF THE GREAT WAR

1. S. Andreski, *Military Organisation and Society* (1954); R. Titmuss, *Essays on the Welfare State* (1958); A. Marwick, *The Deluge* (1967).
2. House of Commons (HC) Debates, 7 Aug. 1914, c.2158; Home Office letter, 21 Aug. 1914, Suffragette Fellowship paper Z6067.
3. E. Pankhurst, circular letter, 13 Aug. 1914.
4. Fawcett to Miss E. Atkinson, undated (1915), Fawcett Library Autograph Collection.

5. *Common Cause*, VI, no. 282, 4 Sept. 1914.

6. Imperial War Museum, EMP 49/2/2.

7. Guildhall speech, Plymouth, 17 Nov. 1914.

8. Imperial War Museum, EMP 13/2, E. Pankhurst circular, 9 July 1915; *Daily Chronicle*, 19 July 1915; *Weekly Dispatch*, 24 Apr. 1921.

9. Jill Liddington, *The Long Road to Greenham: Feminism and Anti-Militarism in Britain since 1820* (1989), pp. 96–102.

10. WIL Annual Report, 1918–19.

11. Julia Bush. *Behind the Lines: East London Labour 1914–18* (1984), pp. 72–3, 149–50; P. Romeiro, E. *Sylvia Pankhurst* (1987), pp. 105, 118–20.

12. *Chronicle of Youth: Vera Brittain's War Diary 1913–17*, ed. A. Bishop (198 1), pp. 84, 102.

13. Fawcett to Miss E. Atkinson, 19 Feb. 1916, Fawcett Library Autograph Collection.

14. Jill Liddington, *The Life and Times of a Respectable Rebel* (1984), pp. 264–5.

15. Cecil to Mrs Fawcett, 5 Aug. 1914, Fawcett Library Autograph Collection.

16. WFL, executive minutes, 29 Nov. 1917.

17. *Anti-Suffrage Review*, 77 (Mar. 1915).

18. *Handbook for Housewives*, National Food Economy League (1917).

19. J. M. Winter, *The Great War and the British People* (1985), pp. 103–53.

20. Imperial War Museum, LAND 8/6,8/10,8/30. Inez Jenkins, *The History of the Women's Institute Movement of England and Wales* (1953), pp. 1–31.

21. M. G. Fawcett, *What I Remember* (1925), p. 218.

22. Liddington, *Respectable Rebel*, p. 275.

23. Imperial War Museum, WEL 2/5.

24. *Women's Industrial News*, XVIII, 67 (Oct. 1914), 298.

25. Imperial War Museum, EMP 2/I; 22/39,53,55.

26. Imperial War Museum, EMP 55/6.

27. Board of Trade Report on 'The Increase in Employment of Women During the War: Individual Industries' (1917), IWM, EMP 25/10.

28. *Report of the War Cabinet Committee on Women in Industry*, Cd. 135, HMSO (1919), p. 107.

29. *Daily Mail*, 29 Oct. 1917.

30. *East Anglian Daily Times*, 17 Mar. 1916, see Imperial War Museum, LAND 2/3.

31. *Birmingham Post*, 25 Apr. 1915.

32. *Western Daily Mercury*, 22 May 1915; *East Anglian Daily Times*, 17 Mar. 1916; *Montgomeryshire County Times*, 5 Aug. 1916.

33. *Summary of the Work of the Women's War Agricultural Committees*, HMSO (1916).

34. Home Office Report, 'Substitution of Women in Non-Munitions Factories During the War', HMSO (1919).

35. *Report on the Increased Employment of Women During the War* (1916), p. 11, Imperial War Museum, EMP 25/2.

36. Imperial War Museum, EMP 22/2/19.

37. *Dundee Advertiser*, 31 Aug. 1917.

38. Harold L. Smith, 'The issue of "equal pay for equal work" in Great Britain, 1914–19', *Societas*, VIII, 1 (1978), 40–3.

39. Ibid. p. 45.
40. 'Final Report of the Civil War Workers' Committee on Substitute Labour', Cd. 9228 (1918).
41. 'The Position of Women After the War', SJCIWO, n.d., p. 13, Imperial War Museum, EMP 28/2.
42. 'Report of a Conference on the Position of Women in Industry After the War', Mar. 1918, Imperial War Museum, EMP 28/1.
43. Anne Summers, *Angels and Citizens: British Women as Military Nurses* (1988).
44. Lady Frances Balfour, *Dr.Elsie Inglis* (1920), p. 144.
45. *Blackpool Herald*, 12 Mar. 1915.
46. National Service press cuttings, Imperial War Museum, EMP 49/2/27.
47. *Daily Express*, 10 June 1918.
48. *Time and Tide*, 4 June 1920.
49. Lady Londonderry, *Retrospect* (1938), pp. 127–8.
50. *Church Family News*, 26 May 1915.
51. Gail Braybon and Penny Summerfield, *Out of the Cage* (1987), pp. 109–10.
52. 'Women's Patrol Committee', NUWW pamphlet, Oct. 1917.
53. *Weekly Dispatch*, 15 July 1917.
54. See Martin Pugh, *Electoral Reform in War and Peace 1906–18* (1978), pp. 67–9.
55. W. H. Dickinson to Miss Barry (copy), 20 Jan. 1943, Dickinson Papers (GLC Record Office); HC Debates, 22 May 1917, c. 2213–14.
56. S. S. Holton, *Feminism and Democracy* (1986), pp. 134–50.
57. Asquith to M. G. Fawcett, 7 May 1916, Fawcett Library Autograph Collection.
58. Dated 13 Dec. 1915, Labour Party Archives, WNC 29/5.
59. Liddington, *Respectable Rebel*, p. 271.
60. Dickinson to M. G. Fawcett, 19 Jan. 1917, Fawcett Library Autograph Collection.
61. CAB 24/6/1, 13 Feb. 1917.
62. 'The 1917 Deputation to Lloyd George', Suffragette Fellowship papers Z6065.
63. Cicely Hamilton, *Life Errant* (1935), p. 67; H. M. Swanwick, *The War and Its Effects on Women* (1918), p. 24; Elizabeth Robins, *Ancilla's Share* (1924), xxxvi.
64. C. Hartley, *Motherhood and the Relationship of the Sexes* (1917), pp. 14–15.
65. HC Debates, 16 Aug. 1916, c. 1959–60; E. S. Pankhurst, *The Suffragette Movement* (1931), p. 601.
66. Anne Summers, *Angels and Citizens*, pp. 273, 287–8.
67. Quoted in Summers, *Angels and Citizens*, p. 287.
68. HC Debates, 29 Feb. 1924, c. 872.
69. W. Long to H. A. Morton (copy), 14 June 1917, Long Papers; CAB 24/6/1, 13 Feb. 1917.
70. *Letters From Lord Oxford to a Friend* (1933), pp. 125–6.
71. A Memorandum on Franchise Reform, n.d., Grey Papers, 236/3.

3 STRATEGY AND TACTICS OF THE WOMEN'S MOVEMENT INTHE 1920s

1. Ray Strachey, *The Cause* (1928), p. 368.
2. *Britannia*, 30 Nov. 1917.
3. Lloyd George to A. Bonar Law, 21 Nov. 1918 (copy), Lloyd George papers F/30/2/55.
4. *The Labour Woman*, no. 21 (Jan. 1918), p. 67.
5. Teresa Lucas, 'The Pankimrst Sisters After 1914', Sheffield University PhD thesis, unpublished (1988), p. 155.
6. Ibid.
7. WFL, Political and Militant Sub-Committee, minute books, 1917–35, Fawcett Library, Box 56.
8. Lady Rhondda, *This Was My World* (1933), pp. 135–6, 151–3.
9. *Time and Tide*, 9 July 1920.
10. Ibid., 18 May 1923, 16 May 1924.
11. *Good Housekeeping*, Mar. 1957, p. 162.
12. Mary Grieve, *Millions Made My Story* (1964), p. 143.
13. Lady Rhondda, *This Was My World* (1933), p. 299.
14. Glasgow Society for Women's Suffrage, executive minutes, 21 Feb. 1921.
15. *Time and Tide*, 21 Jan. 192 1.
16. Ibid., 8 Nov. 1922, 14 Dec. 1923.
17. Jill Liddington, *The Life and Times of a Respectable Rebel* (1984), pp. 310–11.
18. NUSEC, executive minutes, 22 Nov. 1927.
19. Ibid., 4 Mar. 1920.
20. *The Woman's Leader*, 1 Apr. 1920.
21. NUSEC, executive minutes, 11 Jan. 1923; Glasgow Society for Women's Suffrage, executive minutes, 27 Mar. 1929.
22. NUSEC, executive minutes, 27 Nov. 1924.
23. Glasgow Society for Women's Suffrage, executive minutes, 15 Apr. 1929.
24. *The Woman's Leader*, 11 Nov. 1921.
25. Liddington, *Respectable Rebel*, pp. 299–300.
26. *The Woman's Leader*, 5 Nov. 1920, 12 Nov. 1920, 1 July 1921.
27. Women's Local Representation Joint Committee (Glasgow), minutes, 17 Mar. 1919, 25 Oct. 1919.
28. Jonathan Billings, 'The First Lady Members on the Councils of the Newcastle and Gateshead Corporations', Newcastle University dissertation (1985), pp. 10–15.
29. Cambridge Women's Citizens' Association, minutes, 17 Aug. 1925, 9 Oct. 1925.
30. *The Woman's Leader*, 10 Nov. 1922.
31. Conservative Party, Annual Conference Report, Nov. 1917.
32. Martin Pugh, *The Tories and the People, 1880–1935* (1985), pp. 56–62.
33. Women's Unionist Organisation, Annual Conference Report, Apr. 192 1.
34. Women's Labour League, Conference Report, Jan. 1918.
35. Ibid., Jan. 1918, pp. 43–46.
36. Ibid., June 1919, p. 80.

358 Women and the Women's Movement in Britain

37. *The Woman's Leader*, 10 June 1921, p. 288.
38. CGWO minutes 1 Mar. 1921, 13 Apr. 1921, Fawcett Library Collection, Box 342.
39. Ibid., 28 Oct. 1926, 24 Oct. 1927.

4 THE ANTI-FEMINIST REACTION

1. *Time and Tide*, 31 Oct. 1925.
2. Ibid., 12 Aug. 1927.
3. Gail Braybon and Penny Summerfield, *Out of the Cage* (1987), pp. 222–3.
4. Arabella Kencaly, *Feminism and Sex Extinction* (1920), p. v.
5. Janet Courtney, *Countrywomen in Council* (1933), p. 151.
6. Lady Rhondda, *Notes On The Way* (1937), p. 94.
7. *Daily Mail*, 5 Feb. 1920.
8. *Eve*, 27 Sept. 1922, p. 404.
9. Quoted in Sheila Jeffries, *The Spinster and Her Enemies* (1985), pp. 94–5.
10. Ibid., p. 97.
11. In Ray Strachey (ed.), *Our Freedom and Its Results* (1936), p. 271.
12. Quoted in Brian Harrison, *Prudent Revolutionaries* (1987), pp. 21, 197, 311.
13. Alice Head, *It Could Never Have Happened* (1939), p. 187.
14. *Daily Mail*, 20 Apr. 1927.
15. Daily Express, 27 Nov. 1927, quoted in Billy Melman, *Women and the Popular Imagination in the Twenties* (1988), p. 44.
16. Kenealy, *Sex Extinction*, pp. 245–6.
17. Daily Express, 12 Nov. 1924, quoted in Melman, *Women and the Popular Imagination*, p. 23.
18. Barbara Cartland, *The Isthmus Years* (1942), p. 106.
19. Quoted in Melman, *Women and the Popular Imagination*, p. 23.
20. HC Debates, vol. 145, 4 Aug. 192 1, c. 1799–1806.
21. Kenealy, *Sex Extinction*, p. 249.
22. Cartland, *Isthmus Years*, pp. 15–16.
23. *Good Housekeeping*, Nov. 1934, pp. 10– 11.
24. Notes on a deputation to Lloyd George, 31 Jan. 1920, Imperial War Museum, EMP 59/8.
25. Ibid.
26. *Edinburgh Evening News*, 16 June 1919.
27. Minutes of the Women's Employment Committee, Ministry of Reconstruction, Imperial War Museum, EMP 29/2, p. 23.
28. See Weekly Reports by the Ministry of Labour (Department of Civil Demobilisation and Resettlement), Imperial War Museum, EMP 80/25, 32, 50,68.
29. *Daily Mail*, 18 Apr. 1919.
30. *The Times*, 16 Apr. 1919.
31. Weekly Reports, Ministry of Labour, 4 Jan. 1919, 5 July 1919.
32. Labour Party Archives, 'Report on First Steps Towards a Domestic Workers' Charter', DOM/30/33.

33. Labour Party Archives, 'Synopsis: Domestic Workers' Charter', DOM/ 30/28.
34. *Good Housekeeping*, Mar. 1922.
35. Head, *It Could Never Have Happened*, pp. 187–8.
36. Mass Observation Report, in *Good Housekeeping*, Jan. 1950, p. 11.
37. Enid Charles, *The Twilight of Parenthood* (1934), p. 12.
38. Kenealy, *Sex Extinction*, p. 97.
39. HC Debates, 15 Apr. 1935, c. 1634.
40. *Home Chat*, 7 Feb. 1920, p. 201.
41. *My Weekly*, 25 Jan. 1919.
42. Ibid., 'What's the Matter With Marriage?', 26 Apr. 1919.
43. Charles, *Twilight*, pp. 75–6.
44. Cartland, *Isthmus Years*, p. 157.
45. NBW Council Report, 1921, Astor Papers 1416/1/1/397.
46. Jane Lewis, *The Politics of Motherhood* (1980), p. 154.
47. Ibid., p. 129.
48. Hilda Martindale, *Women Servants of the State 1870–1938* (1938), p. 156.
49. *Manchester Guardian*, 31 Jan. 1930.
50. Cardiff Women's Citizens Association, minutes 23 Jan. 1922, DDX/158/ 2–1.
51. NUSEC, subcommittee minutes 17 Nov. 1921, Fawcett Library Box 342.
52. HC Debates, 29 Apr. 1927, c. 1185–92.
53. Ray Strachey, *Careers and Openings for Women* (1935), pp. 22–3.
54. Elizabeth Roberts, *A Woman's Place* (1984), p. 137.
55. Report of the War Cabinet Committee on Women in Industry, Cd. 135 (HMSO, 1919), p. 7.
56. *Time and Tide*, 21 May 1920, 19 Jan. 1923.
57. Mike Savage, 'Trade unionism, sex segregation, and the state: women's employment in "new industries" in inter-war Britain', *Social History*, 13, 2 (1988), 210.
58. Ibid., pp. 221–2.
59. N. C. Solden, *Women in British Trade Unions 1874–1976* (1978), pp. 117–19.

5 THE DOMESTICATION OF BRITISH POLITICS

1. H. Swanwick to C. Marshall, 10 June 1917, Marshall Papers, Box 22.
2. E. Barton, *Woman in the Home, the Store and the State* (WCG, n.d., late 1920s).
3. Astor to Sir John Baird, 14 Dec. 1923, Baldwin Papers. vol 35, fol 129; Malcolm Fraser to Austen Chamberlain, 30 Dec. 1921, Chamberlain Papers, AC/32/4/16.
4. Jill Liddington, *The Long Road to Greenham: Feminism and Anti-militarism in Britain since 1820* (1989), pp. 109–19.
5. Women's Labour League, *Annual Conference Report*, May 1927.
6. Women's Co-operative Guild, Central Committee Minutes, 13 Nov. 1937.

360 Women and the Women's Movement in Britain

7. Women's Unionist Association, Annual Conference Report, 1925, pp. 66–7.

8. M. G. Fawcett, *What the Vote Has Done* (NUSEC, 1926), p. 1.

9. Brian Harrison, 'Women's Suffrage at Westminster 1866–1928', in *High and Low Politics in Modern Britain*, ed. M. Bentley and J. Stevenson (1983), p. 91.

10. *The Woman's Leader*, 12 Aug. 1921.

11. *Equal Franchise 1918–28* (NUSEC, 1927), p. 5.

12. *Daily Mail* 20, 23, 28 Apr. 1927.

13. Ruth Hall, *Marie Stopes* (1978), pp. 169, 206; HC Debates, 25 July 1923, c 480; 30 July 1924, c 2050.

14. Women's Unionist Association, Annual Report, 1935, p. 45.

15. *Time and Tide*, 26 May 1922.

16. Joan Lock, *The British Policewoman* (1979), pp. 153–4.

18. 'The Need for Women Police', NCW pamphlet, n.d.

19. C. T. Stannage, *Baldwin Thwarts the Opposition* (1980), p. 291.

20. Martin Pugh, *The Tories and the People 1880–1935* (1985), pp. 179–80.

21. Based on Women's Unionist Association, Annual Conference Reports.

22. *The Guardian*, 22 Mar. 1983, p. 2.

23. *The Woman's Leader*, 10 Nov. 1922, p. 232.

24. NUSEC, Executive Minutes, 22 Nov. 1923.

25. *Home and Politics*, No 38 (June 1924), p. 11; No 48 (Apr. 1925), pp. 2, 6, 8.

26. Women's Unionist Association, Annual Conference Reports, 1921, pp. 9–13, 1925, p. 67.

27. Ibid., 1924, pp. 15–16.

28. Ibid., 1921, pp. 6–7.

29. Ibid., 1921, p. 21; 1927, pp. 17, 30; 1930, pp. 46–62.

30. Conservative Party, Campaign Guide, 1922, p. 981.

31. See Olive Banks, *Faces of Feminism* (1981), p. 164; Lucy Middleton (ed.), *Women in the Labour Movement* (1977). For the opposite view Harold Smith, 'Sex vs Class: British Feminists and the Labour Movement 1919–29', *The Historian*, 47 (Nov. 1984). For an intermediate position see Pat Thane, 'The Women of the British Labour Party and Feminism, 1906–45', in Harold Smith (ed.), *British Feminism in the Twentieth Century* (1990), and Brian Harrison, 'Class and Gender in Modern British Labour History', *Past and Present*, 124 (Aug. 1989).

32. Labour Party Women's Organisation, Annual Conference Report, 1921, p. 85, 1923, p. 88.

33. Ibid., 1918, p. 41.

34. *The Labour Woman* carried regular pages on 'The Housewife' and 'Housing'; see also A. D. Furniss and M. Phillips, *The Working Woman's House* (n.d.).

35. Labour Party Women's Organisation, Annual Conference Report, 1935, p. 97.

36. Michael Savage, *The Dynamics of Working-Class Politics: the Labour Movement in Preston 1880–1940* (1987), pp. 164–70.

37. Ibid., p. 181.

38. *The Labour Woman*, VI (7 Oct. 1918), 82.

39. See Smith, 'Sex vs Class', p. 21.
40. *The Labour Woman*, v (21 Jan. 1918), 2; Labour Party Women's Organisation, Annual Conference Reports, 1920, pp. 77–8, and 1923, p. 87; *The Woman's Leader*, 2 Mar. 1923; M. Phillips (ed.), *Women and the Labour Party* (1918), p. 6.
41. NUSEC, Executive Minutes, 27 Sept. 1927.
42. Ibid., 25 Jan. 1923.
43. Labour Party Women's Organisation, Annual Conference Reports, 1921, p. 90.
44. Ibid., 1928, p. 76.
45. Ibid., 1929, p. 33.
46. Ibid., 1930, p. 58.
47. Ibid., 1925, p. 123.
48. Dora Russell, *The Tamarisk Tree* (1975), p. 172.
49. LPWO, Annual Conference Reports, 1927.
50. Ibid., 1928, p. 27.
51. Ibid., 1927, pp. 36–7.
52. Ibid., 1932, pp. 96–7.
53. Ibid., 1930, pp. 48–9.
54. Ibid., p. 43.
55. LPWO, Annual Conference Reports, 1928, pp. 18–20.
56. Ibid., 1930, pp. 53–4.
57. *The Labour Woman*, XXVI (Feb. 1938), 18–19; (Mar. 1938), 34.
58. LPWO, Annual Conference Reports, 1930, p. 60.
59. *Liberal Woman's News*, No 4 (Feb. 1920), 50; No 5 (Mar. 1920), 62.
60. R. M. Wilson, *Wife: Mother: Voter. Her Vote – What Will She Do With It?* (1918).
61. *Time and Tide*, 8, 24 Nov. 1922, 23, 30 Nov. 1923, 24 Oct. 1924.
62. *Richmond Times*, 4, 11, 18 Nov. 1922.
63. *Chiswick Times*, 24 Nov. 1922.
64. *West Herts and Watford Observer*, 17, 24 Nov. 1923, 1 Dec. 1923.
65. See M. Benney, A. P. Gray and R. H. Pear, *How People Vote* (1956), p. 107; D. Butler and D. Stokes, *Political Change in Britain* (1971), p. 164; R. McKenzie and A. Silver, *Angels in Marble* (1968), pp. 88, 91; F. Parkin, 'Working Class Conservatives', *British Journal of Sociology*, XXVIII (Sept. 1967); Judith Evans, 'Women and Politics: a Reappraisal', *Political Studies*, XXVIII, 2 (1980); J. S. Rasmussen, 'Women in Labour: the Flapper Vote and Party System Transformation in Britain', *Electoral Studies*, 3, No 1 (1984); B. Campbell, *The Iron Ladies* (1987).
66. Evans, 'Women and Politics', p. 215.
67. *The Times*, 21 Nov. 1918.
68. J. Turner, 'The Labour Vote and the Franchise After 1918: an Investigation of the English Evidence', in P. R. Denley and D. I. Hopkin (eds), *History and Computing* (1987), pp. 138–41.
69. D. Marquand, *Ramsay MacDonald* (1977), p. 235.
70. E. Pethwick-Lawrence, *My Part in a Changing World* (1938), pp. 322–3.
71. Stuart R. Bell, 'Asquith's Decline and the General Election of 1918', *Scottish Historical Review*, LXI, 171 (1982); see also K. O. Morgan, *Consensus and Disunity* (1979), pp. 152–3.

362   *Women and the Women's Movement in Britain*

72. Peter Rowland, *Lloyd George* (1975), p. 469.
73. R. Holt to W. Runciman, 17 Dec. 1918, and A. Haworth to W. Runcirnan, 17 Dec. 1918, Waiter Runciman Papers, Box 169.
74. *The Woman's Leader*, 1 July 1921.
75. Ibid., 14 Dec. 1923.
76. *Bucks Free Press*, 23 Nov. 1923.
77. Rasmussen, 'Women in Labour', pp. 47–63; Butler and Stokes, *Political Change in Britain.*
78. Stuart Ball, *Baldwin and the Conservative Party* (1988), pp. 220–1; Butler and Stokes, *Political Change*, pp. 105–15.
79. Rasmussen, 'Women in Labour', p. 57.
80. The constituencies were: N. Midlothian and Peebles, S. Battersea, Bishop Auckland, Wansbeck, Liverpool (E. Toxteth), Eddisbury, Bath, Holland-with-Boston, and N. Lanarkshire.
81. Rasmussen, 'Women in Labour', p. 58.

6 THE POLITICAL CONTAINMENT OF WOMEN 1918–1939

1. Austin Ranney, *Pathways to Parliament* (1965), p. 96.
2. Jill Hills, 'Candidates, the Impact of Gender', *Parliamentary Affairs*, xxxiv, 2 (1981), 221–2, 225–7; R. L. Leonard, *Guide to the General Election* (1964), p. 97.
3. Jill Liddington, *The Life and Times of a Respectable Rebel: Selina Cooper 1864–1946* (1984), pp. 295–7, 325–9.
4. Women's Unionist Organisation, Annual Conference Reports, 1922, pp. 3–4; K. 0. Morgan, *Consensus and Disunity* (1979), p. 153.
5. *Berwick Advertiser*, 23 Nov. 1923.
6. *Louth and North Lincolnshire Advertiser*, 17 Sept. 1921.
7. Corbett Ashby to A. B. Ashby, 16 Oct. 1918, Corbett Ashby Papers Box 482, B6.
8. Lloyd George to Megan Lloyd George, 22 May 1928, Lloyd George Papers (National Library of Wales), 20475C/3147; Thelma Cazalet, *From the Wings* (1967), pp. 50–1; Duchess of Atholl, *Working Partnership* (1958), p. 126.
9. Women's Unionist Organisation, Annual Conference Reports, 1932, pp. 32–5; John Ramsden, *The Age of Balfour and Baldwin* (1978), pp. 245–6, 248.
10. Cazalet, *From the Wings*, p. 90.
11. Leah Manning, *A Life for Education* (1970), pp. 79, 99–100.
12. Jennic Lee, *My Life With Nye* (1980), p. 63.
13. Mary Agnes Hamilton, *Remembering My Good Friends* (1944), pp. 71, 172–3.
14. Labour Party Women's Organisation, Annual Conference Reports, 1930, p. 28.
15. Women's Co-operative Guild, Central Committee Minutes, 14 Dec. 1923, 20 Sept. 1929; also *Annual Reports* for 1922 and 1923.
16. WCG, Central Committee Minutes, 11 Apr. 1933.
17. Labour Party Women's Organisation, Annual Conference Reports, 1925, p. 84.

18. Ibid., 1927, p. 27; 1928, p. 11.
19. Hills, 'Candidates', p. 222.
20. Ibid., p. 227.
21. J. S. Rasmussen, 'Women Candidates in British By-Elections: a National Choice Interpretation of Electoral Behaviour', *Political Studies*, 29, 2 (1981) 271.
22. *Berwick Advertiser*, 11 May 1923.
23. *Staffordshire Sentinel*, 22 Apr. 1929.
24. *Express and Echo*, 24 May 1929, Walter Runciman Papers, Box 332.
25. Florence Horsbrugh Papers, Box 2/3, Scrapbook 1931–2.
26. *Newcastle Evening Chronicle*, 15 Feb. 1928.
27. Edith Summerskill, *A Woman's World* (1967), pp. 50–3; Manning, *Life for Education*, p. 104.
28. *Western Morning News*, 24 Oct. 1919, 4 Nov. 1919.
29. Ibid., 4 Nov. 1919.
30. Ibid., 3 Nov. 1919.
31. Quoted in Anthony Masters, *Nancy Astor* (1981), p. 147.
32. *Berwick Advertiser*, 18 May 1923.
33. *Staffordshire Sentinel*, 22 Apr. 1929, 24 May 1929.
34. Ibid., 22 Apr. 1929, 25 May 1929.
35. *Manchester Guardian*, 24 Sept. 1921; *The Woman's Leader*, 10 Mar. 1922.
36. *The Woman's Leader*, 16 Sept. 1921; *Lincolnshire Chronicle*, 27 Aug. 1921, 24 Sept. 1921.
37. *Manchester Guardian*, 12 Sept. 1921, 23 Sept. 1921.
38. *Daily Chronicle*, 3 Mar. 1928.
39. Ibid.
40. *Western Morning News*, 7 Mar. 1928.
41. *Northampton Mercury*, 30 Nov. 1923; *Newcastle Chronicle*, 28 June 1926.
42. *Sunderland Echo*, 23 May 1929.
43. *East Ham Echo*, 14 Dec. 1923.
44. See election material in Atholl Papers 90/11 and 22/1.
45. *Newcastle Chronicle*, 28 June 1926.
46. *Walsall Observer*, 4 Nov. 1922, 11 Nov. 1922.
47. Leonard, *Guide to the General Election*, p. 97.
48. *Oldham Chronicle*, 14 Oct. 1922.
49. *Derby Daily Telegraph*, 30 Oct. 1924.
50. *Blackburn Times*, 1 Nov. 1924.
51. Ibid., 4 May 1929, 11 May 1929.
52. Chamberlain to Hilda Chamberlain, 23 Nov. 1919, Chamberlain Papers NC/1 8/1/234; J. R. Vincent (ed.), The Crawford Papers (1984), p. 500; Summerskill, *Woman's World*, p. 61.
53. Summerskill, *Woman's World*, p. 60.
54. Cazalet, *From the Wings*, p. 126.
55. Manning, *Life for Education*, p. 87–8.
56. Summerskill, *Woman's World*, p. 62.
57. Hamilton, *Remembering*, p. 181; *Daily Mirror*, 28 Nov. 1933.
58. Summerskill, *Woman's World*, p. 59.

59. Ibid., p. 60.

60. *Glasgow Herald*, 20 Dec. 1933, Horsbrugh Papers 2/8.

61. See press cuttings, Florence Horsbrugh Papers 2/7 (1936).

62. Elizabeth Vallance, *Women in the House* (1979), p. 15.

63. Brian Harrison, 'Women in a Men's House: the Women MPs, 1919–1945', *Historical Journal*, 29,3 (1986), 630.

64. Jean Mann, *Woman in Parliament* (1962), pp. 18, 23.

65. Hamilton, *Remembering*, p. 180.

66. *Yorkshire Post*, 11 Aug. 1930.

67. See Lloyd George Papers (National Library of Wales), press cuttings 1930–2, 20486E.

68. Ellen Wilkinson, *Peeps at Politicians* (1930), p. 25.

69. Ibid., p. 78.

70. Harrison, 'Women in a Men's House'.

71. David Lloyd George to Megan Lloyd George, 1 Dec. 1936, Lloyd George Papers (National Library of Wales), 20482C/3151.

72. S. J. Hetherington, *Katharine Atholl 1874–1960* (1989), pp. 136–7.

73. *The Times*, 12 Mar. 1932; *Daily Express*, 24 June 1932; *News Chronicle*, 25 June 1932.

74. *Daily Mirror*, 28 Nov. 1933.

75. *South Wales News*, 27 Mar. 1928.

76. Harrison, 'Women in a Men's House', pp. 642–3.

77. E. Picton-Turbervill, *Life Is Good* (1939), p. 173.

78. Hamilton, *Remembering*, pp. 169, 181.

79. Beatrice Webb, *Diaries 1924–1932* (1933), p. 133.

80. Picton-Turbervill, *Life is Good*, p. 173.

81. Margaret Bondfield, *A Life's Work* (1948), p. 253.

82. Rodney Lowe, *Adjusting to Democracy* (1986), pp. 39–40.

83. Ibid., p. 139.

84. Hetherington, *Katharine Atholl*, pp. 109–10.

85. Ibid., pp. 110–16.

86. Harrison, 'Women in a Men's House', p. 634.

87. Atholl to Colonel Butter (copy), 14 Aug. 1935; Atholl to J. Spittal (copy), 24 Sept. 1935, Duchess of Atholl Papers, 22/3.

88. Atholl, 'My Answer' (August 1937), and Atholl's letter to the Constituency Association, 6 May 1938, Duchess of Atholl Papers 22/3.

89. Cazalet, *From the Wings*, p. 123.

7   THE CULT OF DOMESTICITY IN THE 1930S

1. Cynthia L. White, *The Women's Periodical Press in Britain 1946–76*, Royal Commission on the Press Working Paper No 4 (HMSO, 1977), p. 9.

2. *Woman*, 5 June 1937, p. 7.

3. Robin Kent, *Aunt Agony Advises: problem pages through the ages* (1979), pp. 27, 247.

4. *Woman*, 5 June 1937, p. 20.

5. J. M. Golby and A. W. Purdue, *The Monarchy and the British People* (1988), pp. 110–17.
6. Mary Grieve, *Millions Made My Story* (1964), p. 157.
7. *Woman's Own*, 15 Oct. 1932, p. 5.
8. Ibid., 4 Mar. 1933, pp. 704–5.
9. Ibid., 6 Jan. 1934, p. 3 8 1.
10. Ibid., 14 July 1934, p. 417.
11. Ibid., 28 July 1934, p. 481.
12. Ibid., 30 Apr. 1938, p. 7.
13. Ibid., 15 Oct. 1932, p. 10.
14. Ibid., 22 Oct. 1932, p. 56.
15. Ibid., 5 Jan. 1935, p. 449.
16. Ibid., 13 Apr. 1935, p. 57; see also Barbara Cartland, *The Isthmus Years* (1942), p. 164.
17. *Woman's Own*, 6 Jan. 1934, p. 381.
18. Ibid., 3 Feb. 1934, p. 493.
19. Ibid., 22 Oct. 1932.
20. Ibid, 31 Dec. 1932, 24 Feb. 1934.
21. *Woman*, 5 June 1937, pp. 12–13.
22. Ibid., 14 Aug. 1937, pp. 7–8.
23. Grieve, *Millions Made My Story*, pp. 80–1.
24. Cynthia L. White, *Women's Magazines 1693–1968* (1970), p. 112.
25. Grieve, *Millions Made My Story*, p. 89.
26. Ibid., pp. 114–16.
27. Ibid., pp. 105–7.
28. *The Labour Woman*, 1 Nov. 1923.
29. Elizabeth Roberts, *A Woman's Place* (1984), pp. 125–8.
30. Ibid., p. 161.
31. Ibid., pp. 82–3; Lady Bell, *At the Works* (1907), pp. 180–1.
32. Jeffery Weeks, *Sex, Politics and Society* (1981), p. 209.
33. A. H. Halsey (ed.), *British Social Trends Since 1900* (1988), p. 75.
34. Inez Jenkins, *The History of the Women's Institute Movement of England and Wales* (1953), p. 13.
35. Ibid., pp. 15–20.
36. *Good Housekeeping*, Sept. 1922, p. 15.
37. Janct Courtney, *Countrywomen in Council* (1933), pp. 145–51.
38. Gervas Huxley, *Lady Denman G. B. E. 1884–1954* (1961), p. 74.
39. Ibid., p. 84.
40. Honora Enfield, *The Importance of Women for the Co-operative Movement* (n.d.); and *The Women's Co-operative Guild: Notes on Its History, Organisation and Work* (1920).
41. Margaret Liewelyn Davies, *Women as Organised Consumers* (1921), pp. 2–3.
42. WGC Central Committee Minutes, 13 May 1919.
43. Mary Stott, *Forgetting's No Excuse* (1975), p. 24.

8 THE NEW FEMINISM AND THE DECLINE OF THE WOMEN'S MOVEMENT IN THE 1930s

1. Cicely Hamilton, *Life Errant* (1935), p. 251.
2. Winifred Holtby, *Women in a Changing Civilisation* (1935), p. 6.
3. Dale Spender, *There's Always Been A Women's Movement This Century* (1983), pp. 1–8.
4. Olive Banks, *Faces of Feminism* (1981), pp. 178, 203; S. K. Kent, 'The Politics of Sexual Difference: World War I and the Demise of British Feminism', *Journal of British Studies*, 27, 3 (1988), 232; Sheila Jefferies, *The Spinster and Her Enemies* (1985), pp. 151–4.
5. Victor Gollancz (ed.), *The Making of Women: Oxford Essays in Feminism* (1918), p. 132.
6. See E. Rathbone, *The Disinherited Family* (1924); Mary Stocks, *Eleanor Rathbone* (1950).
7. Eleanor Rathbone, *Milestones* (1929), p. 28; see also 'The Old Feminism and the New', *The Woman's Leader*, 13 Mar. 1925, and M. Stocks, 'What is Equality?' *The Woman's Leader*, 25 Feb. 1927. For the rival view see Elizabeth Abbott 'What is Equality?' *The Woman's Leader*, 11 Feb. 1927.
8. Minutes, 10 May 1926, 10 Sept. 1926, Cardiff WGA, D3DX158/3/1.
9. *The Woman's Leader*, 11 Mar. 1927, pp. 36–7.
10. Ibid., 30 Jan. 1925, pp. 3–5.
11. *Proposed Lines of Expansion for the NUSEC*, Dec. 1928.
12. Mary Stott, *Organisation Woman: the Story of the National Union of Townswomen's Guilds* (1978), pp. 23–4, 44.
13. Minutes, Glasgow Society for Women's Suffrage, 16 Jan. 1933; 30 Jan. 1933.
14. Mary Stocks, *My Commonplace Book* (1970), p. 143.
15. Quoted in Brian Harrison, *Prudent Revolutionaries* (1987), pp. 79–80.
16. See Astor Papers 14/6/1/1/490.
17. Correspondence in the Astor Papers, 14/6/1/1/491,492.
18. Astor Papers, 14/6/1/1/1302,1304.
19. Astor to Sir George Newnes (copy), 9 Feb. 1925, Astor Papers 14/6/1/1/308.
20. Astor to Mrs Butler-Kitson (copy), 26 Nov. 1935, Astor Papers, 14/6/1/1/1007.
21. Astor to D. Thurtle (copy), 20 Dec. 1928, Astor Papers, 14/6/1/1/309.
22. Margery Spring Rice (ed.), *Working-Class Wives* (1981 edn.), p. 28.
23. F. M. L. Thompson, *The Rise of Respectable Society* (1988), p. 55.
24. Spring Rice, *Working-Class Wives*, p. xi.
25. Naorni Mitchison, *You May Well Ask* (1979), pp. 69–70.
26. Annette Kulm, *Cinema, Censorship and Sexuality 1909–1925* (1988), pp. 78–83.
27. Stocks, *My Commonplace Book*, pp. 160–1.
28. R. A. Soloway, *Birth Control and the Population Question in England 1877–1930* (1982), pp. 256–7.
29. Constance Rover, *Love, Morals and the Feminists* (1970); Susan K. Kent, *Sex and Suffrage in Britain 1860–1914* (1987); Carol Dyhouse, *Feminism and the Family in England 1880–1939* (1989).

30. Dora Russell, *Hypatia or Woman and Knowledge* (1925), pp. 24–5.
31. *Time and Tide*, 31 Oct. 1924.
32. Victoria Glendinning, *Rebecca West* (1987), p. 125.
33. Quoted in Johanna Alberti, *Beyond Suffrage* (1989), p. 73.
34. Gollancz, *The Making of Women*, p. 43.
35. Mitchison, *You May Well Ask*, p. 34.
36. H. M. Swanwick, *I Have Been Young* (1935), p. 169.
37. Viscountess Rhondda, *Notes on the Way* (1937), p. 19.
38. *Time and Tide*, 4 Mar. 1935.
39. Cicely Hamilton, *Life Errant* (1935), pp. 273–4, 282.
40. *Woman*, 5 June 1937, p. 7.
41. Mary Stott, *Forgetting's No Excuse* (1975), p. 11.
42. Mitchison, *You May Well Ask*, pp. 69–70.
43. *Good Housekeeping*, Jan. 1935, pp. 33–6.
44. Spender, *Women's Movement*, p. 95; Dora Russell, *The Tamarisk Tree*, 1 (1977), p. 73.
45. Vera Brittain to George Catlin, 8 Mar. 1929, quoted in Deborah Gorham, 'Vera Brittain and inter-war feminism', in Harold Smith (ed.), *British Feminism in the Twentieth Century* (1990), p. 103.
46. 'Committees Versus Professions' (1920), in Paul Berry and Alan Bishop (eds), *Testament of a Generation: the Journalism of Vera Brittain and Winifred Holtby* (1985), pp. 105–6.
47. *Woman*, 5 June 1937, p. 7.

9   WOMEN IN THE SECOND WORLD WAR

1. Mass Observation (MO) Reports, 'Working Women in This War', Dec. 1939, and 'Working Women's Attitudes to Evacuation', 20 May 1940.
2. Ibid., Dec. 1939, p. 6.
3. MO Report, 'The Demand for Day Nurseries', 11 Mar. 1942, p. 4.
4. Gail Braybon and Penny Summerfield, *Out of the Cage: Women's Experiences in Two World Wars* (1987), pp. 236–41.
5. See MO Reports, 'Class and Sex Differences in Morale', 25 May 1940, pp. 1–3; 'Women and Morale', 10 Dec. 1940; 'Summary Report of ATS Campaign', 2 Feb. 1942, pp. 2–3.
6. Quoted in Braybon, *Out of the Cage*, p. 244.
7. MO Report, 'Female Attitudes to Compulsion', 16 Oct. 1941, p. 14.
8. See MO Report, 'Publicity Campaign Questionnaire', 21 May 1940.
9. MO Report, 'The Slogan – Be Like Dad, Keep Mum', 7 Oct. 1940.
10. Mary Grieve, *Millions Made My Story* (1964), pp. 125–6.
11. For an example see P. Donnelly (ed.), *Mrs Milburn's Diaries* (1979).
12. MO Report, 'Women's Organisations in Wartime', 9 Feb. 1940, pp. 4, 29.
13. Ibid., p. 27.
14. MO Report, 'Women in Pubs', 3 Mar. 1943, p. 5.
15. Braybon, *Out of the Cage*, p. 210.
16. A. H. Halsey (ed.), *British Social Trends Since 1900* (1988), p. 73.
17. Ibid., p. 40.

18. Alan Bullock, *The Life and Times of Ernest Bevin*, 11 (1967), pp. 126.

19. Penny Summerfield, *Women Workers in the Second World War* (1984); and Harold L. Smith, 'The effect of the war on the status of women', in *War and Social Change* (1986), p. 212.

20. MO Report, 'Female Attitudes to Compulsion', 16 Oct. 1941, pp. 1–4.

21. MO Report, 'Registration of Women', 21 Apr. 1941, pp. 2–3.

22. Surnmerfield, *Women Workers*, p. 37.

23. MO Report, 'An Appeal to Women?', 20 Mar. 1941, pp. 2–3.

24. Ibid., p. 6.

25. MO Report, 'Women and the War Effort', 3 Dec. 1940, pp. 22–4.

26. Ibid., p. 3.

27. Harold Smith, 'The Problem of "Equal Pay for Equal Work" in Great Britain during World War 11', *Journal of Modern History*, 53 (Dec. 1981), 657–8.

28. MO Report, 'Will the Factory Girls Want to Stay Put or Go Home?' 8 Mar. 1944, pp. 3–8.

29. Ibid., p. 6.

30. MO Report, 'Women's Organisations in Wartime', 9 Feb. 1940, p. 34; also MO Report, 'Appeals to Women', 1 May 1942, pp. 2–3.

31. D. Evans to Ministry of Health, 27 July 1944 (copy) and reply 9 Aug. 1944, Six Point Group Papers Box 526/C2.

32. Reports in *Daily Herald*, 12 Feb. 1940, and *News Chronicle*, 15 Feb. 1940.

33. HC Debates, 20 Mar. 1941, c 376–7.

34. Harold Smith, 'Equal Pay', p. 667.

35. Thelma Cazalet-Keir, *From the Wings* (1967), p. 143.

36. Conservative Party, *Notes for Speakers* (1945), p. 150.

37. *The Labour Woman* (Nov. 1941), 114.

38. *Annual Report*, Labour Women's Conference, 1942, p. 44.

39. Minutes, Six Point Group AGM, 7 Mar. 1940.

40. See memoranda by Theresa Billington-Greig in the Central Women's Electoral Committee/Women for Westminster papers, Box 281 (Fawcett Library).

41. Smith, *War and Social Change*, pp. 219–20.

10　THE NADIR OF BRITISH FEMINISM 1945–1959?

1. *Woman's Own*, 8 Mar. 1956, p. 28.

2. Vera Brittain, *Lady Into Woman* (1953), p. 8.

3. Quoted in Ibid., p. 77.

4. *Guardian*, 18 Apr. 1960.

5. G. Braybon and P. Summerfield, *Out of the Cage* (1987), p. 26 1.

6. BBC Radio 4 recording, 9 Aug. 1989.

7. Quoted in Harold Smith, *War and Social Change* (1989), p. 222.

8. William Crofts, 'The Attlee Government's Pursuit of Women', *History Today* (Aug. 1986), 32–3.

9. Gregory Anderson, *The White Blouse Revolution* (1988), p. 123.

Notes 3

10. *Good Housekeeping*, Feb. 1950, pp. 78–82.

11. Women's Conservative and Unionist Association, Annual Conference Report, July 1947, p. 3.

12. Conservative Party, *Campaign Guide* (1950), pp. 663–4.

13. Labour Party Women's Organisation, Annual Conference Report, Apr. 1952, p. 12; see also *Labour Woman* (Nov. 1951), 214.

14. See Mass Observation report in *Good Housekeeping*, Feb. 1950, pp. 78–82.

15. Mary Grieve, *Millions Made My Story* (1964), p. 197.

16. Cynthia L. White, *The Women's Periodical Press in Britain 1946–76* (1977), p. 9.

17. J. H. Goldthorpe, D. Lockwood, F. Bechhofer and J. Platt, *The Affluent Worker* (1968), p. 20.

18. Theresa M. McBride, *The Domestic Revolution* (1976), pp. 83–98.

19. Jean Mann, *Woman in Parliament* (1962), pp. 160–1, 169–73.

20. Elizabeth Wilson, *Women and the Welfare State* (1977), p. 60.

21. *The Labour Woman*, xxxi (July 1943), 70–2.

22. *Good Housekeeping*, Aug. 1949, p. 21.

23. Report on the Social Insurance and Allied Service, Cd. 6404 (HMSO, 1942), p. 52.

24. Cd. 6404, p. 49.

25. B. Spock, *Baby and Child Care* (1963), p. 460.

26. John Bowlby, *Maternal Care and Mental Health* (1951), p. 11.

27. Ibid., p. 86.

28. Mary Stott, *Organisation Woman* (1978), pp. 169–70.

29. *Onward* (Conservative Party), Apr. 1954.

30. Allen Potter, 'The Equal Pay Campaign Committee: a Case-Study of a Pressure Group', *Political Studies*, 5 (1957), p. 63.

31. Cd 6937 (HMSO, 1946), pp. 119, 143, 167–70.

32. EPCC, minutes, 5 Mar. 1948 and 21 Sept. 1948 (Fawcett Library, Box 157).

33. Ibid., 25 Nov. 1947.

34. Ibid., 20 July 1949.

35. EPCC, Fawcett Library, Box 157, folder 1.

36. EPCC, minutes, 5 Apr. 1954.

37. See Monica Whately to E. Summerskill (copy), 17 Dec. 1947, Six Point Group papers, Fawcett Library, Box 526/C7.

38. Whately to Pethick-Lawrence (copy), n.d., Six Point Group papers, Fawcett Library, Box 526/C7.

39. Women for Westminster papers, Fawcett Library, Box 281.

40. Stott, *Organisation Woman*, pp. 153–4.

41. WCG, Annual Report, 1946–7, pp. 2–3.

42. Elizabeth Valiance, *Women in the House* (1979), p. 66.

43. Melanie Phillips, *The Divided House: Women at Westminster* (1980), p. 59.

44. Ibid., pp. 71–2; Valiance, *Women in the House*, pp. 44–6.

45. Phillips, *The Divided House*, pp. 96–7.

46. Women's Unionist Organisation, Annual Conference Report, July 1947, p. 29.

47. Vallance, *Women in the House*, p. 49; Phillips, *The Divided House*, p. 72.
48. Thelma Cazalet-Keir, *From the Wings* (1967), p. 149.
49. See press cuttings in Horsbrugh Papers (Churchill College), 1/4.
50. Mann, *Women in Parliament*, p. 13.
51. Phillips, *The Divided House*, pp. 159–60.
52. Labour Party Women's Organisation, Annual Conference Report, 1946, p. 16.
53. Ibid., 1952, p. 18.
54. Phillips, *The Divided House*, pp. 162–3.

11   WOMEN'S LIBERATION

1. Hence the title *There's Always Been a Women's Movement This Century* (Pandora Press, 1983).
2. Melanie Phillips, *The Divided House* (1980), pp. 159–60.
3. Peter Paterson, *Tired and Emotional: The Life of Lord George-Brown* (1993), pp. 29–33.
4. Colin S. Gibson, *Dissolving Wedlock* (1994), pp. 99–106.
5. Betty Friedan, *The Feminine Mystique* (1975), p. 32.
6. Jill Liddington, *The Long Road to Greenham: Feminism and Anti-Militarism in Britain since 1820* (1989), pp. 172–94.
7. Angela Phillips in *The Guardian*, 20 January 1998.
8. David Bouchier, *The Feminist Challenge* (1983), pp. 74–81.
9. Germaine Greer, *The Female Eunuch* (1971), pp. 233–7.
10. A. H. Halsey, *British Social Trends Since 1900* (1988), p. 71.
11. Ibid, pp. 75, 78–9.
12. Gibson, *Dissolving*, pp. 106–8.
13. Greer, *Eunuch*, pp. 41–6.
14. Bouchier, *Challenge*, pp. 147, 184–7.
15. Ibid, pp. 133-4.
16. *The Guardian*, 4 February 1982.

12   FEMINISM IN THE ERA OF THATCHERISM, 1979–1999

1. *The Guardian*, 30 November 1989.
2. Bo Sarlvik and Ivor Crewe, *Decade of Dealignment: The Conservative Victory of 1979 and Electoral Trends in the 1980s* (Cambridge, 1983), pp. 132–3.
3. Natasha Walters, *The Guardian*, 17 January 1998.
4. See the valuable account in Jill Liddington, *The Long Road to Greenham: Feminism and Anti-Militarism in Britain since 1820* (1989), pp. 221-45.
5. *Spare Rib*, no. 99, October 1980.
6. See *The Guardian*, 6 December 1989; Melanie Phillips in *The Observer*, 17 October 1993.
7. *The Guardian*, 21 August 1996.
8. *The Guardian*, 14 December 1994.

9. *The Guardian*, 6 July 1990.
10. *Social Focus on Women*, Central Statistical Office, (HMSO, 1995).
11. *Men and Women in Britain*, Equal Opportunities Commission Report, 1990.
12. See reports in *The Guardian*, 19 January 1989 and 1 September 1993.
13. David Bouchier, *The Feminist Challenge* (1983), p. 177
14. Ibid, pp. 165–7.
15. See *The Guardian*, 9 December 1997.
16. *The Observer*, 2 November 1997.
17. *Living in Britain: Preliminary Results of the 1994 Household Survey*, (HMSO, 1995).
18. *The Observer*, 4 May 1997.
19. Female members of selection committees were still apt to ask women applicants 'will your husband come to our coffee mornings?', *The Observer*, 3 December 1995.
20. See a typical Blair article in the *Daily Mail*, 14 June 1999, on teenage mothers.

Bibliography

Primary Sources

Individuals

Nancy, Viscountess Astor Papers – Reading University Library
Katharine, Duchess of Atholl Papers – Blair Castle
Margery Corbett Ashby Papers – Fawcett Library
Florence, Baroness Horsbrugh Papers – Churchill College, Cambridge
Lady Megan Lloyd George Papers (David Lloyd George Papers) –
National Library of Wales
Hilda Runciman Papers (Walter Runciman Papers) – Newcastle
University Library
Julia Varley Papers – Brynmor Jones Library, University of Hull

Organisations

Cambridge Women's Suffrage Association and Women's Citizens
Association, minutes and annual reports, 1918–7 Cambridge County
Record Office
Cardiff and District Women's Citizens Association Papers – Glamorgan
County Record Office
Catholic Women's Suffrage Association Papers – Fawcett Library
Central Women's Electoral Committee/Women for Westminster papers
– Fawcett Library
Conservative Party Annual Conference Reports and Campaign Guides
Consultative Committee of Women's Organisations, minutes – Fawcett
Library
Equal Pay Campaign Committee, minutes 1944–56 – Fawcett Library
Fabian Women's Group Papers (Fabian Society Archives, part 5)
Glasgow Society for Women's Suffrage/Society for Equal Citizenship
Papers, 1915–33 – Mitchell Library
Tom Harrison Mass Observation Archives 1937–49
Imperial War Museum: Women at War Collection
Labour Party Archives (Part 6, Marion Phillips Papers)
National Liberal Club: Election Addresses 1918–31
National Union of Societies for Equal Citizenship Papers – Fawcett
Library
Open Door Council Papers – Fawcett Library

Bibliography

Six Point Group Papers – Fawcett Library
Women's Citizens Association Papers – Fawcett Library
Women's Co-operative Guild Papers – Brymnor Jones Library, University of Hull
Women's Freedom League Papers – Fawcett Library
Women's Labour League/Labour Party Women's Organisation Annual Conference Reports 1918–59
Women's Suffrage, pamphet collection – Fawcett Library
Women's Unionist Organisation Annual Conference Reports 1921–58 – Conservative Central Office

Newspapers and Magazines

The Conservative Woman
Daily Mail
Domestic News
Eve: the Lady's Pictorial
Good Housekeeping
Home Chat
Home and Politics
The Labour Woman
My Weekly
Time and Tide
The Townswoman
Woman
The Woman's Leader
Woman's Liberal Magazine/Liberal Woman's News
Woman's Opinion
Woman's Own
Women's Industrial News

Secondary Sources

Biographies, Autobiographies, Diaries

(Place of publication is London unless otherwise stated)

Duchess of Atholl, *Working Partnership* (Arthur Barker, 1958)
Hilary Bailey, *Vera Brittain* (Penguin, 1987)
Lady Frances Balfour, *Dr. Elsie Inglis* (Hodder & Stoughton, n.d.)
Alan Bishop (ed.), *Chronicle of Youth: Vera Brittain's War Diary 1913–1917* (Gollancz, 1981)

Margaret Bondfield, *A Life's Work* (Hutchinson, 1948)
Vera Brittain, *Testament of Youth* (Gollancz, 1933)
Vera Brittain, *Testament of Friendship* (Macmillan, 1940)
Vera Brittain, *Testament of Experience* (Gollancz, 1957)
Alan Bullock, *The Life and Times of Ernest Bevin*, vol. II (Heinemann, 1967)
Barbara Cartland, *The Isthmus Years* (Hutchinson, 1942)
Barbara Cartland, *The Years of Opportunity 1939–45* (Hutchinson, 1949)
Thelma Cazalet-Keir, *From the Wings* (Bodley Head, 1967)
Ronald Crichton (ed.), *The Memoirs of Ethel Smyth* (Viking, 1987)
Peter Donnelly (ed.), *Mrs Milburn's Diaries* (Harrap, 1979)
Katharine Furse, *Hearts and Pomegranates* (Peter Davies, 1940)
Victoria Glendinning, *Rebecca West* (Weidenfeld & Nicolson, 1987)
Mary Grieve, *Millions Made My Story* (Gollancz, 1964)
Ruth Hall, *Marie Stopes* (Virago, 1978)
Cicely Hamilton, *Life Errant* (Dent, 1935)
Mary Agnes Hamilton. *Remembering My Good Friends* (Cape, 1944)
Mary Agnes Hamilton, *Margaret Bondfield* (Leonard Parsons, 1924)
June Hannam, *Isabella Ford* (Blackwell, Oxford, 1989)
Jose Harris, *William Beveridge* (Clarendon, Oxford, 1977)
Alice Head, *It Could Never Have Happened* (Heinemann, 1939)
Sheila Hetherington, *Katharine Atholl 1874–1960* (Aberdeen University Press, Aberdeen, 1989)
Winifred Holtby, *Women and a Changing Civilisation* (Bodley Head, 1934)
Diana Hopkinson, *Family Inheritance: a life of Eva Hubback* (Staples Press, 1954)
Gervas Huxley, *Lady Denman, G.B.E., 1884–1954* (Chatto & Windus, 1961)
Robert Rhodes James, *Victor Cazalet: a portrait* (Hamish Hamilton, 1976)
Jennie Lee, *My Life With Nye* (Cape, 1980)
Jill Liddington, *The Life and Times of a Respectable Rebel: Selina Cooper 1864–1946* (Virago, 1984)
Jean Mann, *Woman in Parliament* (Odhams, 1962)
Leah Manning, *A Life for Education* (Gollancz. 1970)
Violet Markham, *Return Passage* (Clarendon, Oxford, 1953)
Anthony Masters, *Nancy Astor: a Life* (Weidenfeld & Nicolson, 1981)
Naomi Mitchison, *You May Well Ask* (Gollancz, 1979)
E. Sylvia Pankhurst, *The Life of Emmeline Pankhurst* (Laurie, 1935)

Ĝisela Bock and Pat Thane (eds), *Maternity and Gender Policies: Women and the Rise of the European Welfare States, 1880s to 1950s* (Routledge, 1991)

David Bouchier, *The Feminist Challenge* (Macmillan, 1983)

John Bowlby, *Maternal Care and Mental Health* (World Health Organisation, Geneva, 1952)

Gail Braybon, *Women Workers in the First World War* (Croom Helm. 1981)

Gail Braybon and Penny Summerfield, *Out of the Cage: Women's Experience in Two World Wars* (Pandora, 1987)

Susan Briggs, *Keep Smiling Through* (Fontana, 1976)

Vera Brittain, *Women's Work in Modern England* (Noel Douglas, 1928)

Vera Brittain, *Lady into Woman* (Andrew Dakers, 1953)

Sue Bruley, *Women in Britain Since 1900* (Macmillan, 1999)

G. Bussey and M. Timms, *Pioneers for Peace* (Women's International League for Peace and Freedom, 1980)

David Butler, *The Electoral System in Britain since 1918* (Clarendon Press, 1963)

Angus Calder, *The People's War 1939–45* (Cape, 1969)

Beatrix Campbell, *The Iron Ladies* (Virago, 1987)

Enid Charles, *The Twilight of Parenthood* (Watts & Co., 1934)

Carl Chinn, *They Worked All Their Lives* (Manchester University Press, 1988)

Margaret Cole, *Marriage Past and Present* (Dent, 1939)

Nancy Cott, *The Grounding of Modern Feminism* (Yale University Press, 1987)

Janet Courtney, *Countrywomen in Council* (Oxford University Press, 1933)

Ros Coward, *Sacred Cows: Is Feminism Relevant to the New Millennium?* (HarperCollins, 1999)

Irene Danogyer, *A World of Women: an Illustrated History of Women's Magazines* (Gill & Macmillan, 1978)

M. Llewelyn Davies, *Life As We Have Known It: By Co-operative Working Women* (1931, Virago reprint 1977)

E. M. Delafleld, *The Diary of a Provincial Lady* (Macmillan, 1947)

Carol Dyhouse, *Feminism and the Family in England, 1880–1930* (Blackwell, 1989)

M. L. Eyles, *The Woman in the Little House* (Grant Richards, 1922)

Shulamith Firestone, *The Dialectic of Sex* (Bantam House, 1980)

Betty Friedan, *The Feminine Mystique* (Gollancz, 1963)

Betty Friedan, *It Changed My Life* (Gollancz, 1963)

Colin S. Gibson, *Dissolving Wedlock*, (Routledge, 1994)

Diana Gittins, *Fair Sex: Family Size and Structure, 1900–39* (Hutchinson, 1982)

Victor Gollancz (ed.), *Oxford Essays in Feminism* (Allen & Unwin, 1918)

I. Grant, *The First Sixty Years, 1895–1955* (National Council of Women, 1955)

Germaine Greer, *The Female Eunuch* (MacGibbon & Key, 1970)

Germaine Greer, *The Whole Woman* (HarperCollins, 1999)

A. H. Halsey, *British Social Trends Since 1900* (Macmillan, 1988)

Cicely Hamilton, *Marriage as a Trade* (Chapman & Hall, 1909)

Christina Hardyment, *From Mangle to Microwave: The Mechanisation of Household Work* (Polity Press, 1988)

Brian Harrison, *Separate Spheres* (Croom Helm, 1978)

Brian Harrison, *Prudent Revolutionaries: Portraits of British Feminists Between the Wars* (Clarendon Press, 1987)

Tom Harrison, *Living Through the Blitz* (Collins, 1976)

Brian Heeney, *The Women's Movement in the Church of England 1850–1930* (Clarendon Press, 1988)

Patricia Hollis, *Ladies Elect: Women in English Local Government 1865–1914* (Clarendon Press, 1987)

Sandra Stanley Holton, *Feminism and Democracy* (Cambridge University Press, 1987)

Sheila Jeffries, *The Spinster and Her Enemies* (Pandora, 1985)

Inez Jenkins, *The History of the Women's Institute Movement of England and Wales* (Oxford University Press, 1953)

Arabella Keneally, *Feminism and Sex Extinction* (T. Fisher Unwin, 1920)

Robin Kent, *Aunt Agony Advises: Problem Pages Through the Ages* (W. H. Allen, 1979)

Annette Kuln, *Cinema, Sexuality and Censorship* (Routledge, 1988)

Tony Kushner and Kenneth Lunn (eds), *The Politics of Marginality* (Frank Cass, 1990)

Elsie M. Lang, *British Women in the Twentieth Century* (T. Werner Laurie, 1929)

S. Lewenhak, *Women and Trade Unions* (Macmillan, 1977)

Jane Lewis, *Women in England 1870–1950* (Wheatsheaf, 1984)

Jane Lewis, *The Politics of Motherhood* (Croom Helm, 1980)

Jane Lewis (ed.), *Labour and Love* (Blackwell, 1986)

Jane Lewis, *Women in Britain since 1945* (Blackwell, 1992)

Peter Lewis, *A People's War* (Methuen, 1986)

ıll Liddington, *The Long Road to Greenham: Feminism and Anti-militarism in Britain since 1820* (Virago, 1989)

Joan Lock, *The British Policewoman* (Hale, 1979)

Joni Lovenduski, *Women and European Politics* (Harvester, 1986)

Neil Lyndon, *No More Sex War* (Granta Publications, 1992)

Hilda Martindale, *Women Servants of the State 1870–1938* (Allen & Unwin, 1938)

Arthur Marwick, *Women At War 1914–1918* (Thames & Hudson, 1977)

Arthur Marwick, *British Society since 1945* (Penguin, 1982)

Billie Melman, *Women in the Popular Imagination in the Twenties* (Macmillan, 1988)

Lucy Middleton (ed.), *Women in the Labour Movement* (Croom Helm, 1977)

Kate Millett, *Sexual Politics* (Rupert Hart Davis, 1971)

K. O. Morgan, *Consensus and Disunity* (Clarendon Press, 1979)

Alva Myrdal and Viola Klein, *Women's Two Roles: Home and Work* (Routledge & Kegan Paul, 1956)

Ann Oakley, *Housewife* (Allen Lane, 1974)

Marion Phillips (ed.), *Women and the Labour Party* (Headley Bros, 1918)

Melanie Phillips, *The Divided House* (Sidgwick & Jackson, 1980)

Martin Pugh, *Electoral Reform in War and Peace 1906–1918* (Routledge & Kegan Paul, 1978)

Martin Pugh, *The Making of Modern British Politics 1867–1939* (Blackwell, 1982)

Martin Pugh, *The Tories and the People 1880–1935* (Blackwell, 1985)

Austin Ranney, *Pathways to Parliament* (Athlone, 1965)

Eleanor Rathbone, *The Disinherited Family* (W. H. Allen, 1949)

Margery Spring Rice, *Working-Class Wives* (Virago, 1981)

Elizabeth Robins, *Ancilla's Share: An Indictment of Sex Antagonism* (Hutchinson, 1924)

Elizabeth Roberts, *A Woman's Place* (Blackwell, 1984)

Elizabeth Roberts, *Women's Work 1840–1940* (Macmillan, 1988)

Robert Roberts, *The Classic Slum* (Manchester University Press, 1971)

Sheila Rowbotham, *Hidden from History* (Pluto Press, 1973)

Michael Savage, *The Dynamics of Working-Class Politics: The Labour Movement in Preston 1880–1940* (Cambridge University Press, 1987)

Harold L. Smith (ed.), *War and Social Change: British Society in the Second World War* (Manchester University Press, 1986)

Harold L. Smith (ed.), *British Feminism in the Twentieth Century* (Edward Elgar, 1990)

N. C. Solden, *Women in British Trade Unions 1874–1976* (Gill & Macmillan, 1978)

R. A. Soloway, *Birth Control and the Population Question in England 1872–1930* (University of North Carolina Press, 1982)

Dale Spender, *There's Always Been A Women's Movement This Century* (Pandora, 1983)

Dale Spender, *Time and Tide Wait for No Man* (Pandora, 1984)

Benjamin Spock, *Baby and Child Care* (Bodley Head, 1963)

Margaret Stacey and Marion Price, *Women, Power and Politics* (Clarendon Press, 1981)

Tom Stannage, *Baldwin Thwarts the Opposition* (Croom Helm, 1980)

John Stevenson, *British Society 1914–1945* (Allen Lane, 1984)

Marie Stopes, *Married Love* (Putnam, 1918)

Marie Stopes, *Wise Parenthood* (Putnam, 1918)

Mary Stott, *Organisation Woman: The Story of the National Union of Townswomen's Guilds* (Heinemann, 1978)

Ray Strachey, *Careers and Openings for Women* (Faber & Faber, 1935)

Ray Strachey, *Our Freedom and Its Results* (Hogarth Press, 1936)

Ray Strachey, *The Cause* (G. Bell, 1928)

Penny Summerfield, *Women Workers in the Second World War* (Croom Helm, 1984)

Anne Summers, *Angels and Citizens: British Women as Military Nurses 1854–1914* (Routledge, 1988)

Louise Tilly and Joan Scott, *Women, Work and Family* (1978; Methuen reprint, 1987)

Elizabeth Vallance, *Women in the House* (Athlone, 1979)

Martha Vicinus, *Independent Women* (Virago, 1985)

Natasha Walters, *The New Feminism* (Little, Brown, 1988)

Catherine Webb, *The Woman With the Basket: The History of the Women's Co-operative Guild 1883–1927* (WCG, 1927)

Jeffery Weeks, *Sex, Politics and Society* (Longman, 1981)

Cynthia White, *Women's Magazines l693–1968* (Michael Joseph, 1970)

Cynthia White, *The Women's Periodical Press in Britain 1946–1976* (HMSO, 1977)

Elizabeth Wilson, *Women and the Welfare State* (Tavistock, 1977)

Elizabeth Wilson, *Only Hay-Way to Paradise: Women in Post-War Britain 1945–1969* (Tavistock, 1980)

Virginia Woolf, *A Room of One's Own* (Hogarth Press, 1929)

Articles and Essays

Stuart Bell, 'Asquith's Decline and the General Election of 1918', *Scottish Historical Review*, LXI, 171 (1982)

William Crofts, 'The Attlee Government's Pursuit of Women', *History Today* (August, 1986)

Anna Davin, 'Imperialism and Motherhood', *History Workshop Journal*, 5 (Spring, 1978)

Judith Evans, 'Women and Politics: A Re-appraisal', *Political Studies*, 28, 2 (1980)

Deborah Gorham, ' "Have we really rounded seraglio point?" ': Vera Brittain and interwar feminism', in Harold Smith (ed.) *British Feminism in the Twentieth Century* (Edward Elgar, 1990)

Brian Harrison, 'Women in a Men's House: the Women MPs 1919-45', *Historical Journal*, 29, 3 (1986)

Brian Harrison, 'Women's Suffrage at Westminster 1866–1928', in M. Bentley and J. Stevenson (eds), *High and Low Politics in Modern Britain* (Clarendon, Oxford, 1983)

Brian Harrison, 'Class and Gender in Modern British Labour History', *Past and Present*, 124 (August, 1989)

Jill Hills, 'Candidates: the Impact of Gender', *Parliamentary Affairs*, 34, 2 (1981)

Susan Kingsley Kent, 'The Politics of Sexual Difference: World War I and the Decline of British Feminism', *Journal of British Studies*, 27, 3 (1988)

Hilary Land, 'Eleanor Rathbone and the Economy of the Family', in Harold Smith (ed.), *British Feminism in the Twentieth Century* (Edward Elgar, 1990)

Jane Lewis, 'Beyond Suffrage: English Feminism in the 1920s', *The Maryland Historian*, 6 (1975)

Jane Lewis, 'The Ideology and Politics of Birth Control in Inter-war England', *Women's Studies International Quarterly*, 2 (1979)

Jane Lewis, 'Myrdal, Klein, *Women's Two Roles* and Post-war Feminism 1945-60', in Harold Smith (ed.), *British Feminism in the Twentieth Century* (Edward Elgar, 1990)

Allen Potter, 'The Equal Pay Campaign Committee: a case study of a pressure group', *Political Studies*, 5 (1957)

Frank Prochaska, 'A Mother's Country: Mothers' Meetings and Family Welfare in Britain, 1850–1950', *History*, 74, 242 (1989)

Martin Pugh, 'Politicians and the Woman's Vote 1914–1918', *History*, 59, 197 (1974)

Bibliography

Martin Pugh, 'Women's Suffrage in Britain 1867–1929', Historical Association pamphlet (1980)

Martin Pugh, 'Popular Conservatism in Britain: Continuity and Change 1880–1987', *Journal of British Studies*, 27, 3 (1988)

Martin Pugh, 'Domesticity and the Decline of Feminism, 1930–1950', in Harold Smith (ed.), *British Feminism in the Twentieth Century* (Edward Elgar, 1990)

J. S. Rasmussen, 'Women Candidates in British By-Elections', *Political Studies*, 29, 2 (198 1)

J. S. Rasmusson, 'Women in Labour: the flapper vote and party system transformation in Britain', *Electoral Studies*, 3, 1 (1984)

Mike Savage, 'Trade unionism, sex segregation and the state: women's employment in "new industries" in inter-war Britain', *Social History*, 13, 2 (1988)

Harold L. Smith, 'The issue of "equal pay for equal work" in Great Britain, 1914–19', *Societas*, 8, 1 (1978)

Harold L. Smith, 'The Problem of "Equal Pay for Equal Work" in Great Britain during World War II', *Journal of Modern History*, 53 (December 1981)

Harold L. Smith, 'The Womanpower Problem in Britain during the Second World War', *Historical Journal*, 27, 4 (1984)

Harold L. Smith, 'Sex vs Class: British Feminists and the Labour Movement 1919–29', *The Historian*, 47 (November 1984)

Pat Thane, 'The Women of the British Labour Party and Feminism 1906–45' in Harold L. Smith (ed.), *British Feminism in the Twentieth Century* (Edward Elgar, 1990)

John Turner, 'The Labour vote and the franchise after 1918', in P. R. Denley and D. I. Hopkins (eds), *History and Computing* (Manchester University Press, Manchester, 1987)

Elizabeth Vallance, 'Women Candidates in the 1983 General Election', *Parliamentary Affairs*, 37 (1984)

Index

Index

ardson, Mary, 47
bins, Elizabeth, 38, 260
ver, Constance, 313–14
oyden, Maude, 10, 104, 236, 259, 261
Ruddock, Joan, 338
Runciman, Mrs Hilda, 140, 155, 157, 162, 164, 171, 177–8, 193, 200
Runge, Mrs N. C., 162, 183
Russell, Audrey, 285
Russell, Dora, 135, 136, 255, 258, 259, 262, 318
Russell, Mabel, *see* Philipson

Samuel, Herbert, 16
Selborne, Viscountess, 52, 126, 127, 129
Sex Disqualification (Removal) Act (1919), 51, 90, 93, 116
sexuality, 75, 78–9, 210, 224, 246–8, 258–60, 269–71, 315, 322–3, 324, 326–7, 332, 344, 345
Shaw, Mrs H. B., 162, 183
Simon, Sir John, 35, 36, 93, 111, 119, 139
Six Point Group, 49–50, 69, 70, 142–3, 145, 236–7, 243, 259, 263, 276, 301
Slater, Harriet, 304, 305
Smith, Dr Miall, 93
Smythe, Dame Ethel, 260
Snowden, Ethel, 10, 52, 66, 131, 172
Spock, Dr Benjamin, 296, 329
Spring Rice, Margery, 250, 253
Spurrell, Kate, 167
Steel David, 328
Stevenson, Frances, 23, 87
Stocks, Mary, 52, 72, 237, 238, 239, 240, 241, 244
Stopes, Marie, 75, 116, 254–6, 257, 259
Stott, Mary, 261
Strachey, Pippa, 237, 261, 278
Strachey, Ray, 11, 43, 94, 144, 172, 237, 261, 277
Summerskill, Edith, 164, 170, 172, 304; as a candidate, 158, 162, 165, 170, 172, 305; as a feminist,

281, 284–5, 301, 309; and equal pay, 277–8, 299; as an MP, 192, 195, 196; as a minister, 307–8
Sutherland, Mary, 131, 135, 169, 280, 299
Swanwick, Helena, 10, 38, 48, 75, 101, 104, 135, 260

Tate, Mrs Mavis, 162, 197, 202, 276, 277, 278, 298, 301
Termant, May, 8
Terrington, Lady Vera, 149, 183, 201
Thatcher, Mrs Margaret, 297, 298, 303, 304, 306, 309, 335–7
Thurtle, Ernest, 111, 116, 197
Time and Tide, 48–9, 142–3
Townswomen's Guilds, 68, 240–1, 268, 297, 302
trade unions, 26–7, 29, 68, 99–100, 133, 152, 166, 274, 313, 329–30

Underwood, Florence, 47, 243
unemployment, 19, 99, 124, 205, 340–1
Union of Democratic Control, 10, 103

Varley, Julia, 100
Vickers, Dame Joan, 307, 308, 309
Voluntary Aid Detachments, 8, 30, 39

Walters, Natasha, 336, 352
Ward, Irene, 165; and Conservative Party, 126, 155, 162, 165; as a candidate, 155, 183, 306–7; as a feminist, 197, 274, 276, 277, 300; as an MP, 196, 197, 300
Ward, Mrs S. A., 162, 183
Webb, Beatrice, 28, 134
Weldon, Fay, 346
West, Rebecca, 48, 49, 72, 81, 258
Whately, Monica, 47, 56, 69, 100, 135, 167, 239, 243, 301
Wheatley, John, 116, 193
White, Eirene, 299, 304, 305, 308–9, 310
widows' pensions, 16, 92, 110, 122–3